Arthur Conan Doyle and the Meaning of Masculinity

This book is dedicated to the memory of
William George Basham
(1917–87)

Arthur Conan Doyle and the Meaning of Masculinity

DIANA BARSHAM

Routledge
Taylor & Francis Group

LONDON AND NEW YORK

First published 2000 by Ashgate Publishing

2 Park Square, Milton Park, Abingdon, Oxfordshire OX14 4RN
52 Vanderbilt Avenue, New York, NY 10017

Routledge is an imprint of the Taylor & Francis Group, an informa business

First issued in paperback 2019

British Library Cataloguing in Publication Data

Barsham, Diana.
  Arthur Conan Doyle and the Meaning of Masculinity.
  (The Nineteenth Century series)
  1. Doyle, Sir Arthur Conan, 1859–1930—Criticism and
  interpretation. 2. Masculinity in literature.
  I. Title.
  823.9'12

Library of Congress Cataloging-in-Publication Data

Barsham, Diana.
  Arthur Conan Doyle and the meaning of masculinity/Diana Barsham.
    p. cm. (The Nineteenth Century series)
  Includes bibliographical references and index.
  ISBN 1–85928–264–4 (alk. paper)
  1. Doyle, Arthur Conan, Sir, 1859–1930. 2. Doyle, Arthur Conan, Sir,
1859–1930—Knowledge—Psychology. 3. Doyle, Arthur Conan, Sir,
1859–1930—Characters—Men. 4. Autobiographical fiction, English—
History and criticism. 5. Authors, Scottish—Biography—History and
criticism. 6. Spiritualists—Biography—History and criticism.
7. Physicians—Biography—History and criticism. 8. Masculinity in
literature. 9. Self in literature. 10. Men in literature. 11. Autobiography.
I. Title. II. Nineteenth Century (Aldershot, England).
PR4623.B37   2000
823'.8—dc21   00–42047

ISBN 13: 978-1-85928-264-9 (hbk)
ISBN 13: 978-0-367-88809-1 (pbk)

Contents

The Nineteenth Century
General Editors' Preface

The aim of this series is to reflect, develop and extend the great burgeoning of interest in the nineteenth century that has been an inevitable feature of recent decades, as that former epoch has come more sharply into focus as a locus for our understanding not only of the past but of the contours of our modernity. Though it is dedicated principally to the publication of original monographs and symposia in literature, history, cultural analysis, and associated fields, there will be a salient role for reprints of significant texts from, or about, the period. Our overarching policy is to address the spectrum of nineteenth-century studies without exception, achieving the widest scope in chronology, approach and range of concern. This, we believe, distinguishes our project from comparable ones, and means, for example, that in the relevant areas of scholarship we both recognize and cut innovatively across such parameters as those suggested by the designations 'Romantic and 'Victorian'. We welcome new ideas, while valuing tradition. It is hoped that the world which predates yet so forcibly predicts and engages our own will emerge in parts, as a whole, and in the lively currents of debate and change that are so manifest an aspect of its intellectual, artistic and social landscape.

Vincent Newey
Joanne Shattock

University of Leicester

Acknowledgements

I am indebted for information and advice to a large community of Doyle scholars. My thanks are due especially to Richard Lancelyn Green for his invaluable help in supplying details of Doyle's life, to Owen Dudley Edwards for his hospitable introduction to Doyle's Edinburgh, and to Christopher and Barbara Roden of the Arthur Conan Doyle Society for their willingness to talk about Doyle on a twenty-four hour clock. Thanks for practical help is due also to the Society for Psychical Research and especially to their librarian, Mrs Wyllys Poynton. I would also like to acknowledge the constant support I have received from Heather Watkins, Subject Librarian for Humanities at the University of Derby. I am indebted to Fred Inglis for some valuable reference books, to Stephen Knight, Mark Wheeler, Mike Sanders and Trev Lynn Broughton for some helpful discussions and to Joseph Kestner for directing my attention to some relevant theoretical material. My greatest debt of gratitude is to Hester Barsham who has helped in innumerable ways with the production of this book. And then, of course, there are the spirits themselves ... .

Diana Barsham
2000

Introduction

As an exponent of the late-Victorian adventure culture which served to fashion the masculinities of the British Empire between 1880 and 1920, Arthur Conan Doyle (1859–1930) structured his own life to embody the chivalric, comedic and competitive manhood that was the subject of all his writing. His career was an attempt to promote the profession of letters as a definitively masculine pursuit, one that combined literature with an active engagement in those fields of public endeavour – medical, legal, military, political and religious – which would situate his name among the larger inscriptions of nation and empire. It was the career of someone who, in the heroic iconography of the time, wanted to be seen as 'a great man' but who was, at the same time, pathologically afraid of the the attributes of genius and subversively opposed to the politics of greatness. His writing, whether as fiction, history or propaganda, taught the attributes of self-effacing leadership to a reading public not, by and large, born to lead. Doyle's autobiography, *Memories and Adventures* (1924, 1930), provided a model of the masculine life – one based on his extensive and critically articulate study of life-writing genres. As a follower and defender of Thomas Carlyle, he was fascinated by those genres through which the cultural meaning of masculinity was expounded and commodified.

Doyle's version of authorship derived from the orthodoxies and writing contexts of his Edinburgh upbringing. The masculine *écriture* of Victorian Scotland was one that developed in association with the Cheap Literature Movement vigorously promoted by the Edinburgh publishers, Robert and William Chambers. In imitation of their success, Doyle's writing career carried an ambitious project: that of modernizing and strengthening the representation of British manhood to match the directives of more secular, scientific and empire-conscious culture. This task involved the reworking of archetypal configurations. Doyle recast the dominant masculine archetypes – of the warrior, the lover, the king-father and the priest-magician[1] – in the serial heroes of his short fiction: Brigadier Gerard, Professor Challenger and, above all, Sherlock Holmes. As the priest-magician, Sherlock Holmes was Doyle's most inspired diagnostician of breaches and vulnerabilities in the modern domain of the masculine sign. 221B Baker Street became a magical site at which deformed, anxious and estranged masculinities encountered the corrective resymbolizations of a manhood predicated on an advanced and intelligent control of language codes.

Masculinity is represented in Doyle's writing as a bifurcated concept, as both a pathology and an order, a set of ludic rules which
could be copied, learned and publicly performed, and a problematic
essentialism activated and defined by its relationship to written and
spoken language. For this reason, the archetype of the clown, magician, priest and healer is the dominant one of Doyle's career, configuring
a transgressible border between essence and construct, predatory animal and performative spirit. The figure of the magician appears, too,
as a transformer of stories on the interface between autobiography
and fiction. In the most important friendships of Doyle's life, those
with Dr George Turnavine Budd and later with the escapologist
'Houdini', the magician-figure mediates and exchanges the representation of self and other.

For Doyle the meaning of masculinity was located in the writing
practices and ideological interpolations which compelled masculine bodies
to respect the privileged laws of their own representation. As the prescribed reading of a British boyhood, Doyle's writing imprints on its
readership powerful expectations of ethical conduct that are closely
allied to the language codes of the Holmes stories. Formulaic and
entrapping, the comedic apparatus of Doyle's fiction is, in Foucault's
terms, a literary panoptican, 'a machine for creating and sustaining a
power relation independent of the person who exercises it'. Doyle's
readers, like the prison inmates of Discipline and Punish, are 'caught up
in a power situation of which they are themselves the bearers'.[2]

The masculine sign-surveillance of Doyle's writing, however, is under
the eye of the 'Comic Spirit' and owes more to the comedic theories of
his literary mentor, George Meredith, than to nineteenth-century prison
technology. Adopting Meredith's approach to the policing of masculine
interiority, Doyle saw comedic surveillence as a distinctively British
form of ideological control and cultural supremacy.[3] Where Sigmund
Freud, a conscious imitator of the Holmesian diagnostic method,[4] saw a
puzzling attribute of the super-ego in humour,[5] Doyle identified it as
one of the fundamental qualities of the spirit. For him, humour was a
sign of spiritual survival, flowing through the discontinuities of the
death experience and reconnecting the broken threads of individual
identity with the same persistence that the British army in Afghanistan,
Sudan and South Africa recovered from its recurrent defeats. Sherlock
Holmes in particular was designed to associate Meredithian notions of
the Comic Spirit with the new theories of genius postulated by Doyle's
admired colleague in the field of psychic research, F. W. H. Myers.
According to Myers, 'the subliminal personality' operating at 'supraliminal' levels produced 'a surviving self', a core of identity relatively
unchallenged by death.[6]

While Holmes and Watson offer the reassurances of a moral order within the very structures of the English language, they do so in the name of a manhood which requires a relentless policing of its own criminal shadows. Fantasies of the concealed and invisible self and its covert activities are everywhere the subject of Holmes's deciphering panoptican. Significantly, Holmes uses his own experience of narcotic trance to mirror and penetrate the fantasies of his opponents and to prohibit the kind of interiority that believes itself free of surveillance. Written from the edges of a taboo articulation, the Holmes stories excite, not just by their deductive reasoning, but by their teasing suggestion of alternative and more *outré* disclosures. As part of their unofficial policing of British manhood, they ingeniously silence the articulation of the forbidden materials of masculine fantasy. They find comedic devices to trope the emotional and sexual repressions and indiscretions of a morally responsible masculine code. Animals – especially dogs or the notoriously sibilant swamp adder in *The Speckled Band* – are used as criminal scapegoats for the repressed material of stories in which, to decipher this famously enigmatic title, to speak all is banned.

It is, above all, the presence of Dr Watson, the literary emblem of an unimaginative decency, which controls and guarantees this continual suppression. As the normative, unexceptional Englishman, Watson understands lust, greed, addiction and gambling, but the more intricately perverse forms of criminal subjectivity are beyond his range. Where Doyle himself collected details of sexual perversion, the unEnglish vices of the Holmes stories invariably have dog kennels drawn decently in front of them. In the very last Holmes story, 'The Adventure of the Retired Colourman' from *The Case Book of Sherlock Holmes* (1927) a miserly and impotent old painter turns his strongroom into a gas chamber to provide the final solution for his unfaithful wife and her chess-playing lover. Attempting to explain such vengeful fantasies to a puzzled Watson, Holmes attributes to the murderer the mindset of a 'medieval Italian' rather than that of a 'modern Briton'.[7] As the icons of a distinctively British masculinity, Holmes and Watson stand for the surveillance and suppression of the kind of male interiorities graphically catelogued by Klaus Theweleit in his study of Nazi masculinity, *Male Fantasy* (1989).

Germany and Austro-German culture became, for Doyle, the murderous other of his writing about British manhood, and also a covert part of its meaning. Austria, where he himself was partly educated, is represented in his autobiography as a place of satisfied hungers and disproportionately large instruments. His only 'memory' of his year in Feldkirch is of having his bed linen stuffed up his Bombardon by his fellow students.[8] Sherlock Holmes of course has, as he reminds his

German counterpart, the spymaster Von Bork in *His Last Bow*, 'done a good deal of business in Germany' since his first European triumph of separating Irene Adler from the King of Bohemia.[9] In the final collection of Holmes stories, *The Case Book of Sherlock Holmes*, Watson's 'case-book' itself is matched and mirrored by the 'lust-diary' of the Austrian wife-murderer, Baron Adelbert Gruner.

Holmes is himself, in many ways, a totemic figure of the kind of male fantasy detailed by Theweleit. His unemotional repudiation of women, his subjection of what Theweleit calls ' the whole desiring production of the unconscious' to repression and, above all, the massive egotism and sense of limitless power which accompanies his erasure of human parentage all conform to the fascist pattern.[10] Placed in the writing context of John H. Watson, however, the sadistic fantasy components of Holmes are refathered and subject to the symbolizations of a covert Christian schema which reinscribes manliness as a desirable presence. Holmes and Watson detect the masculine absences of their culture, supply the deficiencies of the patriarchal father and control the signification of an unacceptable fantasy whose exposure threatens the status of manhood. Specifically, the Holmes stories utilize a private and playful language by which Doyle covertly encodes autobiographical impulses of his own.

The role of Holmes in Doyle's own life involves a similar surveillance, a strict control of fantasy through a formulaic repetition of the father–son relationship. In repeated acts of self-invention, Doyle moved steadily, throughout his career, closer to the centre of an English culture whose masculine models he, like the Scottish biographer, James Boswell, felt compelled to refashion. Through their double language of private reference, the Holmes stories act to affirm Doyle's links with his paternal grandfather, the Irish political cartoonist, John Doyle. They also act as a talisman against more treacherous and more dangerous affiliations. Holmes is the guarantor of Doyle's remarkable creation of himself, in the face of many counter-impulses, as the embodiment of a composite 'British' manhood whose private history exists in subversive graffiti beneath its dominant modes of representation.

Doyle's version of what Graham Dawson, in his now well-known study *Soldier Heros* (1994), has collectively labelled 'Empire-Man', does not altogether conform to the stereotypical figure that cultural histories of Victorian masculinity have increasingly tended to invoke. British imperialism for Doyle involved complex negotiations with his own most troubled sources of identity, his religious beliefs, the Irish nationalism of his father, Charles Altamonte Doyle, and his own deep identification with Scotland. His autobiography, *Memories and Adventures*, offers the conflicted history of the United Kingdom as a distinctive geography, the 'landscape for a good man' whose prosopopeia configured the nation itself. The varied genres of Doyle's writing self-consciously inform this topography: his historical fiction is a construct of his own attempt at Englishness, the authority of his war correspondence and military history is Scottish in affiliation, while his Spiritualism attempts to locate itself in the lost poetry of Wales. The mainstay of his career, however, remained the Anglo-Irish partnership of Holmes and Watson.

Doyle's life was wide-ranging in its literary productions and increasingly combative in its commitments. Noisy causes attracted him. He was as willing to investigate poltergeist phenomena as he was to fight legal campaigns against miscarriages of justice or to write instant histories of the British at war. This broad and public-spirited approach concealed what might be considered a literary failure – his refusal to challenge the silencing censorship of Holmes or to engage in the direct representation of politically controversial issues. Taboo areas of discourse are configured in Doyle's fiction as a recurrent landscape of bog and mire, whose treacherously sinking surface only dogs and spirits could cross in safety. Consequently, while he has often been acknowledged for his seminal contribution to the detective story, the rest of his work has received relatively little critical attention. Nonetheless, it remains a varied and interesting *oeuvre*, one shaped by his preoccupation with the national determinants of masculinity and the uncertain face and mission of British imperialism.

Inheriting a nineteenth-century mythology derived largely from Carlyle and Macaulay which equated Protestant manhood with a privileged version of truthfulness, Doyle's literary career was informed by his compulsive interest in 'truth-genres', especially those of history, biography, journal, oral witness, legal testimony and scientific case-study. A Catholic by birth, he taught himself the accents of English Protestantism by inscribing truthfulness as a framing device in his representations of masculinity. For Doyle, however, whose propaganda for the British cause during the Boer War earned him a knighthood, the domain of truth, like that of the Empire itself, was mapped and troped as an improved and memorable versionality, whose boldness of outline could exonerate potentially de-authenticating inconsistencies within. His model of manhood was a similar one but in 1916, acknowledging the exclusions of that broad outline, he decisively broke the mould.

Whether learning to read or wrestling with addiction, facing the fear of battle or the threat of the uncanny, Doyle consistently defined masculinity, whether in men or women, as the courageous encounter with a potentially annihilating otherness. It was an encounter with which he became personally familiar following his controversial and often ridiculed conversion to Spiritualism in 1916. Hoping for recognition as a serious military historian following his six-volume history of the First

World War, he became known instead by the apparently irreconcilable polarities of his career: his creation of Sherlock Holmes on the one hand, and his support for the seance on the other. These stark polarities collapse once the inner history of his writing is read in its entirety. Just as Holmes was a reassuring prophylactic against the dangerous lures of Theosophy and the secret societies it fostered, so Spiritualism was a prophetic intelligence device, a preventive against cultural collapse and a continuation of propaganda by other means.

Doyle's Spiritualism and his Sherlock Holmes stories are dialogic in their mutual fascination with cryptic writing ciphers and the secret intelligence codes of the alphabet. The opposition they invoke is not one between reason and irrationality; instead, it is located in their incompatible cultures with regard to naming and identification. Himself a celebritized name, Holmes's function is that of correctly identifying problematic bodies. The spirits, on the other hand, revel in their freedom from sign, whether verbal or physical, and their insistent rejection of public identity. Skilled in the reconstruction of missing letters, Doyle also found in Spiritualism the occluded body of Victorian medical science and an antidote to the poisonous silences of his own past. After the execution of his friend and colleague, Roger Casement, whom he had already inscribed as the hero of his novel, *The Lost World*, Doyle came to believe that his own writing was itself a haunted site, not just a burial ground of desperate gambles and corpse-like configurations but a necrophylic art of safe bets and accurate predictions.

Despite the relative neglect of his work, Doyle's life story has been the subject of repeated biographical and fictional reconstructions. As recent biographies of him continue to testify, his version of the adventurous manly life retains considerable nostalgic appeal. *Memories and Adventures*, significantly written in the early 1920s at the height of his Spiritualist mission, is the anchoring text for these admiring biographies. This anchor is a deceptive one, encrypting the political nature of Doyle's engagement with Christianity and Christian Spiritualism during the last phase of his life. In his book, *The Sinews of the Spirit* (1985) Norman Vance has traced a progressive decline in the ideal of Christian manliness from the mid- to the late nineteenth century and the eventual 'unmanning of manliness' during the First World War: 'What was left of Christian manliness', Vance claims, 'was desperately wounded in the trenches.'[11] Kaja Silverman, in her seminal study *Male Subjectivity at the Margins* (1992), has reiterated Theodor Reik's contention that Christianity as a religion represents 'the utter negation of all phallic values', arguing further that Christianity is intrinsically incompatible with the pretensions of masculinity.[12]

Christian Spiritualism, however, appears to be something of an exception to these theoretical rulings, replacing 'phallic values' of mastery and domination with a more explorative ethic of continuity and responsible development. The construction of masculinity in these terms was particularly significant for those sectors of society without a major investment in the institutions of state power or the ideological strategies of the English public schools. The movement at whose head Doyle placed himself had a strong and coherent appeal for many articulate and intelligent members of an increasingly educated working class, from the Chartist poet, Gerald Massey to the socialist editor, Robert Blatchford. The testimonials of obscure but impressively self-educated artisans like the Coventry ribbon weaver, Joseph Gutteridge, illustrate the importance of Christian Spiritualism in sustaining notions of manhood through the deprivations of a working life spent under what Gutteridge, in his autobiography, calls 'the blighting influence of the dark shadows of Materialism' and its 'philosophy of non-responsibility'.[13] According to Gutteridge, who made Stradivarius violins in his spare time, it was 'the investigation of spiritual phenomena, guided by works that were within the means of a working man' that enabled him to reaffirm his manhood and 'emerge towards the sunlight of reason'.

Like the contestations of Doyle's own fiction, Spiritualism spoke directly to and from the inner man. Sceptically attending a seance in Bedworth, Gutteridge records how a spirit, writing through an entranced medium, suddenly announced itself as 'Satan'. The moment changed his awareness of himself:

> With the bravado and self-consciousness characteristic of a youth with a smattering of science, I was bent on discovering and exposing imposture, and said, 'You are just the chap I want.' ... I had not finished the sentence before I was apparently transported to the frigid zone; I felt like a statue of ice, every fibre in my body being frozen and rigid – a most horrible sensation. Fearlessly and defiantly exercising my will power, which had been momentarily paralysed by the suddenness of the ocurrence, I freed myself from this uncanny condition. Another member of the party felt a similarly chilling influence.[14]

Just as Gutteridge went on to became a convert, so, for Doyle, Spiritualism was the culmination of a literary career devoted to the language of masculinity and its lifelong demonization of the inner being.

While *Memories and Adventures* outlines a model life, it is a model which now rings hollow with the repetitions of biographers content to redeploy Doyle's own self-epistemology while ignoring the Spiritualist context within which it was written. In trying to restore some of the missing contexts of Doyle's writing career, I have also tried to read some of the silences of his own life story, deconstructing his own fiction where necessary to supply the inner texts of a very public man. A post-modern or post-structural art of biography still needs to be formulated and, in writing this book, I have been conscious of such a theoretical lack. Following recent scholars of Romanticism such as Mary Jacobus and Jerome Christensen, I have tried to dissolve 'the protective divisions between persons and texts'[15] in an attempt to explore the tortured and sometimes hilarious tensions between the inner and the outer man joined together in the name of Arthur Conan Doyle.

There is no excuse for writing a dull book on Doyle. As his work is known and valued by a wide community of readers outside academia, I have tried as far as possible to balance the often contradictory requirements of gender theory, cultural history, literary criticism and readability. While each chapter has a distinct focus organized according to the different genres of Doyle's writing, there is an orchestration between them in which Holmes has to take his place as the subliminal and surviving centre of the diverse and sometimes diffuse strands of Doyle's writing identity.

Notes

1. See Moore, R. and Gillette, D., *King, Warrior, Magician, Lover: Redis-covering the Archetypes of The Mature Masculine*, New York: Harper Collins Pulishers, 1991.
2. Foucault, M., *Discipline and Punish: The Birth of the Prison*, Harmondsworth: Penguin Books, 1991, p. 201.
3. See Meredith, G., 'An Essay on Comedy', in W. Sypher, *Comedy*, New York: Doubleday Anchor Books, 1956, and also Meredith, G., Prelude to *The Egoist*, Harmondsworth: Penguin Books, 1968.
4. See Shepherd, M., *Sherlock Holmes and the Case of Dr Freud*, London and New York: Tavistock Publications, 1985.
5. Freud writes: 'If it is really the super-ego which speaks such kindly words of comfort to the imtimidated ego, this will teach us that we have still a great deal to learn about the nature of the super-ego': Freud, S., 'Humour' in *Art and Literature*, The Penguin Freud Library, vol. 14, Harmondsworth: Penguin Books, 1990, p. 443.
6. Myers, F. W. H., *Human Personality and its Survival of Bodily Death*, vol. 1, Cambridge: Longmans, Green and Co., 1903, p. 73.
7. Doyle, A. C., 'The Adventure of The Retired Colourman', in *The Penguin Complete Adventures of Sherlock Holmes*, Harmondsworth: Penguin Books, 1981, p. 1120.
8. See Doyle, A. C., *Memories and Adventures*, London: John Murray, 1930, pp. 24–5.
9. Doyle, A. C., 'His Last Bow', in *The Penguin Complete Adventures of Sherlock Holmes*, p. 979.
10. Theweleit, K., *Male Fantasies*, vol. 2, Cambridge: Polity Press, 1989, p. 241.

11. Vance, N., *The Sinews of the Spirit: The Ideal of Christian Manliness in Victorian Literature and Religious Thought*, Cambridge: Cambridge University Press, 1985, p. 201.
12. Silverman, K., *Male Subjectivity at the Margins*, London: Routledge, 1992, pp. 196–8.
13. Gutteridge, J., *Lights and Shadows in the Life of an Artisan*, Coventry: Curtis and Beamish, 1893, p. 275.
14. Ibid., p. 132.
15. Chase, C. (ed.), *Romanticism*, London and New York: Longman, 1993, p. 114.

CHAPTER ONE

Model with Damaged Eyes:
Autobiographical Writings

'Was it for this the clay grew tall?'

Wilfred Owen, 'Futility' (1918)

Representing masculinity

This book is *not* a biography of Arthur Conan Doyle (1859–1930), but it is impossible to engage in any discussion of Doyle's career without acknowledging the biographical frames within which his writing was situated. He planned for himself a life of public meaning, and biography is his literary element. His favourite reading consisted of work in this genre – the inumerable biographies, autobiographies, memoirs and diaries whose literary accents he could replicate and parody with such ease and humour. His own diverse writings constitute a body of work in search of its own autobiographer.

While Sherlock Holmes and his half-infatuated, half-infuriated biographer, Dr Watson, have retained their place in our culture, studies of other aspects of Doyle's career have been relatively rare. His significance has been located less in his fiction or war histories than in his life story. A popular subject for repeated biographies, Doyle has also existed as a quasi-fictional character in a number of novels, plays and films devoted to some of the more controversial aspects of his life. These include his war writing, his legal campaigning, his willing suspension of disbelief in fairies and his resolute championship of the spirit world. His high-profile stance on these issues has enabled reconstruction of him as a post-modern literary hybrid, a figure who crosses and reconstitutes the boundaries of fictional representation.

Although this book is not a biography of Doyle, it does offer a reading of his career which emphasizes his engagement with Victorian biographical debate. It also addresses the main controversies of recent biographical scholarship. These controversies have been listed by Jon Lellenberg in *The Quest for Sir Arthur Conan Doyle: Thirteen Biographers in Search of a Life* as influential in shaping and preserving Doyle's uncertain literary reputation. The ambiguity surrounding him derives from his high status as an icon of British masculinity compared to the more modest placing of his literary achievements. His version of author-ship was socially engaged and combative, his task as much the social performance of masculinity as the production of texts. A 1907 review of Doyle describes him as having established the profession of letters on a footing equivalent to that of law, medicine or banking

> He is a publicist, he is a philosopher, he is a man of affairs, he is a combatant in the political arena, and he is a philanthropist ... In a way, he may be taken as the John Bull of Letters, with all the virtues and many of the limitations of that traditional and compos-ite personality.[1]

Doyle himself considered that the popularity of the Sherlock Holmes stories had been detrimental to his reputation as a serious writer.

Jon Lellenberg has identified five recurrent problems for the biogra-pher of Doyle, three of them relating to his literary persona. What, he asks, was the 'real mind' of the man behind works whose reassuring propaganda on behalf of British manhood was their most influential quality? How can his intelligence and achievement be assessed? On the one hand, Doyle once claimed, in a piece of bravura rhetoric, to be simply 'the man in the street',[2] a Briton of representative ordinariness who could (and did) use the pseudonym 'Smith' to represent himself. On the other hand, Doyle was famous as the creator of the mastermind, Sherlock Holmes, and of the ingenious detective puzzles it was his function to decipher. A third line of argument again follows Doyle's own self-description, presenting him as not the creator of Sherlock Holmes, but merely as the copier of a brilliant original, replicating the detective methods of his Edinburgh medical professor, Dr Joseph Bell. Holmes, in Doyle's account, was a figure of composite masculine achieve-ment, as reliant on the famous illustrations of Sidney Paget as on his real-life model, Dr Bell.

The penultimate and most intractable problem, according to Lellenberg, concerns Doyle's Spiritualist crusade. The issue here is one of masculine definition and a perception that his Spiritualism under-mines that identification with post-Enlightenment reason used to guarantee the masculinity of the Holmes stories. 'Real men' like Doyle simply do not – or at least should not publicly – believe in spirits. Harry Houdini, Doyle's friend and opponent on this issue in the early 1920s, took a more appropriate public stance, using his own tricks to expose as fraudulent any medium claiming contact with the spirit world.

By the late nineteenth century, biography had become established as the main literary forum for the public configuration of an idealized manhood. As Dr Watson repeatedly illustrated, the male biographer and his subject combined to produce a work which sustained the trans-mission of a culturally produced masculinity while rewriting the life-text between father and son. Although Doyle's 1979 biographer, Julian Symons, describes him as 'a bluff Imperialist extrovert' and a 'Victorian Phillistine',[3] most biographies, including *Teller of Tales* (1999) by Daniel Stashower, retain a strong admiration for their subject that resembles hagiography.

Doyle himself was an adept in the creation of masculine stereotypes. The grandson of an Irish portrait painter turned political cartoonist, he was a writer whose family had, for three generations, specialized in the depiction of a masculinity which inoffensively interrogated the dominant representational practices of the nineteenth century. The instantly recognizable figure of Sherlock Holmes has behind it the equally familiar icons of Punch and John Bull as etched by his uncle, Richard, and his grandfather, John Doyle.

Partly because of the prolonged unavailability of Doyle's private papers, the interpretation of his life has remained fixed for longer than is usually the case with controversial or significant writers. He remains an author whose reputation – for manliness, moral integrity, chivalry, sportsmanship, and good-natured gullibility – has been fixed in time as a museum piece of British manhood. There are, however, obviously haunted silences surrounding this display: the story of Doyle's sisters, of his first wife Louise ('Touie'), and of his relationship with his eldest daughter, Mary. Painstaking research by Michael Baker and by Owen Dudley Edwards has provided material for an understanding of Doyle's Edinburgh childhood, his mother's unorthodox domestic, and perhaps sexual, arrangements and the sad story of his estranged, incarcerated, alcoholic father. Despite these discoveries, however, Doyle's model of the manly life has not been subject to iconoclastic acts of literary vandalism. His carefully crafted version of British manhood remains a cherished and protected part of national literary culture. In a post-feminist age, the name of Arthur Conan Doyle continues to stand for masculine presence. It is a presence still subject to investigation and debate.

At the level of the individual reader, Doyle's name is associated primarily with the literature of boyhood, with the books and stories which fathers recommend to sons and by which phases of adolescence are often recalled. From a wider cultural perspective which includes the Great War, Doyle's name and autobiography convey a set of values identified as distinctly British through one of the deepest crises in the nation's history. Significantly, he offered his 'life' as a version of manliness in subtle opposition to that formed and articulated through the English public school system, one that spoke the additional Celticism of his Scottish birthplace and Irish family background. Like the mythic King Arthur, after whom he was not named, Doyle attempted to represent British culture at a point of crisis and disaster, when the masculinities of the Victorian era were recast through the new directives of the First World War and Georgian democracy.

Behind the long list of largely admiring biographies of Doyle which followed the Reverend John Lamond's 1931 family-commissioned *Memoir* stands the text which authorizes them all and ensures their readability: Doyle's *Memories and Adventures* (1924). This autobiography is remarkable for its success in combining some of the opposing conventions of Victorian life-writing. It is both a saint's life, displaying the characteristics and oratorical gifts used to emblematize the life-text of the religious leader, and a secular career autobiography after the model of Anthony Trollope. Doyle's most informed and astute critic, Richard Lancelyn Green, sums up *Memories and Adventures* as a 'romance':

> Arthur Conan Doyle left no mark on history, but he remains a larger-than-life figure, and his career has a certain glamour enabling him to be named in a variety of other contexts. There is also a world set apart from the real one in which Conan Doyle holds centre stage as the 'big man' of his dreams: the champion, the lover of justice, the man of action, the friend of the opressed. It is the world he created around himself, and it was not purely a dream. His autobiography becomes the sequel to his historical novels, for here Sir Arthur vanquishes his foes and wins glory for himself. His life becomes a romance. Indeed many of the illustrations for *The Strand* serializations were drawn as if for an adventure story.[4]

Like the realism that was its representational mode, Victorian masculinity was predicated on the successful copying of ideological models. By the 1870s, however, realism had become associated with notions of containment and confinement, an entrapment of masculine enterprise at odds with the requirements of late-Victorian imperialism. Doyle had determined early on not to become a second Branwell Brontë – a talented Irish wild boy eclipsed by more industrious sisters. He sought support from, and continuity with, models of male professional praxis, seeking to link himself to the achievements of other men, as he did through his tributes to Joseph Bell. In literature he attached himself to that tradition of historical fiction established by Sir Walter Scott, despite the groans of his *Cornhill* editor, James Payn, who considered it an outdated form. Re-energizing and repopularizing the Scottish Romanticism of Byron and Scott, Doyle's career was built around knowing and showing what and how to copy for the achievement of masculine effects.

Memories and Adventures is a culmination of writing expertise committed to this enterprise. It offers at the same time a model life, one which embodies particular manly values in a narrative of triumphant combat, and a mere model, a shell into which different interiorities can be fitted.

Richard Lancelyn Green attributes to Doyle 'a fear of intimacy' which renders his autobiography primarily an act of self-publication: 'When he describes his life, he omits the inner man. There are no revelations, no great pangs of remorse, and no sense of personal injustice.'[5]

Doyle's skill as a propagandist for British manhood partly depended on his outsider status as a Scottish-born Irishman with a Catholic upbringing, a position illustrated by the causes for which he fought. His active commitment to divorce reform, his fight against racist victimization in the *Edalji* case, his exposure of the atrocities of imperial exploitation in the Congo, his petition for the reprieve of Roger Casement, his public attacks on the blindnesses of British justice, the incompetence of British military command and the failings of the English public school system, as much as his faith in the existence of spirits and fairies, all serve to highlight this anomaly in Doyle's career. He may have represented what his son Adrian called 'the true meaning of three words – an English gentleman',[6] but his ability to do so rested uncannily on the fact that he was not what he represented.

Pierre Norton, Doyle's 1964 biographer, takes the same view as Lancelyn Green. He concludes that Doyle was a reluctant autobiographer, unwilling 'to occupy the centre of his own stage'.[7] This lack of intimacy compounds, for Doyle's biographers, the principal problem of his life story: his departure in 1916 from the solidarities of the masculine tradition and his eccentric acceptance instead of fairyland and the spirit world. Written after his high-profile public conversion, the first edition of *Memories and Adventures* nonetheless excludes the main body of Doyle's Spiritualist work, emphasizing the secular rather than the spiritual dimensions of the text's quest. The model life it describes was one that he personally had already left behind.

In place of personal relevation, Doyle's autobiography charts the gradual convergence of two histories – the story of his own life conjoining with that of the British Empire. Providence itself, he claims, used coincidence and uncanny events to affect this conjunction and its gradual sculpting of a representative 'empire' masculinity:

> I believe that Providence one way or another gets a man's full powers out of him, but that it is essential that the man himself should co-operate to the extent of putting himself in the way of achievement. ... Deep in my bones I felt that I was on earth for some big purpose.[8]

As 'signs' and 'prodigia' of Doyle's fitness to represent the collective manhood of his culture, the uncanny events in his life-course, however, indicate a dissident and rebellious energy partly at odds with what it serves. There is a joke-force in the secular story of his career which anticipates the sudden change of identity that concludes it.

This rictus between Doyle's worldly career and his spiritual vocation is first located in 1900 when he returned from the Boer War and stood as a Liberal Unionist parliamentary candidate for Central Edinburgh. Although unelected, Doyle discovered at the hustings his powers of oratory. Hearing him address an audience of hecklers, his brother, Innes, was deeply impressed:

> 'It would be strange, Arthur,' said he, 'if your real career should prove to be political and not literary.'
> 'It will be neither. It will be religious,' said I. Then we looked at each other in surprise and both burst out laughing ... . It was a curious example of that unconscious power of prophecy which is latent within us.[9]

Whatever their providential design, the recurrence of such 'psi phenomena' in Doyle's autobiography often 'speak' the hidden words of personal memory. The Edinburgh location of this outburst of laughter is important. Doyle remarks in passing that there may have been 'some sentimental call' behind his decision to stand for this seat as it was 'the section of the city where I was educated and where much of my boyhood was spent'.

Autobiography is a teleological form, aimed towards a particular outcome. In an essay on its use in the writing of biography, Kenneth Silverman has drawn attention to the danger of treating autobiography as fact rather than 'personal mythology', insisting that autobiographies owe their allegiance primarily to the time and context of their writing: 'They represent the subject's attempt at that moment to explain how he came to be what he is'.[10] Integral to the structure of his autobiography was Doyle's tracing of the linkage between his own life and that of the nation whose military historian he also became. 'Thus it was', he writes, 'that we learned of the next adventure which was opening up before both us and the British Empire'[11] and, again, 'My life was filled with alternate work and sport. As with me so with the nation'.[12] Throughout his narrative, the British Empire provides Doyle with his main source of intersubjectivity, his partnership with history being the visible process of a masculinity repeatedly reinscribed. This process of connection had begun in 1896 when the illness of his wife, Touie, had taken the Doyles to Egypt for the winter. An excursion across the Libyan desert bought Doyle in contact with the opening phases of the British reconquest of the Sudan. Although he saw little more than a glimpse of Kitchener and a camel recruitment drive, Doyle's brief spell as a volunteer war correspondent began a process of writerly self-transformation. It would lead him to become the historian of, and propagandist for, the British position in the Boer War, and then to produce, from 1916, a contemporaneous six-volume account of *The British Campaign in France and Flanders*.

Doyle wrote and published *Memories and Adventures* in the aftermath of a demoralizing war whose history he had also written. As a memorializing autobiography, it is an evocation and reminder, during the defacements of the post-war years, of what the values and traditions of nineteenth-century British manhood had been. In a famous First World War sonnet, 'When You See Millions of the Mouthless Dead', Charles Sorley had described such an erasure of identity as one of the most chilling effects of the war

> should you
> Perceive one face that you loved heretofore,
> It is a spook. None wears the face you knew.[13]

Like Doyle's simultaneous advocacy of spirit photography, *Memories and Adventures* was an attempt to restore the features, and ensure the continuing vitality, of a lost generation whose lives had been influenced by his own fiction. Victorian codes of masculinity had been grimly interrogated by the poets of the Great War. Unlike Tennyson's Light Brigade in the Crimea, the poets of the First World War considered that it *was* for them very distinctly to reason why. Perhaps the most direct and formidable question was posed by Wilfred Owen in his short poem, 'Futility', which tries to address the ultimate meaning of a masculine life. 'Was it', he asks rhetorically of a dead comrade, 'for this the clay grew tall?' The question might well be posed to Doyle himself, for his writing had consistently inscribed the encounter with death as the signifier of an essential, and essentialist, masculinity.

In his prophetic elegy, 'Strange Meeting', Wilfred Owen had mourned some irreparable loss of healing essence following the war experience and had posited a resulting separation between poetry and the masculine experience. 'Now', the poem contends, 'men will go content with what we spoiled'.[14] While the War Poets offered their mutilated images of a formerly vital body of truth, male autobiographers of the immediate post-war period tried to reintegrate the trauma of war, contextualizing their war experience within the category of a continuing masculine adventure. Winston Churchill's *My Early Life* (1930), Sir Patrick Hastings's *Autobiography* (1848) and Jack Seeley's *Adventures* (1931) all assert continuity with the late Victorian adventure tradition. Robert Graves's *Goodbye to All That* (1929) – a poet's autobiography – tries, at the cost of its own integrity, to pull the work of the two genres together. Doyle's *Memories and Adventures* does not offer itself as a farewell but, it goes without saying, registers with exemplary force a dislocation in its central masculine concept.

Doyle's autobiography offers a classic account, not so much of the inner man, but of that phase of British manhood which had found, in war, adventure and nationhood its most reliable source of identity. Eliding the celebrity writer with his national culture, Doyle concludes *Memories and Adventures* with an account of the Armistice Day celebrations in 1918. As he joins the singing and cheering crowds assembled outside Buckingham Palace, he is able to merge the end of his life story with the reassurances of a renewed colonial fertility:

> They say that it was when the Australian wounded met the War Office flappers that the foundations of solid old London got loosened. But we have little to be ashamed of, and if ever folk rejoiced we surely had the right to do so. We did not see the new troubles ahead of us, but at least these old ones were behind. And we had gained an immense reassurance. Britain had not weakened. She was still the Britain of old.[15]

Only one image contests this version of closure – a 'blot' in the writing that speaks of a different spirit. A drunken civilian in the company of three uniformed officers ignores the singing and pours a bottle of whisky down his throat instead. This 'Irish' saboteur of uniformity is condemned with uncharacteristic venom:

> I saw this civilian hack at the neck of a whisky bottle and drink it raw. I wish the crowd had lynched him. It was the moment for prayer, and this beast was a blot on the landscape.

Unbuttoning an autobiography which conflates self and nation, this episode illustrates a remarkable feature of Doyle's writing: his ability graphically to image contestation of his own discourse. In 1930, six years after its initial publication, Doyle returned to *Memories and Adventures* and, in the manner of a post-modern novel, produced an alternative ending, a second final chapter which asserts not Britain's military achievements, but the more controversial aspects of his own psychic research. His book, *The Coming of the Fairies*, may, he unsettlingly suggests, 'be recognized some day as opening a new vista of knowledge for the human race'.[16]

It is this dislocation in the ending(s) of an autobiography committed to the communal story of the British Union and its empire which makes it such an interesting chronicle of British masculinity at its moment of most decisive change. At the same time, Doyle's alternative ending uses Spiritualism to reformulate the encounter with death as the essential signifier of the masculine life. This encounter and the spiritual meaning that it could generate remained, for Doyle, the ground for the conquest of which the clay had indeed grown tall.

As Byron had illustrated a century earlier in his epoch-making Romantic autobiographical poem *Childe Harold's Pilgrimage* (1812–17), the adventure autobiography celebrates personal and historical discontinuity as a fashioning principle of the masculine. Byron's *Childe Harolde* records as a spiritual 'pilgrimage' his journey across the ruined landscapes of Europe, mourning the interior damage through which he is compelled to view and chronicle revolutionary history. These damaged landscapes reappear in even more fragmented form in T. S. Eliot's Modernist revision of this pilgrimage, *The Waste Land* (1922). Where Eliot's quest fails to supply answers to the post-war crisis, finding only the broken images of a hallucinating culture, Doyle's writing remains as it had begun, a continuous attempt to trace predictive figures of the spirit in the landscapes of the desert.

While a great deal of critical and cultural attention has been focused on Doyle's involvement with the Cottingley Fairies, little has yet been given to the more radically challenging issues that emerge from his Spiritualist beliefs and his commitment to psychic research. The fairies, their cultural context restored to them, are relatively easy to integrate into Doyle's life story, as he himself reintegrated the legacy of his fairy-painting father by organizing a commemorative exhibition of his work in 1924. The fairies are both the nemesis of 'the Great Man' biographical tradition that Doyle's writing had served, and an emotional resource deep in British culture. Less destructive than great men with their murderous war machines, the fairies represented a lost pleasure principle, their light, slight bodies dispersable but not able to sustain the mutilations and amputations of a more robustly damageable human body. The fairies represent that which, in always being lost, provided a continuous geneology of British culture, linking it back to Shakespeare and the earliest traditions of folklore. E. M. Forster in *Howard's End* (1910) had identified this form of mythology as quintessentially English:

> Why has not England a great mythology? Our folklore has never
> advanced beyond daintiness, and the greater melodies about our
> country-side have all issued through the pipes of Greece. Deep and
> true as the native imagination can be, it seems to have failed here.
> It has stopped with the witches and the fairies.[17]

The fairies also symbolize rejected identity paths for Doyle, associated particularly with his lost father, the mentally unstable Charles Altamonte Doyle whose confinement, first in a nursing home and then in a mental asylum, coincided in 1879 with the start of Doyle's literary career. In fairness to Doyle's reputation, it should be stated that, although he wrote a book about fairies, he did not actually endorse belief in them. He championed believers in fairies as he championed the mediumship of many humble and obscure people, particularly if they happened to share his Scottish background.

Doyle was aware, in adding a new conclusion to his autobiography, that he was radically decentering the text that preceded it: 'It is hardly fair to the unsuspecting reader to lure him so far and then to precipitate him into a final chapter of psychic propaganda.'[18] The final chapter of *Memories and Adventures* tries to normalize the weirdness of that journey and to bring it into conformity with the generic demands of the masculine career autobiography. He does not describe his Spiritualist mission in any detail, offering *Memories and Adventures* as the record of a vocation rather than a spiritual autobiography.

In retrospect, however, the nature of that vocation is less easy to define. Despite his formidable reputation as a man of his word, Doyle was also a brilliant liar. His concept of truth, like his version of masculinity, was twofold, hinging together opposing aspects of truthfulness. In his autobiography he frequently employs anecdotes about animals to signal acts of literary deception or to trope the non-representation of occluded material. He also used books to figure acts of autobiographical substitution. Named texts in his narrative often signal, and stand in for, the unspeakable or absent signifiers of the self-story. In a discussion of Victorian discourses of sexuality, Simon Szreter has identified 'a culturally engendered denial of the body and physical aspects of sexuality, through the withdrawal from usage of the signifying words and linguistic resources'. Although 'medically trained adult males' in particular possessed these linguistic resources, their use was suppressed in the interests of the patriarchal culture:

> A patriarchal culture ... prized the eternal self-vigilance necessary for the cultivation of personal, rational, bodily self-control, as the key to manliness, moral worth and material and social success.[19]

Doyle's use of books as a reversible image for such suppressed discourse is a characteristic strategy in his self-definition. After the excitements of his Sudanese adventure in 1896, for example, he began his return journey to Cairo and the sick wife he had left there. He found himself on board an intolerably slow cargo boat, travelling up the Nile with nothing to eat except tinned apricots and nothing to read except a copy of Rousseau's *The Confessions*. The nauseous taste of these interiorities stayed with him for life:

> I never wish to see a tinned apricot so long as I live. I associate their cloying sweetness with Rousseau's 'Confessions', a French edition of which came somehow into my hands and was my only reading till I saw Assouan once more. Rousseau also I never wish to read again.[20]

The rejection of *The Confessions* tropes a similar rejection of his own inner story at this point of redefinition, as Doyle's adventures begin to link him with the needs of the British Empire rather than those of his sick wife. In his substitutive strategies for truth-telling, books metonymically signal what he managed to forget while reading them. This former Irish medical student, returning to a wife whose invasive illness receives little mention once it had dictated the course of his travels, must have started uncomfortably at what he read in Book 6 of the *Confessions* for it offered a mirroring reversal of his own story. Travelling in search of a cure for an illness as ill-defined as Touie's, Rousseau found himself staying at an Irish boarding house where the food was so bad that it gave him indigestion. Here he was taught English by a group of Irish medical students, for whose profession he expressed little respect:

> It was clear that my doctors, who had discovered nothing about my illness, regarded me as a hypochondriac ... doctors only admit to be true such things as they are able to explain ... . These gentlemen understood nothing about my complaint; therefore I was not ill.[21]

The rejected text in this instance is not merely Rousseau and his French confessional mode of life-writing. Here the *Confessions* stand in place of confessions, switching stories with the guilts of his own private life while at the same time allowing them this marginal and disguised voice within his own writing. Unsurprisingly, Doyle's lifelong interest in Spiritualism and psychic phenomena derived initially from uncanny encounters with books. His first experience of a convincing psychic phenomenon was recorded in a letter written in 1887 to the Spiritualist magazine, *Light*. It concerned a seance in Southsea with a medium called Mr Horstead. Prior to the seance, Doyle had been debating whether or not he should read a particular book, Leigh Hunt's *Comic Dramatists of the Restoration*. His published account of this seance, stating his belief that intelligence could exist apart from the body, runs as follows:

> Last week I was invited by two friends to join them in a sitting with an old gentleman who was reputed to have considerable mediumistic power ... . On sitting, our medium came quickly under control, and delivered a trance address ... . We then proposed writing. The medium took up a pencil, and after a few convulsive movements, he wrote a message to each of us. Mine ran 'This gentleman is a healer. Tell him from me not to read Leigh Hunt's book ... .'[22]

Doyle's love of books is closely related to the masculine intimacies of the biographical tradition. It is not by accident that his essays and critical writings present him at his most familiar, supplying in his discussion of books the intimacy lacking in his formal autobiography. Nineteenth-century biography, in particular, linked subject, biographer and reader into a synergy dedicated to the cultural transmission of masculinity, offering access to the shared achievements of masculine lives. Doyle's only collection of critical essays, *Through the Magic Door*, originally written in 1894 but not published in book form until 1907, is distinctive for its celebration of life-writing as a genre or even *the* genre perhaps, for as he claims: 'Each cover of a true book enfolds the concentrated essence of a man. The personalities of the writers have faded ... yet, here are their very spirits at your command.'[23] Doyle defines the ideal biographer as:

> ... a perfectly impartial man, with a sympathetic mind, but a stern determination to tell the absolute truth. One would like the frail, human side of a man as well as the other. I cannot believe that anyone in the world was ever quite so good as the subject of most of our biographies.[24]

The essays in this collection were addressed to young men aged between seventeen and twenty-two who wanted guidance in their reading. Doyle's aim in his own writing was to increase the literacy skills of this male readership by resymbolizing the works of great literary authorities in more accessible form. Books, he insisted, carried a double inscription of the masculine. In addition to their content, they possessed a strongly gendered physicality and a psychic history of their own: books formed part of the physical exchange, as well as the intellectual currency, of manhood. Describing that part of his library dedicated to military memoirs, Doyle stresses this physicality: 'There is this old brown volume in the corner. ... Take it out and handle it! See how swarthy it is, how squat, with how bullet-proof a cover of scaling leather.'[25] His critical essays are unusual in their insistence that books are, in their own right, forms of personal memory and autobiographical record. Individual volumes have life histories of their own. He vividly invokes this secret life of the book in his description of his favourite volume, Macaulay's *Essays*:

> It seems entwined into my whole life as I look backwards. It was my comrade in my student days, it has been with me on the sweltering Gold Coast, and it formed part of my humble kit when I went a-whaling in the Arctic. Honest Scotch harpooners have addled their brains over it, and you may still see the grease stains where the second engineer grappled with Frederick the Great. Tattered and dirty and worn, no gilt-edged morocco-bound volume could ever take its place for me.[26]

Next to Macaulay who had 'the gift of reconstructing a dead celebrity to a remarkable degree', the novels of Sir Walter Scott are those which, he claims, 'started me on to rhapsody'. Yet this rhapsody is associated with guilty pleasures. He recalls reading Scott surreptitiously 'by candle ends in the dead of night'. Rather than contextualizing this guilty pleasure, however, and telling the story behind his own reading, Doyle tells the story of the book. His copy of *Ivanhoe*, for example, is a replacement one for an original volume which had suicidal instincts:

> The first copy was left in the grass by the side of a stream, fell into the water, and was eventually picked up three days later, swollen and decomposed, upon a mud-bank. I think I may say, however, that I had worn it out before I lost it.[27]

This anecdote of an Ivanhoe-turned-Ophelia invokes a watery landscape that is a recurrent trope in Doyle's fiction whenever he confronts a particular problematic of masculinity – one that involves its disappearance from written representation. It signals a place where lies must be told or substitutions for truth be made.

Through the Magic Door is the most self-revealing of all Doyle's writings. As its title suggests, the library door is a magic door opening on the ideological hinges that link masculine interiority to the externalities of national, cultural life. For Doyle this point of intersection is a place of the spirit, one manifest also in battle cries and chants in which the inner language of the masculine body finds its most intense expression. Confirming Carolyn Steedman's observation that soldiering in the nineteenth century was 'the most common metaphorical expression of a man's life',[28] Doyle's reading preference at this stage of his life was for military memoirs:

> I have found that if I am turned loose in a large library, after hesitating over covers for half an hour or so, it is usually a book of soldier memoirs which I take down. Man is never so interesting as when he is thoroughly in earnest, and no one is so earnest as he whose life is at stake upon the event.[29]

Discussing the soldier's experience of battle, he finds himself suddenly considering the alternative figure of the writer in close encounter with his source of inspiration. This confrontation too had been classically configured as a dangerous, potentially annihilating one. Just as the soldier found in battle an encounter with death that drew upon the masculinity of the spirit, so too the writer could be released from the individual embodiments of truth and enter a subliminal reservoir of meaning. The encounter with death had, as its correlate in both fields, an experience of traumatic namelessness and sign-loss.

Doyle's ambition at the start of his career was to represent a Scottish version of manhood in which fighting and writing were equally figured, a formulation that established strong common ground with contemporary American fiction. While Doyle wished to be, and was often described as, a second Sir Walter Scott, there was, however, an additional dilemma for the late-Victorian writer of soldier stories – one which Scott had been able to ignore. While representations of soldiering carried the glamorous sheen of the essential masculinity, the lessons of the Crimea in 1856–57 had highlighted the squalid impoverishment of the average soldier's lot. Kipling's resymbolization of this impoverishment in *Barrack Room Ballads* presented a working-class masculinity stoically swallowing its own wrongs while salting the earth of Empire with its physical exertions. Describing Kipling's poetry as 'part of my very self',[30] Doyle, in *Memories and Adventures*, positions his own identity at a point of class exchange where he is simultaneously someone and no-one. Repeated self-anecdotes construct him on the verge of being mistaken for someone or something else. When, prior to the Boer War, he took part in a military parade reviewed by the elderly Duke of Cambridge, some minor aberration in Doyle's uniform threw the Duke into hysterical outrage and his company into hysterical laughter. The repeated question 'What is this?' screamed by the Duke 'in a sort of ecstasy'[31] at the rigid figure of the quasi-soldier is one that reverberates through the text to the accompaniment of subversive laughter.

Writing books became Doyle's profession only from 1891 when he abandoned his attempt to acquire celebrity in the medical profession. Throughout the 1880s, Doyle had led two intersecting lives, one as an aspiring writer fascinated by masculine criminality, the other as a GP with an interest in 'locomotor ataxy', that form of spinal paralysis, formerly believed to be associated with venereal disease, which he called 'the special scourge of the imaginative man'.[32] These points of exchange between divergent life stories, different careers and alternative identities are the distinctive territories of Doyle's self-definition, places where the tortured and interrogated male body displays its power of silence against a counter-impulse to emotional articulation or confession.

In *Memories and Adventures*, he describes the ordeals of physical punishment inflicted on him by the Jesuits during his schooldays at Stonyhurst. He adds with approval:

> To take twice nine upon a cold day was about the extremity of human endurance. I think, however, that it was good for us in the end, for it was a point of honour with many of us not to show that we were hurt, and that is one of the best trainings for a hard life ... .
> I went out of my way to do really mischievous and outrageous things simply to show that my spirit was unbroken.[33]

Doyle's autobiography, and indeed his whole career, can be read as a determined attempt to resist the pressures of interiority by repeated changes of location, occupation and representational form. *Memories and Adventures* is remarkable both in its commitment to a code of silence, gendered masculine in its denial of personal subjectivity, and in its ability to outwit that censorship through a range of transgressive representational devices.

The nineteenth century was, for Doyle, the age of charting masculinity through the medium of biography, a much-needed development from the fiction-oriented eighteenth century which had excelled in representations of 'the most delightful ... the most perfect women.'[34] His interest in life-writing formed part of a conscious determination to remodel the masculine image of the literary career. During the later part of the century, literary work had been increasingly represented as erasing the masculinity-sustaining divide between the workplace and the domestic sphere. A seminal figure for Doyle in the context of this debate was Thomas Carlyle, the most important and – by the time Doyle began his own writing – the most vulnerable exponent of a Romantic and heroic ideal of masculinity. Rector of Doyle's own University, embodiment of the Scottish tradition of charting masculine lives, Carlyle had usurped James Boswell's more deferential and objectifying stance and had troped the masculine literary life as a demon controlled, a battle fought in subterranean soils, a problem of divinity worked out in the mundane world.

In terms that would be reiterated throughout the century, Carlyle had defined masculinity as the outcome of these negotiations, its individuality measured by the outline of tasks attempted and the success of its plans. Goethe, Carlyle's model for a life shaped by the true force of masculine selfhood, had achieved 'the harmonious adjustment of Necessity and Accident, of what is changeable and what is unchangeable in our destiny; the calm supremacy of the spirit over its circumstance'. He had instigated a new model of masculine culture, one forged 'in the rugged school of Experience' but freed equally from the Catholic imitation of Christ and the Jewish tendency to moan:

> A gay delineation will give us notice of the dark and toilsome experiences, of business done in the great deep of the spirit; a maxim, trivial to the careless eye, will rise with light and solution over long perplexed periods of our own history. It is thus ... that the life of one man becomes a possession to all.[35]

Carlyle himself, on the other hand, had been an irritable, dyspeptic snob. That at least had been the reluctant conclusion of his own biographer and disciple, J. A. Froude, based on the evidence with which Carlyle himself had supplied him. It is difficult to decide whether it was a commitment to truthfulness, a remorseful self-destructiveness or an unshakeable self-complacency that had accompanied Carlyle's decision to hand over to his biographer-elect the full range of his private papers, along with the responsibility for deciding how much of it should be made public. Within weeks of Carlyle's death in 1881 Froude had published Carlyle's intimate biographical sketches, the *Reminiscences*, written in 1866 after the death of his wife and full of guilty and remorseful self-accusation. Froude's biography of Carlyle began to appear in 1882, attracting immediate controversy for its portayal of a violent and unhappy marriage, and of Carlyle as a needy, domestic tyrant. The issue on which it focused was not merely Carlyle's personal reputation but the appropriate mode of representing a culturally significant masculinity. Leslie Stephen rewrote his essay on 'Autobiography' to include his shocked response to the *Reminiscences*, while Frederick Harrison spoke for many late Victorian readers (and writers) when he commented:

> The biographies and autobiographies ... are intensely interesting. But they have told us things we would rather not have heard ... . Those who love good men and good women, those who honour great intellects, those who reverence human nature, have been wounded to the heart. Foul odours, as from a charnel-house, have been suddenly opened on us.[36]

Froude, who described his biographical task as hanging like a nightmare over him for eleven years, was aware of the controversial issues that he had aroused. In seeking to tell 'the whole truth', he had disturbed an ideologically valuable icon of lettered masculinity. He had also undermined some of the holy ground upon which Victorian cultural icons were erected.[37] Carlyle might have been an inspired writer but he had been appalling to live with, even for a woman like Jane Welsh who was committed to nurturing his genius. Froude – indeed Carlyle himself – had revealed the emotionally exploitative economy of masculine literary achievements, showing how, as Doyle delicately put it with reference to his own childhood, 'The world, not the family, gets the fruits of genius'.[38]

The late Victorian debate about the masculine 'life' invariably involved a wider discussion about cultural representation in general – a debate about history and historians as well as about biography and autobiography. To reassert the active masculinity of authorship, and to associate that masculinity with Scotland, was Doyle's first plan for the construction of his literary career. In 1886, while he was still seeking a publisher for his first novel, he had chosen 'Thomas Carlyle' as the topic for his second public lecture to the Portsmouth Literary and Scientific Society. (His first had been on the Arctic Seas, the region of his first masculine 'adventure'.) When the talk was criticized in the local newspaper for not mentioning 'the darker side of Carlyle's character', Doyle sprang at once to his defence, replying that as 'flies settle on the least sound portion of the meat, so critics love to dwell on the weaker side of a great mind'.[39]

This impulse to protect the reputation of the man who had done so much to create heroic images of the masculine life was to stay with Doyle until the end of the century, and he championed Carlyle's domestic life again in his 'marriage question' novel of 1899, *A Duet*. Doyle's early defence of Carlyle had a further resonance, for Carlyle himself had, in his writing, attacked an Edinburgh contemporary whose public champion Doyle also insisted on becoming. When Carlyle decided to pass on to his biographer that most damaging of texts, the *Reminiscences* of Jane Welsh Carlyle, he had included within it some provocative passages about contemporary masculine decline. One example was particularly outspoken and personalized. Discussing his father-in-law, John Welsh, he comments:

> What year he first went to Edinburgh or entered the University I do not know; I think he was first a kind of apprentice to a famous Joseph or Charles Bell (father of a surgeon still in great practice and renown, though intrinsically stupid, reckoned a sad falling off from his father, in my own time); and with this famed Bell he was a favourite, probably, I think, attending the classes, etc.[40]

Carlyle's attack on Joseph Bell as 'a sad falling off from his father' is now forgotten in the fame attaching to the name as a result of Doyle's widely publicized insistence that he was the original model for Sherlock Holmes. While Holmes was both Doyle's antidote to any theory of masculine decline and a riposte to the rising force of the Women's Movement, his tributes to both Bell and Carlyle were part of his determined advocacy of Scottish manhood, whether past, present or in spirit. He wrote in particular to mediate images of masculinity to the new and newly literate generation of readers for whom the Carlylean traditions of the 'Great Man' were already being replaced by the celebritized middle-class professional icons of *The Strand Magazine*.

In his essay 'Autobiography', revised in the light of the Froude/ Carlyle controversy, Leslie Stephen had pondered the question of what was the best model for masculine self-description. Perhaps for personal reasons, he selected Gibbon as the autobiographer offering the surest exemplum of a life shaped by qualities which were themselves the most desirable signifiers of Victorian masculinity. Gibbon had shaped his own manhood by the perfection of his life-plan, realizing himself through its achievement:

> I know, as everybody knows, what may be said against Gibbon ... .
> And yet ... one cannot help asking, did not Gibbon succeed in solving the problem of life more satisfactorily than almost anyone one knows? ... He has not aimed, perhaps, at the highest mark, but he has hit the bull's eye. Given his conception of life, he has done his task to pefection ... . Though his plan ripened slowly and with

all deliberation, he acted as if he had foreseen the end from the beginning.[41]

If Doyle's first public address on literary matters had been his paper on Carlyle, his second, significantly, had been on Edward Gibbon. In late Victorian discussions of autobiography, Gibbon was used to represent Carlyle's antithesis. Gibbon, as Leslie Stephen made clear, was the man who had avoided the pitfalls of marital partnership and emotional disclosure by excising the female altogether and wedding himself to that more flattering mirror of masculinities, the muse of history. In *Through the Magic Door* Doyle took issue with this assessment of Gibbon:

> Some men are greater than their work. Their work only represents one facet of their character, and there may be a dozen others, all remarkable, and uniting to make one complex and unique creature. It was not so with Gibbon. He was a cold-blooded man, with a brain which seemed to have grown at the expense of his heart.[42]

A prototype of Holmes, Gibbon was a calculating machine who needed, not a wife, but a biographer to humanize him.

In his critical essays on life-writing, Doyle expresses reservations about autobiography as a masculine form. It was, he felt, a genre at odds with the values and ideals of British manhood. He wrote scathingly of Gibbon's six accounts of his own career 'each differing from the other, and all equally bad'. A man, he claimed, must have more heart and soul than Gibbon to write a good autobiography:

> It is the most dificult of all human compositions, calling for a mixture of tact, discretion, and frankness which make an almost impossible blend ... . No British autobiography has ever been frank, and consequently no British autobiography has ever been good. Trollope's, perhaps, is as good as any I know, but of all forms of literature it is the one least adapted to the national genius. ... In one way it is to the credit of the race that it should be so.[43]

Arguing that Pepys's *Diary* with its private cipher for the secret life of its author was the one really great autobiography in the language, Doyle continues:

> As a race we are too afraid of giving ourselves away ever to produce a good autobiography. We resent the charge of national hypocrisy, and yet of all nations we are the least frank as to our emotions ... . Those affairs of the heart, for example, which are such an index to a man's character, and so profoundly modify his life – what space do they fill in any man's autobiography?[44]

Doyle's account of Pepys in *Through the Magic Door* illustrates his view of masculinity as a phenomenon seeking its own double, both in terms of its need for private codes and in the dual focus required to 'sight' the 'greatness' of a particular individual:

> The wonderful thing about Mr. Pepys is that a man should succeed in making himself seem so insignificant when really he must have been a man of considerable character and attainments. Who would guess it ... ! The effect left upon the mind is of some grotesque character in a play, fussy, self-conscious, blustering with women, timid with men, dress-proud, purse-proud, trimming in politics and in religion, a garrulous gossip immersed always in trifles. And yet, though this was the day-by-day man, the year-by-year man was a very diferent person, a devoted civil servant, an eloquent orator, an excellent writer, a capable musician, and a ripe scholar who accumulated 3,000 volumes – a large private library in those days – and had the public spirit to leave them all to his University. You can forgive old Pepys a good deal of his philandering when you remember that he was the only official of the Navy Office who stuck to his post during the worst days of the Plague. He may have been – indeed, he assuredly was – a coward, but the coward who has sense of duty enough to overcome his cowardice is the most truly brave of mankind.[45]

Where Pepys had written himself small in the day-to-day transcripts of the diary, the Scottish biographer, James Boswell, had done the exact opposite, erecting Samuel Johnson as a monument of English manhood:

> If Boswell had not lived I wonder how much we should hear now of his huge friend? With Scotch persistence he has succeeded in inoculating the whole world with his hero worship ... .
> ... it is not by chance that a man writes the best biography in the language.[46]

Trying to explain how a man whose opinions on nearly every important subject were wrong, whose literary output was largely drudgery and whose poetry at best contains only 'a few vigorous lines' could acquire such cultural significance, Doyle concludes that the answer lay with the Scottish writing skills of 'his humble, much-ridiculed biographer':

> It is just these pen-pictures of his of the big, uncouth man, with his grunts and his groans, his Gargantuan appetite, his twenty cups of tea, and his tricks with the orange-peel and the lamp-posts, which fascinate the reader, and have given Johnson a far broader literary vogue than his writings could have done.[47]

While British biography constructs its masculinity through the strength of its intersubjective partnerships, autobiography offers only the solipsistic spectacle of the fantasist and his mirrors.

If Pepys, writing in the secret codes of his private diary, represents for Doyle the acceptably hidden face of masculinity's interior inscriptions, he found in the work and localities of George Borrow a determinant for the outer man. In *Through the Magic Door*, Doyle devotes a chapter to Borrow, first placing him 'in contact' with the worldly Pepys as key figures in the Anglo-celtic alliance of British letters:

> It is a long jump from Samuel Pepys to George Borrow – from one pole of the human character to the other – and yet they are in contact on the shelf of my favourite authors.[48]

Whereas Pepys is Doyle's image of an English tension between the inner and the outer man, Borrow invokes a celtic version of manhood defined by its place of origin and its masculine rituals, particularly those of the aggressive encounter. Doyle's description of himself as a fighter and a boxer in *Memories and Adventures* is itself quite literally 'Borrowed':

> I have always been keen upon the noble old English sport of boxing ... . I suppose I might describe my form as that of a fair average amateur. As I was just over six feet high and was forty-three round the chest, weighing over sixteen stone in the buff, I was well qualified for the heavy-weight division, and I came of that brown-haired, grey-eyed stock which George Borrow declares to be apt at the game.[49]

In *Through the Magic Door* Doyle describes the pleasure he received from hearing that his own boxing novel, *Rodney Stone*, had been read to an Australian prizefighter on his deathbed and had held the interest of the dying gladiator. Who, he asks, cares about criticism after that!

If Doyle found in George Borrow a celtic masculinity to set against the Brontë sisters, he considered Anthony Trollope to have provided the best model for the literary life. The timely publication of Trollope's posthumous *Autobiography* (1883) had done much to readdress the masculine problematics of the literary career so disturbingly exposed by Carlyle. For Trollope, manhood had been achieved through a double identification with letters, his career as a writer developing alongside his travels as a civil servant to extend the postal service. While doubling his inscription of career and emphasizing the non-domestic contexts of his writing, Trollope had also reinstated the single masculine figure as the subject of autobiography, relegating his marriage to the private sphere as 'of no special interest to anyone except my wife and me'.[50] No female gaze disturbs this masculine representation, as the lettered perspective of Jane Welsh had disturbed the reputation of Carlyle. Both Trollope and Doyle grew up in matriarchal families saved from economic and social disaster by the energy and enterprise of strongminded women. Like Doyle, Trollope learned his masculinity as much from his energetic mother as from the profession of letters with which he replaced his unworldly father. Both having watched paternal lives slide into disaster, Doyle and Trollope wrote model autobiographies, exempla for other men to learn from, though lacking a subjectivity of their own.

Doyle's paternal grandfather, the artist John Doyle, had come to London from Dublin in 1821, having made a name for himself as a painter of horses. In England he set up initially as a portrait painter before specializing as a political cartoonist producing lithographs of famous figures under the pseudonym HB. This insignia was produced by a double inscription of his actual initials, J. D., one set overlaying the other so that the doubled copy produced a different identity. Much of Doyle's writing draws on John Doyle's special view of Regency society, for his good-humoured lithographs, often using literary parables, were printed individually for display in shop windows, and became collectors' items to be found in gentlemen's libraries. Doyle's fascination with the Napoleonic period has these 917 detailed illustrations drawn from his grandfather's memory of celebrity appearances to support it. Both his Sherlock Holmes stories and the Brigadier Gerard series use these cartoons as models, the same figures recurring in designs which are both formulaic and diversified. Regarded as the inventor of the cartoon as distinct from the caricature, John Doyle's political 'conversation-piece' figures were reduplicated as political stereotypes. In cartoons from 1829 relating to Catholic Emancipation and the Irish question, John Doyle drew a new type of 'John Bull', the heavy-set, perplexed figure of the English squirearchy endlessly confused between rival political factions.[51]

The politics of masculine representation took on an altogether more sinister and original aspect in the case of Doyle's father, Charles Altamonte Doyle. He had been sent to Edinburgh at the age of seventeen to work as an assistant surveyor and draughtsman in the Scottish Office of Works. Marrying Mary Foley, the daughter of his landlady, the couple produced seven surviving children, of whom Doyle was the second child and eldest son. With the birth of his children, Charles Altamonte became a failure as a father, succumbing first to alcoholism and eventually to what was diagnosed as epilepsy. From 1879, these conditions were regarded as requiring confinement in a series of nursing homes and mental hospitals until his death in 1893 in Montrose Lunatic Asylum. As Charles failed more and more conspicuously to provide for his family, his place was taken by a young doctor, not much older than Doyle himself, Dr Bryan Waller – a man who also had literary aspirations. Waller receives no mention in Doyle's autobiography, despite his lifelong support for Doyle's mother and the fact that Doyle was married from his home.[52] Doyle spent most of his childhood away from his family, sent first to stay with friends in Edinburgh before, in 1868, being sent to a Jesuit preparatory school, and finally to Stonyhurst.

The unworldly, eccentric talent and tragic example of his father appears to have haunted Doyle in an entirely beneficial way throughout his writing career. He provided an example not to be copied, a story of an originality seriously misplaced and lacking in context and a creativity that weakened into addiction. Like his famous brother, Richard

Doyle, Charles was a fairy painter but his creations inhabit a fairyland bereft of the usual rich resources of the genre. Trapped in the discomforts of the body, Charles's fairies have to make do where they are.

It was his own story too. The trouble with Charles Doyle was not just his alcoholism and his epilepsy. It was also his troublesome sense of humour and its lack of shared community. In 1867 he had illustrated *The Book of Humorous Poetry* and, to his great detriment, his estranged, unhappy notions of joke and humour stayed with him to the end of a life which lacked convivial companions. Confined in the lunatic asylum, Charles insisted that the diagnosis of insanity derived from a misunderstanding of this humour, from a Scottish inability to understand his jokes. He continued to produce vividly illustrated journals full of verbal and pictorial puns, of split identities making compulsive contact with each other. The journal form is significant, for Charles understood himself as part of a creative, diary-writing family whose shared solipsisms had, in childhood, provided him with a sense of community and a world of intersubjective reference.

The history of Charles Doyle is, in his son's account, essentially a tragedy of an Irish artist in an alien, unappreciative environment. Neglected until Doyle staged a commemorative exhibition in 1924, Charles Doyle's work was subsequently championed by George Bernard Shaw, who hailed him as an Irish genius. Doyle writes in *Memories and Adventures*:

> His painting was done spasmodically and the family did not always reap the benefit, for Edinburgh is full of water-colours which he had given away ... . His brush was concerned not only with fairies and delicate themes of the kind, but with wild and fearsome subjects, so that his work had a very peculiar style of its own, mitigated by great natural humour. He was more terrible than Blake and less morbid than Wiertz. His originality is best shown by the fact that one hardly knows with whom to compare him. In prosaic Scotland, however, he excited wonder rather than admiration, and he was only known in the larger world of London by pen and ink book-illustrations which were not his best mode of expression.[53]

The power of brotherly partnership, on the other hand, had been illustrated for Doyle throughout his formative years, by that of the famous Edinburgh bookseller and magazine proprietor, William Chambers, and his pioneering brother, Robert, whose conversion to Spiritualism in 1866 would provide a model for the later developments of Doyle's own career.

Edinburgh

Doyle's autobiography opens with a statement about his birthplace: 'I was born on May 22, 1859, at Picardy Place, Edinburgh, so named because in old days a colony of French Huguenots had settled there.'[54] While this opening is a conventional one, the Edinburgh setting of Doyle's childhood and its destructive containment of his father's talent became the topography for a certain kind of memory formation. Edinburgh is represented as neither visual, nor imaginative: it is essentially 'prosaic', a place of writing and of written law. Doyle's public memories of childhood are memories of prose encounters – memories of texts and of reading. While he was later to draw on his fascination with the Huguenots in his historical novel, *The Refugees*, Doyle makes it clear that Edinburgh was the wrong place for his Catholic father, who had arrived there from London in 1849. He writes in *Memories and Adventures*:

> I have a little bundle of my father's letters written in those days, full of the appreciation of the kindness which he met with and full, also, of interesting observations on that Scottish society, rough, hard-drinking and kindly, into which he had been precipitated at a dangerously early age, especially for one with his artistic tempera-ment. He had some fine religious instincts, but his environment was a difficult one.[55]

Edinburgh is more important than it appears in the schema of Doyle's autobiographical writing and the location haunted his dreams until the end of his life. Its failure to provide a context for his father's artwork was offset by its beneficial impact on his own career. Prosaic though it may have been, the prose of Edinburgh provided some of the strongest models for the construction of his own writing identity. His mentor in the adventure novel and in the use of the case study as fiction, Robert Louis Stevenson, had written a history of their mutual birthplace – one dedicated to the reforms brought about by the Chambers brothers.

Enterprising young writers and booksellers who had become central to 'the Cheap Literature Movement' with the publication of *Chambers' Edinburgh Journal* in 1832, the brothers had set out their aim to put literature and information within the reach of the ordinary man in the street in the first issue. Robert Chambers wrote:

> The principle by which I have been actuated, is to take advantage of the universal appetite for instruction which at present exists; to supply to that appetite food of the best kind, in such form and at such price as must suit the convenience of every man in the British dominions. Every Saturday, when the poorest labourer in the coun-try draws his humble earnings, he shall have it in his power to purchase with an insignificant portion of even that humble sum, a meal of healthful, useful, and agreeable mental instruction.[56]

Fifty thousand copies of *Chambers' Edinburgh Journal* were sold in Scotland within the first few days. Feeding the mind assuaged the pangs of a more political hunger. During the Lancashire famine of 1863, the MP for Ashton-under-Lyme claimed that it was 'to the information contained in the excellent cheap papers of this country' that he 'attributed much of the calm forbearance with which the distressed had borne their privations'.[57] As William Chambers himself had done, Doyle records how, as a schoolboy, he often preferred to spend his lunch money on cheap secondhand books from the market stall:

> I used to be allowed twopence for my lunch, that being the price of a mutton pie, but near the pie shop was a second-hand book shop with a barrel full of old books and the legend 'Your choice for 2d' stuck above it. Often the price of my luncheon used to be spent on some sample out of this barrel.[58]

When Sir Walter Scott died in 1863, Robert Chambers produced a *Memoir* of him 'from such materials as were within reach, as well as from personal recollections. The memoir was issued by us in a popular fom, and had an extraordinary sale – as many as eighty thousand copies.'[59] Robert Chambers also wrote copiously about Scottish history and Scottish places – Edinburgh in particular – mapping a literary region with its own masculine correlatives. This Edinburgh-specific literary identity enabled Doyle to establish himself as a writer and to feel at home, as his artistic father had never done, in prosaic Scotland. It was, he claims, on the strength of his lunchtime fare of secondhand books that he sat down and 'wrote a little adventure story which I called "The Mystery of Sassassa Valley"'. It was to the Chambers brothers that he sent what was to become his first publication: 'To my great joy and surprise it was accepted by "Chambers Journal", and I received three guineas.'[60]

His entrance fee to the masculine world now in his possession, Doyle's life story, from this point of first publication, closely follows that of his first publisher. At times the resemblance between William Chamber's *Memoir* (1872) and Doyle's account of his Edinburgh years is so close as to raise questions whether it was his own life or the autobiography of his first publisher that Doyle was actually recalling. Certainly they had a number of formative experiences in common.

In February 1859, a few months before Doyle's birth, Robert Chambers gave a well-attended lecture at an evening *conversazione* of the Merchant Company of Edinburgh, a company of which he was at that time master. As William reports it in his *Memoir*, the object of Robert's talk was 'to shew how, by a course of sobriety and diligence in his calling, a man may rise to fortune, not only for his own advantage, but that of his descendants; and to remind many who occupy a high social position what they owe to the thrift and plodding industry of their ancestors'.[61] Had Charles Doyle been among the audience at this lecture, he would have clearly been unimpressed, but Robert and William Chambers knew what they were talking about. Their own lives had begun inauspiciously when their father had, like Charles Doyle, arrived in an Edinburgh of stale jokes and ruthless conviviality. Chambers comments:

> ... they related the same jokes perhaps daily for years ... it was a standing rule in this club of convivialists to laugh at every whimsicality, no matter how often repeated, the old jokes were always as good as the new.[62]

When Charles Doyle subsequently complained, in *The Doyle Diary*, that he had been confined as a madman due to the 'narrow Scotch misconception of jokes',[63] he was reopening a subject with which the Chambers brothers had always been closely associated. In 1831 Robert Chambers had published his *Scottish Jests and Anecdotes*, an anthology intended 'to vindicate, for the first time, the pretensions of the Scottish nation to the character of a witty and jocular, as they are already allowed to be a painstaking and enlightened, race'. This provocative book went through two editions before the subject of Scottish humour was taken up by the Very Reverend Dean Ramsay in what William describes as 'that more earnest spirit which has ensured a great share of public approbation'.[64] Despite his brother's wish to 'extend the geography of Fun beyond the Tweed', William Chambers himself, like Dr Watson after him, remained a firm believer in the importance of being earnest.

Doyle drew from Edinburgh the first stage of his self-definition, identifying closely with the kind of Scottish literary tradition that the Chambers brothers had succeeded in establishing. Local tradition was a concept much favoured by the brothers, with Robert publishing his often reprinted and highly successful *Traditions of Edinburgh* in 1824. The Chambers' enterprise specialized in the popularization of historical and military narratives, consciously providing a link between Scott and Macaulay. Also part of the enterprise was their determination to purvey models of masculine lives and careers drawn from local examples that could be used to construct a distinctively Scottish version of contemporary manhood. Defined as purposeful, intolerant of distraction and, above all, based on a partnership of shrewd business sense and artistic imagination, William saw his relationship with his brother as embodying a model manhood:

> A happy difference, yet some resemblance, in character, proved of service in the literary and commercial union of Robert and myself.

Mentally, each had a little of the other, but with a wide divergence in matters requisite as a whole. One could not have done well without the other. With mutual help there was mutual strength.[65]

It was a model which Doyle set to duplicate as he described his own ventures into professional life, using the same Crusoe-esque motif of self-sufficient resourcefulness and improvisation which had informed William Chambers' account of his early years in the book business. Like *Memories and Adventures*, Chambers' *Memoir* is an Edinburgh autobiography shaped by the theme of the improvident father whose failure is a stimulus to his sons. However, in striking contrast to the lengthy grievances and hilarious anecdotes with which William Chambers details the impecunious habits of his father, Doyle maintains a discreet reserve about the details of his childhood. Doyle's Edinburgh, which both contains and excludes his father's story, is represented as a place of worldly practicalities, home of a manhood stronger and more independent than that produced by the English system. Of his university he writes:

> Edinburgh is, I believe, more practical than most other colleges. It is practical too, in its preparation for life, since there is none of the atmosphere of an enlarged public school, as is the case in English Universities, but the student lives a free man in his own rooms with no restrictions of any sort. It ruins some and makes strong men of many.[66]

This construction of Edinburgh as instrumental in the development of a free and hardy manhood corresponds to Doyle's inner development as he recalls it: the sins and suffering of Catholicism are replaced by a Darwinian view of life as struggle and fight more fitting to the masculinities of his own generation. Charles Doyle's life is elegized as 'full of the tragedy of unfulfilled powers and of undeveloped gifts', his 'unworldly and unpractical' nature the result of his 'developed spirituality'.[67] Doyle is insistent about the dramatic discontinuities of Victorian manhood:

> A gap had opened between our fathers and ourselves so suddenly and completely that when a Gladstone wrote to uphold the Gadarene swine, or the six days of Creation, the youngest student rightly tittered over his arguments.[68]

It was within this 'gap' that much Victorian autobiography had been written. The genre had been used by writers as diverse as J. S. Mill, Samuel Butler and Edmund Gosse to redefine masculinity, in narrative form, through dislocations in the father–son relationship. Gosse defined the territory of his autobiography as 'the record of a struggle between two temperaments, two consciences and almost two epochs'.[69] *Memories and Adventures* was written at the end of the second of these two epochs, during the reappraisals following the First World War. Reinvoking this earlier 'gap' between fathers and sons, Doyle's autobiography frames a distinct phase in the history and representation of masculinity, enclosing within its timeframe a phase of masculine definition discontinuous with what followed or preceded it.

Edinburgh is constructed by Doyle as a place dedicated to the production of masculine 'doubles', one specializing in the literary and historical representation of manhood. Following Stevenson and the Chambers brothers, he defines Edinburgh as the region where masculinity, becoming literate, encounters its own written signs. In James Hogg's classic gothic thriller, *The Private Memoirs and Confessions of a Justified Sinner* (1824), Edinburgh had been written through the concept of identity-split, bearing as its uncanny 'Brocken Spectre' memories of its own former autonomy and power. In William Chambers' *Memoir* the moment of masculine sign acquisition is both actual and symbolic, for the signboard he purchases for himself is larger than his shop:

> I painted the sign-board in well-defined letters in chrome yellow on a black ground ... the inscription anounced that I was a 'Bookseller and Printer', and with this bold intimation, the huge sign-board was hoisted to the tiled roof which covered my small establishment ... . On the whole, things were looking up.[70]

This moment of reidentification through the book business is one that unites both Chambers and Doyle. In *Through the Magic Door* Doyle states bluntly: 'Hereditary impulses, personal experiences, books – those are the three forces which go to the making of a man.'[71] Books in particular had the power to reconstruct masculinity, and Edinburgh, for Doyle, was essentially a city of writing, its emblem being Lockhart's famous biographical anecdote of Sir Walter Scott as the 'man outlined on the blind' of the house opposite his own in Castle Street:

> All evening the man wrote, and the observer could see the shadow hand conveying the sheets of paper from the desk to the pile at the side. He went to a party and returned, but still the hand was moving the sheets. Next morning he was told that the rooms opposite were occupied by Walter Scott.[72]

This image from Lockhart's *The Life of Sir Walter Scott* is one that informs Doyle's account of his own Edinburgh upbringing. The masculine eye across the Edinburgh street watches the writing of a manhood it will come to participate in and duplicate. Doyle uses a similar motif as the shared signature of his own boyhood.

Robert Louis Stevenson in his short guidebook, *Edinburgh*, is unequivocal in his support for the reforms and alterations affected by the Chambers brothers:

> It is almost the correct literary sentiment to deplore the revolution-
> ary improvements of Mr. Chambers and his following. It is easy to
> be a conservator of the discomforts of others; ... But what slices of
> sunlight, what breaths of clean air, have been let in! And what a
> picturesque world remains untouched![73]

He is equally clear about the hardships and romance of an *Edinburgh*
boyhood, using his own departure from the city to image its reiterated
loss of manhood:

> Edinburgh pays cruelly for her high seat in one of the vilest cli-
> mates under heaven ... . The weather is raw ... . The delicate die
> early, and I, as a survivor, among bleak winds and pumping rain,
> have been sometimes tempted to envy them their fate ... . Happy
> the passengers who shake off the dust of Edinburgh, and have
> heard for the last time the cry of the east wind among her chimney-
> tops! And yet the place establishes an interest in people's hearts; go
> where they will, they find no city of the same distinction; go where
> they will, they take a pride in their old home.[74]

Feminized as maternal, gothic and marginal, Edinburgh retains a vestigal
power to rewrite its own epitaph:

> There is a spark among the embers; from time to time the old
> volcano smokes. Edinburgh has but partly abdicated, and still
> wears, in parody, her metropolitan trappings. Half a capital and
> half a country town, the whole city leads a double existence; it has
> long trances of the one and flashes of the other; like the king of the
> Black Isles, it is half alive and half a monumental marble.[75]

It is the project of Stevenson's writing to continue the reinscription
begun by the Chambers brothers, using his own work to create a
continuity out of the gaps, contrasts and duplicates of the city's archi-
tectural history. Doyle, both in his early career and in his later
autobiographical account of Edinburgh, is indebted to this continuity.
As a writer, he was quick to identify himself with the work of his fellow
student from Edinburgh University. The two men never met but they
corresponded briefly and praised each other's work in magazine articles
and letters. Both build on the work of the Chambers brothers to define
their own writing, Chambers describing 'the Cheap Literature Movement' as a renovation and renaissance of the 'Cheap Book' which
'furnished amusement to the humble fireside. These books appealed to
the popular love of the heroic, the marvellous, the pathetic, and the
humorous.'[76] Stevenson and Doyle both specialized in an adventure
fiction which inscribed a readership at the place of transition between
boyhood and manhood and unobtrusively identified this place with
Edinburgh.

Stevenson writes about the city as a place where boundaries of normality and fantasy, of power and make-believe, privileged class and

inner space are transgressed and reorganized as part of the dramatic
move from the old gothic city to the new commercial centre:

> There was such a flitting, such a change of domicile and dweller, as
> was never excelled in the history of cities: the cobbler succeeded the
> earl; the beggar ensconced himself by the judge's chimney ... the
> hearth-stone of the old proprietor was thought large enough to be
> partitioned off into a bedroom by the new.[77]

His Edinburgh is a place of intersecting visions, a city built, not to
music, but to glimpses and glances. It is a city of the eye in which it is
'scarce possible to avoid observing your neighbours'.[78] The high houses
contain their own dialectics for literary transformation:

> In the first room there is a birth, in another a death, in a third a
> sordid drinking-bout, and the detective and the Bible-reader cross
> upon the stairs ... children have a strange experience from the first;
> only a robust soul ... could grow up in such circumstances without
> hurt.[79]

Located at 221B Baker Street, a similar crossing of paths and identities
between the detective and the Bible-reader would become Doyle's solution to the damage done to his own childhood by the birth, deaths and
drinking bouts of Edinburgh life. For both Doyle and Stevenson, Edinburgh is pre-eminently a city of the masculine 'gap', a place of strange
disappearances imaged most literally and dramatically in the collapse of
the *lands* or old tenements in the High Street. In 'the black hours of a
Sunday morning, the whole structure ran together with a hideous up-
roar and tumbled storey upon storey to the ground'. Edinburgh's capacity
for disappearance has implications throughout the British Empire as
people in London, Canada or New Zealand exclaim 'The house that I
was born in fell last night!'.[80]

The house in which Doyle was born had not fallen at the time he
wrote his autobiography but it had certainly degenerated. His Edinburgh, too, is an uncanny place, prosaic and literal as the scene of an
unhappy childhood and yet also a place of strange representational
returns. In his autobiography, it is both birthplace and final point of
autobiographical recall. Significantly and in striking contrast to
Stevenson, Doyle in *Memories and Adventures* provides no description
of the city. Under the shadow of its own 'practicality', Edinburgh represents a terrain from which anything that is visually, imaginative, magical,
original or uncopied has been excised.

Nineteenth-century literary autobiography from Wordsworth to Thomas Hardy is, to a significant extent, grounded in the power and
privileged sightedness of the masculine eye. Doyle's engagement with
the subjectivities of Romanticism was complex and sometimes covert,
but his view of his own literary significance depended entirely on the

nineteenth-century elision of masculinity and the seeing eye. Recalling the streets of Edinburgh, he defines his vocation in terms of the conflictual politics of the eye resolved there. His life-task will become the realignment of crooked or defective vision and the assimilation of partial and opposing viewpoints into one narrative of shared masculine perspective. Doyle is not 'the man in the street' but a writer who defines places of perceptual consensus across both the British Isles and the British Empire.

Memories and Adventures is an autobiography themed on the construction of masculine identity. It is not a particularly accurate or reliable self-history but it is skilfully crafted in terms of its self-representation, placing Doyle in a series of subject positions which make him the ideal mediator of conflicting views. Childhood, that *locus classicus* of Romantic subjectivity, is largely rejected by Doyle as a subject for memory. The punished and beaten body that he describes as his own denies its own interiority and remembers itself only through its reading matter and the written adventures of others. Of an Edinburgh childhood painstakingly reconstructed by Owen Dudley Edwards, Doyle writes succinctly:

> Of my boyhood I need say little, save that it was Spartan at home and more Spartan at the Edinburgh school where a tawse-brandishing schoolmaster of the old type made our young lives miserable. From the age of seven to nine I suffered under this pock-marked, one-eyed rascal who might have stepped from the pages of Dickens. In the evenings, home and books were my sole consolation ... . My comrades were rough boys and I became a rough boy, too.[81]

The motif of damaged eyesight introduced by this 'one-eyed rascal' configures Doyle's Edinburgh years while a discussion of Mayne Reid's adventure fiction is used to substitute for more personal recollections of boyhood. Edinburgh generates only two types of memory for Doyle – one of street fighting, the other of sitting on William Thackeray's knee during a brief visit to his father. Reading and fighting create interchangeable sites of masculine identity located in the injuries and consolations of the eye. Doyle uses anecdotes about Edinburgh to place him socially as an outsider – someone fighting with, and for, the poorer boys of the district:

> We lived for some time in a *cul de sac* street with a very vivid life of its own and a fierce feud between the small boys who dwelt on either side of it. Finally it was fought out between two champions, I representing the poorer boys who lived in flats and my opponent the richer boys who lived in the opposite villas ... . When I got home after the battle, my mother cried, 'Oh, Arthur, what a dreadful eye you have got!' To which I replied, 'You just go across and look at Eddie Tulloch's eye!'[82]

At the same time, these anecdotes of damaged eyes and street-injured masculinities are combined with a privileged interiority, a dreaminess which places him on Thackeray's knee, as someone linked through his grandfather to the most famous names of the English cultural establishment:

> I was so young that it seems like a faint dream, and yet it pleases me to think that I have sat on Thackeray's knee. He greatly admired my dear little mother with her grey Irish eyes and her vivacious Celtic ways – indeed, no one met her without being captivated by her.[83]

Both types of boyhood memory focus on the eye, whether his own, those of his opponents, or those of his mother. Other recollections of street fights further define his position. He recalls being knocked unconscious by the boot of the 'bookmaker's boy' and getting a glimpse of 'the periodical troubles which poor Ireland has endured' as 'a gang of rough men' who turned out to be Fenians threatened the house of some Irish relatives. These four childhood memories serve to link Scotland, England, Ireland and unconsciousness in a British union of poverty and privilege – a union, too, of different kinds of problematic, antagonistic or uncertain seeing.

Having established Edinburgh as a place of embattled reading, the narrative of *Memories and Adventures* moves forward through anecdotes which foreground the eye. Doyle's unhappy schooldays under the Jesuits at Stonyhurst are concluded with recollections of a visit to an Irish relative, his godfather, Michael Conan, in Paris. Associated with the founders of Sinn Fein, Michael Conan invokes the perceptual antagonism of that other damaged eye watching Britain from across the Irish Sea. Sharing the passion for heraldry and geneology which contributed so largely to the fantasy life of Doyle's mother, Michael Conan traced his descent from the Dukes of Britanny. Doyle comments smoothly, 'indeed Arthur Conan was the ill-fated young Duke whose eyes were put out, according to Shakespeare, by King John'. This anecdote is an important one in the geography of Doyle's self-consciousness. Placed to mark the end of his boyhood, it is also figures an identity traceable to this literary–historical act of blinding: 'hence my name Arthur Conan'. Noting that it was not only name but also his body-shape that he had inherited from Michael Conan, Doyle returned to Edinburgh, 'conscious that real life was about to begin'.[84]

Real life meant, from 1876, training as a medical student at Edinburgh University. He obtained his MD in 1881 and set up in general practice in Portsmouth, drawn there by the proximity of a fellow student from a famous west-country medical family, George Turnavine Budd. The two young doctors had spent a tense, hilarious and highly charged six months in practice together in Plymouth before a quarrel led Doyle to strike out on his own, almost as far away from Edinburgh as he could get. It appears to have been Budd who advised him to develop a new specialism in ophthalmology, although he later attributed this advice to Malcolm Morris. After testing eyes and correcting astigmatisms in Portsmouth Eye Hospital, Doyle went to Vienna in search of prestigious qualifications to attract wealthy patients to a new London practice in Devonshire Place. He had begun publishing short stories in 1879 and by 1891 he had published three novels and the first two Holmes novellas, A Study in Scarlet (1887) and The Sign of Four (1889). As the collection of short stories later to be published as The Adventures of Sherlock Holmes began appearing in The Strand Magazine, Doyle decided to abandon medicine for a literary career.

Doyle's account of the writing of the Sherlock Holmes stories emphasizes a creative dissonance between the outer form taken by his life and its alternative inner story. He wrote The Adventures while waiting for eye-patients who never materialized:

> We took rooms in Montague Place, and I went forth to search for some place where I could put up my plate as an oculist. I was aware that many of the big men do not find time to work out refractions, which in some cases of astigmatism take a long time to adjust when done by retinscopy. I was capable in this work and liked it ... . But to get it, it was clearly necessary that I should live among the big men so that the patient could be easily referred to me. I searched the doctors' quarters and at last found suitable accommodation at 2 Devonshire Place ... close to the classical Harley Street ... .
>
> Every morning I ... reached my consulting-room at ten and sat there until three or four, with never a ring to disturb my serenity. Could better conditions for reflection and work be found? It was ideal, and so long as I was thoroughly unsuccessful in my professional venture there was every chance of improvement in my literary prospects.[85]

The above anecdote is both carefully crafted and unreliable. According to Richard Lancelyn Green, Doyle gave an interview to The World in 1892 in which he told a very different story. According to that account, he had been working at the Westminster Eye Infirmary in addition to attending to his own patients, only finding time at night for his literary pursuits. Struggling with two careers, he abandoned his medical work when his health became seriously affected by the strain.[86]

The discrepancy in these two accounts emphasizes Doyle's use of autobiographical anecdote to position and define himself in a male professional hierarchy. Placed insecurely among the big men, the master oculists, he waits to undertake the humbler work for which they have little time. In Kiplingesque mode, Doyle can wait and not be tired by waiting. Instead, he creates stories of a great detective whose perfect vision corrects that of greater men – the princes, dukes and patriarchs who consult him whenever their identity or social position is under threat. This double story of ophthalmic loss and literary gain has, in both inner and outer frames, its prime referent in the eye and begins a new phase of masculine development:

> Up to now the main interest of my life lay in my medical career. But with the more regular life and the greater sense of responsibility, coupled with the natural development of brain-power, the literary side of me began slowly to spread until it was destined to push the other entirely aside.[87]

In his famous essay 'The Uncanny' (1919), Sigmund Freud identified 'a substitutive relation between the eye and the male organ' which turned anxiety about the eye into fears of castration by a punishing father:

> A study of dreams, phantasies and myths has taught us that anxiety about one's eyes, the fear of going blind, is often enough a substitute for the dread of being castrated.[88]

Doyle's career was an attempt to replace the anxieties of his Scottish upbring with a narrative which turned the castrating sandman of Freud's oedipal drama into its own brainchild, reversing the *dramatis personae* of this mythic identity formation by a different reading of the sand. The castrated father becomes a creative child supplying the spiritual vision of the son's career. Having remodelled a masculinity damaged both in the family and in the nation, *Memories and Adventures* records a mythic manhood which can generate alternative narratives of masculine development from its own doubleness.

The story of Doyle's double vision took him through a series of accidents and catastrophes to a vantage point from which he could supply the defective seeing of the British Empire itself. The climax of his autobiography occurs in 1918 when he receives a fortuitous invitation to visit the war front and witnesses the breaking of the Hindenburg Line by the Allies at the end of September:

> I found myself by most unlooked-for chance an actual eyewitness of this, one of the historical episodes of the greatest of wars. Yes, with my own eyes I saw the rent while the men who made it were still pushing forward from the farther side of it.[89]

This historic event is used as the final link in a chain of events connecting name and nation as the ultimate signifier of a masculine career. It supplies the climax of *Memories and Adventures* and is given as an Appendix to his major history of the First World War, *The British Campaign in France and Flanders 1914–1918*. Climbing on to a tank for his grandstand view of this rupture of the German defences, Doyle writes of this culminating moment and its curious capacity for anti-climax:

> ... there, at our very feet, and less than 500 yards away, was the rift which had been torn a few hours before in the Hindenburg Line. On the dun slope beyond it, under our very eyes, was even now being fought a part of that great fight where at last the children of light were beating down into the earth the forces of darkness. It was there. We could see it. And yet how little there was to see!
> ... With my glasses I saw what looked like Tanks, but whether wrecked or in action I could not say. There was the battle – the greatest of battles – but nowhere could I see a moving figure.[90]

Beyond the privileged eye, stands a tradition of masculinity faced with its own disappearance. Doyle concludes his history of *The British Campaign* with a reminder that the true message of the seen can no longer be read in the empiricism of written history:

> Here the historian's task is done ... . Not to change rival frontiers, but to mould the hearts and spirits of men – there lie the explanation and the justification of all that we have endured. The system which left seven million dead upon the fields of Europe must be rotten to the core. Time will elapse before the true message is mastered, but when that day arrives the war of 1914 may be regarded as the end of the dark ages.[91]

Or its beginning, perhaps. From the gaps and vantage points of Edinburgh to his providential station above the broken Hindenburg Line, Doyle constructs his autobiography in terms of a masculine archetype: that of the clown turned priest or magician who learns by comedic juggling to see what is missing in the field of vision and to supply its presence. According to Jungian archetypes, the role of the magician-priest or shaman is that of the healer who replaces absence with presence and loss with meaning:

> The shaman in traditional societies was the healer, the one who restored life, who found lost souls, and who discovered the hidden causes of misfortune. He was the one who restored wholeness and fullness of being to both individuals and communities.[92]

'This gentleman is a healer': the spirit message from Mr Horstead's Southsea seance in 1887 had identified Doyle in this way, and his healing became increasingly literary and spiritual as he moved away from his medical career. If, as he suggests, his ability to make writing stand in place of sight derived from the prosaic lessons of Edinburgh, the magic that makes language disappear has a different place of origin.

The land of mist (and snow)

In his useful discussion of the historical study of masculinity, John Tosh has argued for the dual reference of this term:

> Masculinity ... is both a psychic and a social identity: psychic, because it is integral to the subjectivity of every male as this takes shape in infancy and childhood; social, because masculinity is inseparable from peer recognition, which in turn depends on performance in the social sphere.[93]

Tosh identifies three linked arenas in which the public demonstration of masculinity occurs – 'home, work and all-male associations'. Each of these arenas, including Tosh's assertion that 'setting up a new household is the essential qualification for manhood',[94] is clearly figured and foregrounded in *Memories and Adventures*, but Doyle also defines a fourth arena, that of masculine 'spirituality' and its representation. It is interesting to note Tosh's late twentieth-century avoidance of this term, despite its crucial role in nineteenth-century identity formation. The psychic and subjective dimension of Doyle's masculinity is inseparable from his spiritual quest.

Supporting Tosh's argument that 'all-male associations are integral to any notion of patriarchy beyond the household',[95] Doyle's first real adventure was his voyage to the Arctic in 1880 as surgeon on the whaler, *Hope*. In the all-male community of the ship, both Doyle and his writing undergo a sea change. This voyage is a magical and comical journey of substitutions, of swapping one body and one identity for another. It is perhaps worth noting that, according to Owen Dudley Edwards, Doyle's mother had already made this act of substitution, replacing her unworldly, alcoholic husband with the far more substantial and reliable Dr Bryan Waller. This swap of bodies is the stuff of boyhood fantasy, the more especially as literacy and illiteracy change places in the hierarchies of adventurous manhood. This exchange between the lettered and the unlettered man is vital to the ship's community:

> There was one curious thing about the manning of the *Hope*. The man who signed on as first mate was a little, decrepit, broken fellow, absolutely incapable of performing the duties. The cook's assistant, on the other hand, was a giant of a man, red-bearded, bronzed, with huge limbs, and a voice of thunder. But the moment that the ship cleared the harbour the little, decrepit mate disappeared into the cook's galley, and acted as scullery boy for the voyage, while the mighty scullery-boy walked aft and became chief mate. The fact was, that the one had the certificate, but was past sailoring, while the other could neither read nor write, but was as fine a seaman as ever lived; so by an agreement to which everybody concerned was party, they swapped their berths when they were at sea.[96]

A similar reversal transforms the one possibly criminal member of the crew into its silent law-maker. For three nights running, the cook's rum drinking had caused him to ruin the ship's dinner:

> On the third day our silent outlaw approached the cook with a brass saucepan in his hand. He said nothing, but he struck the man such a frightful blow that his head flew through the bottom and the sides of the pan were left dangling round his neck. ... We heard no further complaints of the cooking.[97]

The trip to the Arctic provided Doyle with two landscapes which he uses to symbolize the beginning and the end of the masculine quest. On the voyage out, the *Hope* takes refuge from bad weather in the lee of one of the outlying islands and Doyle encounters a landscape that he was to make peculiarly his own, a place of bogs and marshes in which the sign of the masculine is absent. He writes:

> I got ashore and wandered among peat bogs, meeting strange, barbarous, kindly people who knew nothing of the world. I was led back to the ship by a wild, long-haired girl holding a torch, for the peat holes make it dangerous at night – I can see her now, her tangled black hair, her bare legs, madder-stained petticoat, and wild features under the glare of the torch. I spoke to one old man there who asked me the news. I said, 'The Tay bridge is down,' which was then a fairly stale item. He said, 'Eh, have they built a brig over the Tay?' After that I felt inclined to tell him about the Indian Mutiny.[98]

The wet lands of the peat bogs, where time and men's achievements pass unmarked, are soon replaced in this adventure by one in dramatic contrast to them and even more haunting. Doyle describes the Arctic as a landscape of purity and romance beyond the terrain of home and human sexuality:

> It is a region of purity, of white ice and blue water, with no human dwelling within a thousand miles to sully the freshness of the breeze which blows across the icefields. And then it is a region of romance also. You stand on the very brink of the unknown.[99]

These landscapes are configurations in Doyle's writing that challenge his dominant models of thought and the Edinburgh linguistic culture. A dangerous visuality asserts its counterpower in the context of this new location. He invokes the 'peculiar other-world feeling of the Arctic regions',[100] seeing in this spiritual landscape signs of an intelligence that is alien to the discourses of the world, but linked to it through the speaking bodies of animals. He describes a seal cull on the open ice fields:

> From the crow's nest at the top of the main mast, one can see no end of them. On the furthest visible ice one can still see that

sprinkling of pepper grains. And the young lie everywhere also, snow-white slugs, with a little black nose and large dark eyes. Their half-human cries fill the air; and ... you would think you were next door to a monstrous nursery.[101]

In his essay entitled 'Becoming Animal', the French aesthetic philosopher, Gilles Deleuze, has described the alternative routes of potential development or 'becoming' which affect the process of human identity formation. These alternative routes exist alongside that of the 'Oedipal symbolic community' and bear witness 'to an inhuman connivance with the animal' which can counterbalance and disturb entrance to the human symbolic order:

> ... for all children, it is as though, independent of the evolution carrying them towards adulthood, there were room in the child for other becomings, 'other contemporaneous possibilities' that are not regressions but creative involutions bearing witness to 'an inhumanity immediately experienced in the body as such, "unnatural nuptials' outside the programmed body'. There is a reality of becoming-animal, even though one does not in reality become animal.[102]

Such experiences of 'becoming-animal' are particularly pronounced in nineteenth-century boys' adventure fiction. For Doyle, the Arctic is a 'zone of proximity' to other forms of becoming which offer escape from the symbolic order of print-dominated Edinburgh. His description of the Arctic seal cull tries to balance the slaughter of the young seals and their mothers with the exigencies of the masculine workforce they bring into being:

> ... at dawn upon the third [day], the ship's company took to the ice, and began to gather in its murderous harvest. It is brutal work, though not more brutal than that which goes on to supply every dinner-table in the country. And yet those glaring crimson pools upon the dazzling white of the icefields, under the peaceful silence of a blue Arctic sky, did seem a horrible intrusion. But an inexorable demand creates an inexorable supply, and the seals, by their death, help to give a living to the long line of seamen, dockers, tanners, curers, triers, chandlers, leather-merchants, and oil-sellers, who stand between this annual butchery on the one hand, and the exquisite, with his soft leather boots, or the savant, using a delicate oil for his philosophical instruments, upon the other.[103]

For Doyle, the seal cull is a moment not of 'becoming-animal' but of 'becoming-man' instead, although the land of mist and snow is written as one of the territories of fall and guilt where the masculine symbolic order faces its own disappearance and annulment.

Ordered back to the ship on account of his inexperience, Doyle did not take part in the cull but fell into the water instead. Two further falls led to his being sent to bed, consoled only by the knowledge that his clowning had served to amuse the ship's captain after his ill-luck on the seal hunt. Doyle's newly acquired nickname, 'the great Northern Diver', after the sea bird that swims under water, stayed with him for the rest of the voyage, emphasizing his experience of the Arctic as a zone of 'becoming-bird', rather than one of 'becoming-animal'.

This section of *Memories and Adventures* has earned Doyle sharp criticism from his most acerbic biographer, Ronald Pearsall who sees in it those 'signs of insensitivity that were to baffle his admirers' – signs which simultaneously establish Doyle's 'manhood', for 'the sang froid with which he watched the slaughter of the seals demonstrated to the seamen an admirable lack of squeamishness'.[104] In the text, Doyle moves directly from the seal cull to an account of a whale-killing, giving quite specific details of the whale's death-throes. He describes lancing as 'a more exciting because a more prolonged experience' than harpooning and concludes of the death 'Who would swap that moment for any other triumph that sport can give?'[105]

Signifying a rite of passage, this section of the autobiography invites criticism such as Pearsall's by offering this slaughter as a masculinity-esablishing ordeal. 'I went on board the whaler a big, straggling youth,' Doyle writes, and 'I came off it a powerful, well-grown man'. The change in body size which results from entering a zone of bestial reversals is, however, also a form of magical exchange. In the Arctic, Doyle learnt how to leave behind the 'monstrous nurseries' of his Catholic Edinburgh childhood and to internalize instead the spiritual energies of the whale. He writes:

> I have no doubt that my physical health during my whole life has been affected by that splendid air, and that the inexhaustible store of energy which I have enjoyed is to some extent drawn from the same source ... .[106]

Doyle's experience in the Arctic had given him access to another kind of masculine language, one that was crude and spiritual and in opposition to the dominant discourse of literary Edinburgh. Doyle's subsequent returns to his birthplace, as recounted in *Memories and Adventures*, are fraught with complex energy currents and inexplicable bouts of laughter: his sudden hilarious glimpse of his ultimate vocation when he was defeated as a Liberal Unionist candidate for Central Edinburgh in 1900 has already been quoted. In 1905 he was persuaded to stand for another Scottish parliamentary seat, 'The Border Burghs', but again without success. Subsequently, he came to reconstruct his political failures as a training that would ultimately benefit his Spiritualist mission. At the time, however, he merely 'followed blindly where some strange inward instinct led me on'.

That 'inward instinct' not only led forwards, it also led back to his experiences in the Arctic. It is the whale, rather than Doyle, that 'speaks' in the incident which concludes his attempt to enter politics. After an exhausting campaign contesting against the Radicals in which he faced the 'peculiar dry Scottish wit' of his hecklers, Doyle waits to travel home:

> ... as I stood on the platform waiting for the London train, one of my own people, an exuberant young bounder, came up with a loud familiar greeting and squeezed my right hand until my signet ring nearly cut me. It opened the sluice and out came a torrent of whaler language which I had hoped that I had long forgotten. The blast seemed to blow him bodily across the platform, and formed a strange farewell to my supporters.
> Thus ended my career in politics.[107]

This re-emergence of whaler language signals a moment of redefinition in the course of which Doyle will come to speak, not for the human constituency, but for that of 'the other-world' he first encountered in the guilty purity of the Arctic landscape. It was this voyage to the Arctic which Doyle took as the subject for his first public address to the Portsmouth Literary & Scientific Society in 1883. He used it to establish a masculine reputation somewhat at odds with his actual experience:

> [The lecture] ... gave me a quite unmerited reputation as a sportsman, for I borrowed from a local taxidermist every bird and beast that he possessed which could conceivably find its way into the Arctic Circle. These I piled upon the lecture table, and the audience, concluding that I had shot them all, looked upon me with great respect. Next morning, they were back with the taxidermist once more.[108]

This impressive image of himself as the successful sportsman replaces an altogether different story which threatened to emerge from the icy landscapes of the Arctic: a story told most definitively by Leopold von Sacher-Masoch, the German historian and novelist, whose notoriously 'masochistic' novel, Venus in Furs, was written in 1870. In Masoch's work, the identity problem is not that of 'becoming animal', but rather that of 'becoming man', and the key figure in this psychosexual drama is that of the cold, cruel, 'oral' mother who punishes the likeness of the father in her 'victims' so that a 'new man' can emerge. Gilles Deleuze identifies the role played by the 'oral mother' in the development of masculinity as one of conspiracy with the ego against the father's likeness:

> But what is the significance of this constantly recurring theme 'You are not a man, I am making a man of you?' What does 'becoming a man' signify? Clearly it does not mean to be like the father, or to

take his place. On the contrary, it consists in obliterating his role and his likeness in order to generate the new man.[109]

Masochism, Deleuze concludes, 'is a story that relates how the superego was destroyed and by whom, and what was the sequel to this destruction'.[110]

Masoch's 'new man' is one essentially 'devoid of sexual love' who provides an alternative to the power imperatives of the Marquis de Sade. Nineteenth-century accounts of 'masculinity', as distinct from the more ideological formulations of 'manhood' and 'manliness' – in so far as they exist at all – develop in large part from an enforced dialectic between these positions. *Memories and Adventures* is a text full of puzzling images of powerful matriarchal figures, from the haughty, plate-throwing eccentric of his Southsea days to the Empress Eugenie, a jigsaw addict described by Doyle as 'at the root of all modern history'.[111] His own mother, who sits knitting through a car crash, is another variant of this figure.

According to Deleuze, the masochist experiences the symbolic order of the law as represented by the mother; it is also the mother who 'generates the symbolism through which the masochist expresses himself'.[112] Many of Doyle's early gothic stories reveal this imaginative structure, describing 'femme fatales' who offer, in exchange for the successfully constructed masculine career, a deeply compelling inner life. One of Doyle's early stories, *The Captain of the 'Polestar'* (1890) fuses the Arctic landscape with a law-articulating image of the 'oral mother'. The captain of this tale is driven to a gratifying destruction by the spectral figure of an ice maiden, whose powerful portrait dominates his cabin:

> It was evidently a portrait ... . The languid, dreamy eyes, with their drooping lashes ... were in strong contrast with the clean-cut, prominent jaw, and the resolute set of the lower lip ... strength of will ... was stamped upon her face.[113]

Whereas Edinburgh represented a symbolic order dominated by the cold oral mother, the Arctic, paradoxically, signifies blood warmth and masculine community, a symbolic order in which illiteracy is king and lawlessness the sign of the father. Unlike the instructing sadist, the masochist is, according to Deleuze, essentially an educator, and the compelling part of this educational process is the masochist's power to subvert guilt and to effect its transformation into humour:

> There is no doubt that the masochist lives in the very depth of guilt; but far from feeling that he has sinned against the father, it is the father's likeness in him that he experiences as a sin which must be atoned for. Hence guilt is completely turned upside down: it is

both at its deepest and its most absurd. It is an integral part of the masochist's triumph, and ensures his liberation. Indeed it is indistinguishable from humor.[114]

Doyle's autobiography plays with the reversability of these two psychosexual roles, substituting a masochistic but educative humour for a sadistic masculine authority initially figured by the one-eyed, tawse-brandishing instructor of his boyhood.

Through the discontinuous endings of his autobiography, Doyle represents masculinity at a point of reappearance and of choice. While his trip to the Arctic had enabled him to configure Edinburgh as the cold *alma mater* or 'oral mother' whose punishing directives must be obeyed, his late conversion to Spiritualism offered him an opportunity to reshape his memories of his birthplace and to revisit the legacy of his father. Edinburgh reappears in Doyle's seldom-mentioned dream life as a place particularly associated with problems of masculine interiority. Promised at a seance that he would be given a glimpse of the spirit world, Doyle found himself in an Edinburgh of his own inner being:

> My first impression was that of a row of rather delapidated stone villas, such as one would see in the suburbs of Edinburgh. They looked well in front but were only half finished within, though I observed pictures upon the walls – frescoes rather, since they seemed to be part of the wall. There was waste ground around, untidy and weed-covered. I saw no dwellers in these uncomfortable buildings, but I was aware all through that I had a companion at my side, whose face I never saw. This invisibility did not seem to worry me at the time, and I made no attempt to get past it.[115]

These half finished interiors surrounded by wasteland lead, in his spirit-dream, into a large assembly hall also with coloured frescoes on its walls. Here he is approached by a strange man in Elizabethan dress whose 'plum coloured doublet and trunk hose' give him an aspect of superiority:

> We eyed each other and I was so completely myself that I smiled and said, 'Well, if you fellows are going to dress like that we poor moderns have no chance.' He made no answer, and his face was quite unresponsive. I could recognize the man now if I saw him, ruddy-faced, about thirty-five years of age, short, crisp, black hair and a black moustache, well-built and vigorous. He was sullen and sinister in his expression. I was conscious of someone else approaching with a black Spanish cloak. Then it all disappeared.[116]

Throughout his life, Doyle had dressed up as a man in preparation for this sinister but suggestive meeting with his own spiritual double. Its colourful, Catholicized masculinity no longer made him feel plain and insecure in comparison.

His final autobiographical return to Edinburgh occurs in the chapter he added to *Memories and Adventures* during the last year of his life. Although this chapter is ostensibly taken up with Doyle's Spiritualist mission, one 'worldly matter' occupies the central space of this section. It concerns Doyle's seventeen-year campaign on behalf of Oscar Slater, the German–Jewish immigrant sentenced to death by an Edinburgh judge on a charge of murdering an elderly Glaswegian lady, Miss Gilchrist, in 1909 – a sentence subsequently commuted to life imprisonment. Slater spent eighteen years in gaol before being allowed a retrial also in Edinburgh, largely as a result of Doyle's campaign on his behalf. Slater emerged with his name cleared and with a meagre compensation award but Doyle ended up having to pay a large proportion of Slater's legal costs and was left feeling deeply hurt at his ingratitude.

This final act of belated justice in Edinburgh is resonant with autobiographical echoes, Slater's release perhaps atoning for the confinement of that other victim of Edinburgh's laws and injustices, his own father. Certainly, Doyle's conversion to Spiritualism altered his memories of his birthplace. His travel writing lingers over descriptions of cities that most closely remind him of it: 'Edinburgh is the nearest analogy which I can recall', he writes enthusiastically of Melbourne in Australia.[117] His image of Edinburgh as a city of prosaic writing was gradually replaced by a more visual and idealized location which eventually subsumed his interest in the written life. After the war, the American publisher, George H. Doran, visited Doyle in his psychic bookshop at Westminster with the suggestion that he might like to conclude his career by writing a biography of Dr Watson. Doyle listened with mild receptivity, but indicated that he had lost all interest in the written life. Instead, he insisted on showing his guest a picture of Heaven 'given under guidance to an inspired artist'. Doran thought it looked like Monte Carlo.[118]

Memories and Adventures is, like his Edinburgh dream, an autobiography of finely finished facades, masculine mirrors and an incomplete picture of its own interiority. At the outset of his career and again at the end of it, Doyle's self-definition was challenged by two men who acquired a special status in his writing. One of them was Houdini, Doyle's close associate while writing *Memories and Adventures*, and the other was George Turnavine Budd, the Edinburgh student with whom he briefly shared a medical practice in 1882. Both charismatic materialists who offered showmanship in place of spirituality, each forced him to define the grounds of his own manhood. Trying once to compose a prayer, Doyle found he had written 'a legal document'[119] instead. Between the Arctic and Edinburgh, magic and medicine, literature and law, he finally situated his chambers in a writing beyond autobiography.

Notes

1. Gibson, J. M. (ed.), 'Conan Doyle in the Daily Mail' in *The Journal of the Arthur Conan Doyle Society*, vol. 9, June 1999, Ashcroft: British Columbia, pp. 129–30.
2. Doyle, A. C., *The Wanderings of a Spiritualist*, Berkeley: Ronin Publishing, 1988, p. 97.
3. See Richard Lancelyn Green, 'Victorian Philistinism Reconsidered' in Jon L. Lellenberg (ed.), *The Quest for Sir Arthur Conan Doyle: Thirteen Biographers in Search of a Life*, Carbondale and Edwardsville: Southern Illinois University Press, 1987, p. 169.
4. Green, R. L., 'His Final Tale of Chivalry' in ibid., p. 62.
5. Ibid., p. 43.
6. Ibid., p. 114.
7. Ibid., p. 128.
8. Doyle, A. C., *Memories and Adventures*, London: John Murray, 1924, pp. 234–5.
9. Ibid., p. 235.
10. Silverman, K., 'Biographers and the Art of Biography' in O'Conner, U. (ed.), *The Literary Biography: Problems and Solutions*, London: Quartet Books, 1991, pp. 111–12.
11. Doyle, *Memories and Adventures*, op. cit., p. 157.
12. Ibid., p. 177.
13. Hibberd, D. and Onions, J. (eds), *Poetry of the Great War*, Basingstoke: Macmillan, 1986, p. 156.
14. Hibberd, D. (ed.), *Wilfred Owen: War Poems and Others*, London: Chatto and Windus, 1973, p. 103.
15. Doyle, *Memories and Adventures*, op. cit., pp. 437–38.
16. Ibid., p. 448.
17. Forster, E. M., *Howard's End*, Harmondsworth: Penguin, 1910, 1941 edn, p. 249.
18. Doyle, *Memories and Adventures*, op. cit., p. 439.
19. Szreter, S., 'Victorian Britain, 1831–1963: Towards a Social History of Sexuality', *Journal of Victorian Culture*, 1(1), Spring 1996.
20. Doyle, *Memories and Adventures*, op. cit., p. 168.
21. Rousseau, J.-J., *The Confessions*, trans. J. M. Cohen, Harmondsworth: Penguin Classics, 1953, p. 245.
22. Quoted in Stavert, G., *A Study in Southsea*, Portsmouth: Milestone Publications, 1987, p. 101.
23. Doyle, A. C., *Through the Magic Door*, London: Smith Elder and Co., 1907, p. 2.
24. Ibid., p. 37.
25. Ibid., p. 162.
26. Ibid., pp. 6–7.
27. Ibid., p. 22.
28. Steedman, C., 'Linguistic Encounters of the Fourth Kind', *Journal of Victorian Culture*, 1(1), Spring 1996, p. 65.
29. Doyle, *Through the Magic Door*, op. cit., p. 182.
30. Doyle, *Memories and Adventures*, op. cit., p. 293.
31. Ibid., p. 18.
32. Doyle, *Through the Magic Door*, op. cit., p. 44.

33. Doyle, *Memories and Adventures*, op. cit., p. 22.
34. Doyle, *Through the Magic Door*, op. cit., p. 139.
35. Carlyle, T., *Selected Writings*, Harmondsworth: Penguin, 1971, pp. 37–40.
36. Clubbe, J., 'Introduction', *Froude's Life of Carlyle*, London: John Murray, 1972, p. 2.
37. See Broughton, T., 'The Froude–Carlyle Embroilment: Married Life as a Literary Problem', *Victorian Studies*, Summer 1995.
38. Doyle, *Memories and Adventures*, op. cit., p. 16.
39. Quoted in Stavert, *Study in Southsea*, op. cit., p. 73.
40. Carlyle, T., *Reminiscences*, New York: Harper & Brothers, 1881, p. 225.
41. Stephen, L., 'Autobiography' in *Hours in a Library*, vol. 3, London: John Murray, 1919, pp. 247–8.
42. Doyle, *Through the Magic Door*, op. cit., p. 75.
43. Ibid., p. 82.
44. Ibid., pp. 83–4.
45. Ibid., pp. 84–5.
46. Ibid., pp. 48–9.
47. Ibid., pp. 52–3.
48. Ibid., p. 91.
49. Doyle, *Memories and Adventures*, op. cit., p. 316.
50. Trollope, A., *Autobiography*, The World's Classics, Oxford: Oxford University Press, 1950, p. 71.
51. See Everitt, G., *English Caricaturists and Graphic Humorists of the Nineteenth Century*, London: Swan Sonnenschein and Co., 1893.
52. For the best account of Doyle's Edinburgh years see Edwards, O. D., *The Quest for Sherlock Holmes*, Edinburgh: Mainstream Publishing Co., 1983.
53. Doyle, *Memories and Adventures*, op. cit., p. 15.
54. Ibid., p. 11.
55. Ibid., p. 15.
56. Chambers, W., *Memoir of Robert Chambers with Autobiographic Reminiscences of William Chambers*, Edinburgh and London: W. & R. Chambers, 1872, p. 235.
57. Ibid., p. 319.
58. Doyle, *Memories and Adventures*, op. cit., p. 37.
59. Chambers, *Memoir*, op. cit., p. 244.
60. Doyle, *Memories and Adventures*, op. cit., p. 37.
61. Chambers, *Memoir*, op. cit., p. 294.
62. Ibid., p. 210.
63. Doyle, C. A., *The Doyle Diary*, London: Paddington Press, 1978, p. 56.
64. Chambers, *Memoir*, op. cit., p. 199.
65. Ibid., p. 241.
66. Doyle, *Memories and Adventures*, op. cit., p. 31.
67. Ibid., p. 38.
68. Ibid., p. 40.
69. Quoted in Gagnier, R., *Subjectivities: A History of Self-Representation in Britain, 1832–1920*, Oxford: Oxford University Press, 1991, p. 235.
70. Chambers, *Memoir*, op. cit., p. 159.
71. Doyle, *Through the Magic Door*, op. cit., p. 136.

72. Ibid., pp. 39–40.
73. Stephenson, R. L., *Edinburgh*, London: Seeley, Service & Co., 1879, pp. 37–8.
74. Ibid., pp. 16–17.
75. Ibid., p. 20.
76. Chambers, *Memoir*, op. cit., p. 225.
77. Stephenson, *Edinburgh*, op. cit., p. 30.
78. Ibid., p. 40.
79. Ibid., p. 44.
80. Ibid., pp. 47–8.
81. Doyle, *Memories and Adventures*, op. cit., pp. 16–17.
82. Ibid.
83. Ibid., p. 17.
84. Ibid., pp. 27–8.
85. Ibid., pp. 112–13.
86. Richard Lancelyn Green, 'His Final Tale of Chivalry' in Lellenberg, *The Quest for Arthur Conan Doyle*, op. cit., p. 50.
87. Doyle, *Memories and Adventures*, op. cit., p. 86.
88. Freud, S., 'The Uncanny' in *The Penguin Freud Library*, vol. 14, Harmondsworth: Penguin, 1990, p. 252.
89. Doyle, A. C., *The British Campaign in France and Flanders, 1914–1918*, vol. 6, London: Hodder and Stoughton, 1919, p. 307.
90. Doyle, *Memories and Adventures*, pp. 432–3.
91. Doyle, A. C., *The British Campaign*, vol. 6, p. 305.
92. Moore, R. and Gillette, D., *King, Warrior, Magician, Lover: Rediscovering the Archetypes of the Mature Masculine*, San Francisco: HarperCollins, 1991, p. 111.
93. Tosh, J., 'What Should Historians do with Masculinity? Reflections on Nineteenth-century Britain', *History Workshop*, (38), Autumn 1994, p. 198.
94. Ibid., pp. 184–5.
95. Ibid., p. 186.
96. Doyle, *Memories and Adventures*, op. cit., p. 44.
97. Ibid., p. 46.
98. Ibid., p. 48.
99. Ibid., p. 57.
100. Ibid., pp. 53–4.
101. Ibid., p. 49.
102. Boundas, C. V. (ed.), *The Deleuze Reader*, New York: Columbia University Press, 1993, p. 123.
103. Doyle, *Memories and Adventures*, op. cit., pp. 49–50.
104. Pearsall, R., *Conan Doyle: A Biographical Solution*, Glasgow: Richard Drew Publishing, 1977, p. 16.
105. Doyle, *Memories and Adventures*, op. cit., p. 53.
106. Ibid., p. 57.
107. Ibid., p. 243.
108. Ibid., p. 109.
109. Deleuze, G., 'Coldness and Cruelty' in Deleuze, G. and Sacher-Masoch, Leopold von, *Masochism*, New York: Zone Books, 1989, p. 99.
110. Ibid., p. 130.
111. Doyle, *Memories and Adventures*, op. cit., p. 374.

112. Deleuze, 'Coldness and Cruelty', op. cit., p. 63.
113. Doyle, A. C., *The Conan Doyle Stories*, London: John Murray, 1929, p. 351.
114. Deleuze,'Coldness and Cruelty', op. cit., p. 101.
115. Doyle, A. C. *The Edge of the Unknown*, New York: Berkley Publishing Corporation, 1968, p. 67.
116. Ibid.
117. Doyle, *The Wanderings of a Spiritualist*, op. cit., p. 95.
118. Orel, H. (ed.), *Arthur Conan Doyle: Interviews and Recollections*, London and Basingstoke: Macmillan, pp. 259–60.
119. Doyle, *Memories and Adventures*, op. cit., p. 86.

CHAPTER TWO

When Did You Last See Your Father?
The Early Fiction

Masculinity and narration

Just as Stevenson had written of Edinburgh as a city constructed from oppositions between a gothic past and a commercial present, so Doyle's early fiction shows experimentation across a range of similarly contrasting forms. In his first three novels, gothicism competes both with contemporary realism and with historical fiction to define the direction of writing whose main imperative is the exploration of masculine doubles. The father–son relationship is the main site for this exploration – one that is coupled with the act of narrating itself. This relationship is used to image a complicity between filial stories and the paternalistic, law-embodying truth modes, the sworn statements, legal testimonies and evidential diaries which they employ for their narration. In the name of truth, and sometimes in competition with it, these filial narrators tell improbably tall stories. In Doyle's first historical novel, *Micah Clarke*, this process is reversed. As Judge Jefferies interrogates the Sedgmoor rebels, legal discourse loses its authority, becoming instead the hysterical tool of a failing regime. At issue in Doyle's first three novels, *The Mystery of Cloomber* (1888), *Micah Clarke* (1889) and *The Firm of Girdlestone* (1890) is the truth status of a newly formulated narrative of masculinity.

It is difficult to establish a clear chronology for Doyle's early fiction, as the gaps between composition, completion, revision and publication make for an erratic sequence. What this range of early fiction has in common, however, is a preoccupation with unsafe and treacherous landscapes. Whether as tall tale or truthful testimony, contemporary gothicism or historical realism, these early narratives head compulsively towards the same fatal destination – a marsh, mire, bog or sinking ground like that of the historic battlefield of Sedgmoor in *Micah Clarke* where the Duke of Monmouth's rebel forces were defeated by the army of James II in 1685. These unstable grounds are places of masculine disappearance, as well as places where the masculine story loses contact with its own duality and credibility. As Doyle attempted to forge a literary career for himself, these watery landscapes are also the signifiers of dangerous identity determinants and of damaging causes. His early fiction was not only an attempt to identify by elimination a safe ground for masculine narration, it was also an attempt to find a burial ground for the true story of his own father. Whether encrypted in a gothic mansion, drowned in a realism at sea with its own belief system or sunk in the subversive swamps of British history, the traumatically unavailable story of the real father creates a vulnerability in the truth-discourses particularly affiliated with patriarchy.

Doyle began publishing his short stories, as distinct from his novels, in 1879, the year that Charles Doyle was first removed to a nursing home and while he himself was still obtaining his medical qualifications. His first story, 'The Mystery of Sasassa Valley' (1879) hinges on the fertile Irish brain of a young man who succeeds in transforming a ghost story into a mineral reserve, correctly identifying as the gleam of rock salt what others had perceived to be demonic eyes peering up from the ground. Doyle published several stories a year until 1887 when the first Holmes novella, *A Study in Scarlet*, written a year earlier, appeared unsensationally in *Beeton's Christmas Annual*. These early stories are what they set out to be – small triumphs of narration which self-consciously dramatize the problematics of male testimony in the act of narrating. The stories inscribe the storyteller in masculine communities as someone able to resymbolize gender anxieties in a configuration which releases doubt and tension as laughter and amazement.

Doyle's second published story, 'The American's Tale', (1880) in which swaggering loudmouthed Joe Hawkins gets eaten by a Venus Fly-Trap (*Dianoea*) in Montana, draws particular attention to the narrative performance of its main speaker. The American tale-teller, Jefferson Adams, is initially described as gleaming 'across our ordinary quiet conviviality like some brilliant meteor',[1] his story of the male body trapped by the devouring feminine leaving uncertainty in its wake:

> 'A most extraordinary narrative!' said Dawson. 'Who would have thought a Dianoea had such power!'
> 'Deuced rum yarn!' said young Sinclair.
> 'Evidently a matter-of-fact truthful man,' said the doctor.
> 'Or one of the most original liars that ever lived,' said I.[2]

'The American's Tale' demonstrates Doyle's formula for writing about the landscape as a place where both men and stories are both likely to be swallowed. The Venus Fly-Traps grow in the treacherous marshes of Montana, a vaginal territory of almost parodic terror: 'This here gulch was a marshy gloomy place … . Some parts of the marsh, too, were soft and deep, and a body thrown in would be gone by the morning.'[3]

While the great Grimpen Mire in the *The Hound of the Baskervilles* (1902) is Doyle's most famous sinking ground, this landscape appears early in his writing partly as a warning that it is trespassing on the unsayable, disturbing a dangerous ground of verbal taboo where the masculine story and the insecure career could easily founder. Its recurrence as a trope in his writing gives it the status of an authorial code whose formula can be contextualized and deciphered. This marsh landscape conjures up powerful symbolic associations as well as supplying a physical threat, eliding a conventional Catholic hell of sexual transgression with the new topography of the unconscious – a place of emotional struggle, repression and lost memories. In imitation of Wilkie Collins, this landscape also tropes Irishness for Doyle, providing a fictional repository for dangerous but tempting personal practices and political alignments.

This landscape is a place of story-exchange with a throat-like capacity for swallowing. It conflates those stories that are *swallowed* in the sense of being choked back and repressed with those that are *swallowed* in the sense of being believed and accepted as truths. Both as a novelist and as a propagandist, Doyle, in his writing, patrols these places of story-exchange which can, at times, secrete a disturbing gothic darkness. The marsh designates a place of personal struggle for characters and author alike; it is the site where an autobiographical and confessional impulse is transformed into a representation controlled by cultural censorship. A place of memory erasure which reduces the stories that can be told of it, the marsh is the contested and Oedipal territory of masculine practices which meet and merge there with their own suppression and punishment. As masculine stories are alternately suppressed and consumed, the marsh also mirrors its own fiction-hungry readership. After an uncertain start, Doyle's fiction seeks known ground for its encoding of the rules by which late-Victorian masculinity can be both learnt and recognized.

Many of Doyle's early narrators are earnest dupes or gullible self-publicists, insecurely isolated in their own egotism. Their version of events and of their own subjectivity is not just unreliable, it is subtly, self-complacently, even defiantly at odds with the reality clues of their story. In 'That Little Square Box' (1881), a neurasthenic narrator mistakes a box of racing pigeons for an IRA bomb; in 'Selecting a Ghost: The Ghosts of Goresthorpe Grange' (1883), a parvenu grocer tries to have a ghost installed in his newly acquired stately home and discovers that he has bought himself a burglar instead. Such a commodification of implausible beliefs and unlikely objects is a major preoccupation of these early stories.

In 'The Heiress of Glenmahowley' (1884) two young Irishmen find themselves monotonously holidaying 'in the centre of an enormous area of peat cuttings and bog land'.[4] As the would-be Byronic narrator and his friend adjust to this unpromising landscape by opting to pursue a

local heiress, they find themselves in difficulties owing to their ignorance of the physical ground they have to cover in order to reach her.
Penniless as it turns out, and in any case already married, the 'heiress'
greets the proposal that she should 'fly with me! Be mine! Share with
me the wild free life of a barrister'[5] with peals of laughter. Her amusement at this male performance identifies as 'boyish' their failure accurately
to read the manifest signs of the land. Aimed at an inexperienced
readership, often that of the *Boy's Own Paper*, these comedic stories
insist on the importance of ground-reading as an essential skill of
masculine reading. Manhood, they punningly reiterate, is acquired
through the practice of mastering signs not through the erections of
fantasy. Boys must learn through the hilariously painful lessons of
masochism to read the ground rules of modern manhood and avoid the
self-delusions of the bog.

In contrast to his comedic fantasists, another group of early stories
offer serious, often bemused, narrators who employ the codes of male
professionalism to try to read the puzzle of the marvellous. In some of
these instances Doyle's ability to replicate truth-discourse is so convincing that the stories pose successfully as 'statements' or factual eye-witness
testimonies. For Doyle, this mode of evidential writing came to represent the most significant and interesting form of narrative, one in which
the epistemological status of the masculine eye and voice was most
obviously at stake. What men saw and believed converted into a truth-
practice which then defined and guaranteed agreements about what
constituted masculinity itself. Doyle's first story for the prestigious
Cornhill Magazine, 'J. Habakuk Jephson's Statement' (1884) is a purported attempt to solve the mystery of the disappearance of the *Marie
Celeste* and her crew. According to Doyle's bibliographers, the reception of this story was provocatively mixed:

> When it was published the following January one reviewer paid the
> author the compliment of attributing it to Stevenson, and it had
> interesting repercussions. The Advocate General in Gibraltar an-
> nounced that it was 'a fabrication from beginning to end'; the
> *Boston Herald*, on the other hand, took it as the truth.[6]

The accurate reading and interpretation of signs, as well as their verbal
reconstruction, encodes as masculine those stories which have the capacity to represent truth.

In her well-known study, *Between Men: English Literature and Male
Homosocial Desire* (1985), Eve Kosofsky Sedgwick has established as
endemic in late-Victorian culture 'a homosexual panic'[7] derived from
the proximity of masculine imperatives and taboos in the formation of
the male homosocial constitution:

> Because the paths of male entitlement, especially in the nineteenth
> century, required certain intense male bonds that were not readily
> distinguishable from the most reprobated bonds, an endemic and
> ineradicable state of what I am calling male homosexual panic
> became the normal condition of the male heterosexual entitle-
> ment.[8]

For Sedgwick, this strangling double bind whereby intense male
homosocial desire was at once 'the most compulsory and the most
prohibited of social bonds' laid claim to its own literary genre through
which to represent the 'eschatological harrowings and epistemological
doublings' of its irresolvable dilemma. Men must bond if the purposes
of imperialism are to be fulfilled but face the possibility of losing their
privileged masculine designation if they do so too intimately. The 'paranoid Gothic'[9] is, according to Sedgwick, the genre which offered an apt
embodiment for the resulting homophobia 'where one man's mind could
be read by that of the feared and desired other', its narrative doubling
leaving 'a residue of two potent male figures locked in an
epistemologically indissoluble clench of will and desire'.[10] Stevenson's
Dr. Jekyll and Mr. Hyde is a classic example of this genre inscribing the
tension between a necessary homosociality and a prohibited homosexuality in the construction of late-Victorian masculinity.

In Doyle's early fiction these tensions are particularly acute. Such
stories as The Sign of Four and The Mystery of Cloomber exhibit a
degree of doubling and redoubling which almost parodies formulaic
practice. Doyle contributed to 'the paranoid Gothic' one of its most
famous configurations, that of Sherlock Holmes plunging down the
Reichenbach Falls locked in the deadly embrace of that 'feared and
desired other', Professor Moriarty. It is only in his fourth full-length
novel, The White Company (1891), that Doyle finds a way of escaping
the paranoid clutches of this genre which suspects, and fulfils itself in
suspecting, its own masculine legitimation. In a novel full of the rough
embrace of warriors, he envisages a non-domestic sphere in which
homosociality is the tension-free norm as men, like Alleyne Edricson,
set out in pursuit of their own masculinity rather than that of other
men. An intensified concern for reputation relegates the threat of homosexual intimacy. In The White Company Sir John Chandos, a mutilated
septuagenarian, embodies the ultimate in masculine desire – one for
'name' rather than face:

> ... what knight was there in that hall of St. Andrew's who would
> not have gladly laid down youth, beauty, and all that he possessed
> to win the fame of this man? For whom could be named with
> Chandos, the stainless knight, the wise counsellor, the valiant war-
> rior, the hero of Crecy, of Winchelsea, of Poitiers, of Auray ... .[11]

Doyle's heroines themselves reinforce the homosocial imperative as the avenue to fame, often preferring the public performance of manhood to the man himself. A publicly agreed and witnessed code of manhood replaces the opposing otherness and doubled identities of 'the paranoid Gothic', allowing it to be exchanged for the comedic and chivalric narratives of masochism in which Doyle and his readers delighted. Lady Mary, the heroine of *Sir Nigel* (1906), a late prelude to *The White Company*, firmly reminds her medieval lover that, in the conflicting demands of heterosexual 'love' and homosocial 'honour', he must always chose the latter.[12] Simultaneously reinforcing and parodying this message, the 'womanly' Gladys Hungerton of *The Lost World* (1912) tells her would-be fiancee that it is only performance in the Victorian biographical tradition that makes a man desirable:

> It is never a man that I should love, but always the glories he had won, for they would be reflected upon me. Think of Richard Burton! When I read his wife's life of him I could so understand her love. And Lady Stanley! Did you ever read the wonderful last chapter of that book about her husband? These are the sort of men that a woman could worship with all her soul and ... be ... honoured by all the world as the inspirer of noble deeds.[13]

The doubling capacity for identity exchange in the father–son relationship had been the subject of an early story of comedic gothicism, 'The Great Keinplatz Experiment' (1885). Taking part in a mesmeric experiment, a respectably married academic professor finds that he has exchanged souls, personalities and behaviour traits with a bohemian student, to the mutual disturbance of the professor's domestic circle and the student's drinking cronies. As a key component of his career, Doyle inscribed a masculine relationship with literacy and literature as itself a variant of the father–son relationship. In his influential writing for boys, Doyle was contributing to an ideological project which carried a heavy investment during the late-Victorian period. The impact of adventure fiction on 'the Peter Pan generation' – the men who had grown up with the imperialism of the 1890s – would be subject to critical scrutiny in the aftermath of the First World War. Doyle's close friend, Roger Casement, faced public execution for treason with the bewildered perception that, in hanging him, 'they' were 'killing a boy',[14] one who had uncritically absorbed the ideological directives of his early reading and mapped them on to his subsequent career.

One of Doyle's stories from 1886, 'Cyprian Overbeck Wells: A Literary Mosaic', inscribes the moment of partnership with literature as simultaneously a moment of entry into the symbolic community of manhood. In the story of a young man who dreams of literary fame but cannot think of what to write, the aspiring author is visited in a dream by the great masters of the masculine romance. Published in the *Boy's Own Paper*, this story rather deviantly addresses itself to the reading constituency solemnly described by John Springhall:

> Under its first and greatest editor, George Andrew Hutchinson (1842–1913), the *Boy's Own Paper* quickly became the most important and influential periodical ever published, despite its firmly moral and Christian tone ... .
>
> In the pages of the *Boy's Own Paper*, manly, intrepid lads wandered around the world, proving their character as plucky Englishmen and, eventually, finding fame and fortune. The portrayal of manliness became the most essential staple of the *Boy's Own Paper*, so much so that it has been called by Patrick Dunae the 'unofficial organ' of the 'muscular Christianity' movement. Manliness was held, in its pages, as the highest virtue to which a British schoolboy could aspire.[15]

Neither very muscular, nor very Christian and certainly not wandering about the world, the narrator of 'Cyprian Overbeck Wells: A Literary Mosaic' encounters his version of manliness from an armchair during an after-dinner nap. The impressively named 'Cyprian Overbeck Wells' is not the story's narrator but the name of the hero of his dream adventure story. The actual narrator is simply called Smith – a Smith whose dream it is to produce 'some great work which should single me out from the family of Smiths, and render my name immortal'.[16]

Smith is initially one of Doyle's boyish fantasists, unable to join his singular perception of himself to any community of male viewpoint:

> From my boyhood I have had an intense and overwhelming conviction that my real vocation lay in the direction of literature. I have, however, had a most unaccountable difficulty in getting any responsible person to share my views ... . From the age of seventeen to that of three-and-twenty I was a literary volcano in a constant state of eruption. Poems and tales, articles and reviews, nothing came amiss to my pen. From the great sea-serpent to the nebular hypothesis, I was ready to write on anything or everything ... . Alas! I could find no one to join me in my appreciation, and solitary admiration for one's self, however genuine, becomes satiating after a time.[17]

The masturbatory ease and self-gratification of these productions gives place, under pressure from his father, to a job as a clerk from which he is sacked for inserting 'pieces of word-painting into the most commonplace business letters'.

Finally in a position to begin his masterpiece, Smith makes a study of the masters of English prose, then sits down and finds that, despite all the new pens he has bought, his imagination is sterile and his mind a complete blank. In sleep, he is visited by a gathering of great authors, from Defoe and Smollett to Dickens and Stevenson. Taking turns to share the narration, these dream writers compose the adventures of Cyprian Overbeck who, in an interesting reversal of patriarchy, assumes the name of his wife's family on marriage. The story begins in 1617 and travels the history of adventure writing in a series of brilliant parodies, finally disappearing into the quagmires of Bulwer Lytton's prose. In a quarrel with Scott about the nature of originality, the derisive laughter of Bulwer's audience wakes Smith from his dream. Left with the hope that the great masters of originality will one day return and finish his story, he is in the meantime content to copy their inspiration.

For all its playfulness, this is a significant story. Written while Doyle was working on *A Study in Scarlet*, it does more than introduce its *Boy's Own* readers and the aspiring Smiths among them to a community of name and achievement. It also raises the question of masculine originality *vis-à-vis* masculine copying as the best guarantee of manhood. This was a vexed issue for Doyle himself, for his father, Charles, and for that group of Scottish writers associated with Stevenson who saw the correct modelling of boyhood as their specific territory. In his essay, 'The Boy' (1905), the publisher and author, Andrew Lang, had discussed this subject in different contexts, contrasting the 'extremely original, imaginative, and almost poetical' qualities of the solitary boy with the savage reversions to which boyhood in the plural was generally liable.[18] While Charles Doyle, according to the evidence of his 1889 *Sunnyside Journals*, was still desperately trying to prove his sanity by producing finely detailed drawings of leaves, flowers and mushrooms, and labelling them as 'exact copies', Doyle himself was carefully aligning himself with the lost originalities of the adventure tradition.

In an 1894 essay for The *Idler* series on 'First Books' to which Doyle later contributed an account of *Micah Clarke*, Robert Louis Stevenson had written a parable about the creative genesis of that classic boy's adventure story, *Treasure Island*, a parable which inscribes copying and plagiarism as the necessary acts of a masculine literary identity. Stevenson described a summer spent with an artistic schoolboy who used his holidays to create a gallery of his own work – an exhibition to which Stevenson himself contributed a beautifully coloured map called 'Treasure Island'. His account of the story inspired by this coloured map emphasizes a collective authorship in which he, his own father, the artistic schoolboy and a number of male friends and acquaintances all collaborated to produce a work from which 'Women were excluded'. On the subject of plagiarism, Stevenson was cavalier:

> No doubt the parrot once belonged to Robinson Crusoe. No doubt the skeleton is conveyed from Poe. I think little of these, they are trifles and details; and no man can hope to have a monopoly of skeletons or make a corner in talking birds. The stockade, I am

> told, is from *Masterman Ready*. It may be, I care not a jot. These
> useful writers had fulfilled the poet's saying: departing, they had
> left behind them Footprints on the sands of time, Footprints which
> perhaps another – and I was the other![19]

While copying is inscribed as the sign of an all-male community, a lost originality is the inevitable cost of membership. When the publishers sent back the proofs of *Treasure Island* for correction, the original map was found to have vanished from among them. Stevenson, with the help of his father, was left to re-create his own inspirational design from the cues of the written story: 'my father himself ... elaborately *forged* the signature of Captain Flint, and the sailing directions of Billy Bones. But somehow it was never *Treasure Island* to me'.[20]

An originality anterior to language had thus been resymbolized by it, losing its boyish authenticity under the forged signature of the father. As its fantasy constituent, the adventure story celebrates and re-inscribes this lost place of origins under the sign of the masculine community. In contrast to Stevenson, however, Doyle's 'lost' originality was his own father and where Stevenson was able, with the help of his father, to reproduce his lost map, Doyle's early fiction was a fantasy in search of its own source of masculine legitimation.

The Mystery of Cloomber

In 1889, the year that Doyle began to establish himself as a writer with the publication of his third novel, *Micah Clarke*, Charles Doyle copied into his Journal a misspelt review of his son's gothic novel, 'Mystery of Cloomber'. Dated 11 January 1889, the review from the *Literary World* runs as follows:

> The so called 'Occult Science' of the East has been intruded upon
> by Mr. Conan Doyle for the Plot of his interesting book – 'The
> Mystery of Cloomber' – For Forty years, General Heatherstone is
> haunted by an Astral Bell whose wringing constantly reminds him
> that the cutting down in battle of Ghoolab Shah ... an Arch Adept
> of the First Degree ... will in due course be avenged – The Chelas
> or deciple [sic] of Ghoolab eventually appears in Scotland – and
> carries off the General and a Servant, who was also concerned in
> the Arch Adept's fall, to their deaths in an almost trackless Morass
> in Wigtownshire – Two Love Stories run thro' the Book – and there
> are other exciting incidents of a Strictly Natural Kind.[21]

While the plot of Doyle's novel sounds even more disturbed than his father's inner world, Charles Doyle was sane enough to provide illustrations for it and it remains the novel on which his influence was most apparent. Because of rewritings and rejections, it is difficult to construct a clear order of composition for the first three novels, but there are good reasons for regarding *The Mystery of Cloomber* as belonging to an earlier phase of imaginative mapping than *The Firm of Girdlestone*, which Doyle subsequently selected as the starting point for his literary career. Doyle's bibliographers remark of the book:

> *The Mystery of Cloomber* was written between April and July 1888. It was not among the author's favourite works, as he considered it very immature. It was the only novel excluded from the Crowborough Edition.[22]

If for no other reason, this exclusion of the novel from the Crowborough Edition of Doyle's work, puts *The Mystery of Cloomber* in an uncanonical category of its own – one that is antecedent to the acknowledged body of his work. It is unclear whether Doyle rejected it on grounds of its aesthetic form (paranoid gothic), its religious position (Theosophist), its political perspective (anti-English and anti-imperialist) or the painful personal memories it encoded in its joking reminders of his father's fate. It is pre-eminently a book of burial places and bereavement anxiety, and its shortlived history in Doyle's own memory – it was a book that he often forgot having written – further emphasizes the unresolved interaction of autobiographical material and aesthetic form.

Simultaneously first novel and lost original, *The Mystery of Cloomber* is the novel in which Doyle buried alive part of his own identity and the affiliations which he considered inimical to a successful career. His first three novels all focus on different problematics of the father–son relationship in the contrasting geography of different fictional genres and opposing value systems. *The Mystery of Cloomber* deploys a gothic narrative of masochistic suspense set on the west coast of Scotland, while *The Firm of Girdlestone* moves away from its early Edinburgh setting into the realist domain and Oedipal dramas of commercial London. *Micah Clarke* revives a Puritan defeat of the later seventeenth century, using the father–son relationship to hinge together the manhood of the seventeenth century with that of the late nineteenth. In each novel, the father figure is differently construed. The evil, hypocritical, capitalist of *The Firm of Girdlestone* is at the same time a devoted father to his son, Ezra, while the kindly, eccentric scholar of *The Mystery of Cloomber* is too self-centred and unworldly to give a thought to the welfare of his children. The apolitical Micah Clarke is sent as his father's representative to fight for Monmouth at the Battle of Sedgmoor, despite the fact that he shares none of his father's religious or political beliefs. Each version of this relationship shows Doyle envisioning a different burial place for the masculine lack around which his fiction is constructed.

'Wigtownshire', the setting for *The Mystery of Cloomber*, is so named on account of its lawyers and legal writing but the bleak and remote coastline, which two contrasting fathers have, for different reasons, each chosen as their retreat, is figured as beyond all but the peripheral vision of British law. Both John West and General Heatherstone face problems of the spirit for which there is no visible jurisdiction. Like *Wuthering Heights*, *The Mystery of Cloomber* contrasts two houses to invoke cultural differences that nonetheless maintain an uneasy dialogue with each other, as do the Scots and English families whose interlinked stories form the main narrative and the marital alliances that conclude it. A similar alliance grounded the first stage of Doyle's writing identity.

Gothic symbolism reverberates across a landscape full of images of living death and places of unmarked burial. Cloomber Hall itself is described as 'a giant sarcophagus', a lonely landmark in a desolate region: '... there was no sign of the works of man save only where the high, white tower of Cloomber Hall shot up, like a headstone of some giant grave, from amid the firs and larches which girt it round'.[23] Unlike other Victorian gothic locations, Cloomber is distinctive for the emptiness of its symbolism: it stands for nothing, containing no history of its own but providing the final retreat of a paranoid imperialism. If Cloomber stands for burial, it is also the site of grim Scottish jokes on the subject of madness and its places of confinement. The house agent who has let Cloomber is convinced that his new tenant, General Heatherstone, is mad because of his obsessive anxiety about the privacy of the location and his complete disregard for its cost. The agent claims:

> 'If every man had his due, our friend would find himself in a house with a high wall round the grounds, and that without costing him a farthing,' ...
> 'Where then?' I asked, humouring his joke.
> 'Why, in the Wigtown County Lunatic Asylum,' cried the little man, with a bubble of laughter, in the midst of which I rode on my way, leaving him still chuckling over his own facetiousness.[24]

Son of one of the novel's reclusive patriarchs, the principal narrator, John West junior, is a law student who describes himself as the editor rather than the author of his story. The only literary ambition he claims for himself is the accurate arrangement and sequencing of a narrative whose primary sources are acts of legal witness or evidential testimony. The novel opens with this claim:

> I, John Fothergill West, student of law in the University of St. Andrews, have endeavoured in the ensuing pages to lay my statement before the public in a concise and business-like fashion.[25]

In a novel where all the narrators are men and where writing and inscription is used to designate entry into a masculine community composed equally of law and storytelling, great care is taken to present these statements as truthful forms of fact. John West rejects any notion of literary embellishment as he recounts the peculiar life aims of his own eccentric father and the bizarre life story of his eventual father-in-law, General Heatherstone.

The more prosaic the code of law, however, the more bizarre are the forces that are sent to try it. *The Mystery of Cloomber* is a gothic novel which sides with its own strangeness and refuses to defeat or exclude it – a text of masculine doubling and of paranoid gothic which cheerfully endorses its own paranoia and inscribes it as indisputable truth. Like the house itself, the masculine interiority at the centre of the story is one of a masochistic emptiness, containing a spiritual guilt that is forced into a prolonged wait for its own punishment. It is a novel whose only plot is one of mysterious but emasculating suspense, as the retired English general waits for a fate which has haunted him for forty years. In place of the unworldly heroine conventionally haunted by patriarchy, this gothic novel shows patriarchy haunted by the notion of unworldliness itself.

This unworldliness takes other forms than that of General Heatherstone's mysterious retreat from society. It is also the chief characteristic of the narrator's father, an eccentric ex-lawyer whose notion of law is not limited by border, creed or coastline. John West senior is an Orientalist and Sanscrit scholar who has gradually relinquished his lucrative legal practice for the delights of abstruse research. He has been successful in his spiritual studies although they have cost him his worldly career:

> He had been brought up to be a solicitor, or Writer to the Signet, as it is termed in Scotland, but ... as his learning accumulated his practice dissolved, until at the very moment when he had attained the zenith of his celebrity he had also reached the nadir of his fortunes.[26]

Doyle's portrayal of this familiar Victorian figure of the unworldly scholar is, like much else in this masculine gothicism, a reversed one. The value system that sustains West's scholarship is a spiritual knowledge which he dreams of translating into the English language. For John Hunter West, the Victorian obsession with lineage is a purposeful one, for he believes his family to be the vehicle for a specific cultural task in the achievement of which the individual life is of little significance. The task of the West family is a gradual decipherment of Eastern spiritual wisdom and the eventual completion of an English translation of the 325 volumes of the Buddhist Djarmas, with appropriate scholarly annotation. In commencing this task, John Hunter West has carefully calculated the family resources necessary for its undertaking:

> 'The abridged edition in the Imperial Library of Pekin', said my father, rubbing his hands together, 'consists of 325 volumes of an average weight of five pounds. Then the preface, which must embrace some account of the Rig-veda, the Sama-veda, the Yagur-veda, and the Atharva-veda, with the Brahmanas, could hardly be completed in less than ten volumes. Now, if we apportion one volume to each year, there is every prospect of the family coming to an end of its task about the date 2250, the twelfth generation completing the work, while the thirteenth might occupy itself upon the index.'[27]

When his pragmatic son enquires how the family are to live during the progress of the great undertaking, his father replies:

> 'That's the worst of you, Jack ... . There is nothing practical about you. Instead of confining your attention to the working out of my noble scheme, you begin raising all sorts of absurd objectives. It is a mere matter of detail how our descendants live, so long as they stick to the Djarmas.'

In this novel father and son operate a combined intelligence in which the son's practical sense and legal training attempt to balance the father's spiritual wisdom and visionary intellectualism. This family combination of law and higher law is linked to the cities and coastlines of Scotland, in obvious contrast to the worldly materialism and arrogant superiority of the English General Heatherstone whose uniform and impeccable class credentials cannot protect him from the avenging spiritual forces of the East. Significantly, General Heatherstone has no dialogue with his own son to match that of the Wests but lives in a perpetual silence and lack of language on the one subject that concerns him most. He cannot explain his spiritual terror without compromising a masculine authority predicated on the denial of its own interiority.

The Mystery of Cloomber commences Doyle's lifelong fascination with the British Empire and the varying enthusiasms he felt for the subject. Significantly, the early novels are anti-imperialist in stance and, while he came to acquire the reputation of a staunch supporter of Empire, he could only do so by reformulating the colonializing culture. The novel dramatizes the beginnings of this process. Among the damaged masculinities of Doyle's fiction, the figure of the returned colonial is the most haunting. Characters throughout the Holmes canon return, like Watson himself, to the mother country carrying wounds that are both psychic and physical, guilts and secrets that can only be inscribed in unintelligible ciphers, not read in the formal discourses of the dominant culture. General Heatherstone is the first of this speckled band who have lost contact with their own manhood, living in a state of vulnerability and paranoia which no amount of surveillance can render secure.

Major General J. B. Heatherstone, formerly a colonel in the Indian Army, five times mentioned in dispatches and a veteran of the First Afghan War (1839–42), has taken up the tenancy of remote Cloomber Hall, and is living there in a state of paranoid defensiveness, under siege from unknown, apparently invisible enemies. Heatherstone is the first of many British ex-public school boys whom Doyle represents as defective sign readers, bound to the codes of their own culture, but blindly unable to read the spirit of other masculinities. The General's long-withheld guilty secret, his murder of a Buddhist holy man during the First Afghan War, is finally revealed in an old dairy account relating to General Pollock's successful crossing of the Khyber Pass, after an earlier massacre of the British army on their way to the relief of Jalalabad.[28]

The haunting of Heatherstone is psychological, its only external manifestation being the sound of an astral bell, which rings to remind him that his crime is unforgotten. Embodiment of British colonial power and the English class system though he is, neither courage, class nor military status can protect him from a spiritual power that can penetrate all his material and physical defences. This vulnerability to spiritual penetration is the source of his apparent madness, and the unfinished nature of his story brings with it a wracking suspense that resembles torture.

The location of his guilty secret, the Terada Pass, is a site for the reversal of meanings and power signs. In October 1841, following the collapse of the British garrison at Kabul, General Heatherstone had allowed a rout of the native forces to turn into a slaughter, determined to teach the native Afridis 'such a lesson that the sight of a single scarlet uniform would in future be a passport in itself'.[29] In this borderland territory, however, the meaning of power is suddenly reversed when an ancient holy man emerges from his cave to interpose himself between the two armies. Warning the British that they are desecrating holy ground, that the place they occupy is one 'for prayer and meditation, not for murder', the old man significantly addresses them in 'excellent English'.[30] His mastery of their language signals the point at which power changes hands as the British under Heatherstone betray their own moral code. Following the murder, the scarlet uniform of the Indian Army becomes a scarlet letter, a badge of dishonour that cannot protect the General from enemies who can penetrate and direct his thoughts.

The General's diary records the events that form the nucleus of the story. After the massacre of the Afridis he writes in his day-book:

> I have only just got back, tired and weary, stained with blood and dust, but I have sat down before either washing or changing to have the satisfaction of seeing our deeds set forth in black and white – if only in my private log for no eye but my own. I shall describe it all fully as a preparation for an official account, which must be drawn up when Elliott gets back. Billy Dawson used to say that there were three degrees of comparison – a prevarication, a lie, and an official account.[31]

His own unwashed body the original record of his deed, Heatherstone sets down his account of what he calls his 'vermin-killing' and the murder that preceded it. The following day he experiences himself in the grip of a mesmeric sleep as something takes control of him. He feels like a bird under the influence of a snake: 'My mind was clear enough, but my body was as torpid as though I was asleep.'[32] He sees a man dressed in Asiatic costume standing at the entrance to his tent and learns from him that his crime has placed him in the power of occult laws from which there will be no protection. The diary is broken off after a four-day silence with the words ' – God help us!'

This strange novel illustrates the dialectical tensions which sustained Doyle's fiction, his public identity, and a considerable part of his career. His Scottish narrator, John West, finds himself in the position of having to defend General Heatherstone, a man he dislikes but his future father-in-law, against an avenger, the Buddhist master, Ram Singh, to whom he feels strongly attracted. Doyle's own rejection of Theosophy in favour of positivism and psychic research required a similarly counter-emotional positioning. The growing tension in John West as he tries to anticipate the dangers threatening the General is reinforced by a covert threat to his own Western heterosexual manhood:

> I tried to read, I tried to write, I paced about the lawn, I walked to the end of the lane, I put new flies upon my fishing hooks, I began to index my father's library – in a dozen ways I endeavoured to relieve the suspense which was becoming intolerable. My sister, I could see, was suffering from the same feverish restlessness.[33]

As a similar suspense invades all the characters surrounding the General, John West finds himself addicted to the mysterious problem for which he can find no clear explanation and no appropriate solution:

> It was in vain ... to direct my mind into some healthy channel. Do what I would ... I would still find myself puzzling over this one question, until it obtained such a hold upon me that I felt it was useless for me to attempt to apply myself to anything until I had come to some satisfactory solution of it.[34]

The problem is so absorbing that West even suggests that he has fallen in love with the General's daughter, Gabriel, in order to justify his obsession with it. Gabriel herself complicates the picture by insisting that the repulsive General is the kindest of fathers. The fascination of this patriarchal enigma, and West's attempt to discover what the General is waiting for with such overwhelming anxiety, creates a suspense so acute it threatens to unhinge mind from body, in a separation of inner and outer man which resembles the madness of the General himself. This notion of unhingement is the dominant motif of the novel, readable as both madness and spiritual mastery. While John West and the General cannot escape the physical torments of suspense, the three avenging Buddhist chelas have the ability to release their souls from their bodies and to practise astral travel at will.

The Mystery of Cloomber is a distinctly masochistic novel, with General Heatherstone embodying Theodor Reik's description of the masochistic ego as 'closed and self-referential', this self-containment dispensing with the need for an external object, since victim and victimizer become one. Exploring the link between masochism and fantasy, Kaja Silverman explains how masochism 'prolongs preparatory detail and ritual at the expense of climax and consummation, endlessly delaying the moment at which suffering yields to reward.'[35] The masochist, she argues, following Deleuze, 'liberates himself in preparation for a rebirth in which the father will have no part'.[36]

This certainly was the rebirth for which Doyle himself was waiting as he produced his curious manuscript of patriarchal victimization. General Heatherstone's prolonged ordeal of waiting was one shared by Doyle's own father. Charles Doyle's Sunnyside diary returns repeatedly to his own long-awaited encounter with death. A journal sketch depicts him with two separated bodies, one physical and the other spiritual, lying above and below each other on a long sofa. This is, he claims in the text, another of his exact copies: 'People say true as Life – but this is true as Death'.[37] *The Mystery of Cloomber* cathects Charles Doyle's predicament with his son's growing fascination with the British Empire – a fascination which weds him to an Englishness in tension with his own inner story.

When the long-fantasized and dreaded act of spiritual vengeance eventually occurs, General Heatherstone and the corporal who shared his guilt are mysteriously spirited away from Cloomber at the dead of night by the three chelas and disposed of in the great bog or Hole of Cree, a saltwater marsh that 'no man would venture through unless he had the guidance of one of the few peasants who retain the secret of its paths'.[38] A knowledge of the paths which circumnavigate these sinking grounds is another secret of the book, one handed down from great-grandfather to great-grandson, and now only possessed by one man and his lurcher – a dog with phenomenal tracking powers. It is with the help of this animal that the narrator, West, and the General's son are able to follow the tracks of the General's disappearance.

The Bog of Cree is described in stridently symbolic text, in which landscape maps the contours of a sick physiological interior:

> Great purple and yellow fungi had broken out in a dense eruption, as though Nature were afflicted with a foul disease, which manifested itself by this crop of plague spots ...
> ... Never had I ventured into so pestilent and forbidding a place.[39]

John West and Heatherstone's son finally find themselves at the hellish opening to which the tracks lead:

> At last ... we came on a spot the gloomy horror of which might have furnished Dante with a fresh terror for his 'Inferno'.
> The whole bog in this part appeared to have sunk in, forming a great, funnel-shaped depression, which terminated in the centre in a circular rift or opening about forty feet in diameter. It was a whirlpool – a perfect maelstrom of mud, sloping down on every side to this silent and awful chasm.[40]

Kneeling at the edge of the hole, the narrator hurls a great stone into the abyss from which a 'faint, sickly exhalation seemed to rise'. As the stone disappears into the bowels of the earth, the faint musical tinkle of an astral bell can suddenly be heard.

In case the reader has missed the symbolic significance of the Great Bog, Doyle draws attention to it as the last remaining 'mystery of Cloomber', the 'one point which is still dark' in the narrative. There may be, the narrator suggests, some occult connection between this place of disappearance and 'the sacrilege which had been committed' in the Terada Pass.[41] In the genre of 'paranoid gothic', power, place and identity are reversible propositions, easily deconstructed. If the bog is a recurrent trope for the masculine story's place of disappearance, that of the borderland pass between two countries is Doyle's symbol for identity exchange.

Among the testimonies that make up this narrative is one by 'Dr Easterling', the physician attending General Heatherstone. The significantly named doctor provides West with a medical memorandum. As a man of science he is puzzled by the extreme exhaustion of his patient's much injured body and by its apparently scheduled refusal to die. The suffering, mesmerized General, who knows that his body is controlled by alien spirits, gives his doctor a lecture on the superior knowledge of body-magic to be found in the East, distinguishing between mere conjurers and those who have a higher spiritual knowledge of the body's powers. Annoyed at this challenge to his medical authority but puzzled to find his patient's pulse has suddenly become normal, the doctor makes some passes of his own and finds that he has performed an unexpected trick of discovery. Stretching out a hand to pick up his gloves from a bedside table, he disturbs a linen cloth arranged over an object in its centre. What he has revealed is a model of the principal passes between India and Afghanistan, scene of the crime and nerve centre of the General's illness and sudden recovery. Wondering if he, too, has become subject to autosuggestion, the doctor suddenly hears the faint ringing of an astral bell, the sound of external forces working on the spirit. This trick unexpectedly performed by the doctor is one performed by the novel too, as it casually reveals the hidden places at the heart of the story.

As East and West connect and exchange with each other, the occult link between the General's crime and his place of punishment is found in the text which contains the story of his guilt. In his Afghan diary, the General had reflected on the total nature of colonial war, favouring an unlimited extermination of subject people:

> If you are making war you should throw no chance away. I hate half-and-half measures. The Children of Israel seem to have been the only people who ever carried war to its logical conclusion – except Cromwell in Ireland.[42]

It is this exception which proves the occult rule, that Ireland is the hidden connection linking crime and punishment. In Doyle's writing, Ireland and Irishness articulate themselves through a different set of representational practices and occulted symbols, which operate like a secret, cipher language within the dominant discourse of the text. It is a tempest in the Irish Sea, described as 'a water full of lost souls'[43] that delivers the agents of Buddhist retribution to the General's door, forcing him to acknowledge colonial deeds and things of darkness as his own. In its hidden preoccupation with Irish history, *The Mystery of Cloomber* uses a masochistic suspense narrative which simultaneously avenges his own father while banishing his image in the emergence of a new man. Marrying the General's daughter, John West establishes an Anglo-Scottish alliance in which spiritual disassociation and dangerous bogs are both left behind.

As a novel, *The Mystery of Cloomber* represents both the 'pass' where national identities confront each other and the mesmeric sleight of hand through which variants of inner and outer stories, of East and West, are magically exchanged. Such border passes are sites of ideological conflict in the novel and those who report from them are liable to fierce punishment and suppression. 'Proposed to shoot our inform-ant',[44] the General writes in his day-book about the messenger who had brought him information about the planned attack in the Terada Pass. Such borderlands are troped throughout Doyle's fiction as representing a truth mode which cannot articulate itself 'in perfect English' without suffering immediate attack. Imaging places of confused connection in the masculine identity which polices them, the pass is simultaneously an impasse – a place of violent suppression and story exchange.

While General Heatherstone disappears in body to leave his written story behind, the three Eastern adepts who are his avengers do the opposite, leaving their bodies behind while their spirits engage in astral travel. As the climax to the narrator's personal adventures, the sane and practical young lawyer is given a privileged sight, allowed, as the chapter heading tells us, to 'see that which has been seen by few', a glimpse of meditating bodies from which the spirit has been removed:

> They were so still and silent that they might have been two bronze statues but for the slow and measured rhythm of their breathing. Their faces, however, had a peculiar, ashen-grey colour ... and I observed, on stooping my head, that only the whites of their eyes were visible, the balls being turned upwards beneath the lids.

Witnessing what the adept, Ram Singh, describes as 'the grandest results of our occult philosophy, the dissociation of spirit from body', West is told that, in the East, the astral bodies of these men are standing on the banks of the Ganges, their spirits 'clothed in a material covering so identical with their real bodies' that none who saw them would doubt the reality of their presence.[45] Behind the facticity of its narrative, the novel endorses its own supernatural conclusions and justifies the apparent 'madness' of the impoverished, unworldly Sancrit scholar, John West senior, by making him a centre of understanding between Western knowledge and Eastern spirituality. His faith in his family task is rewarded with a remunerative appointment at the University of Edinburgh.

The connection between the empty towers of Cloomber and the British failure to colonize Afghanistan is an obvious and reversible one. The novel exchanges English manhood and the English class system for the inner strengths of a sign-literate, spiritually-informed Scottish manhood, eventually establishing Edinburgh as a place of power in its own right. The association between the Khyber Pass, with its fierce Afridi inhabitants, and Scotland was not Doyle's alone. Mr Beeton, in whose *Christmas Annual* Sherlock Holmes had made his first appearance, had other claims to fame apart from being the husband of a famous cookery writer. His impressive *Dictionary of Universal Information* compiled in 1860 draws attention to this comparison. His reference for the Afridis reads:

> ... a clan of Afghans, who inhabit the Khyber Hills ... . Like the Scottish Highlanders of the last century, they command the passes of their hills ... . They are a warlike, determined race of clansmen.[46]

The Mystery of Cloomber was a novel of rejections, one which explored the fascinations of Theosophy and the Irish nationalism of Doyle's father, and rejected them in favour of an Anglo-Scots alliance whose readjusted power relationship privileged Scotland. It was the direction in which Doyle himself was to move, and the novel is an interesting illustration of his method of using fiction to map and envisage political directions. Exploring the power play between rival fictional modes, Doyle departed from the dangerous paths of his own creativity, choosing instead to copy the dominant discourse models of late-Victorian culture and to become, like his narrator, the exponent and defender of an imperial and military masculinity. The identities buried in this rejected novel were forgotten but they were not gone, and they would in time resurface from their boggy burial places with all their fascinations intact. The glamorous flowing robes and sweeping gestures of the Eastern adept, Ram Singh, would eventually clothe the figure of Doyle's own personal spirit guide, the Arabian physician 'Pheneas' when, after the First World War, he emerged through the seance circle of Doyle's second family. While Doyle continued to converse with spirits who worked exclusively for Scotland, Ireland would remain an undecipherable blot on his autobiographical landscape – an unstable terrain whose navigatable paths remained a family secret.

In this early story of suspense, masculinity itself hangs in the balance of truths to be weighed and tested. The vulnerability of General Heatherstone to psychic penetration invites questions about the truth status of his personal history, probing the extent to which fantasy can lie at the heart of a guarded and uniformed masculine story. Everything that the narrator can provide by way of truth credentials to guarantee the General's story is lavishly supplied. A whole system of names, professions and narratives are invoked along with genuine information sources such as the Indian Army List, which provides details of General Heatherstone's career. Dialect narrative also guarantees local authenticity, as does the complete excision of 'unreliable' female narrators from the text. The sign of the cross authenticates the 'Statement' of the coachman, Israel Stakes, itself followed by a professional memorandum from the well-qualified Dr Easterling. A cultural system of truth modes is used to validate the bizarre story of the British General's disappearance into the Great Bog of Cree.

Most authentic of all is the General's own day-book from the war zone in Afghanistan which captures the terse, rather indiscreet preoccupations of the British officer and demonstrates Doyle's ability to replicate the style of military journals and diaries. The day-book references real-life events, such as the relief of Jelalabad and, in particular, the rescue of Lady Florentia Sale who was captured at Kabul and whose real diary offered a vivid account of British sufferings. The General records on 3 October: 'Glorious news from the Front to-day ... Polluck entered Cabul triumphantly on the 16th of last month, and, better still, Lady Sale has been rescued by Shakespear, and brought safe into the British camp.'[47]

But diaries are a peculiar literary form, situated on the border between public and private discourse – a border as uncanny perhaps as the Terada Pass where stories and identities are exchanged and masculine meanings carefully generated. One date is crucial in *The Mystery of Cloomber*, for it is the anniversary of 5 October 1841 that annually weakens the General's nerve and it is forty years to the day that retribution descends on him. The only problem is, it is the wrong date. Pollock invaded Afghanistan in 1842, not 1841 and Lady Sale had to wait considerably longer for her rescue than the October recorded in the General's diary.

Error lies in the very centre of this heavily referenced masculine story. It is this missing lady who most conclusively establishes the systematized fictionality of its truth modes. The over-emphases on truth in this novel points to the excision of the female narrative within it. Lady Sale's own dairy, incidentally, offers a very different account of active female experience, heroism and suffering, to that contained in the General's day-book. In *The Mystery of Cloomber* it is women who generate the courage on which a demoralized masculinity re-erects itself, the General's daughter, Gabriel, being the only one to voice the view that it is more manly to confront enemies than to hide from them. The elision of Gabriel's voice with that of John West articulates masculinity in this novel as a doubled silence, one in which the female voice and the guilty or painful secrets of the inner man are equally forbidden expressions. The 'mystery' of Cloomber is General Heatherstone's weakness of spirit, his inability to put into words the secrets of his own guilt.

The narrator of *The Mystery of Cloomber* is concerned throughout to avoid any connotation of 'romance' in his narrative. Despite the book's two love stories, his own marriage and that of his sister are omitted from the account as 'mere domestic episodes' which he cannot avoid alluding to, though not wishing to 'parade his private affairs before the public'.[48] The romance with which it does deal is that of an exotic masculine spirituality which usurps the place of heterosexual love. The flowing robes and Romanticised spirits of Cloomber are, however, much more corsetted in the novel that accompanied it. In *The Firm of Girdlestone* Doyle takes a radically different approach to the masculine romance.

The Firm of Girdlestone

Despite his insistence in *Memories and Adventures* that *The Firm of Girdlestone* (1890) was his 'first attempt at a connected narrative'[49] there is significance evidence that *The Mystery of Cloomber* belongs to an earlier phase of imaginative work. Its composite, compiled rather than 'connected' narrative aligns it with such early stories as 'Cyprian Overbeck Wells: A Literary Mosaic'. As Geoffrey Stavert has pointed out,[50] Doyle is remarkably careless of detail in his description of the three Buddhist masters in his Eastern mystery, whereas *The Firm of Girdlestone* is prefaced by an acknowledgement of thanks to Mr P. G. Houlgrave for his help in supplying accurate details for the book's African chapters. Also carrying a Dedication to Professor William Burton for encouraging Doyle to continue with the story, *The Firm of Girdlestone* establishes itself from the outset as arising from male conversation and embodying male professional knowledge and expertise. This anchoring in the 'real' is reinforced by the novel's city setting first in Edinburgh and then in London, and by the hard-hitting, power-playing worldliness of its concerns. The short gothic section it contains is focused conventionally on the plight of the rich but powerless heroine, Kate, imprisoned in a lonely mansion as the two desperate businessmen of 'the firm of Girdlestone' attempt to murder her for her money. The mystery, unworldliness, remoteness and spirituality of Cloomber Hall have vanished in one of Doyle's rapid exchanges of place and identity.

The dramatic contrast between these novels suggests the polarities in Doyle's thinking about the masculine adventure novel and the ideological modelling in which it engages. For all their generic differences, however, the novels have similar preoccupations and signal to each other in an intertextual dialogue of proper names. In *The Mystery of Cloomber*, the ship the wrecking of which lands the three avenging Buddhists on Scotland's west coast is named the *Belinda*. It is a ship so leaky and well-insured that the owner is well compensated for her loss. That owner appears to be none other than Mr Girdlestone from the rival novel, for Mr. Girdlestone's office contains in pride of place a watercolour painting of the barque *Belinda*, going down on a reef north of Cape Palmas.[51] The painting is important in Girdlestone's office because it is the visual sign of a duality and ambiguity in the representation and interpretation of Girdlestone himself. As he ostensibly suffered heavy losses from the wreck of the *Belinda*, the presence of the painting in his office is considered by some observers to be a sign of his strongmindedness, in his ability to look calmly upon 'so melancholy a souvenir'. The other view is that the painting commemorates a highly successful insurance scam. Another name that slips easily through the passes between the two texts is that of 'Farintosh'. In *Cloomber* he is the real Laird of Branksome, the 'ministering angel' and kinsman who lends his house to the impoverished Wests at the very nadir of their fortunes. In *Girdlestone* 'Farintosh' appears as a demonic defrocked vicar who outsmarts young Ezra Girdlestone during his South African diamond scam.

Doyle's carelessness about the names and details of his characters is legendary in the annals of the Holmes canon. These small acts of inattention in the clued world of the great detective fascinate Doyle's readers who treat them with the seriousness given to textual ambiguities in the Holy Writ. Such errors also draw attention to sometimes significant slips of meaning – acts of passage between writer, reader and text – which invite ingenious additional narratives to be threaded through them. These signs of carelessness are also signs of an authorial presence which acts as a crossing point for different stories. In *Memories and Adventures,* Doyle had stressed the role of coincidental and synchronistic linkages in the construction of his life story, his own name a playful signifier across different contexts and discourses. Frequently mistaken for 'Canon Doyle', he was once asked to say Grace at a Chicago dinner 'as being the only ecclesiastic present'.[52] He also had a Hull steam trawler named after him, the *Conan Doyle* acting as flagship to a group of trawlers in a military engagement with a German submarine.[53] The *Belinda* is not the only ship which draws lines of lateral meaning between two texts. The ship on which Ezra Girdlestone embarks for his South African diamond scam with Farintosh is the mail boat, *Cyprian,* eponymous hero of the collective male adventure story in 'A Literary Mosaic'.

These moments of sign crossing and narrative interconnection show Doyle attempting to fit together some of the contradictions in late-Victorian discourses of masculinity. They also represent the pragmatic enactment of that discourse by pointing to the intersections of a busy professional life and the contradictory calls it made on him. Doyle insists on these points of intersection as integral to his early writing, as in the following fascinating anecdote about the composition of *The Firm of Girdlestone.* He describes himself as a young doctor hard at work upon 'an exceedingly sensational' first novel:

> I may urge in extenuation of all shortcomings that it was written in the intervals of a busy though ill-paying practice ... . How often have I rejoiced to find a clear morning before me, and settled down to my task, or rather, dashed ferociously at it, as knowing how precious were those hours of quiet. Then to me enter my housekeeper, with tidings of dismay. 'Mrs. Thurston's little boy wants to see you, doctor.' 'Show him in,' say I, striving to fix my scene in my mind that I may splice it when this trouble

is over. 'Well, my boy?' 'Please, doctor, mother wants to know if she is to add water to that medicine.' 'Certainly, certainly.' Not that it matters in the least, but it is well to answer with decision. Exit the little boy, and the splice is about half accomplished when he suddenly bursts into the room again. 'Please, doctor, when I got back mother had taken the medicine without the water.' 'Tut, tut!' I answer. 'It really does not matter in the least.' The youth withdraws with a suspicious glance, and one more paragraph has been written when the husband puts in an appearance. 'There seems to have been some misunderstanding about the medicine,' he remarks coldly. 'Not at all,' I say, 'it really didn't matter.' 'Well, then, why did you tell the boy that it should be taken with water.' And then I try to disentangle the business, and the husband shakes his head gloomily at me. 'She feels very queer,' says he; 'we should all be easier in our minds if you came and looked at her.' So I leave my heroine in the four-foot way with an express thundering towards her, and trudge sadly off, with the feeling that another morning has been wasted, and another seam left visible to the critic's eye in my unhappy novel. Such was the genesis of my sensational romance ... .[54]

What seeks attention in this passage is not just the small boy with the sick mother, not just the tug of identity between doctor and author, not even the substitution of father and son; it is the 'seam left visible to the critic's eye'. Doyle's errors of carelessness are precisely these seams in the flesh of his literary material which connote nodes of intersection between a life and its fictions. These apparently opposing stories are junctions which signify the masculinity of the author as both a healer and destroyer of the female body.

In contrast to *The Mystery of Cloomber*, *The Firm of Girdlestone* is subtitled ' a romance of the unromantic', but the meaning of the term 'romance' has changed between texts. In the former, romance connotes a personal history and its partnerships, with the secondary connotation of fantasy, flowing robes and free-floating stories. In *Girdlestone* the connotation is different: the partnerships depicted are largely unromantic and between men, informed not by sexual or spiritual magic but by proximity, kinship and money.

The Firm of Girdlestone uses three contrasting male partnerships in its attempt to find an effective form for the male homosocial romance. The principal partnership is that between the men who make up the firm of the title, the African merchant, John Girdlestone and his entrepreneurial son, Ezra. Girdlestone senior is a sinister mid-Victorian patriarch with a dual reputation for religious virtue and shrewd business dealing, a capitalist struggling to preserve his firm from bankruptcy by a series of increasingly risky stratagems; first, by a speculation and scam in the diamond markets of South Africa, then by brokering a marriage between Ezra and his wealthy ward, Kate. Finally, when both expedients fail, he attempts to murder Kate, his best friend's daughter, so that her inheritance reverts to himself.

The second father–son relationship is that between Dr Dimsdale and Tom, who at the start of the novel has just failed to follow his father into the medical profession by fluffing his University of Edinburgh exams. Secretly engaged to the heroine, Kate, Tom takes up commerce and becomes an employee of the Firm of Girdlestone. As the novel's rugby-playing hero, Tom contrasts strongly with Ezra, its anti-hero and life force. The third partnership of the novel is also one of financial expediency as two indigent but contrasting men decide, like Holmes and Watson, to set up shared living quarters. One is a retired Irish soldier, Major Clutterbuck, a raconteur, gambler and man about town; the other is an *emigré* German socialist, Von Baumser, who belongs to a group of exiles and anarchists. It is with the help of these two 'Bohemians' that Tom eventually manages to rescue the beleaguered Kate from the murderous clutches of Girdlestone senior who has immured her in a gloomy house on a Hampshire marsh, spreading the rumour that she is confined there as a result of mental illness.

As the murderers and the rescue team converge on Kate, she herself is attempting to carry out a plan of escape. Although a murder is committed in the dark gardens of the lonely house, it is one that involves a Doylean act of substituted bodies. The girl murdered is not the gentle, home-loving Kate, but a far more impassioned female character, Kate's maid and Ezra's mistress, Rebecca Taylforth. Described as a tigress, Rebecca is the embodiment of female sexuality, motivated by murderous jealousy of Kate in a narrative where women are either kindly, maternal, extremely old or altogether absent. Rebecca's jealousy fuels a passionate misreading of events which eventually leads her to assume the clothing of her mistress and consequently to take her place as the murder victim. This murder of the female sexual body in a novel of male partnerships signifies a fundamental displacement in Doyle's writing. If sexuality signifies one form of romance, Doyle's 'romance of the unromantic' ruthlessly removes the female body and romances the unpartnered male body instead. Rebecca's murder is described as a destruction of female physical power, 'a magnificent woman in all the pride of her youthful beauty ... left ... a poor battered senseless wreck',[55] which, like the murder of the holy man in *The Mystery of Cloomber*, invokes its own avenging spirit.

Kate arrives at the murder scene just as her mistaken assassins are dragging the cloaked corpse of her maid on to the railway line. Seeing her in the moonlight, the terrified men believe they are being confronted by her ghost. This is, of course, the dramatic moment that Doyle chose to inscribe in his anecdote of the novel's interrupted composition, when he left his heroine on the railway line to attend to Mrs Thurston. The supposed 'ghost' is the sign of this interruption, signalling the moment where an exchange of identities has taken place both in the writing, which substitutes one female body for another, and in Doyle's own transformation from murdering writer to healing doctor. This point of connection and exchange between one story and another, between an outer and an inner body is, for Doyle, a moment of masculine identification under the sign of the spirit for books and bodies are the reversible signifiers of his own life text. 'Thurston', incidentally, was the name of a contemporary at Stonyhurst who became a Catholic priest and one of Doyle's main opponents as a spokesman for Spiritualism.

This ghost scene is the climactic episode of the novel, the moment of power reversals when a murdered female sexuality appears to reassert itself as an avenging spirit in a mercenary male adventure. It is the only time that the heroine is empowered for, otherwise, Kate receives little attention in the novel. The real romance lies elsewhere, in the deceptions, exchanges and power-shifts of the commercial world. Doyle writes a mode of masculine romance which replaces heterosexual passion with masculine game play, from rugby and gambling to international speculation. The romance narrative is generated out of readings and misreadings of signs, situations and characters, offering reading skill as the determining factor in the success or otherwise of the male player. Although the male body remains the focus of descriptive attention, and is the 'unromantic' subject of this romance, the text is ambivalent about its subtitle, uncertain as to whether or not masculinity should carry the sign of romance.

This ambiguity is explored through contrasts between the two young men at its centre. Although he plays rugby for Scotland and performs the actions of the conventional romantic hero, Tom Dimsdale is designated as 'unromantic'. He declares his love for Kate on a road crossing, his proposal interspersed by the 'animated semaphore' of the traffic policeman. Tom himself embodies a type of British masculinity which is predicated on a mistrust of language and articulateness; he is a doer rather than a sayer:

> Shy, and yet strong; plain, and yet pleasing; it was the face of a type of man who has little to say for himself in this world, and says that little badly, but who has done more than all the talkers and the writers to ring this planet round with a crimson girdle of British possessions.[56]

Saying little and saying it badly and in the wrong places is a guarantee of masculine integrity in a novel where the dominant English patriarch, Girdlestone senior, is a master of lying, verbal substitutions and false letters. The relationship between language and masculinity is everywhere implicit in Doyle's concern with romancing the unromantic. Tom's hilarious failure of the chemistry component in his Edinburgh medical viva – significantly he produces the wrong word for the common marsh gas – is contrasted with the relentless masculine writing which constitutes the Firm of Girdlestone and through which it is first introduced.

Tom embodies the limited romance of a manhood that is not dictated by his own father. He chooses his own profession, his own associates and his own partner and eventually succeeds in each area of choice.

Ezra Girdlestone, on the other hand, *is* romantic. Broad-shouldered and bull-necked, with a bright, bold glance, the heir of the firm is introduced as presiding masterfully over a room full of scribbling clerks. The exotic and dangerous master of the firm's writing, Ezra is viciously free of sentiment but not evil and he is capable by his courage and sometimes comedic resourcefulness, of engaging the reader's sympathy. Physically impressive, the romance he represents is not one which the novel is willing overtly to endorse. Doyle writes of Rebecca Taylforth's infatuation with Ezra:

> In her poor, dim, eventless life the sole bright spot had been the attention which the young merchant had occasionally shown her. To her distorted fancy he was a man among men, a hero, all that was admirable and magnificent. What was there which she would not do for him?[57]

Rebecca here is, like the novel itself, romancing the unromantic, transforming a masculinity largely devoid of 'spirit' or inner meaning into a desirable icon for her distorted fantasies. Ezra's romanticism lies elsewhere.

In a striking departure from the conventions of Victorian villainy, Ezra is quite without that commercial lust for the wealthy heroine that shadow and doubles the Victorian hero from Dickens's Uriah Heep to Hardy's Donald Farfrae. Ezra is not interested in Kate and is reluctant to marry her, even for her money. While recognizing her sweetness and gentleness, he finds these qualities unappealing. 'Kate has', he complains to his father, none of the 'go and snap about her'[58] that he enjoys in women's company. Cruel, callous and self-seeking though he is, Ezra stands for the risk-taking adventurer of the masculine romance. The problematic associated with him clearly fuels the interest Doyle took in writing a 'sensation novel' in which the criminal protagonist was male rather than female.

Where Tom struggles to gain entrance into a range of masculine language communities, Ezra is a man apart, his only dialogue that with his father who increasingly infuriates him by his unlucky speculations. Doyle's interest in masculine speech and dialogue mirrors his concern with the animating spirit of his masculine models. Because Ezra lacks any inner life, he fails to read other people, though he has enormous skill in handling situations. The quietest level of action in the book concerns Ezra's developing awareness of the resources of evil in his father's gift for manipulating words and replicating discourses as verbal traps for his intended victims. When he discovers that his father has forged a love letter to persuade Kate that Tom has been unfaithful to her, Ezra is entertained by his father's deviousness, combined as it is with religious self-justification:'"Capital, dad; very good!" cried Ezra, chewing his toothpick. "I like to hear you argue. It's quite refreshing."'[59]

This father–son relationship is, like that between Tom and Dr Dimsdale, depicted in terms of a mutual misreading, the amoral sensuality of the son set in counterpoise to the treacherously bifurcating discourses of Girdlestone senior. Ezra's inability to read other people derives from his father's utter lack of verbal integrity and, in Ezra's life, a driven and ludic resourcefulness comes to replace any notion of truthfulness. This absence of paternal truth allows Ezra eventually to represent a deviant life force released from the masculine signifying system of the Firm into a nameless life of travel, adventure and loneliness.

Despite his manifold villainies, which range from shooting cats to causing suicides and which conclude with the effective murder of his own father, Ezra stands for an unrealized, because unpartnered, form of masculine romance. With the drowning of his father, his partner becomes the disembodied spirit of his former mistress. Just as the novel exchanges heterosexual romance for masculine adventure, so Ezra himself becomes the substituted ghost of the story, haunting its conclusion but excluded from the plethora of marriages which provides closure and happiness. As the narrative loses track of his fleeing figure, he remains in the text as an unconfirmed rumour, 'a melancholy broken man who haunted the low betting-houses of San Francisco'.[60] Like that classic Victorian adventuress, Thackeray's Rebecca Sharp, the resourceful, immoral Ezra survives at the cost at exclusion from patriarchal structures, reduced to the play of his luck and the loss of his name sign. He acquires freedom at the cost of his identity: 'There was much about this desperado which tallied with the description of young Girdlestone, but nothing certain was ever known about the matter.' Ezra remains the nameless focus of a romance freed equally from heterosexuality, the symbolic order of patriarchal language and a colonialism which circles the globe with its own controlling girdle of possessions. Outside the language system whose praxis he initially controlled, the man described as devoid of spirit becomes the gambling ghost of the novel's own spiritual project.

Between these two young men – the sporting but unludic and inarticulate Tom, and the unfixed sign-playing of Ezra – is the novel's talker and fantasist, the Irish Major Clutterbuck, whose verbal play eventually counters that of Mr Girdlestone himself. Like all the male characters in this novel, the Major is an ambivalent figure, using his social connections and game skills to dupe sappy young men out of their money. In a novel that celebrates ludicity as the sign of the masculine, the Major's games are whist, billiards and a skilful reading of men's faces. He succeeds in rescuing himself and his German socialist partner, Von Baumser, from poverty and exposure by an astute piece of blackmail and gamesmanship.

In this network of game play which leaves the honest and affectionate heroine utterly resourceless, the Major stands for linesmanship, a recognition of good form and acceptable limits. His anecdotes encode and affirm this commitment to ludic good form, as in his story of the duelist who shoots his second because of his lack of punctuality. In contrast to, and apart from, his love for his son, Girdlestone senior acknowledges no limits to the dishonesty of his play and he embodies masculine bifurcation at its most intense point of self-blindness. Presented initially as a great man, a masculine model who combines religious integrity with business acumen, Girdlestone's determination not to be beaten in the game of life turns him into a figure of demonic evil who keeps a religious diary while planning the murder of his best friend's daughter.

The moment that Ezra steps beyond both patriarchal community and the novel's own sphere of representation is one in which he overcomes the taboo against patricide. As father and son flee from the scene of their crimes aboard one of those leaky vessels that had introduced the Buddhists to Scotland in *The Mystery of Cloomber*, the ship founders and sinks, leaving father and son clutching at rocks for safety. On finding a secure niche on a cliff ledge in the surging waters, Ezra clings on for dear life and, seeing his father's face and arm emerge from the waves, he denies assistance to the drowning man:

> 'There's no room here,' said the young man, brutally.
> ... 'Help me, Ezra.'
> His son brought down his heavy heel upon the bloodless hands. The old African trader gave a wild shriek and fell back into the sea. Looking down, Ezra saw his despairing face gazing at him through the water. Slowly, it sank until it was but a flickering white patch far down in the green depths. At the same instant a thick rope came dangling down the face of the cliff, and the young man knew that he was saved.[61]

Finally identified with the drowned god of fertility ritual, John Girdlestone comes to represent an outdated paternal model, a masculinity associated with both British colonialism and Victorian evangelicism. *The Firm of Girdlestone* concludes, not with the bankruptcy of a corrupt commerce but with its takeover by two Scottish partners. As 'Dimsdale and Gilray', it becomes 'among the most successful and popular of all the English firms connected with the African trade',[62] able even to count on the support of the socialist group who attend Tom's wedding to Kate. As Mr Girdlestone followed General Heatherstone into watery annihilation, Doyle began constructing yet another version of this sinking ground for the masculine double. In *Micah Clarke*, Doyle wrote the novel he subsequently selected to represent the formal beginning of his career as a novelist who could speak for England as well as for Scotland.

It was a revolutionary England for which he spoke. *Micah Clarke* is a historical novel about the Monmouth Rebellion against James II and its disastrous culmination at the Battle of Sedgmoor in 1685. Sedgmoor itself, the battlefield where the rebel army finds itself trapped in the marshy grounds between the dykes and ditches of the Bussex Rhine, is definitive Doyle territory. Micah, fighting in Monmouth's army in place of his Cromwellian father, emphasizes this uncanny disaster zone:

> To this day I have never been able to make up my mind whether it was by chance or by treachery on the part of our guides that this fosse was overlooked until we stumbled upon it in the dark. There are some who say that the Bussex Rhine, as it is called, is not either deep or broad, and was therefore, unmentioned by the moorsmen, but that the recent constant rains had swollen it to an extent never before known. Others say that the guides had been deceived by the fog, and taken a wrong course ... . However that may be, it is certain that we found it stretching in front of us, broad, black and forbidding, full twenty feet from bank to bank, with the cap of the ill-fated sergeant just visible in the centre as a mute warning ... .[63]

Although this watery landscape is personal to Doyle, the novel as a whole draws upon that fascination with the mid-seventeenth century so important in the historiography of Victorian self-representation. Seen, especially by Macaulay, as the heroic age of the British constitution when parliamentary government emerged out of religious and political conflict, the seventeenth century was inscribed as the Protestant origin of British political identity and as a mirror for the spiritual crises of the nineteenth. It was a mirror which carried an idealized image of a masculinity whose earnest energies the Victorians sought to reproduce and to emulate. Carlyle had famously identified the Puritan Revolution as the site of a specific disappearance, providing the last glimpse of the godlike vanishing from England.

If the godlike had vanished from England in the seventeenth century, it had reappeared with remarkable frequency on the canvasses of

Victorian artists, particularly those of the St John's Wood School who specialized in historical genre painting intended to re-create this period. The St John's Wood School gained fame through the use of their paintings as illustrations for the new history textbooks produced in the wake of the 1870 Education Acts. The most famous painting in this genre was W. F. Yeames's *And when did you last see your father?* in which the son of a Royalist is shown facing interrogation by the victorious officers of Cromwell's army. By an appropriate coincidence, this painting had been exhibited at the Royal Academy in 1878, just before Charles Doyle first disappeared into a nursing home.

Micah Clarke

Doyle's account of 'his first novel' in *Memories and Adventures* presents the book in several interesting ways, one of which emphasizes the importance of re-imaging the English Puritans after the caricatures of earlier representations. Given his own Catholic upbringing, this indicated an important realignment of familiar perspectives. Certainly, Doyle used his first excursion into English history as a forum for the redefinition of his own subjectivity. *Micah Clarke* was written while Doyle was waiting for his Holmes novella, *A Study in Scarlet*, to appear in print:

> ... feeling large thoughts rise within me, I now determined to test my powers to the full, and I chose a historical novel for this end, because it seemed to me the one way of combining a certain amount of literary dignity with those scenes of action and adventure which were natural to my young and ardent mind. I had always felt great sympathy for the Puritans, who, after all, whatever their little peculiarities, did represent political liberty and earnestness in religion. They had usually been caricatured in fiction and art. Even Scott had not drawn them as they were. Macaulay, who was always one of my chief inspirations, had alone made them comprehensible – the sombre fighters, with their Bibles and their broad swords.[64]

Micah Clarke thus derives from Doyle's own deepest sources of reading pleasure – in particular, his love for Macaulay's essays and histories. He read the *Essays* while at Stonyhurst and found that the book had transformed his view of history, bringing it alive as Scott's novels had also done. For Doyle, Macaulay was a centre of English meaning. Visiting London for the first time at the age of fifteen, he went to see Macaulay's grave in Westminster Abbey, describing it as 'the one great object of interest which London held for me'.[65] It was Macaulay's writing which helped Doyle to develop an English identity, for the *Essays* were, as he claimed, 'entwined into my whole life as I look backwards'.[66] Macaulay's *The History of England*, of course, begins at the genesis of Doyle's own Englishness in 1685, when the accession of James II was challenged at the Battle of Sedgmoor. Monmouth should have been supported by the Duke of Argyle but his Scottish ally was captured, taken to Edinburgh, condemned and executed. In conformity with this, the Scottish element in Doyle's early writing disappears with *Micah Clarke*, and his novels of the 1890s articulate a London-centred writing identity held in place by the masculine rituals of English history.

The book's experiences on the road to publication, however, were, according to Doyle, nearly as injurious as Micah's adventures on the way to Sedgmoor. *Micah Clarke* was initially rejected as an uninteresting historical novel, the vogue for which had long since passed. In a last-ditch effort, Doyle rescued his injured manuscript for one final sortie:

> I was on the point of putting the worn manuscript into hospital with its mangled brother 'Girdlestone' when as a last resource I sent it to Longman's, whose reader, Andrew Lang, liked it and advised its acceptance. It was to 'Andrew of the brindled hair', as Stevenson called him, that I owe my first real opening, and I have never forgotten it. The book duly appeared in February, 1889, ... and it has sold without intermission from that day to this. It was the first solid corner-stone laid for some sort of literary reputation.[67]

This rescue significantly reaffirmed Doyle's Edinburgh connections. Lang, like Stevenson, was part of that often unacknowledged group of Scottish writers who undertook the task of representing an alternative version of boyhood to that associated with the most distinguished English public schools. In his essay on 'The Boy', Lang argued for this alternative tradition:

> The British authors who understand boys best are not those who have written books exclusively about boys ... . The Rugby boy is distinguished by 'moral thoughtfulness'. Now the characteristic of the ordinary boy is his want of what is called moral thoughtfulness.

Predictably, Lang championed Doyle as the best living writer for boys:

> Were I a school master in possession of wealth, and about to found a library for boys, my corner-stone should be a large mass of the works of Sir Arthur Conan Doyle: The White Company, Micah Clarke, Brigadier Gerard (the best) and Sherlock Holmes.[68]

Boys, Lang believed, 'on the whole change very little. They remain the beings whom Thackeray understood better than any other writer: Thackeray, who liked boys so much and was so little blind to their defects'.[69]

Significantly seated on the knee of Thackeray in one of his few boyhood 'memories', Doyle had, by the time he wrote *Memories and Adventures*, positioned himself as Thackeray's successor. It was a position of some dialectical discomfort, like that of Monmouth's ill-equipped army at Sedgmoor, trapped between dykes with an unforeseen twenty-foot ditch preventing their attack. *Micah Clarke* enacts a catastrophic drama of boyhood, as Monmouth's forces take arms against a king who wishes to deny their manhood and force them back into a stage of political and religious thought which they have already outgrown. The lack of a bridge at Sedgmoor literally replays an episode from Micah's childhood when, in mock battle with a rival gang, he had sawn through a river bridge and nearly drowned the local vicar. A positivist model informs Doyle's reconstruction of history, justifying his own departure from the faith of his fathers as Micah articulates the anti-Royalist and Protestant position:

> There are, to my thinking, stages of human progress for which the Church of Rome is admirably suited. Where the mind of a nation is young, it may be best that it should not concern itself with spiritual affairs, but should lean upon the old staff of custom and authority. But England had cast off her swaddling-clothes, and was a nursery of strong, thinking men, who would bow to no authority save that which their reason and conscience approved. It was hopeless, useless, foolish, to try to drive such men back into a creed which they had outgrown.[70]

While Sedgmoor represents a moment of defeat and savage suppression for the rebel army, the importance of the battle lies in the accurate sign-reading of those ostensibly defeated. The message of Micah's narrative flows in the opposite direction to its own events. Read backwards from the bloodless revolution of 1688, the small catastrophe of Sedgmoor appears as a harbinger of major change, an avant garde action that foretells, through its own watery catastrophe, the bloodless revolution to follow. This issue of the right reading of events is crucial to Doyle's interest in Micah's Statement, for it links to a major preoccupation in his own life story, that of the great opportunities that flow from reversal. As part of its subliminal story of manhood, Doyle offers superior reading skills as the hidden revolutionary power of a newly emergent masculinity. The novel flatters its readership into a double identification with literacy, the spiritual sign-reading of the rebel army underlying the late-Victorian inscriptions of the literary text.

This insistence on popular literacy had a contemporary political agenda for the disturbed, potentially insurrectionary, years of the 1880s. While Doyle drowned his own socialist sympathies in the swamps of Sedgmoor, *Micah Clarke* affirms the prophetic vision of common people and their correct reading of history's direction along with their wrong reading and choice of battleground. Micah explains this to his listening grandchildren, as the ill-equipped west country army in his narrative prepare to do battle against the massed forces of the Crown:

> For though these poor peasants, in their dumb, blundering fashion, would have found it hard to give all their reasons in words, yet in the inmost heart of them they knew and felt that it was England's cause which they were fighting for ... . Three more years made all this plain, and showed that our simple unlettered followers had seen and judged the signs of the times more correctly than those who called themselves their betters ... . In three years the nation would understand it, and the King would be flying from his angry people; but at present, sunk in torpor after the long civil wars and the corrupt reign of Charles, they failed to see what was at stake, and turned against those who would warn them, as a hasty man turns on the messenger who is the bearer of evil tidings. Is it not strange, my dears, how quickly a mere shadowy thought comes to take living from, and grow into a very tragic reality?[71]

Micah Clarke himself rejects the stories and 'Lives' of 'giant men',[72] gamely lending his support to the common man fighting for the cause of civil liberty, even though the army fights without any effective leadership. Monmouth himself is portrayed as clearly not worth fighting for and the romantic heroism of his private life extensively detailed by Macaulay receives no mention from the family-oriented Micah. The men of the South West 'fought on with a dogged, desperate courage for a ruined cause and a man who had deserted them'.[73] Micah concludes:

> Should ye hear or read, then, my dear children, that Monmouth's rising was easily put down, ... remember that I, who was concerned in it, say confidently that it really trembled in the balance, and this handful of resolute peasants with their pikes and their scythes were within an ace of altering the whole course of English history. The ferocity of the Privy Council, after the rebellion was quelled, arose from their knowledge of how very close it had been to success.[74]

Just as the disaster of Sedgmoor and the subsequent sadistic cruelty of Judge Jeffreys clarify the causes for which the battle was fought, so too do Micah's personal misfortunes set up a dialectical dialogue with providence that proves to his advantage. The popularity of *Micah Clarke* made a signal contribution to the conventions underlying representations of British manhood. The novel defines a manhood predicated upon a doubled literacy, one that indicates both spiritual strength and a skilful reading of external signs. In offering this model of masculine reading, *Micah Clarke* drowns the radicalism of its own political agenda, replacing it with an engaged ludicity, a willing ability to take part in the struggles and contests through which a national culture defines itself.

The culturally persistent stereotype of the English 'stiff-upper lip' derives, in Micah's Statement, from a Protestant reading of signs in which providence works through misfortune, rendering unnecessary any downward turn of the mouth at the appearance of disaster. Micah explains:

> And if you once take this into your hearts, it is a mighty help in enabling you to meet all your troubles with a stiff lip; for why should a man grieve when he hath not yet determined whether what has chanced may not prove to be a cause of rejoicing?[75]

For all its confident articulation of the directives of English history, *Micah Clarke* cannot escape a paranoid doubling of its own field of masculine representation. On their way to Sedgmoor, Micah and his friends encounter three ferocious black dogs which double their own newly acquired identity as rebel soldiers. While the battlefield itself is a paranoid setting caught between two entrapping ditches, the Civil War fought on it is equally an encounter between outer form and inner content, between the Puritan notion of truthful individual testimony and the systemic deceptions of war itself. The verifications of personal witness are undercut by the lie of the land and the valorized betrayals of war. As the novel's most canny old soldier, Decimus Saxon, asserts, the lie is the condition of warfare: 'For what are all stratagems, ambuscades and outfalls but lying upon a large scale? ... What is an adroit commander but one who hath a facility for disguising the truth?'[76]

The novel's extended title offers the story as a truthful testimony 'from his own narration' passed down from Micah to his grandsons 'during the hard winter of 1734' and compiled by his eldest grandson, Joseph. It concludes: 'Now for the first time collected, corrected, and rearranged from the original manuscripts by A. Conan Doyle.'[77] As Doyle identifies himself as the editor of a plain and truthful Protestant narrative, he slips into the frame of history graphic images of a masculinity more colour-oriented than it is prepared to admit.

Balanced against the plain truthfulness of Micah's statement is the verbal sign-shifting of the mercenary soldier, Decimus Saxon, who can mimic and move between the discourses of different positions, praying with the Puritans as convincingly as he can roister with the rebels, his identity tied to no tongue, the epitome of the liar and strategist who is simultaneously the novel's image of soldierly resourcefulness. The emotional centre of the novel, however, lies in the figure of Sir Gervas Jerome, the impoverished Cavalier who, having squandered his family fortune, is cheerfully fighting for the opposite side. Uninterested in the political narratives of history, motivated only by 'the old story' of debt, Sir Gervas embodies a defiant pleasure principle which is figured as one extreme of masculinity, his Catholic homosocial gayness a counter to the heterosexual earnestness of the Puritans. To him all causes are more or less equal and he claims that he has 'never had so much honest amusement out of my prosperity as hath been caused in me by my downfall'.[78] The tension between inner and outer story in the case of each character predicates a soldier-masculinity caught, like the narrative itself, at a point of intersection between truth and lie.

The issue of the novel is less political alignment than the right degree of colour in the performance of masculinity. While Sir Gervas exhibits a cavalier willingness to make a masque of himself, the Puritans, unless playing the hypocrite, reject such modes of dramatization as their insignia of manhood. Faced with hanging, Micah calmly studies the tattoo marks on a companion's arm. Saved from hanging, he disgusts his Royalist captors by his lack of dramatic flair:

> 'Nay, that is but a sullen way to take your deliverance,' cried the smaller officer. 'The situation is as flat as sutler's beer. Otway would have made a better thing of it. Can you not rise to the occasion?'[79]

For the Puritans the meaning of their manhood lies in a spiritual control over the dramas of the body and an excision of the dramatic colour of its own blood. After the battle, Micah describes his audiencing of the kind of performance expected of the Puritan spirit:

> Pushing aside the branches, we came upon a man, seated with his back up against a great stone, cutting at his own arm with a broad-bladed knife, and giving forth the Lord's prayer the while, without a pause or a quiver in his tone. ... His arm had been half severed by a cannon-ball, and he was quietly completing the separation in order to free himself from the dangling and useless limb. Even Saxon, used as he was to all the forms and incidents of war, stared open-eyed and aghast at this strange surgery; but the man, with a short nod of recognition, went grimly forward with his task, until, even as we gazed, he separated the last shred which held it, and lay over with blenched lips which still murmured the prayer.[80]

A footnote informs the reader:

> The incident is historically true, and may serve to show what sort of men they were who had learned their soldiering under Cromwell.

Micah himself uses colourful pictorial images to dramatize moments of spiritual meaning, just as he had used a tattoo to obviate his fears of hanging. While battle cannot be described by a participant who 'has stamped forever upon his mind just the few incidents which may chance to occur before his own eyes',[81] Micah offsets this limited physical vision by invoking the larger interpretive frame of the historical painter: 'Could I but paint such a scene with the brush of a Verrio or Laguerre, I should have no need to describe it in these halting and feeble words.'[82] Similar passages of colourful writing organized as visual composition convey the suffering of the prisoners after the battle as they await the bloody assizes to follow:

> Here and there in the shadows dark kneeling figures might be seen, and the measured sound of their prayers rang through the aisles, with a groan now and again, or a choking gasp as some poor sufferer battled for breath. The dim yellow light streaming over the earnest pain-drawn faces, and the tattered mud-coloured figures, would have made it a fitting study for any of those Low Country painters whose pictures I saw long afterwards at the Hague.[83]

Doyle believed that *Micah Clarke* contained some of his best writing, but it was writing that wrestled with its own ambivalence towards colour and exterior display. The powerfully realized chapters describing Judge Jeffreys open up another sphere of disturbed visibility: that of a legal system in the pay of a corrupt and outdated power. In a chapter entitled 'Of the Devil in Wig and Gown', Doyle describes Judge Jeffreys as a Dorian Gray whose outer beauty is no index to what lies within. Micah remarks that, while Jeffreys has often been represented as a study in hideousness, he was in fact 'a man who, in his younger days, must have been remarkable for his extreme beauty'. A footnote attached to this passage reinforces this observation: 'The painting of Jeffrey's in the National Portrait Gallery more than bears out Micah Clarke's remarks. He is the handsomest man in the collection.'[84]

In the novel's exploration of different modes of masculine performance, Jeffreys represents a hysterical play-acting which dramatizes an acute tension between the inner and the outer man, between the law which judges and its own inner vacancy. Possessed by evil, Jeffreys remains one of the most disturbing villains in Doyle's convincing repertoire of criminal masculinities. Of his field of power at the Taunton assizes, Micah comments:

> Folk may call it a trial that they received, and a trial it really was, but not in the sense that we Englishmen use it ... .
> The court-house was the thorny path which led to the scaffold. What use to put a witness up when he was shouted down, cursed at, and threatened by the Chief Justice ... ? I have heard from those who were there that day that he raved like a demoniac, and that his black eyes shone with a vivid vindictive brightness which was scarce human. The jury shrank from him as from a venomous thing when he turned his baleful glance upon them. At times, as I have been told, his sternness gave place to a still more terrible merriment, and he would lean back in his seat of justice and laugh until the tears hopped down upon his ermine. Nearly a hundred were either executed or condemned to death upon that opening day.[85]

In contrast to the phlegmatic Micah, Jeffreys is a man of violently externalized emotions uncontained by either Protestant selfhood or the ritual theatre of his legal clothing. He raves and froths at the mouth 'like a madman', his interrogation emphasizing the filial disobedience of the rebels:

> 'Generation of vipers!' he cried, throwing up his hands. 'The best of fathers! The kindest of kings! See that my words are placed upon the record, clerk! The most indulgent of parents! But wayward children must, with all kindness, be flogged into obedience.'[86]

Instructing the recording clerk to 'write "sobs" in the margin', Jeffreys's histrionic performance is in direct contrast to his victims who lack even the language to attempt a defence:

> ... in Taunton alone there lay a thousand hapless prisoners, many of whom were so little trained to express their thoughts, and so hampered by the strange dialect in which they spoke, that they might have been born dumb for all the chance they had of making either judge or counsel understand the pleadings which they wished to lay before them.[87]

The statement of *Micah Clarke* fills in this lack of language, identifying a constituency for whom Doyle's writing would always attempt to speak. Visible through the framed intensities of *Micah Clarke* is Doyle's subsequent work as a legal campaigner, his crusades on behalf of victims of injustice or of colonial power systems that had naturalized themselves as law.

One voice is set in opposition to the story of *Micah Clarke*. It is that of a child whose home has become part of the Sedgmoor battlefield. Like Jeffreys, 'the maid of the marsh' also judges the soldiers as boys rather than men, though she condemns war not as filial disobedience but as an affront to Christian brotherhood. Far from a means by which men distinguish temselves, war for her is a sinking ground in which the butcher and the cavalier become one. The 'maid of the marsh' is a memorial flower in a text of masculine burials. It is outside her cottage that Micah finally drowns the treacherous opponent who speaks 'in the same white, cold, bitter manner' and is the double of his own wintry narrative:

> It had been ordained, ... my dear children, that he should die not the death of a man, but that of the reptile which he was, for even as I closed upon him he sank of a sudden with a gurgling sound, and the green marsh scum met above his head. No ripple was there and no splash to mark the spot. It was ... as though some strange monster of the marshes had seized him and dragged him down into the depths.[88]

As this final body is swallowed by the man-hungry marshes of his early fiction, Doyle finds one more burial ground for the lost spirituality of his father and the paranoid doubling of his own masculine identity.

The novel ends its engagement with truth-testimony in a final para-graph of animal-speak as Micah hands the narrative to his warhorse, Covenant. Despite the bond to defend his plain religion encoded in his name, Covenant is 'much given ... to telling in equine language to all the poor, silly country steeds the wonderful passages which had befallen him in the West'.[89]

Following the success of *Micah Clarke*, Doyle wrote another historical novel, *The White Company*, based on Froissart's fourteenth-century *Chronicles* of the Hundred Year War between France and England. Led by the diminutive Sir Nigel Loring, a real, though relatively insignificant, personage in the *Chronicles*, *The White Company* finally shakes off the dark doubles of Doyle's early fiction, combining accuracy of historical research with a depoliticized and desexualized version of the masculine adventure story. In a novel dedicated to 'the reunion of the English-speaking races' and their 'common ancestry', there are no bogs challenging the cleanliness of this company or its celebration of the English language as the true spirit of manhood. The only dissident voice in the novel is that, significantly, of an Italian painter who comments 'Take a Goth, a Hun, and a Vandal; mix them together and add a Barbary rover; then take this creature and make him drunk – and you have an Englishman.'[90] The book was written, as Doyle recalled, as a testimonial to the 'martial women'[91] who sustained feudalism and the English archers who ensured its demise. He considered this novel and its companion, *Sir Nigel*, (1906) as together forming a single piece of work that stood as his most satisfy-ing and ambitious literary achievement. With these books, he had himself joined the archers and arrived as an Englishman:

> I remember that as I wrote the last words of 'The White Company'
> I felt a wave of exultation and with a cry of 'That's done it!' I
> hurled my inky pen across the room, where it left a black smudge
> upon the duck's-egg wall-paper. I knew in my heart that the book
> would live and that it would illuminate our national traditions.[92]

One of several eloquent blots in *Memories and Adventures*, the black smudge on the duck's-egg wall paper articulates both a well-aimed shaft and a masculinity established, albeit at some cost to his interior decora-tion! *The White Company* was, he says, 'the last book which I wrote in my days of doctoring at Southsea, and marks an epoch in my life'.[93]

Notes

1. Doyle, A. C., 'The Americans Tale' in Gibson, J. M. and Green, R. L. (eds), *The Unknown Conan Doyle Uncollected Stories*, London: Secker and Warburg, 1982, p. 11.

2. Ibid., p. 17.
3. Ibid., p. 14.
4. Doyle, A. C., 'The Heiress of Glenmahowley' in Gibson and Green, *The Unknown Conan Doyle*, op. cit., p. 144.
5. Ibid., p. 157.
6. Green, R. L. and Gibson, J. M., *A Bibliography of A. Conan Doyle*, Oxford: Clarendon Press, 1983, p. 30.
7. Sedgwick, E. K., *Between Men English Literature and Male Homosocial Desire*, New York: Columbia University Press, 1985, p. 89.
8. Sedgwick, E. K., *Between Men: English Literature and Male Homosocial Desire*, New York: Columbia University Press, 1985, pp. 245–7.
9. Ibid., p. 114.
10. Ibid., p. 246.
11. Doyle, A. C., *The White Company* in *The Historical Novels, Vol.1*, Poole: New Orchid Editions, 1986, p. 209.
12. Doyle, A. C., *Sir Nigel*, Ware, Hertfordshire: Wordsworth Classics, 1994, p. 113 .
13. Doyle, A. C., *The Lost World*, London: John Murray, 1934, p. 6.
14. Montgomery Hyde, H., *Famous Trials 9: Roger Casement*, Harmondsworth: Penguin Crime, 1964, p. 156.
15. Springhall, J., 'Building Character in the British Boy: The Attempt to Extend Christian Manliness to Working Class Adolescents, 1880–1914' in Mangan, J. A. and Walvin, J. (ed.), *Manliness and Morality*, Manchester: Manchester University Press, 1987, p. 65.
16. Doyle, A. C., 'A Literary Mosaic' in *The Conan Doyle Stories*, London: John Murray, 1929, p. 748.
17. Ibid., p. 747.
18. Lang, A., 'The Boy' in *Adventures Among Books*, London: Longmans, Green & Co., 1905, p. 305.
19. Stevenson, R. L., 'My First Book: Treasure Island' in *Essays in the Art of Writing*, London: Chatto & Windus, 1910, p. 125.
20. Ibid., pp. 133–4.
21. Doyle, C. A., *The Doyle Diary*, London: Paddington Press, 1978, p. 28.
22. Green and Gibson, *A Bibliography of A. Conan Doyle*, op. cit., p. 14.
23. Doyle, A. C., *The Mystery of Cloomber*, Elstree: Greenhill Books, 1987, p. 14.
24. Ibid., pp. 29–30.
25. Ibid., p. 7.
26. Ibid., p. 10.
27. Ibid., p. 128.
28. See Giddings, R., *Imperial Echoes*, London: Leo Cooper, 1996, pp. 89–97.
29. Doyle, *The Mystery of Cloomber*, op. cit., p. 221.
30. Ibid., p. 225.
31. Ibid., p. 217.
32. Ibid., p. 229.
33. Ibid., p. 185.
34. Ibid., p. 45.
35. Silverman, K., *Male Subjectivity at the Margins*, London: Routledge, 1992, pp. 196–8.
36. Ibid., p. 211.

37. Doyle, *The Doyle Diary*, op. cit., p. 41.
38. Doyle, *The Mystery of Cloomber*, op. cit., p. 245.
39. Ibid., p. 247.
40. Ibid., pp. 249–50.
41. Ibid., p. 257.
42. Ibid., p. 214.
43. Ibid., p. 125.
44. Ibid., p. 214.
45. Ibid., pp. 179–80.
46. Beeton S. O. and Sherer, J., *Beeton's Dictionary of Universal Information*, London: S. O. Beeton, 1860, p. 27.
47. Doyle, *The Mystery of Cloomber*, op. cit., p. 213.
48. Ibid., p. 256.
49. Doyle, *Memories and Adventures*, London: John Murray, 1930, p. 74.
50. Stavert, G., *A Study in Southsea*, Portsmouth: Milestone Publications, 1987, pp. 125–6.
51. Doyle, A. C., *The Firm of Girdlestone*, Indiana: Gaslight Publications, 1980, p. 6.
52. Doyle, *Memories and Adventures*, op. cit., p. 117.
53. Ibid., p. 373.
54. Quoted in Tracey, J., 'Afterword' in Doyle, *The Firm of Girdlestone*, op. cit., p. 363.
55. Doyle, *The Firm of Girdlestone*, op. cit., p. 309.
56. Ibid., pp. 33–4.
57. Ibid., p. 300.
58. Ibid., p. 185.
59. Ibid., p. 181.
60. Ibid., p. 356.
61. Ibid., p. 351.
62. Ibid., p. 356.
63. Doyle, A. C., *Micah Clarke* in *The Historical Novels, Vol. 2*, Poole: New Orchard, p. 405.
64. Doyle, *Memories and Adventures*, op. cit., p. 91.
65. Pearson, H., *Conan Doyle: His Life and Art*, London: Methuen, 1943, p. 8.
66. Ibid., p. 27.
67. Doyle, *Memories and Adventures*, op. cit., p. 92 .
68. Lang, 'The Boy', p. 187.
69. Ibid., p. 311.
70. Doyle, *Micah Clarke*, p. 354.
71. Ibid.
72. Ibid., p. 120.
73. Ibid., p. 417.
74. Ibid., pp. 441–2.
75. Ibid., pp. 290–91.
76. Ibid., p. 65.
77. Green and Gibson, *A Bibliography of A. Conan Doyle*, op. cit., p. 15.
78. Doyle, *Micah Clarke*, op. cit., p. 140.
79. Ibid., p. 437.
80. Ibid., p. 419 .
81. Ibid., p. 413.

82. Ibid., p. 175.
83. Ibid., pp. 440–41.
84. Ibid., p. 452.
85. Ibid., p. 454–5.
86. Ibid., p. 457.
87. Ibid., p. 451 .
88. Ibid., p. 391.
89. Ibid., p. 487.
90. Doyle, *The White Company*, op. cit., p. 239 .
91. Ibid., p. 116.
92. Doyle, *Memories and Adventures*, op. cit., p. 96.
93. Ibid., p. 97.

CHAPTER THREE

Sh ... !: Reminiscences of a London Medical Man

Kindling detective vision

In his Preface to the last collection of Holmes stories, *The Case Book of Sherlock Holmes* (1927), Doyle surveyed the long career of London's great consulting detective and his devoted biographer, Dr John H. Watson. Establishing the chronology of that 'broken series' of appearances that constituted Holmes's forty-year history, Doyle remarked on the faulty memory of a male readership who saw Holmes as an unchanging continuum of masculine presence in British culture. He says of Holmes:

> His career has been a long one – though it is possible to exaggerate it; decrepit gentlemen who approach me and declare that his adventures formed the reading of their boyhood do not meet the response from me which they seem to expect. One is not anxious to have one's personal dates handled so unkindly. As a matter of cold fact Holmes made his debut in *A Study in Scarlet* and in *The Sign of Four*, two small booklets which appeared between 1887 and 1889 ... .He began his adventures in the very heart of the later Victorian Era ... and has managed to hold his own little niche even in these feverish days. Thus it would be true to say that those who first read of him as young men have lived to see their own grownup children following the same adventures in the same magazine. It is a striking example of the patience and loyalty of the British public.[1]

In presenting Holmes as an inaccuracy as well as a continuity in the memory of his male readers, Doyle formally inscribes those small defects of masculine recall which had signed his own absentminded authorship since *The Sign of Four*. Inconsistencies in the factual records of Holmes's biographer have fascinated his readers almost as much as the detective puzzles they solve. The bullet wound received by John H. Watson in the shoulder at the fatal battle of Maiwand, but later remembered as afflicting his leg, or even – as his wedding approached – one of his other members, is the most notorious example of those memory problems which affect the biographer and historian of nineteenth-century manhood. Holmes is intimately associated with inaccurate recall, both the slips and substitutions of the common intelligence and the erasures and repressions of painful memory. Without his alphabetical encyclopedias, the numerous bodies of information which pass through 221B Baker Street would become an unorganized narrative, whose post-modern chaos threatens the structure of memory itself. Through the crisis years of 1880 to 1930, this was a structure whose centre, British masculinity, just about holds.

Itself a small masterpiece of literary charm, the 1927 Preface signals a point of reconciliation between Doyle and his most famous literary creation. Throughout his career, Doyle had insisted that the popularity of Holmes had been damaging to his reputation as a serious writer, bifurcating and weakening his literary identity. In 1893 he had described Holmes as 'a sort of nightmare – an old man of the sea about my neck. If I don't kill him soon he'll kill me.'[2] Similar expressions of nausea and rejection litter Doyle's anecdotes about Holmes, indicating a dimension of disturbed interiority: 'I feel towards him as I do towards paté de foie gras, of which I once ate too much, so that the name of it gives me a sickly feeling to this day.'[3] A realization of the Romantic alter ego, this Frankenstein's monster is himself a master scientist, 'a calculating machine'[4] for the identity problems of an unmanageable empire and the muse of a puzzle-oriented reading culture.

Holmes was also a love object and father figure, created out of the absences of Doyle's own childhood, and one for whom the late-Victorian reading public felt an unappeasable hunger. The scientific Holmes paradoxically represents a Eucharistic presence inscribed – along with a series of breakfasts, suppers and dinners – in the writings of his doctor/biographer. Surveying the fortunes of that 'pale, clear-cut face and loose-limbed figure' who had usurped such an 'undue share' of his imagination, Doyle, in 1927, recanted his long-expressed hostility to Holmes, accepting the limits of his literary adventures as policed by this inner demon:

> I have not in actual practice found that these lighter sketches have prevented me from exploring and finding my limitations in such varied branches of literature as history, poetry, historical novels, psychic research, and the drama. Had Holmes never existed I could not have done more, though he may perhaps have stood a little in the way of the recognition of my more serious literary work.[5]

Doyle's many accounts of Sherlock Holmes all emphasize a polarity between the popularity of Holmes and Doyle's wish to be taken seriously as a historian. These two types of writing ran in tandem through his career, the inspired carelessness of the Holmes stories contrasting with the painstaking and detailed research he brought to his histories. It is a partnership first apparent in the co-production of *Micah Clarke* and *The Sign of Four* (1889). In 1891 Doyle published the first series of

Holmes stories, *The Adventures of Sherlock Holmes* and his fictional-ized historical reconstruction of Froissart's *Chronicles*, *The White Company*. In 1892–93, the liaison between Holmes and history contin-ued with the co-publication of *The Memoirs of Sherlock Holmes* and *The Great Shadow*, a fictionalized account of the Battle of Waterloo. It was with the Napoleonic 'Brigadier Gerard' that Doyle sought to re-place Holmes after his encounter with Moriarty, attempting to bind together these two strands of historical research and comedic anecdote. For all the Brigadier's brilliance, however, the two strands became separate again. When Doyle returned from South Africa to write his instant history of the Boer War, Holmes set forth to encounter *The Hound of the Baskervilles* (1901–02). When Holmes completed his escape from Professor Moriarty in *The Return of Sherlock Holmes* (1904–05), Doyle returned to the clutches of history by writing, not a sequel, but a prelude to *The White Company*, describing the boyhood of *Sir Nigel* (1905), subsequently leader of the White Company in the Hundred Years War with France.

The writing of *Sir Nigel* was a terminating return for Doyle, bringing to an end his need to rewrite his own past, and that of England too, as a genealogical adventure fantasy. A tribute and memorial to the influence of his mother, the novel is his last act of specifically English writing. The final phase of his career involved him in a long reconsideration of that hitherto suppressed Irishness that was the legacy of his father. Throughout this task, the partnership–rivalry of Holmes and history persisted. During the First World War he published two Holmes vol-umes, *The Valley of Fear* (1915), based on the Irish-American secret society of the 'Molly Maguires', and *His Last Bow* (1917). He took another bow with the publication of *The Case Book of Sherlock Holmes* in 1927. While the first two of these were accompanied by Doyle's detailed account of the First World War, *The British Campaign in France and Flanders*, *The Case Book* carried with it a history of a different kind, his two-volume *History of Spiritualism* (1926). Signifi-cantly, it was only when Doyle turned to this alternative mode of history that the longstanding tension with Holmes collapsed, leaving Doyle to acknowledge that 'Had Holmes never existed I could not have done more'.

Whereas Doyle's historical writings demonstrate a carefully system-atic organization of information, the Holmes stories revel in carelessness. While his histories attempt to guarantee truth and authenticate detail, the Holmes stories testify to a different hunger, to that inconsistency celebrated by Oscar Wilde in his essay, 'The Decay of Lying', published in *Intentions* (1891): 'Who wants to be consistent? The dullard and the doctrinaire, the tedious people who carry out their principles to the bitter end of action, to the *reductio ad absurdum* of practice.'[6] The Holmes stories, more effectively than any other *fin-de-siècle* literary production, realize the requirements of Wilde's decadent aesthetic: 'A great artist invents a type, and Life tries to copy it, to reproduce it in popular form, like an enterprising publisher.'[7] Deploring the tyranny of fact, Wilde's essay looks to young men 'with a natural gift for exaggeration' to restore the art of lying, producing 'something really great and wonderful' by avoiding the temptation of footnotes and other such 'careless habits of accuracy'.[8] Wilde's essay blames the 'crude commercialism' of America for this commodification of truth, its materialism evidenced by a national iconization of 'a man who, according to his own confession, was incapable of telling a lie'.[9]

The relationship between the Holmes stories and Doyle's histories is not merely the difference between fiction and non-fiction, for Doyle habitually conflates these oppositions, constructing masculinity on the border between them. His masculine models are persuasive because of the Romantic unreliability with which he harnesses his commitment to realist detail and accurate oral testimony. The fundamental site of this tension is Dr Watson himself, perceived as both a reliable recorder and as incurably colour-hungry, relentlessly working love stories into the fifth proposition of Euclid. Holmes, by contrast, is a flamboyant liar in the realm of factuality, spinning elaborate *fabula* that act as definitive reconstructions of past events. The cases often substitute for the lost stories and embarrassing moments of significant figures:

> 'It can't hurt now,' was Mr. Sherlock Holmes's comment when for the tenth time in as many years, I asked his leave to reveal the following narrative. So it was that at last I obtained permission to put on record what was, in some ways, the supreme moment of my friend's career.[10]

The relationship between Holmes and the writing of history is the overt subject of a case from *The Memoirs* (1893), 'The Musgrave Ritual', in which it is symbolized by the antiquated 'double-ring of metal-work' which constitutes the meaning of the ritual. An early case, dated prior to the partnership of Holmes and Watson, it is one which exemplifies Doyle's method of linking together the public and the private inscriptions of 'history'. 'The Musgrave Ritual' also descries a dimension of sexual play amid the serious reconstructions of historical meaning. As in all the Holmes stories, a hidden level of sexual reference anarchically parodies the formal orderings of masculine discourse, playfully concealed in the crime or mystery it investigates.

'The Musgrave Ritual' is structured on an archival motif and the role played by old documents in littering and lettering a past chaotically unaware of its own import. Watson refers to his own writing as 'these incoherent memoirs', their coherence dependent on the arrangement of what is given the privileged status of 'fact'. Putting away the past and picking up the present are the twin devices of the story, with Holmes only supplying the details of the case in order to distract Watson from the untidiness of their shared room. Watson, no novice in criminal evasion, retaliates by comparing Holmes's cases to the dull stones and rusty bits of metal at the centre of 'the Musgrave Ritual': it is only the twist and shine of biographical and historical reconstruction which gives them their lustre and significance. The constant dialogic interplay between Holmes and Watson establishes a field of contestation which provides the essential ground for their shared construction of masculinity, Holmes using his dialogues with Watson to kindle detective vision while Watson takes control of its written symbolization. This cooperative exchange is contrasted with the monologic, non-interactive practices of clients like Reginald Musgrave himself, an aloof and isolated aristocrat unskilled in verbal play. Two opposing models of politic power, as well as two opposing stories of history, are imaged by this contrast between Holmes and Watson, on the one hand, and Musgrave and his butler on the other.

Missing details, memory loss, and the curious mnemonic of the Musgrave Ritual are the centre of this story set in an ancient house significantly 'built in the shape of an "L"'. Despite its long aristocratic history, Hurlstone Manor is mainly memorable, as Musgrave admits, for the extraordinary intelligence of its butler, Brunston. Brunston has surreptitiously reconstructed the forgotten meaning of a singular old observance, 'the Musgrave Ritual', whose cryptic formula is associated with coming of age in his master's family, and the lost burial place of an old family treasure.

Part of the formula of the Holmes stories derives from a hidden identification between Holmes and his criminal opponent, in which matching names or mirrored body language trope resemblance. Where Holmes, in 'The Musgrave Ritual', is situated at the start of this story among untidy bundles of old papers, so Brunston, the intellectual butler of Hurlstone, is caught by his employer, examining old family documents at two o'clock in the morning. Sacked after twenty years' service and given no opportunity to explain, Brunston nonetheless has 'a clearer insight' into the meaning of the old observance 'than ten generations of his masters'.[11] A pun on sacking acts as the pivot of the story, for the meaning of the ritual is found in a bag at the bottom of the lake, containing broken remnants of a crown belonging to the 'sacked' king, Charles I. The L-shaped house establishes a link, and a private communication with, that other ill-fated Charles, Doyle's father.

In mending the broken links of the crown and restoring a lost dialogue between father and son in 'The Musgrave Ritual', Holmes simultaneously rectifies a loss in the Doyle family too. Whether in terms of politics, patriarchy or the adult and child role reversals enacted by Holmes and Watson, the father–son relationship is resituated at the centre of history, replacing the wilder, more erratic courses of sexual passion. The double metal rings of the ancient crown are 'history' in two senses, simultaneously past and powerless yet still speaking and meaningful. In this anecdotal history of tidying up the past, things are put away in odd places, like the tobacco kept by Holmes in the toe of a Persian slipper. While the story unearths the mystery of the lost Stuart crown, it also re-encrypts a troubled part of Britain's past, one inscribed in the recurrent 'HB' motif which initials both the Hurlstone butler and Doyle's grandfather, the political cartoonist, 'HB'. The date over the lintel at Hurlstone, 1607, was an inauspicious year for British relations. It was the date that the English parliament voted against Union with Scotland and also the year in which the Earls of Ireland fled to Spain after their attempted insurrection. In 'The Musgrave Ritual', it is the Welsh woman, Rachel Howells, who avenges herself on this aristocratic English household, causing the death of her unfaithful lover before disappearing with his newly found treasure.

Discovering Brunston's body, Holmes can only guess what had 'suddenly sprung into flame in this passionate Celtic woman's soul when she saw the man who had wronged her – wronged her far more than we suspected – in her power?'[12] The foetus-like enclosure of the corpse symbolizes a possible answer, suggesting that the additional, but unspoken, wrong may have been pregnancy. Rachel herself echoes the Musgrave Ritual 'Whose was it? His who is gone?' – when hysterically announcing the disappearance of Brunston. Rachel's excitable celticism contributes significantly to a story in which she acts as a vengeful Lady of the Lake, burying men in stone vaults and throwing jewels into the mere in a parody of the Arthurian witch, Vivien, from Tennyson's *Idylls of the King*. Finally disappearing overseas, Rachel Howells buries the oppressions of her Welsh past by rejecting her sack of English treasure.

The Sherlock Holmes stories enshrine and enact small dramas of masculine forgetfulness, whose reference is both personal and political. 'The Musgrave Ritual' can also be read, as Rosemary Jahn reads it, as lending support to a decaying feudal system.[13] There is equal evidence for the text's radical subversions and vengeful revisitings of what has become 'history'. In its repetitions and the fact that no one who repeats it can remember what it means, 'The Musgrave Ritual' is, according to the current heir, 'a sort of ceremony peculiar to our family, which each Musgrave for centuries past has gone through upon his coming of age – a thing of private interest ... but of no practical use whatever'.[14] Unlike his butler, the bachelor dandy, Reginald Musgrave, shows no interest in the ritual, despite his own coming of age. His disregard for it, however, threatens the line of one of the oldest families in the country. With the help of Holmes, a tall tree and some fishing tackle, he finally learns how to apply the ritual, locating the mysterious aperture in which the treasure is hidden through the preposition 'under'. Beneath the complicated rituals of history lie the plain, but brilliantly disguised, facts of life.

As with 'The Musgrave Ritual', so with the Holmes stories as a whole. Their coexistence with Doyle's formal history-writing supplies the 'irregular history' of sexuality and injustice which accompanies it. In 'The Bruce-Partington Plans' from *His Last Bow* (1917), Holmes comments on 'that secret history of a nation which is often so much more intimate and interesting than its public chronicles'.[15] The silencing effects of Holmes's initials, 'Sh!', emphasize his role as a suppressor of masculine discourse as well as a solver of crimes. His cases comprise incidents that are prevented from becoming history, matters which might have had an adverse or alternative influence upon European history – or indeed upon Doyle's career, if Holmes had failed to intervene. While Holmes silences what cannot be included in the hegemonic discourses of history, his cases find ingenious ways of representing what they suppress. Both in their private diaries and in their paintings and book illustrations, the Doyle family – following 'HB' – frequently played elaborate games with the letters of the alphabet, often using them to represent parts of the body or physical acts. The Holmes stories are themselves a collection of 'dancing men', to use the cipher name which provides the title for one of the adventures in *The Return of Sherlock Holmes*. Holmes's world is alphabetically arranged, his case histories and his information filed by letter, and the stories themselves image the secret history of bodies through lively letters of an alphabetical code. If my reading of 'The Musgrave Ritual' is accurate, the silent letter 'L' in the Holmes stories, like the silent 'L' in the detective's name, is a phallic inscription for the reversible laws of sexuality, history and personal identity. The secret and sometimes deviant sexuality in homes is the subject of Holmes's investigations in the first volume of stories, *The Adventures*. As in *His Last Bow*, 'L' is the letter that signifies a linkage between Doyle's private concerns and those of his detective. Sherlock Holmes of Baker Street contains the private, familial inscription 'HB' between two slippery 'S's.

If sexuality is one of the essential, but silent, signifiers of history, Justice, initialled by a reversed 'L', is history's blind spot. In its references to the Stuart interregnum, 'The Musgrave Ritual' invokes the seventeenth-century setting of *Micah Clarke* and the evil travesties of law inflicted by Judge Jeffreys on the Sedgmoor rebels. Justice, the most problematic of legal concepts, is Doyle's most overt preoccupation in the

Holmes stories and it is the delivery of justice, rather than the detecting of guilt, which distinguishes Holmes from his precursors. Holmes specifically defines himself as this historical lack, claiming in 'The Musgrave Ritual' that he is 'generally recognised both by the public and by the official force as being a final court of appeal in doubtful cases',[16] 'a last resource' for those desperate for justice. Justice is the key – an old-fashioned brass key in 'The Musgrave Ritual' – attached through the figure of Holmes to Doyle's formal histories. The partnership between history and the sometimes illegal justice of Holmes was the cornerstone, both of Doyle's career and his representation of British manhood.

In his recent study, *Sherlock's Men* (1997), Joseph A. Kestner describes the Holmes stories as providing 'an archive of debate about fin-de-siècle maleness' and the cultural construction of masculinity.[17] For Kestner, Holmes is a mentor of manhood, simultaneously a 'paradigm and outsider'[18] whose function is to model the dominant, hegemonic masculinity constituted by 'the institutionalised codes' which govern and restrict men's lives.[19] Crucial to this modelling is Holmes's policing of 'male desire', and his control over 'the potential for anarchic behaviour by males in the culture',[20] especially those who 'transgress the normative male script' generated by the Victorian ideology of 'manliness'.[21] Kestner claims:

> The nine volumes of the Holmes canon constitute an archive of material about the construction of masculinity during a 40-year period, addressing a wide range of issues concerning the formation of masculinity: male homosocial institutions such as the army, the Empire and the school; male friendships; male surveillance of other males; male spectacle; the idea of the gentleman; the relation of logic to masculine identity; the ideology of chivalry; differences of national masculinities (American, British colonised); male/male relationships (fathers/sons, brothers); domestic affiliations (stepfathers); ethnic, classist, or racialist inflections in culture (German, Irish, blacks); the imprinting of 'games' or 'sport' ideologies; the role of law and punishment; the policing of cultural institutions and practices; criminality as transgressive masculinity; the role of imperialism; the modelling of behaviours; the commodification of women; the idea of comradeship; the question of race degeneration; international tensions; terrorism and male response; and the idea of heroism.[22]

Holmes, Kestner argues, manifests and models a distinctive gender personality reinforced by association with 'qualities gendered masculine in Victorian culture: science, reason, system and principle'.[23] While Doyle 'indisputably aligns Holmes with manliness by linking his character to science, practical application, exact knowledge, logic and system, all elements gendered masculine in the nineteenth century',[24] the genius and play of the stories resides in Doyle's awareness of the conflicting pressures and tensions out of which masculinity must be constructed. All Holmes's associations with systemic and scientific exactitude are contested by his anarchic private habits and subversive humour. His own potential for lawlessness and illegality is demonstrated through his addictions: equally to exaggeration and rodomontage as to morphine and cocaine. In every respect, the Holmes's masculinity is a dialectical one, a wrestle with oppositions situated within the self but located in the criminal opponent. Holmes is able to stand either side of the law whose principle of justice he embodies.

Twentieth-century gender debate tends to be anti-essentialist in supposition. Elaine Showalter's strictures on the cultural construction of masculinity are generally accepted by historians of late Victorian masculinity:

> ... masculinity is no more natural, transparent, and unproblematic than 'femininity'. It, too, is a socially constructed role, defined within particular cultural and historical circumstances, and the fin de siècle also marked a crisis of identity for men.[25]

Kestner quotes with approval Kimmel and Messner's observation: 'We cannot speak of "masculinity" as a single term, but must examine masculinities: the ways in which different men construct different versions of masculinity.'[26] Late-Victorian writers on masculinity, however, like Doyle himself, worked with an essentialist discourse of gender that usefully unified the male sense of identity. While accepting a dialectical duality within the essence, Doyle's career is particularly informed by his refusal to abandon the search for a spiritual centre to masculinity. Kestner's listing of the materials for debate in the Holmes canon significantly omits any mention of spirituality, a persistent signifier of the masculine in Doyle's work. Holmes is as much Eucharist as rationalist, as much spiritual arbiter as avenging scientist. In 'The Blue Carbuncle', from *The Adventures of Sherlock Holmes*, his task is saving souls as much as solving crimes and he releases the thief, James Ryder, as an act of Christian mercy: 'I suppose that I am commuting a felony, but it is just possible that I am saving a soul.'[27]

As central to Doyle's construction of masculinity was his focus on language use and conversational exchange. Speech and writing are the spiritual properties of 221B Baker Street, just as its intellectual resources are located in the eye and the mind. Ronald Pearsall observes this emphasis with surprise:

> ... if one looks through the stories it is surprising what a high percentage of word is conversation, especially the client explaining the problem and Holmes explaining the answer ... . It was in the clients explaining their own predicaments that Doyle was at his most masterly.[28]

The combination of the earnest writings of Watson and the brilliant oral play of Holmes is used, within the structure of the stories, to resymbolize deficiencies in masculine self-representation, producing models of superior language performance whose 'spirit' was largely political. Holmes's international reputation is based on the skill with which he listens to the inarticulate and incomprehensible stories of others, summarizing and eventually reframing them as complete explanatory narratives.

Doyle's frequently acknowledged debt to the table-talk books of the American author, Oliver Wendell Holmes, who visited Edinburgh in the early 1880s, emphasizes their communal project: that of educating English-speaking men into a more authoritative and effective use of oral discourse. 221B Baker Street is a communication centre through which the speech practices of the cultural élite could be passed to the common reader. As Wendell Holmes, the 'pre-text' of the great detective, had argued in an extended metaphor from *The Autocrat of the Breakfast Table*, good language-law was synonymous with justice:

> Let me lay down the law upon the subject. Life and language are alike sacred. Homicide and *verbicide* – that is, violent treatment of a word with fatal results to its legitimate meaning, which is its life – are alike forbidden ... . 'He who would violate the sanctities of his mother tongue would invade the recesses of the paternal till without remorse ... .'[29]

This equation between language use, moral behaviour and masculine crime is embedded in the Holmes stories from the beginning. The first story from *The Adventures of Sherlock Holmes*, 'A Scandal in Bohemia', features a philandering German aristocrat who is as 'uncourteous to his verbs'[30] as to his women.

Both the American and the British Holmeses instate oral discourse as the modelling material of cultural praxis. Oliver Wendell Holmes continues:

> there is another thing about this talking, which you forget. It shapes our thoughts for us; – the waves of conversation roll them as the surf rolls the pebbles on the shore. Let me modify the image a little. I rough out my thoughts in talk as an artist models in clay. Spoken language is so plastic ... there is nothing like it for modelling. Out of it comes the shapes which you turn into marble or bronze in your immortal books, if you happen to write such.[31]

In a characteristic configuration of the Holmes stories, a crude or confused masculine speech energy encounters resymbolization in the language arts of Holmes. His conversational dexterity subjects hysteria and aggression to humour and moral control. The famous meeting between Holmes and the brutally inarticulate Dr Grimesby Roylott in

'The Speckled Band' is the most dramatic illustration of this formulaic ritual. Brandishing his hunting crop, Dr Roylott confronts Holmes with insults and abuse:

> 'I know you, you scoundrel! I have heard of you before. You are Holmes the meddler.'
> My friend smiled.
> 'Holmes the busybody!'
> His smile broadened.
> 'Holmes the Scotland Yard jack-in-office.'
> Holmes chuckled heartily. 'Your conversation is most entertaining,' said he. 'When you go out close the door, for there is a decided draught.'[32]

Draughts and ventilators play a crucial role in this story which attempts to image the unspeakable, using the indeterminacy of 'the speckled band' to generate and symbolize the dread of what cannot be put into words. To speak all – banned! What is finally ventilated in this story is a technique by which the missing discourses of masculinity and the deviant sexualities of Empire can be symbolized by a snake shaped like the sibilants of Holmes's name. The story itself acts as a 'ventilator', a literary apparatus by which fresh air and clean language can be applied to a syphilitically 'speckled' masculinity which cannot address or express itself in words.

Doyle's mentor, Oliver Wendell Holmes, had taken talk as the main topic of his books, describing it as 'one of the fine arts, – the noblest, the most important, and the most difficult'.[33] He had also identified it in terms of male game play, with conversation as a ludic condenser of more physical games, from chess and cricket to boxing and war. Particularly valuable as a skill was that psychic intelligence which read the mind of the enemy, that 'blessed clairvoyance which sees into things without opening them':

> The whole force of conversation depends on how much you can take for granted. Vulgar chess-players have to play their game out; nothing short of the brutality of an actual checkmate satisfies their dull apprehensions. But look at two masters of that noble game! White stands well enough, so far as you can see; but Red says, Mate in six moves; – White looks, – nods; the game is over. Just so in talking with first-rate men.[34]

Holmes and Moriarty play a version of this master game in 'The Final Problem':

> 'Pray take a chair. I can spare you five minutes if you have anything to say.'
> 'All that I have to say has already crossed your mind,' said he.
> 'Then possibly my answer has crossed yours,' I replied.[35]

Doyle himself was an active participant in that revival of conversational art which was so distinctive a feature of *fin-de-siècle* London culture and of which the plays of Oscar Wilde are the best memorial. Doyle considered Wilde the greatest conversationalist of his age and, after meeting him in 1888, was quick to replicate Wilde's manner in his characterization of Holmes in *The Sign of Four*: Doyle wrote of Wilde:

> His conversation left an indelible impression upon my mind. He towered above us all, and yet had the art of seeming to be interested in all that we could say. He had delicacy of feeling and tact, for the monologue man, however clever can never be a gentleman at heart. He took as well as gave, but what he gave was unique. He had a curious precision of statement, a delicate flavour of humour, and a trick of small gestures to illustrate his meaning, which were peculiar to himself.[36]

This *fin-de-siècle* art form, for which the office tea parties of *The Idler* magazine provided an important forum, had a distinct agenda whose roots lay in the literary representations of late Victorian masculinity. Dickens, in the dark masterpieces of the 1850s and 1860s, and George Meredith, particularly in *The Egoist* and *One of Our Conquerors*, had drawn attention to the weakened link between masculinity and language as indicative of deficiencies in British culture as a whole. Dickens depicted silent patriarchs, like Mr Merdle in *Little Dorrit*, whose chronic lack of language signified both financial and spiritual crisis. The darkness of Dickens's later novels references a growing disgust with masculine speech performance. His deliberately unfinished last novel, *The Mystery of Edwin Drood* (1870), inscribed this language deficiency in its own formal incompletion as well as in its obsessive, 'unintelligible'[37] male characters and its encyclopedic collection of masculine speech deformations. 'Better be quiet'[38] is the ominous, anonymous advice of the century's greatest speech impresario.

Dickens's successor, George Meredith, was the novelist most responsible for initiating a revival of interest in social conversation as an index of national culture and its masculinities. In *The Egoist* (1879), Meredith had designated 'egotism' as a mismatch between speech performance and interiority. Sir Willoughby Patterne, a model English gentleman in social life, reveals an anxious hunger for admiration in the private discourses of his own subjectivity. Appalled by the discrepancy between the inner and the outer man, his first fiancée jilts him for a man of action, and his second for a writer. Sir Willoughby's failure to marry acts and words, public and private modes of self-representation, indicates the political weakness of his blind conservatism. An enthusiastic admirer of Meredith, Doyle described Sir Willoughby as 'the eternal type of masculine selfishness'[39] and made 'egotism' – the mismatching of inner and outer stories – a pivotal issue between Holmes and Watson.

Where Oliver Wendell Holmes had claimed 'Audacious self-esteem, with good ground for it, is always imposing',[40] the biographer in Watson is constantly engaged in a surveillance of Holmes's vanity and conceit. In a quarrel over the representation of facts at the start of *The Sign of Four*, Watson's pride is injured by Holmes's privileging of his own 'calculating power':

> I was annoyed at this criticism of a work which had been specially designed to please him. I confess, too, that I was irritated by the egotism which seemed to demand that every line of my pamphlet should be devoted to his special doings. More than once during the years that I had lived with him in Baker Street I had observed that a small vanity underlay my companion's quiet and didactic manner. I made no remark, however, but sat nursing my wounded leg. I had had a Jezail bullet through it some time before, and though it did not prevent me from walking it ached wearily at every change of the weather.[41]

As his own counter-egotistical vulnerability receives another wound, the new story narrated by Watson sends retaliatory poison darts in reply to this criticism, one narrowly missing Holmes's neck and shoulder.

In constructing Sherlock Holmes as a masculine speech model, Doyle was consciously aligning himself with the work of Dickens and Meredith, both of whom had undertaken to reform British conversation in the light of an expanded democratic practice. While the Franchise Acts of the nineteenth century had brought new speakers into 'the national palaver', novelists of the new democracy, like George Gissing, depicted with unease the cruder, ruder language styles emerging from the new culture:

> The democratic Englishman is ... in parlous case; he has lost the ideal by which he guided his rude, prodigal, domineering instincts ... . And, amid all his show of loud self-confidence, the man is haunted with misgiving.[42]

Even more of a problem were those on the edges of literacy and beyond. According to the historian, Denis Winter, the men who made up the ranks of the British army in the First World War had a 'masculine' mistrust of speech:

> ... the majority of the front line soldiers were humble men, further simplified by having been fitted into an army and subjected to constant danger and hardship. At home many had distrusted 'talk', ridiculed men who 'talked posh' and wanted only to 'get on with the job'. Theirs was a simple vocabulary centred on the personal pronoun with a dialogue showing descriptive rather than analytic, interpretative awareness. There was little vocabulary for the

unexpected or speculative; instead, a fatalistic, helpless orientation in a world whose causes could not be grasped.[43]

The men under survey here were clearly not Holmes readers. Directed at a socially diverse, and not necessarily very extensively educated, readership, the Holmes stories challenged what Winter describes as the 'static mindedness' of Edwardian society. They offered reading puzzles which sharpened the intellect by emphasizing observation, deductive reasoning and clear speech as a common masculine property.

Both Dickens and Meredith had placed comedy and humour at the centre of their work on national conversation. In the 1850s Dickens had put forward his 'Proposals for a National Jest Book', ironically describing the 'rich materials for such a collection' to be found in parliamentary debates, courts of inquiry and 'the published correspond- ence of distinguished personages'.[44] Far less facetiously, Meredith developed this project further in his famous essay on the 'Comic Spirit'. Significantly, both men found themselves in contestation with the Spir- itualist movement whose seances were also attempting to remodel the conversational praxis of social leisure. Where Dickens was mercilessly funny in his attacks on Spiritualism, Meredith, in defining the 'Comic Spirit', was forced to draw significantly on the new vocabulary of oral discourse emerging from the seance.

Meredith had begun his work on comedy in the aftermath of the Franco-Prussian War, a context that affected his comparison of differ- ent styles of national humour. His version of comedy was one of sharp, stylized attack ending in laughter – a civilized ritual against actual physical aggression. He had published his lecture on 'The Idea of Com- edy and the Uses of the Comic Spirit' in 1877 at the very start of Doyle's literary career. His theories, republished in 1897, drew nation- ality-conscious responses from George Bernard Shaw, from Bergson in France and from Freud in Vienna. The debate about comedy and hu- mour was a crucial ground for the discussion of cultural difference and for the display of contending masculinities. As Charles Doyle had expe- rienced in the convention-ridden joke-circles of Edinburgh, this could be a site of paranoia, punishment and exclusion as well as one of entertainment and identification.

Brevity, for George Meredith, was the soul of wit. Aiming to leaven the nation's conversation, he had undertaken to condense 'the big Earth book of human egotism' with its 'inordinate unvaried length' and to replace it with what he called 'the laughter of reason refreshed'.[45] For Meredith, comedy was essentially interpretive, our best 'means of read- ing swiftly and comprehensively', but it was also a way of generating and policing a cultural community. The comic spirit was 'born of our united social intelligence', but with citizenship it brought 'a vigilant

sense of collective supervision' through which agreements about be-
longing and behaving could be reached.[46] In 'The Boscombe Valley
Mystery', Holmes gives a demonstration of the Comic Spirit's ability to
detect criminal outsiders through the communication variants of the
Australian bush. Identifying two clues in a welter of evidence, he tells
Watson: 'Those are the crucial points upon which the case depends.
And now let us talk about George Meredith, if you please, and we shall
leave all minor matters until to-morrow.'[47]

In keeping with another British stereotype, Meredith's Comic Spirit
was essentially animal-loving, accompanied by impish 'dogs and pets'
of its own. These creatures were particularly important for Meredith in
their ability, as he put it, 'to kindle detective vision'.[48] Detective vision
had its own supply of dogs' bodies at 221B Baker Street. In *A Study in
Scarlet*, Holmes's failure to poison Mrs Hudson's sick terrier leads to a
remarkable demonstration of this canine kindling power: 'What can it
mean?' cries Holmes, as his hypothesis fails to deliver results:

> 'Surely my whole chain of reasoning cannot have been false. It is
> impossible! And yet this wretched dog is none the worse. Ah, I
> have it! I have it!' With a perfect shriek of delight he rushed to the
> box, cut the other pill in two ... and presented it to the terrier. The
> unfortunate creature ... gave a convulsive shiver ... and lay as rigid
> and lifeless as if it had been struck by lightening ... . There was the
> dead dog to prove that his conjecture had been correct.[49]

Although Doyle thought Meredith had 'the most original brain and
the most clever pen of any man ... of my time', he also saw him as a
writer whose abounding, unpuritanical wit needed further obedience
training:

> His subtle and intricate mind seemed unable to realise the position
> of the plain outsiders who represent the world. He could not see
> how his stained-glass might be less effective than the plain trans-
> parent substance as a medium for vision ... . He had no idea how
> his words would strike a less complex mind. I remember that once
> ... he read out a poem which he had inscribed 'To the British
> Working-Man' in the 'Westminster Gazette'. I don't know what the
> British working man made of it, but I am sure that we ... were
> greatly puzzled as to what it was about.[50]

The Holmes stories, in their use of speech as a method of policing social
order, offered a practical demonstration of the Comic Spirit at its most
well-behaved. Manifest as a collective moral constituency, a shared
vision of justice and a radical abbreviation of the law's inordinate
length, the comic spirit, in its canine doubling with Holmes, set up its
streetwise dialogue with the British Working Man.

The Comic Spirit announces a new law of social intercourse, one
which can compress large tracts of cultural material into a single apposite

image. As Meredith had defined it, this spirit employed an elliptical brevity that was itself the sign of a richly rational intelligence. Refusing to 'accumulate excess of substance',[51] the Holmes stories condense the prolonged verbal anguishes of the Victorian novel into short story form. The marital and mental breakdown detailed so painstakingly by Trollope in *He Knew He Was Right* is graphically resymbolized in Holmes's account of 'the Dundas separation case' in *The Adventures of Sherlock Homes*. Watson believes that this case will contain the usual details of a marriage breakdown, a desperate wife and a drunken, unfaithful husband, with all the humdrum realism of newspaper reportage. On the contrary, Holmes remarks, the marriage problem has already symbolized itself as one of consumption and non-consumption, the husband having, in this case, 'drifted into the habit of winding up every meal by taking out his false teeth and hurling them at his wife'.[52]

Perhaps the most brilliant of these comic condensations occurs in the ebullient adventure of 'The Red-Headed League'. This story parodies Victorian encyclopedism, critiques Pre-Raphaelitism and, in a tale of pawn-broking and bank-robbing, plays on the famous anti-racist dictum of Macaulay – that it would be as reasonable to place all red-haired men under political ban as it would be to pursue a policy of ant-semitism. A similar compression of mental power is evident in Holmes's boasting. In the final story of *The Adventures*, Watson is once again repelled 'by the egotism which I have more than once observed to be a strong factor in my friend's singular character.' Telepathically *en rapport* with his biographer, Holmes contradicts this judgement:

> 'No, it is not selfishness or conceit,' said he, answering, as was his wont, my thoughts rather than my words. 'If I claim full justice for my art, it is because it is an impersonal thing – a thing beyond myself.'[53]

Although a supremely confident manner was Holmes's contribution to the stereotype of British imperial manhood, these verbal practices were not as English as they seemed but were strongly characteristic of the Doyle family. In *Memories and Adventures*, Doyle recalls his father most vividly through his spoken manners:

> ... he had a charm of manner and a courtesy of bearing which I have seldom seen equalled. His wit was quick and playful. He possessed, also, a remarkable delicacy of mind which would give him moral courage enough to rise and leave any company which talked in a manner which was coarse.[54]

Contemporaries such as Janet Ross bear witness to the same charm and 'delicacy' in Doyle's uncle, Richard,[55] while similar qualities of incisive but inoffensive reference are the distinguishing feature of HB's Regency 'conversation pieces' and political cartoons.

If the Holmes stories provide a series of object lessons in how to touch the pitch and pith of masculine sexual fantasy and not let the pure wells of English become defiled, they do so under the permanent sign of John Doyle. Whether as Hugh Boon, Henry Baker or the Hound of the Baskervilles, the initials HB stamp and hallmark the Holmes stories as the secret signifier of family. Where Scotland, for Doyle, provided the writing of manhood, Ireland was the source of its charmed speech. Significantly, Holmes's standards of speech are only modified by his contact with American culture and his years as an infiltrator of secret societies in Chicago. Acting as a double agent in the First World War story, *His Last Bow*, Holmes goes under the name of 'Mr Altamont', 'a real bitter Irish-American' who 'seems to have declared war on the King's English as well as on the English King'.[56] Reverting to his normal speech, Holmes apologizes for the sacrificial changes he has made for his country in using American slang: 'I beg your pardon, Watson, my well of English seems to be permanently defiled'. As the story's denouement makes clear, the real honey in his tone is hidden with the secret codes encrypted in his 'Practical Handbook of [H] Bee Culture'.[57]

Inner and outer stories: *A Study in Scarlet* (1887) and *The Sign of Four* (1889)

Jefferson Hope, the heroic villain of Holmes's first recorded case, *A Study in Scarlet*, is a lone man who becomes connected to his own inner story through the combined talents of Holmes and Watson. Hope's narrative only emerges when Dr Watson places his hands on his chest to feel the 'extraordinary throbbing and commotion which was going on inside'.[58] An act of autobiographical confession, the story's claim to truth is authenticated by the fact that it is spoken 'on the brink of the grave' and its telling resymbolizes a man previously construed as a sinister villain. While Holmes's detective skills can identify the outer man and bring him to justice, Watson's medical writing is necessary to attach the inner man to the public malefactor. Initially glimpsed through the ape-like corpse of his victim, Enoch J. Drebber, Jefferson Hope sheds this likeness of post-Darwinian man, acquiring the soul that comes with a story. He ends his narrative resymbolized as Holmes – no longer a murderer but 'an officer of justice as you are'.[59]

The movement of *A Study in Scarlet* is from the bone-strewn silence of the Nevada desert to this fluent narrative which connects two cultures and the masculinity cults within them. In striking contrast to the swampy landscapes of Doyle's early fiction, *A Study in Scarlet* uses the desert sand of America as the site for a masculinity which has exchanged wordless disappearance for sign. The spiritless silence of the Nevada Desert is mirrored by the loneliness and initial 'wordlessness' of 221B Baker Street: the 'friendless' Watson records his new room-mate's 'Knowledge of Literature' as 'Nil'.[60] Where the desert receives the polygamous 'Word' of the Mormon leader, Joseph Smith, Baker Street becomes home to the solitary monographs of Holmes and a new analytic 'Revelation'. In 'the great wilderness of London',[61] Holmes restores Watson's faith in life just as Watson breaks the depressive silence which Holmes describes as his worst feature: 'I get in the dumps at times, and don't open my mouth for days on end.'[62] It is Watson who encourages him to talk:

> 'How in the world did you deduce that?' I asked.
> 'Deduce what?' said he, petulantly.
> 'Why, that he was a retired sergeant of Marines.'
> 'I have no time for trifles,' he answered brusquely. Then with a smile: 'Excuse my rudeness. You broke the thread of my thoughts; but perhaps it is as well.'[63]

The domestication of masculinity and its search for a home is the shared motif of this Anglo-American story. The movement away from masculine silence affects both Holmes and Watson, whose gradual recovery from the traumatic Battle of Maiwand is dependent on the written word.

Doyle had used the First Afghan War of 1839–42 as the setting for his early novel, *The Mystery of Cloomber* in which the scarlet uniform of the British officer conceals lack of spirituality. The Second Afghan War (1878–80) was a war of reprisals. In 1878 the British had reinvaded the country and established Major Cavagnari as 'British Resident' the following year. When 'Britain's man in Kabul' and his guard were massacred six weeks later, the British hastened to retaliate. Major General Roberts was ordered 'to strike terror, and to strike it swiftly and deeply'. He retook the capital and had eighty-nine Afghans executed outside the ruins of the Residency. The Afghans struck back in the direction of the British Garrison at Kandahar and met the British at Maiwand on 27 July 1880. The British retreat was made possible by the effective rearguard action of Watson's new regiment, the 66th Berkshires, who fought to the death. The only survivor was a small dog called Bobbie who made its way back across the fifty miles to Kandahar. Bobbie later received a medal from Queen Victoria before being run over by a cab in London.[64]

Interestingly, the staff of the field hospital to which Watson was attached reputedly fled, leaving the wounded behind. Some soldiers of the 66th also stayed behind, getting drunk in the officer's mess. The few who survived did so as a result of being slung over horses, if they were sober enough to stay on. This accurate historical detail occurs in Watson's account of Maiwand. He describes how, after being struck on the shoulder by the Jezail bullet, his orderly threw him across a packhorse and brought him safely to the British lines. Initially located in his shoulder but later described as afflicting his leg, Watson's wound may have wandered his body so disconcertingly in search of the alcohol which signalled the breach in his manhood and in his memory.

Watson moves from a state of wounded loneliness to the domestic companionship of 221B Baker Street. His own damaged interiority restored, he begins to keep a journal, the privacy and powerlessness of this form transformed by his fascination with Holmes into a 'small brochure' with a colourful title, which foregrounds the gifts and personality of his new acquaintance. Rescued from the demoralizations of history by his partnership with Holmes, he becomes the author of published 'Reminiscences' and, as Holmes's biographer, a publicly reconstituted image of normative manhood.

For all the colour of its title, *A Study in Scarlet* is essentially a study in surfaces, the sands, soils, walls, window ledges and bruised bodies which delineate the particular territory of Sherlock Holmes. This superficiality is a talisman against those sinking grounds of the masculine story where emotional depth and inarticulateness threaten the male sign. No amount of engagement with the massive archives of Sherlock Holmes's scholarship can silence their celebration of the ingeniously superficial. Their depth lies only in the autobiographical impulses resymbolized within them and the sexuality which they conceal. Famously measuring the sinkage of parsley into warm butter, Holmes and Watson provide a literary specific against depth as an index of the new masculinity. Holmes's eventual plunge to 'death' down the Reichenbach Falls offers a fitting nemesis for this advocate of surface explanations, whose villains make up, in the ingenuity of their crimes, for the paucity of their motivation.

In its task of resymbolization, the Comic Spirit was quick to sink its teeth into the letter 'L'. In *A Study in Scarlet*, the missing 'L' in the word 'Rache' is the clue which connects a dead man in London with Lucy Ferrier in Utah and Jefferson Hope's Mormon vendetta. Holmes's other clue is a wedding ring. Different organizations of sexuality are the subject of this novella which connects polygamy, monogamy and celibacy as alternative articles of belief. In the Valley of Utah, John Ferrier, though joining the Mormons, refuses to endorse their polygamous practices:

> He had always determined ... that nothing would ever induce him
> to allow his daughter to wed a Mormon. Such a marriage he
> regarded as no marriage at all, but as a shame and a disgrace.
> Whatever he might think of the Mormon doctrines, upon that one
> point he was inflexible.[65]

As Holmes waits for his first meeting with his criminal 'other', Jefferson
Hope, that interactive letter 'L' begins to alliterate. Holmes turns over 'a
queer old book' – *De Jure inter Gentes* – published 'in Latin at Liège
in the Lowlands, in 1642' and formerly the possession of a 'lawyer'
whose writing has a 'legal twist'. Drawing attention to Doyle's trick of
substituting books for bodies, Holmes comments cryptically on an earlier breach of law: 'Charles's head was still firm on his shoulders when
this little brown-backed volume was struck off.'[66] Charles Doyle's own
emasculated illustrations of this text were removed from subsequent
editions. When Hope appears dressed as an elderly woman, the law
between bodies, as well as that between peoples, develops its own
jurisprudential twist.

The wedding ring at the centre of this story articulates both a private
concern and a wider cultural debate. Despite, or perhaps because of, his
own inauspicious childhood, Doyle showed a lifelong public commitment to monogamous marriage, rejecting sexual profligacy or infidelity
as a sign of manhood. 'It is a libel on mankind', he wrote of Fielding's
Tom Jones 'to say that a man who truly loves a woman is usually false
to her'.[67] Cultural debate about marriage and the diverse organizations
of sexuality occupied a significant role in the ideological formulations
of the British Empire, though this debate was necessarily conducted in
the elliptically censored discourse of Victorian Britain. The various legal
campaigns surrounding the Contagious Diseases Act, The Hindu Age of
Consent Act, (which controversially raised the age of sexual availability
for Hindu girls from ten to twelve), and the Divorce Acts, as well as the
high-profile scandals surrounding members of the British aristocracy,
necessitated a debate in which cultural supremacy, as well as gender
relations, were high on the agenda.

Monogamy, it was argued by Christians and medical theorists alike,
was 'the ultimate condition of the race' or at least 'an important factor
... in psychological evolution'.[68] The eugenicist, J. F. Nisbet, linked
monogamy to notions of evolutionary progress:

> ... the secret of human progress lies in the freest recognition of the
> rights of the individual woman. If there is one lesson more forcibly
> taught by heredity than another, it is that the interest of the sexes
> are absolutely solidaire. Treated as serfs, as mere instruments for
> the gratification of passion, denied education and the right of
> choosing their consorts, women exact a terrible penalty from the
> ensuing generations of men.[69]

Women mistreated in marriage produced sons who were unable to forward the work of civilization. In *Marriage and Heredity* (1889) Nisbet claimed that civilization itself was driven by the effects of the mother–son relationship, as conversation between literate mothers and their sons refined manhood and increased the sum of cultural knowledge. 'Mormonism, free love, and other new-fangled substitutes for monogamy adopted in America', he argues, are experiments bound to fail, because of their conflict with instincts planted deep in European or American life.[70]

As critics like Christopher Redmond have argued, the problem of marriage rather than the solution of crime is the main issue of the early Holmes stories. Martin Priestman, in his study of detective fiction, has drawn attention to the status of Watson's marriage to Mary Morstan, which concludes the second novella, *The Sign of Four,* as providing 'the series's one irreversible event'.[71] Sexuality in the private sphere is the territory of silence in which Sherlock Holmes is initially configured. As Inspector Lestrade pithily remarks in 'The Noble Bachelor' as he lays down a wedding ring: 'There is a little nut for you to crack, Master Holmes.'[72] From impotence in 'The Blue Carbuncle' to incest in 'The Speckled Band', each of the stories in *The Adventures* images a sexual practice which threatens to break its taboo of silence unless Holmes can supply a covering *fabula* of crime and detection.

'L', the letter of linkage in *A Study in Scarlet*, also stands for Louise, and the initials of Doyle's first wife are woven into the story along with those of HB. *A Study in Scarlet* was written in 1886, a year after Doyle's marriage to Louise Hawkins, the sister of an epileptic patient who died in his care. This marriage provided the creative stimulus for the Holmes stories as well as the guilts on which they fed. When her brother, Jack Hawkins, died in Doyle's house – possibly of meningitis or possibly from the large dose of morphine prescribed to him – Doyle was placed as both benevolent young doctor and scheming, suspected murderer. Touie's family were large farmers and local dignitaries from Minsterworth in Gloucestershire, and, her father having died the previous year, she had a small private income of her own which was increased by her brother's death. Doyle married her four months later from the home of his mother's 'friend', Dr Bryan Waller, during the year that the alcoholic Charles was confined in Montrose Lunatic Asylum.

From the perspective of late-Victorian eugenics, Doyle's marriage was a dangerous alliance. Alcoholism was considered a transmittable characteristic, like insanity or epilepsy, although as readers of J. F. Nisbet's *Marriage and Heredity* (1889) were comfortingly reminded:

> The family of a man who dies insane or epileptic do not necessarily suffer from the same malady; they may be idiotic, paralytic, or

scrofulous. What the parent transmits is not his insanity, but a constitutional defect which may manifest itself under different forms.[73]

The marriage was also an odd match in terms of size. Touie was a tiny woman, in striking contrast to her gargantuan husband. Facing a double bereavement at the time of her marriage, she may have stimulated Doyle's early interest in Spiritualism in the same way that she undoubtedly contributed a good deal to his sense of fun. Her daughter, Mary, described her as a fairytale figure with 'lovely shadowy eyes that always seemed to see beyond what she was looking at':

> There was a gentle all-lovingness about her that drew the simple folk, children and animals to her, as to a magnet. She had the quiet poise that comes rather from the wisdom of the spirit than from the knowledge of the world, and there ran through her a bright ripple of fun, that would glint in the eyes, and hover around her mouth ... she loved the comical aspects of life and the unconscious humour in people and things.[74]

Pierre Norden suggests convincingly that Doyle found a great deal of 'facile pleasure' in the early years of his marriage and concludes that 'his married life might have been a sort of pilgrimage to the lost paradise of his childhood'.[75] In both cases, the paradise was a brief one.

Although seldom discussed as such, the Holmes stories were acts of creative partnership between Doyle and the women to whom he was closest – his two wives, his mother and his sisters. These acts of partnership are well documented. Mary Doyle suggested the plot for 'The Copper Beeches', the last story of *The Adventures*. Writing 'Silver Blaze', the opening story of the *The Memoirs,* Doyle claimed to have bet Touie a shilling that she would not be able to guess the solution. This anecdote may have had something to do with the fact that the solution in question involved marital infidelity, but its interesting implication is that Touie usually could.[76] According to John Dixon Carr, Jean Leckie supplied the plot for the first story in *The Return of Sherlock Holmes*, 'The Empty House', where Holmes reappears disguised as a bookseller with a copy of the phallic 'Origins of Tree Worship' in his hand. In *Memories and Adventures,* Doyle encodes Touie's contribution to the stories in his description of Holmes as a man with 'a thin razor-like face, with a great hawks-bill of a nose, and two small eyes, set close together on either side of it'.[77] As Ronald Pearsall remarks, 'this gives the impression that Holmes had two sets of eyes',[78] but the pun on 'two eyes' silently tropes Doyle's first marriage under this privately referenced sign of four.

The project of the early Holmes stories, that of detecting and reinscribing the lost double or 'spirit' of late-Victorian masculinity, is clearly manifest in the second novella. Compared to the ape-like corpse of Drebber in *A Study in Scarlet*, the first murder victim of *The Sign of Four*, Bartholomew Sholto, appears as a figure of primitive spirituality – a devilish lunar icon or hanged man. Looking through a keyhole, Watson records:

> I stooped to the hole and recoiled in horror. Moonlight was stream-ing into the room, and it was bright with a vague and shifty radiance. Looking straight at me and suspended, as it were, in the air, for all beneath was in shadow, there hung a face – the very face of our companion Thaddeus. There was the same high, shining head, the same circular bristle of red hair, the same bloodless countenance. The features were set, however, into a horrible smile, a fixed and unnatural grin, which in that still and moonlight room was more jarring to the nerves than any scowl or contortion ... . Then I recalled to mind that ... his brother and he were twins.[79]

In *The Sign of Four*, Doyle doubles the process of detection in a determination to clarify the masculine sign. Images of washing and cleaning accompany this laundering of a dirty story. As Holmes ob-serves of the riverside yard workers:

> 'Dirty-looking rascals, but I suppose every one has some little immortal spark concealed about him. You would not think it to look at them. There is no a priori probability about it. A strange enigma is man!'
> 'Someone calls him a soul concealed in an animal,' I suggested.[80]

Blackened from the moment little Tonga put his foot in the creosote and left a print for Holmes and the hound, Toby, to follow, the story's preoccupation with dirt and blackness reaches its climax on the River Thames when Jonathan Small almost drowns in black mud. As Holmes's elaborate detective theories are finally justified, so the story of Jonathan Small, once the criminal mud is wiped off, is transformed into some-thing potentially rich and strange.

Small becomes a man whose sexual wild oats have led him on a mythic adventure combining elements of horror and of fairy story. While the dirt of empire, financial greed, sticks firmly to him, so too do the partnerships he has formed. The Andaman pygmy, Tonga, earlier demonized as an 'unhallowed dwarf' is reidentified as 'staunch and true. No man ever had a more faithful mate'.[81] Small's solidarity with the Sikhs who remained 'true to their salt' during the Indian Mutiny, as well as his fidelity to the strange partnerships of his chequered career, stand in contrast to the betrayals and treacheries by which he is sur-rounded. The darkness and the treasure are woven together in his story and Small resists all attempt to separate them, finally throwing the jewels at the centre of the story into the river with his dead companion.

The Sign of Four was ostensibly commissioned after a literary dinner arranged for the agent of an American publisher, Lippincotts, who wished to meet some new British writing talents. One suspects that the publisher's brief was more precise and that the American firm was looking for specifically Irish connections. The other dinner guests who made up the foursome were Oscar Wilde and 'a very entertaining Irish M.P.' called Gill.[82] It was an interesting meeting, for which we have only Doyle's account in *Memories and Adventures*. The two novellas commissioned have much in common in their concern with the doubling of masculine representation, for the other was Wilde's *The Picture of Dorian Gray*.

Doyle and Wilde were themselves antithetical twins in the representation of late-Victorian manhood. Where Wilde's essay on Shakespeare's sonnets, 'The Portrait of Mr. W.H.' (1889) offered a paeon of admiration for the male genital muse that it claimed as their inspiration, Doyle's image of heterosexual normality, Dr Watson, carried those initials reversed, 'H.W.', as a summarized family history on the back of his watch. Wilde's *The Picture of Dorian Gray* is the classic text for the representation of the beautiful male body and its remodelling into gothic ugliness while Doyle's novella takes a dirty story and shows the masculine splendour underneath. In his study of adventure narrative, *The Adventurous Male*, Martin Green has argued that aestheticism is a component of the adventure story – one which replaces moral judgement with its own values:

> To see social types in their colourfulness and contrastiveness, as picturesque castes rather than economic classes, in an aesthetic panorama, is to see them in adventure terms, even when those looked at are unadventurous in themselves. Adventure is always in some degree aesthetic because it is linked to pleasure and excitement rather than to moral argument.[83]

In *The Sign of Four* Doyle attempts to reverse this association, linking aestheticism with morality as a neurasthenic alternative to manly heterosexual adventure. Thaddeus Sholto is, on the surface, a peculiarly repulsive hypochondriac who has created an 'oasis of art in the howling desert of South London'.[84] His aestheticism is transformed into handsomeness only by what he does in trying to right the wrongs of Miss Morstan and by his moral resistance to his twin brother's greed.

Watson and Holmes are themselves twinned and mirrored in the partnership of their criminal opposites, Small and Tonga. Watson with his limp and the one-legged Jonathan Small both image the aggravation and rewards of partnership with someone more exceptional than themselves. Like Watson, Small has an area of medical expertise, having worked as a chemist dispensing drugs to a surgeon. Little Tonga, on the other hand, shares Holmes's levitational qualities, an ability to rise up walls, ropes and roofs at the slightest stimulation. Where Tonga is an expert with the poisoned thorn and the blow pipe, Holmes cannot resist injecting himself with cocaine and smoking strong tobacco. Just as Watson shows off the freakish and singular genius of Holmes, so Small survives in England by exhibiting Tonga at fairs ' as the black cannibal'.[85] With his fleshly appetites, Tonga represents the power of smallness in this tall story, one of those 'small facts upon which large inferences may depend'[86] in Holmes's 'extraordinary genius for minutiae'.[87]

The drowning of Tonga and the disappearance of the jewels into the river together provide a moment of poetry in this grimy story, invoking that earlier tale of colonial oppression and lost fathers – Shakespeare's *The Tempest*. As Mary Morstan discovers, those were pearls that were his eyes. The buried poetry of the Holmes stories is a device, like the linking 'L's, which carries autobiographical reference. One of the poetic gems afloat in this murky story is Tennyson's famous poem, 'Tithonus', a pearly, mythological moan about the eternal sameness of marriage. Unable to die but always ageing, Tithonus watches sadly from some celestial institution while the youth of his wife, Aurora, the goddess of dawn, is daily renewed. With its particular applicability to the plight of Doyle's father, Tennyson's poem is allusively inscribed, not just in the name of the steam launch, the *Aurora*, around which the final action of the story takes place, but also in Holmes's evasive poeticizing of the dawn: 'How sweet the morning air is! See how that one little cloud floats like a pink feather over some gigantic flamingo. Now the red rim of the sun pushes itself over the London cloud-bank ... '[88] when Watson questions him about the identity of Small's strange associate. Where Oscar Wilde's *The Picture of Dorian Gray* couples homosexual aestheticism with a realist morality, Doyle creates a masculine adventure whose dark, opposing double is the concept of the heterosexual marital home.

In its inception and its imagery, *The Sign of Four* not only encodes Doyle's ambivalent feelings towards his marriage, it also encrypts another aspect of his private history: that of his father's fate and Irish family background. The 'sign of four' is a sign of strange unions, like those combinations of similarity and difference which make up the British Isles. In the sign of four, there is always an odd one out. Doyle's dark imaging of the 'islander', Tonga, is a contradictory one which carries hidden fears of his own Irishness. Initially portrayed as a bloodthirsty and venomous savage, Tonga turns out to have been a loyal partner in an unlikely union. Disappearing into the water, he frees Holmes from a disturbing double.

From Mary Morstan to the pregnant girl abandoned by Jonathan Small at the start of his adventures, the figure of the missing father haunts this story and gives it an uncanny resonance which still disturbs. As *Memories and Adventures* confirms, masculine disappearance and its double, death, is *the* mystery behind the great detective. Doyle concludes his chapter on Sherlock Holmes with a curious unsolved puzzle about a 'gentleman of blameless life' who starts out for a Sunday evening walk with his family, goes back for something he has forgotten and is never seen again.[89] Unable to resolve the history of his father, Doyle created ever more ingenious puzzles to contain it.

The Adventures (1891), *The Memoirs* (1893) and *The Return* (1905) of Sherlock Holmes

Profound clues to superficial stories are buried throughout the Holmes canon, as part of their comic self-surveillance. Written during the early years of Doyle's membership of the Society for Psychical Research, the first two collections, *The Adventures* and *The Memoirs*, emphasize Holmes's stringent reasoning power as the guarantee of a masculinity situated in the internationalism of the city. It is a location in which declarative reason encounters that which seems to challenge it most, a sign system which emphasizes passional incompletion, an elliptical logic of lost parts and severed signifiers, like the abandoned wedding dress in 'The Noble Bachelor'. Between these indeterminate clues and the linguistic riddles, automatic scripts and psychic phenomena investigated by the powerful Cambridge-based Society for Psychical Research (SPR) between 1880 and 1920, there is a great deal of common ground. Ciphers, codes and secret languages, the pivot on which the Holmes stories turn, are a point of connection between the public and the private world, between politics and espionage, between religion and occultism, and between the outer man and the – largely unsignified – inner being.

The partnership between Holmes and Watson is itself a dramatization of ideas about identity and exceptionality put forward by Frederick Myers, a founder member of the SPR, who published his researches in *Human Personality* (1903), a book which Doyle praised in superlative terms. He had instigated a correspondence with Myers in the 1880s, before joining the SPR in 1893 and Myers's formulations about the multiplex nature of human identity spoke strongly to the divisions in Doyle himself. Partnership rather than division, however, had been Myers's theme as he investigated the processes of both genius and criminality. Myers had drawn on the work of his colleague, Cesare Lombroso, a criminologist and psychic investigator, who claimed that 'men of genius must be classed with criminals and lunatics, as persons in whom a want of balance ... has led on to an over development of one side of their nature'.[90] What separated the man of genius from the criminal was a 'power of appropriating the results of subliminal mentation to subserve the supraliminal stream of thought'. Genius, in other words, involved 'a three pipe solution'. In partial disagreement with Lombroso, Myers argued that genius was not a departure from normality but its fulfilment through the effective partnership devices that facilitate individuality. For him 'the man of genius is ... the best type of the normal man, in so far as he effects a successful cooperation of an unusually large number of elements of his personality – reaching a stage of integration slightly in advance of our own'.[91]

Myers concluded that such cooperative integration involved access to a sphere of deep knowledge that he designated the 'subliminal'. For Myers and, eventually for Doyle himself, it was the intelligence which operated in partnership with the 'subliminal' which had the ability to communicate independently of the body and even to survive death:

> Sometimes we seem to see our subliminal perceptions and faculties acting truly in unity, truly as a Self; – coordinated into some harmonious 'inspiration of genius', or some profound and reasonable hypnotic self-reformation, or some far-reaching supernormal achievement of clairvoyant vision or of self-projection into a spiritual world. Whatever of subliminal personality is thus acting corresponds with the highest-level centres of supraliminal life. At such moments the *subliminal* represents (as I believe) most nearly what will become the surviving Self.[92]

In his first two Holmes novellas, Doyle had submitted the American adventure story with its cult of *potestas*,[93] revenge and violence, to the resymbolizations of the detective intellect. The challenge of unriddling the spiritual geography of the physical world, institutionalized at 221B Baker Street, was, however, not confined there. Holmes belongs with that 'moment' in late-Victorian culture when, at the end of the 1880s, a new revelation appeared momentarily to have declared itself. This messianic moment took a variety of different forms. The radical humanist, Annie Besant, records one of them in her autobiography:

> As I turned over page after page the interest became absorbing; but how familiar it seemed ... . I was dazzled, blinded by the light in which disjointed facts were seen as parts of a mighty whole, and all my puzzles, riddles, problems, seemed to disappear. The effect was partially illusory in one sense, in that they all had to be slowly unravelled later, the brain gradually assimilating that which the swift intuition had grasped as truth. But the light had been seen, and in that flash of illumination, I knew that the weary search was over and the very Truth was found.[94]

Light, however, came from some strange sources. The text here is not Holmes's monograph 'On Secret Writings' but *The Secret Doctrine* by

Madame Blavatsky, who Besant eventually succeeded as the leader of the Theosophists. In his early Holmes stories, Doyle was engaging in a contest with the self-professed muse of the new adventure story, the Russian occultist who, incidentally, shared the symbolic initials of his grandfather, HB. This struggle with the muse had been figured initially in a pre-Holmesian short story, 'The Man from Archangel' (1885), in which a reclusive scientist forms a curious, speechless relationship with a young Russian girl who learns to replicate his scientific discourse. In reality it was the other way round. Holmes's function was to place under the sign of masculine reason and scientific control the adventurous life and apparently occult powers of the woman who, in founding the Theosophical Society, had rejected the sign of the cross and the Marion-worship of her Catholic upbringing.

In a close parallel movement of minds, both Annie Besant and Doyle had turned to Theosophy as a possible answer to their informed dissatisfaction with scientific materialism. Gender was a crucial factor in the divergence of their paths following the SPR's highly controversial 'exposure' of Madame Blavatsky in 1885 and her publication of *The Secret Doctrine* in 1888. Whereas Annie Besant became a convert to Theosophy, Doyle rejected Blavatsky, joined the SPR and created, in Holmes, a scientific medium able to command what looked like – and, according to Myers, were – paranormal powers of observation and surveillance.

Doyle had been investigating psychic phenomena, attending seances and recording spirit messages since his marriage in 1885. The nickname 'Touie', given to his wife Louise, had been cited by Myers in an illustrative case of secondary personality.[95] His initial rejection of Spiritualism was based specifically on the unmasculine models of speech that tended to emerge from the seance. Spirits indulged in 'girl talk', like the example he gives in his autobiography: *'"Don't tell the girls when you see them, but they will talk about me. Kiss my baby for me. I watch her always, Francie."* This was the style of messages, mixed up with a good many platitudes'.[96] Theosophy, on the other hand, was dominated by a woman of extraordinary dimensions who weighed as much as Doyle himself and could write as rapidly. Impressed by the literature of Theosophy, particularly A. P. Sinnett's *The Occult World*, Doyle was also fascinated by the testimony of Blavatsky's comrade and biographer, Colonel Olcott, a veteran of the American Civil War who remained convinced of her psychic gifts. Theosophy, however, was a dangerous option for someone making his public declaration of manhood as Doyle was doing in the mid-1880s. Not only did it destabilize the dominant gender ideologies of the late-Victorian period, it replicated the power structures of his childhood, and offered the lure of unworldliness to which his father had so chronically succumbed. In creating Holmes at this critical juncture, Doyle drew instead on a counter-emotional masochism to instruct the writing of a new masculine law.

In his 1885 'exposure' of Madame Blavatsky, the SPR's investigator, Richard Hodgson, a Cambridge lawyer, concluded that Blavatsky was a psychic fraud and probably a Russian spy into the bargain. Hodgson did not accept as genuine the letters of higher knowledge that Blavatsky claimed to have received from her occult masters: he thought she had written them herself. In reaching this problematic conclusion, however, Hodgson was forced to acknowledge Blavatsky's highly literate challenge to the fundamental categories of Victorian social and scientific control. He called her 'one of the most accomplished, ingenious, and interesting impostors in history'.[97] In reply, Blavatsky, by then living in London, wrote her massive key to all mythologies, *The Secret Doctrine*.

In *Memories and Adventures* Doyle's account of writing the early Holmes stories is situated in the blank spaces of personal recall. Holmes 'covers' the period of his marriage and his experience of fatherhood. Moving from a discussion of Blavatsky to his own manly and medical practices, he writes: 'Suddenly, however, there came a development which shook me out of my rut, and caused an absolute change in my life and plans. One daughter, Mary, had been born to us.'[98] The reader might, at this point, be excused for imagining that paternity itself was the startling development, but this is not the case. On the contrary, Doyle records the bizarre and impulsive series of travels which led him, via Berlin and Vienna, away from his settled life in Southsea, to London, an attempted career in ophthalmology, and the writing of the first series of Holmes stories. Seldom at home during his daughter's first two years, Doyle took Touie with him to Vienna in 1891 when Mary was two, leaving her in the care of her maternal grandmother. Touie's second pregnancy brought with it an energetic holiday in Norway and some strenuous horse-riding. A year after Kingsley's birth in 1892 and another trip abroad, Touie was pronounced terminally ill, her illness necessitating further separations from her young family.

In his autobiography, Doyle describes the events of 1891 as a 'crossroads' in his life from which he emerged 'a changed man'.[99] Waiting for eye patients who never materialized, he began writing *The Adventures of Sherlock Holmes*. Then 'Providence' intervened. Having written the first four stories of *The Strand* series, Doyle succumbed to the flu epidemic sweeping London and, according to his own account, nearly died of the illness. While convalescing, he thought over his career and made the momentous decision to give up medicine for literature. *Memories and Adventures* records:

> I remember in my delight taking the handkerchief which lay upon
> the coverlet in my enfeebled hand, and tossing it up to the ceiling

in my exultation. I should at last be my own master ... I would be
free to live how I liked. It was one of the great moments of
exultation of my life. The date was in August, 1891.[100]

Unfortunately, the 'great moments' of autobiography are no more to
be trusted than the great men whose stories are sustained by them. In
his 1943 biography of Doyle, Hesketh Pearson, comments gently on
this passage: 'He gives the month as August in his autobiography, but
the diary tells us May, and the diary is right. As in the case of his
sojourn in Vienna, his memory exaggerated the period of his proba-
tion.'[101] Doyle's memory had a way of slipping free of precision when
there were links to be forgotten or connections disguised, but his accounts of the appearance of Holmes in 1891 and his disappearance in
1893 are particularly unreliable. The flu, as it happened, had claimed
an impressive body of its own in April 1891, the month in which Doyle
wrote his first story. Madame Blavatsky, as addicted to nicotine as
Holmes himself, went down with the virus on the 21 April. On 8 May,
she rolled her last cigarette, handed it to the doctor attending her, and
died. The final year of her life had been dominated by the re-emergence
of an old scandal. In 1889 *The New York Sun* had printed an article
about her Bohemian past claiming that, in her youth, Blavatsky had had
a love affair with Prince Wittgenstein and had lived as one of the *demi-
monde* in Paris during the 1850s. In her flamboyant rejection of the
domestic sphere and her transformation of the marginalizing freedoms
of the fallen woman, first into an adventure text and then into a
religious movement whose Lodges fostered Irish Nationalism, Blavatsky
posed the single most visible threat to the social order of Victorian
patriarchy.

The first story of *The Adventures*, 'A Scandal in Bohemia', is a
resymbolization of some of the scandals and talents, associated with
this extraordinary woman, including her musical career. As many com-
mentators have remarked, the point of the story is its recontainment of
the figure of the adventuress within a law that includes Christian marriage. When the scandal-provoking Irene Adler is married to her lawyer,
Mr Norton, with Holmes as witness, the detective changes places with
the adventuress as the figure who defines the outer edges of the law.
Attaching Holmes to his own ex-military man as biographer and partner, Doyle replaced Europe's most gifted and errant occultist with a
counter-image of British masculine scientific reason magically rooted to
one particular address. In the 'great game' with Russia, this substitution
proved to be a political masterstroke.

The fact that the Holmes stories emerged out of Doyle's interest in
Theosophy had an effect on the stories themselves, which inscribe their
own form of 'secret doctrine'. In not becoming a Theosophist, Doyle

created a homoerotic religion of Western masculinity, located in a space safe from sexuality but charged with its symbols and their control. Sherlock Holmes was a personal solution to the ideological dilemmas of a late-Victorian spirituality freed from the patriarchal god of the Old Testament but a long way from Jean-Paul Sartre's existential formulation: 'There is no good father, that's the rule. Don't lay the blame on men but on the bond of paternity, which is rotten.'[102] The early Holmes stories arise quite literally from a crisis of paternity and Holmes is, first and foremost, a talisman against the bad father.

Dysfunctional fathers and husbands appear in ten out of the twelve stories that constitute *The Adventures* where they are represented as predatory power-seekers guarding their guilts and their gains with equal ingenuity and disregard for their offspring. In 'A Case of Identity' a stepfather disguises himself as his stepdaughter's lover in order to keep control of her money, and a similar scenario is enacted by the evil comedian Mr Rucastle in 'The Copper Beeches' and the inarticulate Dr Grimesby Roylott in 'The Speckled Band'. Verbal underrepresentation is a sign of the father in this early collection. Charles McCarthy in 'The Boscombe Valley Mystery' leaves only half a word, 'ARAT', as the vital clue to his murder while Dr Roylott communicates with the world and his daughters through a language of wild animals. In the centrally placed story of the collection, 'The Man With the Twisted Lip', the one real clue to the double identity of the respectable city-man, Neville St Clair, and the disfigured beggar, Hugh Boon, is his emblem of fatherhood the box of building bricks bought for his son and recognized by his wife in the unlikely environment of Swandam Lane.

After the paterfamilial absences of the Victorian period, *The Adventures of Sherlock Holmes* were partly an attempt to refigure the father by exposing the power abuses to which the role was liable. The Edwardian creation of 'the family man', a version of the masculine which replaced both the Victorian patriarch and the injured adventurers of empire, owes much to the remodelling work of the Holmes stories. Doyle brought to this task his own guilts, failures and jealousies as a father, as well as the unresolved traumas of his own childhood. Like Jephro Rucastle who, in 'The Copper Beeches', uses humorous stories to conceal the criminal substitutions in his family circle, Doyle submits his personal history to the muzzled ferocity of the Comic Spirit. His ambivalent feelings towards his first daughter and his fears that a genetically unsound marriage might have unfortunate offspring provide the main criminal inspiration for this fatherly volume.

The Adventures depict patriarchs maintaining a problematic relationship both with their children and the spoken word. Holmes's task is to correct the dysfunctions between masculine behaviour and verbal sign, between a carnivalesque licence and that fear of visibility dramatized by the heavily vizored king in 'A Scandal in Bohemia'. Where Freud, in collaboration with Josef Breuer, was working on a 'talking cure' for hysterics in Vienna, using association techniques for the laborious 'business of enlarging what was supposed to be a restricted consciousness',[103] Holmes and Watson were moving in exactly the opposite direction, seeking comic symbolization for masculine anxiety and lack of interiority.

Holmes is situated at that threshold of anxiety where the encounter with the spoken word takes place. Watson presides over the written word; Holmes controls interviews and spoken encounters. Hysterical men feature conspicuously among his early clients – victims of loss whose capacity to sign and represent the masculine has been damaged or stolen. Victor Hatherley in 'The Engineer's Thumb' laughs hysterically as he presents Watson with his amputated thumb. 'All my medical instincts', says Watson, 'rose up against that laugh'.[104] Alexander Holder, the banker-father of 'The Beryl Coronet', has a similarly traumatic glimpse of an absence which rapidly severs his connection both with language and the empowerments of masculine identity. He approaches Baker Street looking like 'a madman':

> He was a man of about fifty, tall, portly, and imposing ... . Yet his actions were in absurd contrast to the dignity of his dress and features, for he was running hard, with occasional little springs ... . As he ran he jerked his hands up and down, waggled his head, and writhed his face into the most extraordinary contortions. ... A few moments later he was in our room, still puffing, still gesticulating ... . For a while he could not get his words out, but swayed his body and plucked at his hair like one who has been driven to the extreme limits of his reason. Then, suddenly springing to his feet, he beat his head against the wall with such force that we both rushed upon him ... . Sherlock Holmes pushed him down into the easy chair, and, sitting beside him, patted his hand, and chatted with him in the easy, soothing tones which he knew so well how to employ.
> 'You have come to tell me your story, have you not?' said he.[105]

In contrast to these honourable but ill-judging hysterics, Holmes's most contemptible villains show either a maladroitness in verbal exchange or an aversion to speech altogether. James Windibank in 'A Case of Identity' insists: 'I cannot waste time over this sort of fantastic talk, Mr. Holmes ... If you can catch the man, catch him, and let me know when you have done it.' In a neat demonstration of the seamlessness between speech and action, Holmes immediately locks the door and pronounces the villain caught. 'Sit down, and let us talk it over' is Holmes's final statement of mastery over this typewritten problem.[106]

If speech is the masculine problem of The Adventures, writing is the principal riddle of The Memoirs. Published after the birth of his son,

Kingsley, these stories emphasize male relationships and foreground the crimes and puzzles which link men together. In 'The Stockbroker's Clerk', brotherly affection counteracts criminal practice, while masculine writing provides the clue to crime in 'The "Gloria Scott"', 'The Musgrave Ritual', 'The Reigate Squires' and 'The Naval Treaty'. As previously discussed, 'The Musgrave Ritual' engages in a dialogic reconstruction of the father–son relationship. The HB device stamped on these stories shows Doyle's determination to link them with the successfully mediated Irishness of his grandfather's political cartoons. In 'The "Gloria Scott"', the case that first turned Holmes's mind 'in the direction of criminal research',[107] the written confession of James Armitage to his son, Victor Trevor, concludes with a postscript which inscribes both cipher and its HB decipherment: 'Underneath is written, in a hand so shaky as to be hardly legible, "Beddoes writes in cipher to say that H. has told all. Sweet Lord, have mercy on our souls!"'[108]

The doubled writing of masculinity brings with it a silencing of the body and a concealment of the female that is at its most pronounced in *The Return of Sherlock Holmes* (1905). In 'The Adventure of the Norwood Builder', a junior partner in a firm of solicitors is instructed by an unknown client to copy out a will of which he himself appears to be the main benefactor. The inflating fantasy of the moment is punctured when he discovers that his handwriting has also made him the main suspect in a peculiar murder in which the human corpse has been replaced by some charred animal remains. As the body is replaced by a criminalized writing, so its animal secrets find their own lexicon of escape through the letters of the alphabet. While financial greed motivates most of the male crime in the stories, sexuality 'pepys' out through the articulate ciphers of Doyle's comic control. The letter 'H' in the name of John H. Watson is one such avenue.

This letter seems, during the late-Victorian period, to have suggested a doubled notion of masculinity, one that was verbally 'respectable' but physically transgressive. H. G. Wells and D. H. Lawrence made it the sign of an explicit and proletarian sexuality. Herman Webster Mudgett, the most versatile criminal on the files of Pinkerton's Detective Agency, adopted the name 'H. H. Holmes' as a permanent alias in a career of such phenomenal villainy and cultural style that people seem to have gone out of their way to be murdered by him! Born in 1860 and trained as a doctor, Mudgett in partnership with a young Englishman began kidnapping, starving and gassing his victims, first extorting large sums of money from them and then selling their corpses for dissection. From 1891 onwards the fictional and the fictitious Holmes ran a parallel course of crime and detection, H. H. inventing ingenious ciphers 'for use in communicating' while S. H. worked at deciphering them, until

Holmes went over the edge of the Reichenbach Falls and H. H. Holmes was hung in Moyamensing Prison, Philadelphia on 7 May 1896, accused of multiple murder.[109]

As addicted to confession as he was to crime, the bigamous Holmes claimed before execution that he had made up all but one of his crimes to satisfy the insatiable narrative lust of the detective investigating him. Doyle and Pinkerton, of course, were themselves well-acquainted, their longstanding association finally severed when Doyle allegedly used confidential information supplied by Pinkerton in writing his final Holmes novella, *The Valley of Fear*.

The letter 'H' gets, perhaps, its most extensive airing in 'The Priory School' from *The Return* when a hysterical headmaster, Dr Huxtable, having lost a boy, collapses on the floor of Baker Street:

> I cannot recollect anything more sudden and startling than the first appearance of Dr. Thorneycroft Huxtable, M.A., Ph.D. etc. His card, which seemed too small to carry the weight of his academic distinctions, preceded him by a few seconds, and then he entered himself – so large, so pompous, and so dignified that he was the very embodiment of self-possession and solidity. And yet his first action when the door was closed behind him was to stagger against the table, whence he slipped down upon the floor, and there was that majestic figure prostrate and insensible upon our bearskin hearthrug.[110]

In contrast to 'The Solitary Cyclist', which illustrates the crude, uncontrolled violence of illiterate masculinity, the plot of 'The Priory School' designates a masculine presence that is too dependent on its letters. The case is rendered problematic from its plethora of signs and clues, including a map and diagrammatic representation of cow tracks drawn in Holmes's breadcrumbs. The proud, uncommunicative Duke of Holdernesse has alienated his wife and been complicit in the abduction of his own son by a former, and illegitimate, child. Significantly, this illegitimate son, James Wilder, acts as his father's secretary and the controller of his writing. Although the investigation focuses on the tracks of bicycles and cows, it is resolved by the discovery that a letter from the Duke has been opened and a second note inserted into it. It is this spurious second letter, apparently from his estranged mother, which had lured the missing schoolboy, Lord Saltire, into the hands of his abductors. Lord Saltire, of course, had already appeared in Doyle's autobiographical novel, *The Stark Munro Letters* (1895) where he is himself the father of an imbecile son. The strong patriarchal dysfunction at the centre of this story and its doubled writing is signalled by its foregrounded 'H'.

Consulted about the case, Holmes goes straight to the heart of the matter. He 'shot out his long, thin arm and picked out Volume "H" in his encyclopaedia of reference'.[111] Finding the entry relating to the sixth Duke of Holdernesse, he could with ease have continued his search to include information about many of the other characters in the story: Dr Huxtable himself; the German master, Mr Heidegger; and the man eventually hung for his murder, Reuben Hayes. It was Hayes who, in imitation of the marauding medieval Barons of Holdernesse, concealed his kidnap route by shoeing his horses with irons designed to leave counterfeit cow tracks.

The central story of the *Return* collection, 'The Adventure of Charles Augustus Milverton', is a turning point in Doyle's representation of gender. Pursuing a blackmailer who trades in women's indiscreet love letters, Holmes himself turns amorist and burglar to outwit him, discovering at last his strong natural talent for crime. Holmes and Watson witness the moment when nineteen centuries of female guilt and original sin are finally discharged as Lady Eva 'empties the barrel of a revolver into the blackmailing serpent who has exiled her from happiness.' For similar crimes of silencing women, Watson's writing itself is lucky to escape arrest!

The final story in the volume, 'The Adventure of the Second Stain' responds to that exclusion of women for which the letter 'H' had previously stood. Reversing this appropriation of the female sign, Lady Hilda Trelawney Hope tries to recover her indiscreet early love letters by inadvertently trading for them a political document from her ministerial husband's dispatch box. The two sets of bloodstains on the blackmailer's carpet inscribe a newly doubled womanhood, a second menstrual presence, not just in the life of the blackmailer, Lucas, but in the writing of the Holmes stories themselves.

The power of the letter 'H' to signal a double identity in Doyle's writing is not confined to the Holmes stories. Describing famous people he had met in *Memories and Adventures,* he relays an anecdote about Sir Henry Hawkins, the judge who had once been counsel for the prosecution at Arthur Orton's trial for perjury in the notorious case of 'the Tichbourne Claimant'. Orton had been a butcher at Wagga Wagga in Australia until, in 1865, he claimed the title and estates of the Tichbourne baronetcy after the legitimate heir was drowned. Describing Hawkins as himself a Jekyll and Hyde character, Doyle remarks:

> Of the distinguished lights of the law whom I have met from time to time I think that Sir Henry Hawkins ... made the most definite impression. I met him at a week-end gathering at Cliveden, when Mr. Astor was our host. On the first night at dinner, before the party had shaken down into mutual acquaintance, the ex-judge, very old and as bald as an ostrich egg, was seated opposite, and was wreathed with smiles as he made himself agreeable to his neighbour. His appearance was so jovial that I remarked to the

lady upon my left: 'It is curious to notice the appearance of our *vis-à-vis* and to contrast it with his reputation', alluding to his sinister record as an inexorable judge. She seemed rather puzzled by my remark, so I added: 'Of course you know who he is.' 'Yes', said she, 'his name is Conan Doyle and he writes novels.'[112]

The name 'Hawkins' of course, had its own partnership connotations for Doyle but this conflation of identities is a particularly fitting one. The Tichbourne case, as has often been remarked, provided material for Doyle's most famous Holmes novella, *The Hound of the Baskervilles* (1902) in which a similar claim is plotted against the Baskerville estate. When, in 1904, Sir Henry Hawkins published his autobiography, *The Reminiscences*, he made a notable innovation in this troubled literary genre. Since *The Reminiscences* of Thomas Carlyle, the handling of domestic partnership in male autobiography had been a particularly sensitive one. Lacking a wife, Sir Henry gaily interwove with his own story the reminiscences of his fox terrier, Jack. Jack, apparently, had a comic spirit of his own:

> I was born into the family of my Lord Falmouth, and claim descent from the most well bred of my race in this kingdom, the smooth fox terrier. All my ancestors were noted for their love of sport, their keen sense of humour, and hatred of vermin.[113]

The comedic anecdotes which supply the Holmes stories with their compressed energy often carry lively trails of personal guilt. The doubled identity here of the sinister judge and the jovial novelist leads back to the inception of the Holmes stories and that other 'Jack Hawkins', Doyle's former patient and now deceased brother-in-law.

The Hound of the Baskervilles

In his discussion of the Comic Spirit, Meredith had identified the great houses of the aristocracy as sites peculiarly haunted by comedic imps: 'They will', he claimed, 'dog a great House for centuries.'[114] This dogging of great houses is, in *The Hound of the Baskervilles*, an incarnate metaphor for the sexual proclivities, privileges and perversities which rather erratically ensure the transmission of aristocratic blood. From rapacious Sir Hugo in the seventeenth century to responsive Sir Henry two hundred years later, there is no obvious need for any Musgrave Ritual in the Baskerville family. Nor in the family of HB either, for the story carries the guilty imprint of Doyle's second relationship with Jean Leckie, which deepened when the story was written, on his return from the Boer War. Two suspicious initials, 'LL', provide a crucial clue to the death of Sir Charles and quietly link together the 'L' in Louise with that in Leckie. Touie's presence is inscribed in the narrative under the name of 'Mrs. Oldmore ... an invalid lady' whose 'husband was once mayor of Gloucester'. More poignantly, it might also be found in that 'skeleton with a tangle of brown hair adhering to it'[115] that was the only companion of the lonely dog at the centre of the novella's hidden autobiography. Where Holmes appears to be substituting young Cartwright for his devoted companion of many years, so Doyle himself was gradually replacing 'Mrs. Oldmore' with a new relationship.

The Hound of the Baskervilles represents Doyle's most powerful attempt to outwit Holmes's censorship of discourse and to tell the story both of the masculine body and of his own inner being. Killing the hound rather than catching its owner is the climax of a story which can find no other form of closure than that of a dog's mouth. Significantly, despite the plethora of marriages on the moor, there are no children in this story apart from the one who supplies the primitive needs of Holmes himself. Sir Charles Baskerville, despite his marriage, dies 'childless' and the only 'little curly headed boy' referred to in the story is the Notting Hill murderer, Selden. At the same time, boys and boyhood memories are deeply inscribed in the text, for Sir Henry's return from America to the English county he knew in his boyhood is directly connected to the story of Selden. In a passage which carefully echoes the landscape of Doyle's 'first' novel about boyhood and rebellion, Micah Clarke, Watson describes Sir Henry's reabsorption into the land of his ancestors:

> Over the green squares of the fields ... there rose in the distance a gray, melancholy hill, with a strange jagged summit, dim and vague in the distance, like a fantastic landscape in a dream. Baskerville sat for a long time, his eyes fixed upon it, and I read upon his eager face how much it meant to him, this first sight of that strange spot where the men of his blood ... had left their mark so deep.[116]

On his return from the Boer War, Doyle had stood as a Liberal Unionist candidate for Central Edinburgh in 'the Khaki elections' of 1900. It was, he claimed in Memories and Adventures, 'some sentimental call'[117] which led him back to this boyhood territory. Refusing to be sectarian and 'not yet converted to Home Rule' for Ireland,[118] Doyle lost both the Irish vote and the chance of election when a political opponent ran a last-minute campaign depicting him on street posters as a Jesuit-educated Catholic. It was from this context of loss and revisiting that Doyle wrote his greatest Holmes story. Originally intended as a collaborative venture with a war correspondent, Fletcher Robinson, this partnership proved no more successful than the ones depicted in the story where separation from, and division within, both Holmes and homes is a recurrent condition.

The dog in *The Hound of the Baskervilles* poses Holmes with his greatest challenge. The complex symbolic compression figured by this phosphorescent black mongrel is matched only by the story's masterly and sinister deployment of language not to speak itself or to articulate its concerns. The supernatural gothicism of the hound powerfully opposes the rational ordering of discourse which Watson attempts to supply in his written reports to Holmes. It is a story of being dogged by the criminal otherness of the self, as Holmes is dogged by a man who gives his name as 'Sherlock Holmes', and as Watson is dogged by a stranger who turns out to be Sherlock Holmes. Of all the *fabula* in the Holmes stories, this odd concoction around the entomologist 'Stapleton', whose name goes through as many metamorphoses as the lepidoptera in which he specializes, is the most fabulous of all. Holmes's failure to net the villain and add him to the Baker Street collection renders his solution to the mystery as suspect as the crime itself.

The Hound of the Baskervilles reverses the formulaic devices of the earlier stories. Watson, for once, leads the investigation, while Holmes, like the hound, is figured through the shine of a gothic darkness. The uncertain positioning of Holmes with regard to the strange practices of the moor is one source of confusion and fear in a story that can only be 'seen' from a distance. Holmes is imaged against the Dartmoor landscape as a deeply puzzled icon of the sublime:

> He stood with his legs a little separated, his arms folded, his head bowed, as if he were brooding over that enormous wilderness of peat and granite which lay behind him. He might have been the very spirit of that terrible place.[119]

As with the figure of the mounted soldier, 'hard and clear like an equestrian statue upon its pedestal',[120] this clarified cultural iconization contrasts with the blurred and wavering images of a manhood less easily represented but equally at home on the moor. The 'connection between ... man and ... beast'[121] is the issue at stake in this story which images a fundamental break between them.

In contrast to the primitive animal-men of the moor and the Romantic essentialism of a 'natural' masculinity is set a modern manhood which appears to have taken a different evolutionary route. The small, slim, prim-faced Stapleton figures a question mark over the link between man, beast and butterfly. Described as 'that impassive, colourless man, with his straw hat and his butter-fly net ... a creature of infinite patience and craft', Stapleton is characterized by his moth-like movements and relentless pursuit of 'Cyclopides'.[122] His passionate interest in the Baskerville heir finds 'voice' in his jealous outburst over Sir Henry's flirtation with his own platonic 'wife', Beryl, and she is subsequently prevented from joining their intimate suppers. In trying to fit

Stapleton up with a vicious dog and a rampant heterosexuality, Holmes is disguising and policing an altogether different sexual orientation.

The story of the hound generates in Sir Charles Baskerville the chronic anxiety associated with blackmail in Doyle's earlier stories. Emphatically *not* the aristocratic hound of the Baskervilles, this black mongrel from the Fulham Road threatens to interpose its body between criminal man and his privileged clothing signs, invoking the common blackmailers whose evidence led, in 1895, to the downfall of Oscar Wilde. Significantly, Holmes's pretext for not accompanying Sir Henry to Baskerville Hall is that 'one of the most revered names in England is being besmirched by a blackmailer, and only I can stop a disastrous scandal'.[123] Wilde had died in 1900 and references to him are strewn carefully through the text. As Watson and Sir Henry approach Baskerville Hall for the first time, they drive through a Pre-Raphaelite landscape of yellow leaves, components perhaps of those notorious 'Yellow Books' in which Wilde had published his work. Watson comments: '... we drove through drifts of rotting vegetation – sad gifts, as it seemed to me, for Nature to throw before the carriage of the returning heir of the Baskervilles',[124] a reference to the bouquet of rotten vegetables presented to Wilde by the Marquis of Queensbury. The recurrence of such ingenious intertextual quotation throughout *The Hound of the Baskervilles* helps to explain the story's reputation for literary depth. The signifying power of the hound lies in its ability to leash, muzzle, kennel and silence the hybrid human stories out of which it was bred. Significantly, the London taxi driver whose mysterious fare gives his name as 'Sherlock Holmes' is himself called John Clayton, a later incarnation perhaps of that notorious homosexual bank robber, John Clay, from 'The Red-Headed League'.

The Hound of the Baskervilles was serialized in *The Strand* from August 1901 to April 1902. It was published between Doyle's history of *The Great Boer War*, and the work which would earn him a knighthood, his refutation of atrocity charges brought against the British troops in South Africa: *The War in South Africa: Its Cause and Conduct* (1902). Unlike Doyle's other returned colonials, Sir Charles Baskerville's 'nervous depression' is not caused by the secret guilts of empire or by the goldmines of South Africa which have restored the fortunes of his family. His fear is located at home, among the abandoned tin mines and crumbling miner's cottage at the heart of the Grimpen mire. Offering the most dramatic example of that counterpoint between Holmes and history that is the motive force of Doyle's career, *The Hound of the Baskervilles* uses names and initials to 'staple' together the different texts of his writing identity.

The pseudonym 'Vandeleur', under which Stapleton makes a name for himself as an entomologist in Yorkshire, is one such link. Holmes tells Watson that Stapleton 'so far forgot himself as to tell you a true piece of autobiography'[125] when he revealed this aspect of his past, and this indiscretion is true of Doyle too. Like Stapleton, he made his name through the ephemerality of the Holmes stories rather than through his solid histories of war. 'Vandeleur' was the name of a young British officer killed by the Boers in a war atrocity in August 1901, the month in which the first instalment of *The Hound of the Baskervilles* appeared. Celebrated in the press as a war hero, Cecil Vandeleur had fought in the Sudan as an officer in the Scots Guards before being transferred to the newly formed Irish Guards. In command of a regiment from the West Riding of Yorkshire, he was killed near Waterval on 31 August 1901 while escorting a mixed train to Pietersburg. The incident attracted notice because the train was derailed and the civilians and blacks on it were shot by seventy Boers dressed in the uniform of British officers. According to press reports, Colonel Vandeleur died attempting to save a compartment of women and children from Boer fire.[126]

From the moment of Watson's escape from the disastrous battle of Maiwand, the Holmes stories commemorate those acts of memory failure which accompany the historical representation of British military manhood. In *The Hound of the Baskervilles* Watson himself had clearly recovered from the leg wound troubling him a year earlier. Sprinting after Holmes, he boasts of his running powers, despite the fact that the story is set in 1889, only a year after his limping approach to the altar in *The Sign of Four*. *The Hound of the Baskervilles* formally inscribes memory loss, that 'intense mental concentration' which blots out 'what has passed', as the conclusion to the case.[127] Asked for 'a sketch of the course of events from memory', Holmes refers Watson to his 'notes ... under the heading B in my indexed list of cases', for any forgotten details. He cannot, he says, 'guarantee' that he carries 'all the facts' in his mind. Homosexual blackmail was not one of the issues dealt with by Doyle in his defence of British military conduct during the Boer War, but it appears to have been recorded under the secret inscription of 'HB'.

Where homosexuality is one issue figured by the blackmailing dog, an accompanying Irishness is the other. Hibernia, the 'H' in Britain, remained a problematic letter for Doyle, and Ireland's place in the British union a subject to which he increasingly returned. Wilde's death had led Doyle back to his old fear that Irishness brought with it some unmasculine illness of mind or body, like that which had affected his own father. Unique in its eponymous foregrounding of the 'HB' initials, *The Hound of the Baskervilles* returns to the tell tale footprint of little Tonga in *The Sign of Four*, subjecting the long history of Catholic

Ireland to the condensing influence of the comic spirit. At the time of Sir Charles's murder, Holmes had been tied up with 'that little affair of the Vatican cameos' and in his 'anxiety to oblige the Pope', had 'lost touch with several interesting English cases'.[128]

Significantly, the only eye-witness account of Sir Charles's death is that of Murphy, the gypsy horse-dealer who hears his cries from the moor but is too drunk to respond. As there are no signs of violence on the body, not even a toothmark, Sir Charles's distored facial features indicate the threat of attack rather than its actual occurrence. As Holmes admits, 'there was no direct connection between the hound and the man's death'.[129] Nothing save a single footprint connects the hound with the body of Sir Charles, and most dogs have four. Unlike the combined image of Britain found in *The Sign of Four*, *The Hound of the Baskervilles* carries the sign of one and articulates divorce and Irish insurrection as the darkest fear of this still contemporary gothic novel.

As if in recognition of the fact that the big mongrel had done his best to guarantee British manhood against all redefinitions, subsequent Holmes stories significantly alter the status of the animal. Where animals had previously taken the blame for what they signified – a gap in discourse about the male body – in stories after *The Hound* they are represented as agents of moral truth. In 'The Adventure of the Creeping Man', from *The Case Book of Sherlock Holmes*, Holmes considers 'writing a small monograph upon the use of dogs in the work of the detective' on the grounds that dogs, like children, accurately 'reflect the family life'.[130] In *The Hound of the Baskervilles* the dog is figured as both a fierce ally and a treacherous companion, the ambivalence of its representation finally located in Beryl Baskerville, Stapleton's Puerto Rican wife. The ultimate 'dog', or whipping post, of the story – the figure of Beryl – is, at its climax, so muffled and gagged that 'one could not for the moment tell whether it was that of a man or a woman'. Both lure and warning, anonymous letter-writer and word of truth, Beryl Baskerville-Stapleton articulates bisexuality, not homosexuality, as the missing boot in the mud – the hidden love – which, at the heart of the Holmes stories, dares not speaks its name.

While the ultimate solitude of Holmes's future is figured in the flagellating sands of 'The Lion's Mane' (1927), these stories celebrate the difficult unions, marital and political, scientific and religious, spoken and written, which sustained British manhood for half a century. In *Memories and Adventures*, Doyle recalled his political ambitions after the Boer War, describing as 'one of the tight corners' of his life an occasion when he was obliged, without a moment's notice, to address a meeting of three thousand people. As the 'Irish part' of him came to the rescue, his speech, though he hardly knew what he was saying, had the audience cheering. Reading a newspaper report the following morning, he was astonished at his own conclusion: 'England and Ireland are wedded together with the sapphire wedding ring of the sea, and what God has placed together let no man pluck asunder.'[131] If marriage was the problematic, but obligatory, code both of the Holmes stories and of the private history of the Doyle family encoded in them, that London medical man with the unassuming manner, John H. Watson, had quietly cracked it.

Notes

1. Doyle A. C., 'Preface', *The Casebook of Sherlock Holmes: The Penguin Complete Adventures of Sherlock Holmes*, Harmondsworth: Penguin, 1981, p. 983.
2. Green, R. L. (ed.), *The Uncollected Sherlock Holmes Stories*, Harmondsworth: Penguin, 1983, p. 65.
3. Pearson, H., *Conan Doyle: His Life and Art*, London: Methuen and Co., 1943, p. 96.
4. Doyle, A. C., *Memories and Adventures*, London: John Murray, 1930, p. 128.
5. Doyle, 'Preface', *The Casebook of Sherlock Holmes*: op. cit., p. 983. Note that all further references are from this collected edition.
6. Wilde, O., 'The Decay of Lying' in *The Complete Works of Oscar Wilde*, London: Collins, 1948, p. 971.
7. Ibid., p. 982.
8. Ibid., p. 973.
9. Ibid., p. 980.
10. Doyle, A. C., 'The Adventure of the Illustrious Client', *The Casebook of Sherlock Holmes*, op. cit., p. 984.
11. Doyle, A. C., 'The Musgrave Ritual', *The Memoirs of Sherlock Holmes*, in *The Penguin Complete Adventures of Sherlock Holmes*, Harmondsworth: Penguin, 1981, p. 392.
12. Doyle, 'The Musgrave Ritual', op. cit., p. 396.
13. See Jahn, R., *The Adventures of Sherlock Holmes: Detecting Social Order*, New York: Twayne Publishing, 1995, p. 74.
14. Doyle, 'The Musgrave Ritual', op. cit., p. 390.
15. Doyle, A. C., 'The Bruce-Partington Plans', *His Last Bow* in *The Penguin Complete Adventures of Sherlock Holmes*, Harmondsworth: Penguin, 1981, p. 931.
16. Doyle, 'The Musgrave Ritual', op. cit., p. 387.
17. Kestner, J. A., *Sherlock's Men: Masculinity, Conan Doyle and Cultural History*, Aldershot: Ashgate, 1997, p. 99.
18. Ibid., p. 37.
19. Ibid., p. 39.
20. Ibid., pp. 81–82.
21. Ibid., p. 97.
22. Ibid., p. 39.
23. Ibid., p. 28.

24. Ibid., p. 29.
25. Showalter, E., *Sexual Anarchy: Gender and Culture at the Fin de Siècle*, London: Virago, 1992, pp. 8–9.
26. Kestner, *Sherlock's Men*, op. cit., p. 4.
27. Doyle, A. C., 'The Blue Carbuncle' in *The Adventures of Sherlock Holmes*, in *The Penguin Complete Adventures of Sherlock Holmes*, Harmondsworth: Penguin, 1981, p. 257.
28. Pearsall, R., *Conan Doyle; A Biographical Solution*, Glasgow: Richard Drew Publishing, 1989, p. 64.
29. Holmes, W., *The Autocrat of the Breakfast Table*, London: Walter Scott, 1889, pp. 9–11.
30. Doyle, A. C., 'A Scandal in Bohemia' in *The Adventures*, op. cit., p. 163.
31. Holmes, *The Autocrat of the Breakfast Table*, op. cit., p. 23.
32. Doyle, A. C., 'The Speckled Band' in *The Adventures Of Sherlock Holmes*, p. 264.
33. Holmes, *The Autocrat of the Breakfast Table*, op. cit., p. 43.
34. Ibid., p. 54.
35. Doyle, A. C., 'The Final Problem' in *The Memoirs of Sherlock Holmes*, op. cit., p. 472.
36. Doyle, *Memories and Adventures*, op. cit., p. 94.
37. Dickens, C., *Miscellaneous Papers/The Mystery of Edwin Drood*, London: Hazell, Watson & Viney, 1947, p. 296.
38. Ibid., p. 427.
39. Doyle, A. C., *Through the Magic Door*, London: Smith Elder and Co., 1907, p. 158.
40. Holmes, *The Autocrat of the Breakfast Table*, op. cit., p. 8.
41. Doyle, A. C., *The Sign of Four*, in *The Penguin Complete Adventures of Sherlock Holmes*, Harmondsworth: Penguin, 1981, p. 90.
42. Gissing, G., *The Private Papers of Henry Rycroft*, New York: The New American Library of World Literature, Signet Classics, 1961, pp. 96–7.
43. Winter, D., *Death's Men: Soldiers of the Great War*, Harmondsworth: Penguin, 1979, p. 233.
44. Dickens, C., op. cit., pp. 237–8.
45. Meredith, G., *The Egoist*, Harmondsworth: Penguin, 1968, p. 33.
46. Meredith, G., 'An Essay on Comedy' in Sypher, W. (ed.), *Comedy*, New York: Doubleday Anchor Books, 1956, pp. 49–53.
47. Doyle, A. C., 'The Boscombe Valley Mystery' in *The Adventures*, op. cit., p. 210.
48. Meredith, *The Egoist*, op. cit., p. 37.
49. Doyle, A. C., *A Study in Scarlet*, in *The Penguin Complete Adventures of Sherlock Holmes*, Harmondsworth: Penguin, 1981, p. 49.
50. Doyle, *Memories and Adventures*, op. cit., pp. 289–90.
51. Meredith, *The Egoist*, op. cit., p. 35.
52. Doyle, A. C., 'A Case of Identity' in *The Adventures*, op. cit., p. 191.
53. Doyle, A. C., 'The Adventures of the Copper Beeches' in The *Adventures*, op. cit., p. 317.
54. Doyle, *Memories and Adventures*, op. cit., p. 38.
55. Ross, J., *The Fourth Generation: Reminiscences*, London: Constable & Co., 1912, p. 228.
56. Doyle, A. C., 'His Last Bow' in *His Last Bow*, op. cit., p. 973.
57. Ibid., p. 978.

58. Doyle, *A Study in Scarlet*, op. cit., p. 77.
59. Ibid., p. 82.
60. Ibid., p. 21.
61. Ibid., p. 16.
62. Ibid., p. 19.
63. Ibid., p. 26.
64. See Farewell, B., *Armies of the Raj: From the Great Indian Mutiny to Independence 1858–1947*, London: Viking, 1990.
65. Doyle, *A Study in Scarlet*, op. cit., p. 62.
66. Ibid., p. 38.
67. Doyle, *Through the Magic Door*, op. cit., p. 140.
68. Nisbet, J. F., *Marriage and Heredity: A View of Psychological Evolution*, London: Ward & Downey, 1889, p. 202.
69. Ibid., p. 187.
70. Ibid., pp. 200–201.
71. Priestman, M., *Detective Fiction and Literature*. London: Macmillan, 1990, p. 15.
72. Doyle, A. C., 'The Noble Bachelor' in *The Adventures*, op. cit., p. 296.
73. Nisbet, *Marriage and Heredity*, op. cit., p. 111.
74. Nordon, P., *Conan Doyle*, trans. Frances Partridge, London: John Murray, 1966, p. 176.
75. Ibid., p. 175.
76. Carr, J. D., *The Life of Sir Arthur Conan Doyle*, London: John Murray, 1949, p. 200.
77. Doyle, *Memories and Adventures*, op. cit., p. 125.
78. Pearsall, *Conan Doyle*, op. cit., p. 54.
79. Doyle, *The Sign of Four*, op. cit., p. 109.
80. Ibid., p. 137.
81. Ibid., p. 155.
82. Doyle, *Memories and Adventures*, op. cit., p. 93.
83. Green, M., *The Adventurous Male: Chapters in the History of the White Male Mind*, Pennsylvania: The Pennsylvania State University Press, 1993, p. 2.
84. Doyle, *The Sign of Four*, op. cit., p. 100.
85. Ibid., p. 156.
86. Ibid., p. 93.
87. Ibid., p. 91.
88. Ibid., p. 121.
89. Doyle, *Memories and Adventures*, op. cit., p. 133.
90. Myers, F., *Human Personality*, London: Longmans Green and Co., 1904, p. 71.
91. Ibid., pp. 71–72.
92. Ibid., p. 73.
93. Green, *The Adventurous Male*, op. cit., pp. 5–11.
94. Besant, A., *An Autobiography*, London: T. Fisher Unwin, 1883, p. 340.
95. Myers, *Human Personality*, op. cit., p. 63.
96. Doyle, *Memories and Adventures*, op. cit., p. 102.
97. See Symonds, J., *Madame Blavatsky*, London: Odhams Press Ltd, 1959, p. 222.
98. Doyle, *Memories and Adventures*, op. cit., p. 104.
99. Ibid., p. 107.

100. Ibid., p. 115.
101. Pearson, *Conan Doyle*, op. cit., pp. 92–3.
102. Sartre, J. P., *Words*, Harmondsworth: Penguin, 1967, p. 11.
103. Freud, S. and Breuer, J., *Studies on Hysteria*, The Pelican Freud Library Vol. 3, Harmondsworth: Penguin, 1974, p. 174.
104. Doyle, A. C., 'The Engineer's Thumb' in *The Adventures*, op. cit., p. 273.
105. Doyle, A. C., 'The Beryl Coronet' in *The Adventures*, op. cit., pp. 301–302.
106. Doyle, A. C., 'A Case of Identity' in *The Adventures*, op. cit., p. 199.
107. Doyle, A. C., 'The Gloria Scott' in *The Memoirs*, op. cit., p. 374.
108. Ibid., p. 385.
109. Pinkerton, M. W., *Murder in All Ages*, Chicago: A. E. Pinkerton & Co., 1898, pp. 401–19.
110. Doyle, A. C., 'The Priory School' in *The Return of Sherlock Holmes*, in *The Penguin Complete Adventures of Sherlock Holmes*, Harmondsworth: Penguin, 1981, pp. 538–9.
111. Ibid., p. 539.
112. Doyle, *Memories and Adventures*, op. cit., pp. 309–10.
113. Hawkins, H., *The Reminiscences of Sir Henry Hawkins*, London: Thomas Nelson & Sons, 1904, p. 249.
114. Meredith, *The Egoist*, op. cit., p. 37.
115. Doyle, A. C., *The Hound of The Baskervilles*, in *The Penguin Complete Adventures of Sherlock Holmes*, Harmondsworth: Penguin, 1981, p. 760.
116. Ibid., p. 700.
117. Doyle, A. C., *Memories and Adventures*, op. cit., p. 234.
118. Ibid., p. 236.
119. Doyle, *The Hound of The Baskervilles*, op. cit., p. 726.
120. Ibid., p. 701.
121. Ibid., p. 744.
122. Ibid., p. 742.
123. Ibid., p. 695.
124. Ibid., p. 701.
125. Ibid., p. 742.
126. See Wilson, H. W., *After Pretoria: The Guerilla War*, vol. 2, London: The Amalgamated Press Ltd, 1902, p. 687.
127. Doyle, *The Hound of The Baskervilles*, op. cit., p. 761.
128. Ibid., p. 677.
129. Ibid., p. 747.
130. Doyle, A. C., 'The Creeping Man' in *The Casebook*, op. cit., p. 1071.
131. Doyle, *Memories and Adventures*, op. cit., pp. 109–10.

CHAPTER FOUR

Tortured Bodies and Nervous Narratives: The Novels of the 1890s

Masculinity in crisis

In 1891 Doyle took his wife to Vienna, ostensibly to further his career as an ophthamologist by acquiring some prestigious European qualifications. Instead, he wrote *The Doings of Raffles Haw* (1891), the story of a modern-day alchemist who can manufacture gold but cannot find it in other people. A parable of Doyle's own creative resources, the novel centres on Haw's involvement with a brother and sister who make use of his friendship to escape the clutches of a scheming alcoholic father. The brother, an artist who specializes in historical genre painting, tries to further his career by forming a business partnership with the gold-producing Raffles Haw. In 1891 a similar partnership between history and alchemy was emerging as the motive force for Doyle's career too, for, in writing the Holmes stories, he had learnt how to transform the base metals of his early life into a lucrative fictional commodity.

In the middle of writing the twelve stories that constituted *The Adventures of Sherlock Holmes*, Doyle published a short novel which contrasted sharply with *The Strand* series and its project of resymbolizing the father. *Beyond the City* (1891) offers a radical realization of emancipated womanhood and the main problematic of the emergent Women's Movement. Recalling the novel in *Memories and Adventures*, Doyle drew attention to this act of literary cross-dressing in a largely apocryphal anecdote about the pirated edition which appeared in New York:

> ... the rascal publisher thinking that a portrait – any sort of portrait – of the author would look well upon the cover, and being quite ignorant of my identity, put a very pretty and over-dressed young woman as my presentment. I still have a copy of this most flattering representation.[1]

The suburban location of *Beyond the City* is its controlling image. The novel situates its representation of emancipated womanhood only just beyond that masculine sphere of power play, criminal deviancy and intellectual control which is the domain of Sherlock Holmes. Beginning with the sale of a field inherited by two elderly spinsters, the two Miss Williams watch the conversion of the countryside they have known as girls into a building plot. The new houses built there are, for the most part, purchased by successful men who are now *beyond* the city, attempting to fill the professional and commercial void in their lives created by retirement. The private sphere of the suburban home is celebrated as a feminized space, one desirably 'free from the sordid aims and base ambitions which drag down the man whose business lies too exclusively in the money market of the vast Babylon'.[2]

Novelists of Doyle's generation constructed the interface between city and country as a site for a contest between genders. In *Beyond the City* an unusually radical exchange of gender roles takes place there. One of the new villas is bought by a retired admiral for his wife and son. A second is purchased by a widowed doctor, whose inheritance of a large sum of money has enabled him to concentrate on scientific research, while his two attractive daughters keep house. The occupation of the third villa, however, designates this territory as one of advancing women as well as of retiring men. The nervous sisters watch with alarm the arrival of Mrs Westmacott, a 'new woman' whose nephew seems to have adopted the bull pup once owned by Dr Watson. Witnessing a fracas with the cab driver, the two Miss Williams quickly sense that there is something unusual about this new neighbour:

> The lady passed him a coin, there was a moment of mumbling and gesticulating, and suddenly she had him with both hands by the red cravat which girt his neck, and was shaking him as a terrier would a rat. Right across the pavement she thrust him, and, pushing him up against the wheel, she banged his head three several times against the side of his own vehicle.[3]

Mrs Westmacott is described as 'the type of the woman of the future'[4] and she certainly has more in common with the cinematic superwomen of the 1990s than the doubt-ridden protofeminists of the previous century. As a novel of the 1890s, *Beyond the City* is remarkable for its sympathetic portrayal of an active feminist whose conduct is endorsed so long as she does not threaten, or aspire to, the institution of companionate marriage. Although Mrs Westmacott transforms the image of the single woman, she remains within its categorization. While the widowed Dr Walker is immediately fascinated by the handsome woman with the pet snake in her pocket, his two daughters believe that their mother's memory is sacred and that the quiet doctor would be deeply unhappy were he to marry a woman who is 'all decision'.[5]

To persuade the doctor of the folly of his attachment, his daughters themselves enact a charade of emancipation, adopting the self-oriented life-styles of professional women. Faced with chemistry experiments at the breakfast table and daughters who drink rum while training to be pilots, the doctor is soon brought to see sense. Clara and Ida, who have not the slightest difficulty in assuming their new roles, revert to type once the experiment is over and the threat to their position in the family averted. As Mrs Westmacott had never had the slightest intention of marrying their father, and chooses an academic career in America instead, 'the marriage question' is left undisturbed by a novel presciently aware of the threats to it.

Last heard of as a Professor at Emancipation College in Denver, 'where mighty thunderbolts are being forged which will one day bring the dominant sex upon their knees',[6] Mrs Westmacott is portayed as neither ridiculous nor tragic. She rejects the complex interior discourses of 'the new woman' in favour of more challenging forms of physical exercise. Her view that the subserviency of women is 'largely due to her abandoning nutrious drinks [stout] and invigorating exercises to the male', and her total rejection of the pernicious ideology of 'woman's mission', make her a powerful spokeswoman for her cause:

> What is this mission which is reserved for woman? All that is humble, that is mean, that is soul-killing, that is so contemptible and so ill-paid that none other will touch it. All that is woman's mission ... . Her mission! To be thankful for coppers and not to interfere with the men while they grapple for gold, like swine round a trough, that is man's reading of the mission of woman.'[7]

Entertaining Mrs Westmacott and her nephew, the two Miss Williams feel both terrified and amused 'at the sight of the fiery domineering victim and the big apologetic representative of mankind who sat meekly bearing all the sins of his sex'.[8]

While Mrs Westmacott is gently caricatured by this comedy, her nephew is not represented as castrated by her powerful phallic presence. He wins the hand of Dr Walker's daughter, Ida, and becomes a flourishing ranchman in Texas. Unlike the anguished, renunciatory heroines of Thomas Hardy's fiction, Doyle's 'new woman' is not dogged by original sin or its gothic shadows, but instead reflects his own preference for heroines of the eighteenth-century style. In *Through the Magic Door* he had praised the novelists of the previous century for their model women:

> There is one characteristic, the rarest and subtlest of all, which each of them had in a supreme degree. Each could draw the most delightful women – the most perfect women, I think, in the whole range of our literature. If the eighteenth-century women were like that, then the eighteenth-century men got a great deal more than they ever deserved ... even now they become our ideals. One cannot come to know them without a double emotion, one of respectful devotion towards themselves, and the other of abhorence for the herd of swine who surrounded them.[9]

Unlike Freud who questioned a fundamental female lack, Doyle had little doubt as to what it was that women wanted: they wanted good masculine performance, both within the family and outside it, or space in which to perform themselves. It is the men in this novel who need rescue and support as they attempt to learn a masculinity, no longer located in mastery of the physical world but constructed through the commercial rivalries of the city. While the doctor's elder daughter, Clara, is taught by Mrs Westmacott to be both more aggressive and less self-sacrificing, her fiancée, Harold Denver, a junior partner in a firm of stockbrokers, finds himself in serious trouble when his partner embezzles the firm's money and leaves him facing ruin in an uncongenial profession:

> He had inherited from his father his love of the air of heaven, his affection for a manly and natural existence. To act as middleman between the pursuer of wealth and the wealth which he pursued, or to stand as a human barometer, registering the rise and fall of the great mammon pressure in the markets, was not the work for which Providence had placed those broad shoulders and strong limbs upon his well-knit frame.[10]

The threat of impending bancruptcy is one that confronts, not just a firm of stockbrokers, but the wider masculine community. As Harold's retired father, Admiral Denver, ventures into the city to try to help his son by selling his pension, he quickly finds himself out of his depth among the sharks, money lenders and working women who constitute its inhabitants. Seeing a barrow woman struck by a male companion, he intervenes disastrously to save her from further hurt only to find himself attacked by both parties. Not a stereotypical gender victim, the woman's 'grip was as strong as a man's, and her wrist pressed like an iron bar upon the admiral's throat'.[11] The admiral's class-blind chivalry receives a further blow when the police point out that the woman has stolen his watch with one hand while throttling him with the other!

The separate cultures of class and caste contextualize Doyle's representation of gender in his early novels which are concerned with masculinity in the private sphere. He described his domestic novels as being 'on a very inferior plane' to that more complex questioning of masculine lack found in a novel he identified as 'near the front of my work for merit',[12] *The Great Shadow* (1892). A reconstruction of the Battle of Waterloo, this resymbolization of a historical memoir as Victorian adventure story gives an ample opportunity to copy other men's writing and to don the glamorous costume of Napoleonic history. What men want, in this novel of masculine lack, is to take part in the ludic drama of history – though preferably after the event.

The story of Jock Calder, who has the nickname 'Union Jack' because the borders between England and Scotland run through the bedroom of his house, *The Great Shadow* highlights Doyle's concern with narration as an act which enacts a fundamental gender problem. While the novel's subject is the final defeat of Napoleon, fear of whom 'hung like a black shadow over all Europe',[13] the Battle of Waterloo acquires significance because it allows the story of the common man to be told as part of the collective masculine enterprise of history. The narrative works so effectively because of the changes of perspective affecting its individual testimony and the constantly revised judgements of manhood and masculine value that those changes necessitate. Moving from local rivalries in love to the political rivalries across Europe, the novel simultaneously elegizes Romantic masculinity and problematizes its field of enactment.

The field of Waterloo is itself described after the battle as 'one huge butcher's shop, where poor devils had been ripped and burst and smashed'.[14] The meaning of the battle is represented as the erasure of a type of masculine writing dictatorially imposed on the land itself. While Waterloo removes the military dictatorship of Napoleon, 'the shadow of that great man over yonder, who had scrawled his name in red letters over the map of Europe',[15] a similar shadow-writing threatens the disappearance of the narrative itself. Jock Calder began his memoir lightheartedly:

> ... but as I went on I wakened a thousand sleeping sorrows and half-forgotten griefs, and now my soul is all as raw as the hide of an ill-sheared sheep. If I come safely out of it I will swear never to set pen to paper again, for it is so easy at first, like walking into a shelving stream, and then before you can look round you are off your feet and down in a hole.[16]

The narration of painful memory is troped here as a masculine mire which darkens the glory of the battlefield and erases the Romantic inscription of masculinity imprinted on it. In his reminiscences Jock Calder is left uncertain whether he has been manned or unmanned by his participation in the great military drama.

The Great Shadow is an impressive piece of work but it is remarkable not just for its reconstruction of a major historical event, but also for its treatment of its enigmatic heroine, 'cousin Edie'. As inspirer of the adventure, Edie is herself subject to transformation. Beginning as a female cousin whom the boyish narrator does not want to play with, she returns as romantic object, as seducer and betrayer and, eventually, as traitor. With her strange, far-away gaze which she directs at men, landscapes and horizons, Edie is both a storyteller in her own right and the inspiration of male narratives and masculine rivalry. Hardy had created a similar heroine in Elfrida in *A Pair of Blue Eyes* (1873), one whose emotional betrayals and romantic attachments to ever more successful men are a stimulus to male competition and endeavour. In Hardy's novel, as in Doyle's, the heroine herself finally falls victim to her own sexual mobility as a *femme fatale* married to an aristocrat who dies in childbirth.

For the narrator, Cousin Edie, 'shining and unstable, like a drop of quicksilver'[17] embodies 'the queerness that lies in a woman'.[18] Quickly replacing one man with another, Edie is an adventuress who carries the unstable meaning of the masculine text of war. A sun worshipper in a world of great shadows, Edie is ultimately an airy essence without fixed meaning. In his relationship with her, Jock feels 'a fear that I was like the man who set forth to lay hands upon the rainbow, and that the real Edie Calder, however near she might seem, was in truth for ever beyond my reach'.[19] He is right. In his failure to capture the meaning of his muse, the narrator images the problematic of the glamorous war story.

The question of how to see and tell the essentially masculine story of war in the modern age vexed the most thoughtful of the late-Victorian writers. Sharing Doyle's fascination with the Napoleonic period as a definitive – and lost – site of Romantic masculinity, Thomas Hardy described war as a 'Clash of Peoples, artificially brought about'. He saw its representation as a dilemma for a contemporary culture increasingly located in 'a meditative world' that is 'older, more invidious, more nervous, more quizzical, than it once was ... unhappily perplexed by – Riddles of Death Thebes never knew'.[20] While their wives judged 'beautiful baby' competitions together, Doyle and Hardy engaged in intertextual debate, Doyle's fiction dramatizing practical solutions to the quizzical riddles posed by Hardy's writing. The friendship between these two men, their common interests and their difference of perspective, is itself one of the more interesting grounds of debate in the literature of late-Victorian masculinity.

In the novels that he wrote in the early 1890s Doyle was still trying to assimilate English cultural perspectives and to acquire a narrative voice that could represent with conviction the hegemonic perspectives of the British Empire. In *Micah Clarke* he had tried to replicate and revise the voice of English Puritanism prior to the Bloodless Revolution of 1688. He completed that process in *The Refugees*, a matching story of French Protestantism concerned with the expulsion of the Huguenots by King Louis XIV and their resettlement in the New World. Doyle's account of *The Refugees* in *Memories and Adventures* describes a visit paid by his mother to Fontainebleau after the novel's publication. The party with which Mary Doyle was travelling was told by their guide that 'if they really wanted to know about the Court of the great monarch, they would find the clearest and most accurate account in an Englishman's book, *The Refugees*'. Doyle adds: 'I expect the guide would have been considerably astonished had he then and there been kissed by an elderly English lady, but it was an experience which he must have narrowly missed.'[21]

While this novel succeeded in clarifying Doyle's Englishness, it also generated identity confusion elsewhere. *The Refugees* was, he recalls, read aloud by the Reverend Mother of a 'strict Irish convent' who had inadvertently mistaken him for a Canon Doyle. The nuns, riveted by early scenes of sexuality in the French Court, were eager for her to maintain her error until she had finished the book.[22]

Son of a masterful mother, Louis XIV is shown as fatally divided between two woman who fight for control of his body and spirit. In chosing the virtuous, intelligent, cordon bleu cooking, tool of the Catholic Church, Madame de Maintenon, rather than her arrogant, irreligious rival, Madame de Montespan, Louis opts to expel the most industrious and able sector of the populace from his kingdom. In revoking the Edict of Nantes, he becomes a man divided from his own duality, a single spirit driving out its most vital and productive oppositions: 'France ... had but one voice, with which she spoke through him'.[23]

A reverse image of Louis's absolutism is reflected from the New World through the figure of the American frontiersman, Greysolon du Lhut, who rejects writing, place and religion in a similar bid to represent an adventurous essentialism. Du Lhut is:

> ... a man whose whole life had been spent in pushing westward ... saying little, writing nothing, but always the first wherever there was danger to meet or difficulty to overcome. It was ... pure love of nature and of adventure, with so little ambition that he had never cared to describe his own travels.[24]

Between these two polarities are men, like the expelled Huguenots, forced to identify themselves through the contradictions of their own position. A Huguenot captain of the guards is offered promotion by Louis XIV on condition that he accepts the Revocation of the Edict and abandons his own beliefs. Relatively uninterested in religion himself, Captain De Catinat nonetheless declines the promotion, suddenly becoming aware of his position as a spokesman for others: '... he seemed for the instant to see that countless throng of men, women, and children of his own faith, all unable to say a word for themselves, and all looking to him as their champion.'[25]

The dialectical self-doublings of the relationship with language constitute Doyle's recurrent image for a masculinity energized by the tensions of its own self-representation. When Louis, fearing for his soul if he offends the Catholic Church, insists that 'France's religion should be that of France's king',[26] De Catinat becomes one of a party of refugees to a French colony of Canada.

Doyle described *The Refugees* as 'really two books with the Atlantic rolling between them'.[27] As in all his writing, it is at the point of intersection – the place of narrative crossing – that the meaning of masculinity emerges most clearly. Having rejected the image of the king as father, De Catinat initiates an alternative 'New World' narrative of masochistic pain-play and providential rewards. On the long voyage across the Atlantic, disaster finds its sea legs as part of a comic roll towards the emergence of a new manhood. This crossing point is the place of the magician who transforms stories of disaster into those of opportunity and adventure. This archetype is figured in the novel by the ship's captain, Ephraim Savage, a shark-eating man with an endless capacity for survival. Apparently lost at sea, he reappears in a magical grotto revealed by his ship as it is torn open on an ice cap, disclosing a place of refuge for the travellers within the ice itself. This frozen but beautiful landscape of masochism and inner resource is used in *The Refugees* as the place of passage between the old world with its mono-lithic forms of power and the new world of democratic adventures. The transition is marked by the death of De Catinat's father, an old Hugue-not merchant who dies prophesying the future glory of the New World.

The Refugees is, at the level of plot, a novel about the amorous tensions at the court of King Louis XIV and the racial tensions of new-world America. The link between the two stories is a shared preoccupation with torture. The motif of the tortured body is first introduced through the man most responsible for persuading Louis to revoke the Edict of Nantes, the fanatical Abbé du Chayla who had used his own martyred limbs to image the future damnation of the the king if he refused.

An even more intensified image of torture characterizes the Jesuit missionary, Ignatius Morat, who strolls the forests of the New World involved in a fatal mission to convert the Iroquois Indians. Repeatedly tortured by the recipients of his religious message, Morat remains cheer-fully 'hopeful of martyrdom',[28] regarding his graphically described wrecked body and scalped head as the sign of spiritual grace.

In contrast to the spiritual rigorousness of the Abbé du Chayla, however, Father Morat figures a comedic generosity of spirit, represent-ing his repeated torture as a form of lively dialogue between himself and the ferocious Iroquois. Even with his shins blown off so that he can hardly walk, he remains undaunted. The Iroquois, he insists, are merely 'mischievous children – merry hearted but mischievous ... they are not to be blamed. No, no, it would be uncharitable to blame them ... . They sank little charges of powder into my legs and then they exploded them ... '.[29] Since the rules of his Order and of Holy Church maintain that a maimed man cannot perform holy rites, Father Morat is on his way to Quebec to obtain a special dispensation from his bishop in order to continue his mission.

As aids to conversion, Father Morat carries with him two pictures 'crudely coloured and gaudy', one representing a smiling man at rest with a musical instrument in his hand, while in the other 'a similar man was screaming at the pitch of his lungs, while half-a-dozen black creatures were battering him with poles and prodding him with lances'.[30] The second image of 'the damned soul' is, he admits, more effective in developing the spiritual life of the Iroquois, as the joys of paradise seem poorly represented to them without beavers or tobacco pipes. Crude though they are, these contrasting body images lie at the centre of the novel's preoccupation with religious difference.

Where hell and torture are concepts meaningful to Catholic and Iroquois alike, and where even the adventurous Puritan, Captain Ephraim, sees life as the trial of a fundamentally sinful human spirit, the manhood of the New World strives to refigure this iconized suffering. The woodsman, Amos Green, believes that the world is seeking to realize the signs of its own happiness by creating a new episteme of the body. As Father Morat painfully discovers, the Iroquois Indians already inhabit a different body-map to that of the French colonialists. For the Iroquois nail-biting is not a sign of worry as for their Christian counterparts. Instead they have a habit of biting the nails off their prisoners as a first taste of all the tortures to come. Yet, although they find amusement in their cruelty, the Iroquois are perfectly able to enjoy a joke turned against themselves. Dying with a hatchet in his skull, an old Iroquois warrior is convulsed with laughter. Du Lhut explains: 'It's a custom they have when they get their death-blow. I've known a Seneca chief laugh for six hours on end at the torture-stake. Ah, he's gone!'[31]

Questions of what the body represents are particularly well posed by the Iroquois. From a distance, the soldiers of a French garrison appear to be taking part in a silent drill exercise. Closer up, the account of their body posture is very different:

> They were lashed to low posts with willow withies, some twenty of them, naked all, and twisted and screwed into every strange shape which an agonised body could assume. In front ... was the gray-headed commandant, with two cinders thrust into his sockets and his flesh hanging from him like a beggar's rags. Behind was the line of men, each with his legs charred off to the knees, and his body so haggled and scorched and burst that the willow bands alone seemed to hold it together.[32]

Doyle's fiction of the 1890s demonstrates a former doctor's continuing interest in the masculine body's nervous system and its often puzzling manifestations. He found the torturing humour of the Iroquois alive in the late-Victorian man of letters. In *Memories and Adventures*, he describes James Payn, the literary editor of *The Cornhill Magazine* in the 1880s, whose brilliant wit was closely linked to a serious medical disorder:

> I knew him best in his latter days, when he was crippled with
> illness, and his poor fingers so twisted with rheumatic arthritis that
> they seemed hardly human. He was intensely pessimistic as to his
> own fate. 'Don't make any mistake, Doyle, death is a horrible
> thing – horrible! I suffer the agonies of the damned!' But five
> minutes later he would have his audience roaring with laughter,
> and his own high treble laugh would be the loudest of all.[33]

In the dialectical oppositions and doubled representations of Doyle's
writing of manhood, the site of humour is the point of intersection
between two narratives and two bodies, each pulling in a different
direction. Torture is, therefore, for Doyle one mode of masculine self-
realization.

For Doyle the year in which *The Refugees* was published was one of
crisis and redefinition. His recorded memories of 1893 are subject to
considerable distortion. It was the year of his father's death, and also
the year in which his marriage to Louise was given a terminal sentence.
This break in emotional continuity was famously figured in the simultaneous demise of Sherlock Holmes, offspring of these strangely creative
partnerships. It was also the year that Doyle joined the Society for
Psychical Research, having replaced the temptations of Madame
Blavatsky's Theosophy with a more appropriately masculine and 'scientific' study of the psychic phenomena which so fascinated him.

On a visit to Switzerland that would seal the fate of Sherlock Holmes
and condemn Touie to a prolonged life of invalidism, Doyle began work
on a new literary venture which was published in 1895 as *The Stark
Munro Letters*. Stephen Knight has viewed this novel as an exercise in
vulnerability because Doyle, for once, was writing without the comfort-
ing presence of Holmes.[34] Vulnerability is certainly a theme in *The
Stark Munro Letters* and even more so in the little-known novella, *The
Parasite*, which was serialized by Lloyd's Weekly Newspaper in the
autumn of 1894. While *The Refugees* had been written in conscious
imitation of Scott and Alexandre Dumas (*père*), *The Parasite – A Mesmeric and Hypnotic Mystery. Told in Extracts from the Diary of Austin
Gilroy, Professor of Physiology*, uses a form of comedic gothicism that
was particularly significant for Doyle. He used it to dramatize the
tortures by which masculinity was systematized within a sensitive body.
Novels whose narratives are situated at the autobiographical interface
between literature and medical science, these two texts offer stories of
nervous men and the strategies they use to overcome and still their
nervousness.

In a recent study of this literary–medical meeting point, *Nerves and
Narratives* (1997), Peter Melville Logan defines the 'new body' emerging from medical science during the late eighteenth century as one

peculiarly susceptible to hysteria and neurasthenia. The medical discourse surrounding this newly identified 'nervous body' was a seriously contested one, leading to the development of psychoanalysis on the one hand and to behaviourism on the other. Logan summarizes the relativity of the body's story in the history of medicine:

> Medicine at any given moment produces an all-encompassing narrative of the body, describing its processes of growth and aging, its daily cycles and monthly rhythms. Each disease, from the onset of symptoms to termination, has its own story, case histories their own ploys. Medicine, too, in its historical dimension, creates its own evolving narrative of the body, and its etiologies change and its taxonomies reconfigure. It is in this medical narrative itself, with its inescapable historical relativity, that the authority of medicine to tell the story of the body is most called into question.[35]

For Logan 'the nervous body' is an episteme of a certain stage of cultural definition – one that is particularly useful 'for writers engaged in social criticism',[36] for the nervous body has, as one of its symptoms, a tendency to talk about itself and to produce a critique of the social conditions to which its etiology is linked. Logan thus sees the nervous system as a vital field of interconection between the two disciplines of medicine and literature.

According to Logan, the later nineteenth century worked with a different model of the body to that of the early part of the century, partly as a result of pioneering studies of the nervous system such as Marshall Hall's research into reflexes published as *Memoirs of the Nervous System* in 1837. Hall argued for two distinct nervous systems in the body, one centred in the brain, the other in the spine. His research led to a revisioning of the body as something with 'two distinct stories, one of voluntary action operating through the brain, and a second of a species' distant past, operating independently through the spinal system'.[37] This account challenged earlier thought and contributed to a changed aesthetic of body representation. In place of the Romantic 'sincere body', in which external signs corresponded to, and made manifest internal emotions, Victorian fiction confronted 'two separate epistemologies of the body, one in which signs have a strong connection to a single central meaning ... and the other in which signs have a weak connection to diffused, multiple meanings'.[38] Victorian writers consequently represented bodies as sites of a multiple and sometimes contradictory narrative.

Few were more contradictory than Doyle's. Bodies in his fiction, particularly those of doctors such as John H. Watson, undergo the most excruciating distortions while retaining their identity as characters. This process of distortion is crucial to the trajectory of his career. Doyle's fiction in the 1890s moves dramatically from representations of nervous bodies with their narratives of pain and self-disassociation to those which have, in the service of empire, rejected this narrative as unmasculine and untrue. While Doyle's historical novels invariably fore-ground the brutality of practices against the body, his tales of contemporary life focus on nervous bodies learning to externalize their story and project it as crime, adventure or a struggle against difficult 'others'. This is the subject of the two novels that followed *The Refugees*: fictions which came to be accorded a very different status in Doyle's estimation of them.

Whereas *The Stark Munro Letters* came to stand in place of autobi-ography, Doyle was later dismissive of *The Parasite*, linking it with *Beyond the City* as an inferior text which imaged female power and domination in place of the doubled story of masculinity. Where the earlier novel had featured a formidably emancipated and enterprising new woman, *The Parasite* has the occult shadow of that emancipation, the witch-figure, at its centre.

The encounter between science and occultism at the heart of *The Parasite* is recorded in the diary of a nervous young scientist who finds himself succumbing to the powers of a crippled, middle-aged, Trinadadian mesmerist, Helen Penelosa. The diary exposes the emotional vulnerabilities and sexual repressions hidden beneath Gilroy's scientific pursuits and his middle-class English lifestyle, anchoring the story into a subjectivity that helplessly describes its own disturbance. Ostensibly using his diary to strengthen his own self-image, Gilroy unwittingly illustrates that tendency of the nervous body to supply a narrative of itself that is the very symptom of its own condition. Initially sceptical about mesmerism, Gilroy realizes with horror, that not only is he an excellent subject for it, but also that it has unleashed within him a passionate sexuality every bit as masochistic as his diary habit:

> April 26 – Ten days have elapsed since I have had the heart to make any entry in my journal. Why should I record my own humiliation and degradation! I had vowed never to open it again. And yet the force of habit is strong, and here I find myself taking up once more the record of my own dreadful experiences – in much the same spirit in which a suicide has been known to take notes of the effects of the poison which killed him.[39]

Gilroy is appalled to discover that his passionate sexual feelings have been aroused by a woman who in no way resembles the conventional model of female desirability. While his fiancée is a pink-cheeked middle-class English rose, Miss Penelosa, with her sinister tapping crutch, strongly resembles a Trinidadian Jane Eyre:

> She was a small, frail creature, well over forty, I should say, with a pale, peaky face, and hair of a very light shade of chestnut. Her

presence was insignificant and her manner retiring ... . Her eyes
were perhaps her most remarkable, and also, I am compelled to
say, her least pleasant feature.[40]

Appalled to hear himself, at Miss Penelosa's suggestion, reject his
own fiancée as 'conventional', he nonetheless finds himself compelled
to act out increasingly dramatic erasures of English identity. While his
colleagues are rendered immune to mesmerism by their 'phlegmatic
Saxon temperament', Gilroy says of himself 'I am black and Celtic, and
this hag's clutch is deep in my nerves'.[41] Under the mesmeric influence
of his own interiority, he finds himself disturbing the gravity of the
lecture theatres with silly jokes, drinking songs and intense personal
abuse of his students. While robbing the Bank of England, he experiences complete cultural alienation:

> And the most dreadful part of it all is my own loneliness. Here I sit
> in a commonplace English bow-window looking out upon a com-
> monplace English street ... and behind me there hangs a shadow
> which is out of all keeping with the age and place. In the home of
> knowledge I am weighed down and tortured by a power of which
> science knows nothing.[42]

The novella centres on Gilroy's struggle to reject the double consciousness which the mesmeric experiments have imposed on him and
to retain that unitary Romantic sincerity of the body for which the
solipsistic diary is the ideal literary form. The strength of the story lies
in its ability to describe the unremitting nervous conflict resulting from
his addiction to the alien and yet familiar personality-substance invad-
ing his own. Like De Quincey with his opium addiction, Gilroy can
produce ever more graphic accounts of his own symptoms, but cannot
overcome them:

> It was all wonderfully clear, and yet disassociated from the rest of
> my life, as the incidents of even the most vivid dream might be. A
> peculiar double consciousness possessed me. There was the pre-
> dominant alien will, which was bent upon drawing me to the side
> of its owner, and there was the feebler protesting personality, which
> I recognised as being myself, tugging feebly at the overmastering
> impulse as a led terrier might at its chain.[43]

A reluctant love-slave to the unprofitable Miss Penelosa, he sees himself
as a lapdog rejoicing in his own psychic subjugation.

Far from being the demonic *femme fatale*, however, Helen Penelosa
also emerges as a lonely figure who feels that Gilroy, after making
passionate love to her, now wishes to reject and insult her. The diary
ends as Gilroy, on the verge of throwing vitriol at his fiancée, suddenly
realizes he has the power to resist the mesmeric influence: 'At the
thought of what I might have done my worn nerves broke down and I

sat shivering and twitching, the pitiable wreck of a man.'[44] He only has the power, however, because his mesmerist is dead and the abruptness of the ending leaves unexplored any alternative explanations for his sense of 'possession'. The possibility of genuine mesmeric power contends with nervous exhaustion due to overwork, the sexual repression of intense academic achievement or fault-lines in his own identity which must exclude and label as foreign its own emotional desires.

The Parasite is Doyle's most irresolute account of that battle with the masochistic muse out of which new phases of manhood and writing could be born. The needs and narratives of the inner man – nervous, emotional and sexual – are not to be trusted as they disrupt the conventional representation of English manhood. As the diary reaches the end of what it can say of itself by performing its own narrative castration, its abrupt ending mirrors the sudden death of the mesmerist, offering the description of interiority itself as the second, and most real, parasite of the story.

In the annals of Victorian occultism, the figure of the parasite is a clearly identified psychic reality – that of the 'monstrous dweller on the threshold'[45] who betokens an increase of mental energy and capability if she is successfully confronted, but threatens madness if she is not. Writing The Parasite did indeed involve the crossing of some threshold for Doyle, for it unlocked the novel he really wanted to write, one in which a nervous male body cures its own condition and makes a successfully public declaration of manhood.

This story was told in The Stark Munro Letters, serialized by The Idler in the autumn of 1894 and published by Longmans in book form in 1895. In Memories and Adventures Doyle insists that The Stark Munro Letters is an explicitly autobiographical novel which reproduces, and indeed recycles, the events which brought him to Southsea in the first place. These events concerned his friendship and shared medical practice with George Turnavine Budd, the fellow student whose fortuitous intervention in Doyle's life drew him away from Scotland and the disturbances of his Edinburgh upbringing.

Doyle finished the novel in January 1894, twelve years after the real-life events recalled within it. When he came to write his autobiography nearly thirty years later, what he remembered of the episode was the book he had already written. Nonetheless, despite the time lag, the chapter of Memories and Adventures which records this brief friendship is a compelling one, to which all Doyle's biographers have been drawn, seeing in Budd a figure of lifelong inspiration for Doyle.[46] Budd is ambiguously recalled as a rescuer and a betrayer, a deeply entertaining villain caught in the coils of his own energy and enterprise. Transmuted through Doyle's writing into the character of Dr Cullingworth, Budd becomes a mirror for Doyle's own identity formation, supplying the model of a masculine archetype which Doyle would convert to his own use. Doyle's description of him emphasizes his multifaceted capacity for masculine performance. He is a potentially 'great man' whose tragic flaw is significantly located in the size of his aspirations:

> He was a man born for trouble and adventure, unconventional in his designs and formidable powers of execution – a man of action with a big but incalculable brain guiding the action. He died in early middle age, and I understand that an autopsy revealed some cerebral abnormality, so that there was no doubt a pathological element in his strange explosive character.[47]

Relentlessly self-aggrandizing, Cullingworth promotes himself as larger than life. Leaving England at the end of the novel, with global plans for a new ophthalmic enterprise, he rejects the former practice he has shared with Stark Munro on account of its modest scale:

> 'Too provincial, my boy! What's the good of a village practice with a miserable three thousand or so a year for a man that wants room to spead? My head was sticking out at one end of Bradfield and my feet at the other. Why, there wasn't room for Hetty in the place, let alone me! I've taken to the eye, my boy. There's a fortune in the eye ... . There's money in ears but the eye is a gold mine.'[48]

While Cullingworth is a version of the magician archetype, a clown, conjurer and mountebank, he nonetheless, by his own extremes, teaches the secret of balance to the young practitioner with whom he works. *The Stark Munro Letters* offers an account of manhood gradually established through contact with various kinds of masculine madness. At the troubled outset of Stark Munro's medical career, he finds himself listening to the advice of his fellow student: 'Old Cullingworth always had a very high opinion of lunatics for beginner. "Get a lunatic, my boy! Get a lunatic!" he used to say.'[49] It is precisely these encounters with mental instability, including that of Dr Cullingworth himself, which eventually enable Stark Munro to ground his own manhood in the secure conventions of bourgeois professional life. The 'Letters' of the novel's title record his erratic progress towards this goal and are sent to Herbert Swanborough, a settled and conventionally pious friend in Lowell, Massachusetts who eventually edits them. The piety is important as Stark Munro struggles to ascertain whether his own nervousness is a sign of a lost spirituality or a defective manhood.

The Parasite charted a power struggle with a psychic interiority externalized as middle-aged, celtic and female. In *The Stark Munro Letters*, the contest is between an inner and an outer man and the various writings which connect or separate them in their gradual exchange of identities. Whereas the diarist of *The Parasite* is repelled by the woman who mesmerises him, Stark Munro is frankly fascinated by the forceful eccentric charm of Dr Cullingworth. Part of Doyle's success as a writer lay in his ability to transform into masculine lines the psychic effects associated with the Victorian figure of the *femme fatale* so that masculinity itself became the desired muse of his writing.

Dr Stark Munro writes of Cullingworth 'He is one of those men who make a kind of magnetic atmosphere, so that you feel exhilarated and stimulated in their presence'.[50] Despite his charismatic presence, Cullingworth offers a materialist version of the masculine. He rejects any notion of an inner spirit in favour of a doubled externality, his strong physical presence reinforced by his skill as a self-publicist and his rapport with the local newspaper. This assertive extroversion, however, conceals an inner vulnerability in the places of the spirit that amounts to paranoia. Like General Heatherstone in *The Mystery of Cloomber*, he lives in secluded privacy with his wife, in phobic dread of being poisoned by invisible enemies. With an insider's knowledge of the medical profession, he both rejects and exploits its mystique, justifying his rule-breaking disregard for medical etiquette on the grounds that he 'was born inside the machine' and has 'seen all the wires'.[51]

Stark Munro, however, is less at home with a mechanistic physics and a deterministic medical practice in which showmanship and overprescription are the main panaceas. The growing opposition between the flamboyant praxis of the confident Cullingworth and the spiritual quest of the more nervous Stark Munro ensures that the medical partnership between them is shortlived. In Stark Munro's half-sceptical wish to conjure a *deus ex machina* from that other 'monstrous machine', the physical universe, he finds at first only a missing essence located in the bifurcated narratives of the nervous system. Madness is the sign of this missing spirit:

> Does not lunacy strike you, Bertie, as being a very eerie thing? It is a disease of the soul ... . That a man's individuality should swing round from pole to pole, and yet that one's life should contain these two contradictory personalities – is it not a wondrous thing?
>
> I ask myself, where is the man, the very, most inmost essence of the man? ... He does not lie in the features ... . Nor is he in the body framework ... . In none of these things lies the essence of the man. And now what is left? An arched whitish putty-like mass, some fifty odd ounces in weight, with a number of white filaments hanging down from it. ... This central mass of nervous matter may be pared down on all sides before we seem to get at the very seat of the soul ... the spiritual part of the man. And what is left then? A little blob of matter, a handful of nervous dough, a few ounces of tissue, but there – somewhere there – lurks that impalpable seed, to which the rest of our frame is but the pod.[52]

The Stark Munro Letters is an autobiographical attempt to tell the inner story of early manhood. What it discloses is an epistemelogical confusion over the relationship between inner and outer modes of being, between the physical body and the nervous body, the written word and the spoken. The relationship between the two doctors is constructed in terms of this confusion, the paranoia between them resisting any gothic encoding and retaining its realist mode as a true story of the masculine body and its writing. Cullingworth's ebullient blurring of distinctions between real and fictional versions of his own behaviour and his rejection of his own interiority make it impossible for Stark Munro to read the man with whom he is working. When Stark Munro questions him about a medal he has been awarded for saving the life of a drowning child, Cullingworth relocates the inside story of this public event

> '... It was a little boy. You've no idea the trouble I had to get him in.'
>
> 'Get him out, you mean.'
>
> 'My dear chap, you don't understand! Anyone could get a child out. It's getting one in that's the bother ... I caught a quinsy walking up and down Avonmouth pier before I saw my opportunity. He was rather a solid, fat boy, and he was sitting on the very edge, fishing. I got the sole of my foot onto the small of his back, and shot him an incredible distance. I had some little difficulty in getting him out'.[53]

Just as Stark Munro becomes convinced that the whole episode had been a publicity stunt to advertise the medical practice, Cullingworth's wife shows him a newspaper cutting telling the 'true story' of his brave and near-fatal rescue of a child trapped below the ice in January 1879. Somewhere between the different 'insides' of the telling and the writing is a point of truth that connects men by its absence. In 1879 Doyle's writing had enabled him to begin his escape from the masochistic ice in which his own childhood story was trapped.

This motif of the fishing boy is itself one which links together the personal histories of the two men, for Stark Munro had begun his career as the medical attendant of a deranged young aristocrat who had been 'struck down by the sun while fishing without his hat last July'.[54] The interchangeability of masculine narratives, of hero and villain, father and son, inner man and outer story, inner story and outer man constitutes the comedic economy of this resolutely inexpressive, autobiographical novel. Between the polarities of the text, the masculine story is unable to decide what, apart from its jokes, it can declare of itself. Cullingworth has a Darwinian view of the 'ruthlessness and brutality' of life in which the sensitivies of the inner being must be constantly hidden; Stark Munro, on the other hand, seeks masculine nakedness and revelation. He writes to his friend, Herbert Swanborough:

> I have often wondered why some of those writing fellows don't try their hands at drawing the inner life of a young man from about the age of puberty until he begins to find his feet a little. Men are very fond of analysing the feelings of their heroines, which they cannot possibly know anything about, while they have little to say of the inner development of their heroes, which is an experience which they have themselves undergone. I should like to try it myself, but it would need blending with fiction, and I never had a spark of imagination. But I have a vivid recollection of what I went through myself. At the time I thought (as everybody thinks) that it was a unique experience; but since I have heard the confidences of my father's patients I am convinced that it is the common lot.[55]

According to his own account, Doyle's aim in writing *The Stark Munro Letters* was 'to draw that critical period which comes to so many clever inquiring men when they first see the fallacies of the sect in which they have been raised ... . And then as a second aim I thought how seldom the struggle of a young man to find room for himself in the world has been done in fiction.'[56] The novel offered 'the evolution of a young medico, based largely, on the subjective side, on my own experiences and feelings'. This emphasis on subjectivity is problematic for, as the young man finds room for himself in the world, his inner story vanishes.

At the start of the sequence of letters, Stark Munro resembles the nervous, highly strung diary writer of *The Parasite*, describing himself as 'a much more nervous person than any of my friends will ever credit me with being.'[57] Dr Cullingworth, on the other hand, is a man figured by his aggressive physicality and confident talk. Stark Munro pays tribute to the pathology and power of his friend's conversation:

> I daresay you've quite come to the conclusion by this time that Cullingworth is simply an interesting pathological study – a man in the first stage of lunacy or general paralysis. You might not be so sure about it if you were in close contact with him ... . He has such huge energy at the back of his fertility of invention ... . His conversation when he does not fly off at a tangent is full of pith and idea ... . He shoots off a whole column of aphorisms in single evening. I should like to have a man with a note-book always beside him to gather up his waste ... . On the other hand, it would be dishonest to deny that I think him thoroughly unscrupulous, and full of very sinister traits.[58]

Described as 'a man who prided himself upon never writing a letter', who was 'never apt at stating his views with a pen',[59] Cullingworth is initially perceived as the unlettered antithesis of his friend and colleague. As partners in a very peculiar medical practice, however, the identity of the two men begins to merge into rivalry. Cullingworth becomes increasingly literary, starting his own newspaper, writing both medical and literary articles and 'sending out a perpetual stream of libellous paragraphs, doggerel poems, social skits, parodies, and articles'.[60] Stark Munro, on the other hand, becomes both more aggressive and more confident, at one point taking charge of the practice and running it with the help of Cullingworth's wife, who acts as its dispensing chemist. His letter-writing becomes less frequent. When Cullingworth 'accidentally' shoots him in the finger with an air-dart and his hand turns septic, Munro is physically prevented from writing altogether. Of this magnetic exchange of identities centred on contestations over medical and literary practice, Stark Munro observes 'Our positions were absurdly reversed'.[61]

Stark Munro gradually assimilates the wordly knowledge and physical aggression of his exuberant friend, quarrels with him over some letters sent by his mother and goes on to establish himself in his own practice with a wife of his own. With this exterior masculinity established, the letter writing gradually ceases. From corresponding every two weeks, Munro finds that seven months have elapsed since his last letter to Swanborough. Writing like a man, he finds, has become something of a contradiction in terms:

> Well, there are some things that we don't talk about to another man, even when we know each other as well as I know you. Why should we, when that which is most engrossing ... can scarcely be written at all, far less made interesting to another?[62]

Doyle expressed his dissatisfaction with the conclusion his hero has reached by having him die in a train crash immediately afterwards.

The Stark Munro Letters is a novel with a double frame, relating late-Victorian neurological science to the military fortunes of the British Empire. In *Nerves and Narratives*, Peter Melville Logan discusses the work of Thomas Trotter, an Edinburgh medical student who became a British naval doctor and evenually physician to the Channel Fleet. In 1807 Trotter produced his influential work, *A View of the Nervous Temperament*. Writing during the Napoleonic Wars, Trotter was particularly concerned that the epidemic increase of nervous disorders throughout Britain posed a threat to national security. This epidemic of nervousness must, he claimed, 'inevitably sap our physical strength of constitution; make us an easy conquest to our invaders; and ultimately convert us into a nation of slaves and ideots'.[63]

Trotter's work, which also included 'An Essay on Drunkenesss', offered a thesis to which Doyle was eager to respond. *The Stark Munro Letters* is a reflective exploration of nervously failing masculinities, moving from accounts of the nervousness of Stark Munro and the pathology of Cullingworth to depictions of idiocy, epilepsy and chronic alcoholism. The novel also accepts Trotter's belief that nervous diseases 'are in a manner the inheritance of the fair sex'.[64] The aristocratic Lady Saltire, whose lunatic son, Jimmie, is Stark Munro's first patient, is described as being no more than 'a thin pipe for conveying disease from one generation to another. She was bounded by insanity upon the north and upon the south'.[65] Jimmie's brain disease manifests itself through crude speech and a conversion to socialism. His new doctor comments: 'In substance, I am bound to say that I think his new views are probably saner than his old ones, but the insanity lies in his sudden reasonless change and in his violent blurts of speech.'[66]

Trotter, like Hall after him, concluded that the nervous temperament had, as one of its distinct symptoms, 'a selfish desire of engrossing the sympathy and attention of others to the narration of [its] own sufferings'.[67] Stark Munro's letters chart a careful course along the edge of this symptomatology. Initially he relies on the correspondence to model his own Romantic anxieties and inebriations into a more appropriately intersubjective Victorian form:

> It is difficult to tell you how pleased and relieved I was at your cordial letter. I have no one to whom I can talk upon such matters. I am all driven inwards, and thought turns sour when one lets it stagnate like that. It is a grand thing to be able to tell it all to a sympathetic listener – and the more so perhaps when he looks at it all from another standpoint. It steadies and sobers one.[68]

In Thomas Trotter's study, gender is a crucial factor in the nervous body's relation to narrative. The impressionable, overinscribed female body 'contains a narrative within the fibres of its nerves'. The non-nervous male body, on the other hand, has a history, but it is not pressed into its material structure, waiting to come forth at a moment of crisis: 'The nervous female body, therefore, possesses a constitutive relationship to narrative. It has a story to tell, whereas the healthy male body has none.'[69] According to Logan, the nervous narrative is 'unavoidably gendered female':

> ... the speaker pleads for the listener's sympathy and so will appear blameless or essentially victimized ... . This is also a self-canceling narrative, because the narrator's authority to speak is compromised by the nervous disease that the story reveals. To a trained ear, the form of this narrative immediately identifies the speaker as a medical object, not an authentic speaking subject.[70]

Doyle had experimented with this kind of victim-narrative in *The Parasite*, and Stark Munro himself briefly reverts to it in his account of his final quarrel with Cullingworth. The novel as a whole, however, rejects the message of pain conveyed by the narrative of the nervous body. Stark Munro reflects at length on this question, arguing for the kindness of providence which limits the cruel tortures humanity attempts to inflict on itself:

> All the physical evils of life seem to culminate in death; and yet death, as I have seen it, has not been a painful or terrible process. In many cases, a man dies without having incurred nearly as much pain, during the whole of his fatal illness, as would have arisen from a whitlow or an abscess of the jaw. And it is often those deaths which seem most terrible to the onlooker, which are least so to the sufferer.[71]

He recalls a cautery applied in a case of spinal disease. When the white-hot iron was pressed into the patient's back without any anaesthetic, the young doctor nearly fainted at the smell of burned flesh but the patient assured him that the process was absolutely painless. The surgeon corroborated this: 'The nerves are so completely and instantaneously destroyed ... that they have no time to convey a painful impression.'[72]

On his way to join Cullingworth at the start of the novel, Stark Munro has an adventure on a train which involves a chance meeting with a widow, Mrs La Force, her son, Fred, who has an epileptic fit in the carriage, and her daughter, Winnie, later to become Stark Munro's wife. According to Doyle's biographers this is a clear recollection of Touie Hawkins and her brother, Jack. It is Fred, an invalid who suffers from 'nervous weakness', who completes the picture of masculine pathologies presented in this novel. His eventual death in the care of Stark Munro is the paradoxical making of the young doctor: 'It was really that cold hand which I grasped that morning as I sat by his bed which drew me towards my happiness.'[73] When an anonymous letter to the police suggests suspicious circumstances surrounding the death, it is only Stark Munro's foresight in having called in a second opinion that saves him from a murder inquest:

> If Porter had not seen him that night, it is more than likely that there would have been an exhumation. And then, – well, there would be chloral in the body; some money interests *did* depend upon the death of the lad – a sharp lawyer might have made much of the case.[74]

A sharp lawyer might also have noticed the speed with which the young doctor became engaged to the dead boy's sister, but the reader is not allowed to. A long gap in the correspondence follows from Fred's death; the burial of that nervous body completes the process which separates Stark Munro from his own.

The pain of the inner story, however, had to go somewhere and in 1893, as Doyle began work on the novel, it chose Touie, just as the inner story of the spirit, rejected by Stark Munro, is reinscribed in the simple 'child-like faith'[75] of his new wife, Winnie. Marriage to Winnie is described in terms of a double vision, the augmented interest of life 'when viewed by four eyes instead of two'.[76] As Doyle's tribute to Touie, the novel dramatizes a manhood established through the transfer of the nervous narratives of the male body, including its spirituality, on to that of its female partner. *The Stark Munro Letters* are Doyle's tribute to the friendship that liberated him from the Catholicism of his upbringing and to the 'force' of the domestic partnership that established his literary career, following his marriage to Touie. This marriage should, perhaps, receive more acknowledgement than it has done, as one of the most creative partnerships of the late-Victorian period and Touie's voice, silenced in the formal discourse of Doyle's autobiography, still speaks through the medium of its expressive errors.

This marital solution to the problem of the nervous narrative is not, however, the only exchange performed by the novel. As part of its magical substitutions, Doyle and Budd change places too. It is James Cullingworth, not Doyle's ostensible alter ego, Stark Munro, who takes on Doyle's own story and becomes both a literary man and an eye specialist. Although Stark Munro is the autobiographical subject of the *Letters*, the author, by a Bakhtinian reversal, is articulated through his inscription in the otherness of the heroically flawed Dr Cullingworth.[77] The insider and the outsider change places in *The Stark Munro Letters*. The text becomes, not autobiography, but a dramatization of the process of autobiographical substitution.

At the end of the novel, Cullingworth is on the point of emigrating to South America to pursue a lucrative career in ophthalmics: 'I've taken to the eye, my boy. There's a fortune in the eye ... . There's a great continent from the equator to the ice-bergs, and not a man in it who could correct an astigmatism. What do they know of modern eye-surgery and refraction?'[78] George Turnaville Budd, as a doctor, was primarily interested in rheumatism and gout. The interest in the eye was entirely Doyle's, although it may have been Budd who suggested it to him. This specialization was to inform his subsequent view of himself as the writer who corrected not just defective images of masculinity but faulty perspectives of the British Empire too. *The Stark Munro Letters* is the novel in which Doyle finally exchanged insight into the narratives of the nervous body for the formally constructed histories of the British Empire.

George Turnaville Budd himself died on 28 February 1889, at the age of thirty-four; this was the year in which Doyle's 'first' novel, *Micah Clarke*, was published. His return to the Budd material in writing *The Stark Munro Letters* is linked to the death sentence placed on both Holmes and Touie during Doyle's visit to Switzerland in 1893. The novel's publication in 1895 concluded the second phase of Doyle's career. Emotionally and sexually, he wrote off the marriage which had provided him not only with the motive force for his early achievements but also with two children, his son Alleyne Kingsley having been born in 1892. The shocking end to the novel which, in the first edition, has Stark Munro and his new wife both killed in a railway accident, invokes the death sentence on Doyle's marriage as well as his unease with the conclusions which the letters reach.

Diagnosed as terminally consumptive after their visit to Switzerland in 1893, Touie's illness became the catalyst to Doyle's most significant self-development. The wife's 'illness' reinscribed the masculinity of the husband's career, dictating the new exploits and adventures that opened up for Doyle after the novel's publication. As Stark Munro escapes from Dr Cullingworth to set up a medical practice of his own, he finds that he has arrived in Birchespool just in time to see a regiment of British soldiers leaving for Malta in anticipation of a war in Egypt. He is so moved at the sight 'of these youngsters going out to do their best for the dear old country' that he sets up three cheers and wonders whether he or they have the hardest fight ahead of them.[79] Doyle himself was of the opinion that Egypt might be beneficial to Touie's health and took her there for the winter in September 1895. By fortuitous coincidence or careful planning, Doyle found himself in the very place where a war correspondent might be needed to report on the British reconquest of the Sudan.

If neither *The Stark Munro Letters* nor Doyle's autobiography can be trusted to tell the story of the inner man in the mid-1880s and 1890s, perhaps a glimpse of this vexed passage in Doyle's life can be obtained from one of his critical essays in *Through the Magic Door*. Discussing the masters of the short story, Doyle remarks that he cannot write the name of Guy de Maupassant 'without recalling what was either a spiritual interposition or an extraordinary coincidence in my own life'.[80] Travelling in Switzerland in 1893, he had crossed the Gemmi Pass and visited an inn which, for three months of the year, was entirely cut off by snow. Fascinated by its other-world location, Doyle began to construct a story about 'a group of strong antagonistic characters being penned up in this inn, loathing each other and yet utterly unable to get away from each other's society'.

Travelling back through France a week later, Doyle happened to buy a book of de Maupassant's *Tales* which he had not read before. The first story was called 'L'Auberge'. Glancing through it, Doyle was astonished to discover that it was set in the very inn he himself had recently visited. Furthermore, the plot depended, as his own had done, on the stranded isolation of the people who lived there through the winter months 'Everything that I imagined was there, save that Maupassant had brought in a savage hound.'[81] He continues:

> But what is perfectly marvellous is that in that short journey I should have chanced to buy the one book in all the world which would prevent me from making a public fool of myself, for who would ever believe that my work was not an imitation? I do not think that the hypothesis of coincidence can cover the facts. It is one of several incidents in my life which have convinced me of spiritual interposition – of the prompting of some benificent force outside ourselves, which tries to help us where it can.[82]

Apart from its location, de Maupassant's 'L'Auberge' has in fact little in common with the story that Doyle was planning. It is not about strong, antagonistic personalities and a savage hound. On the contrary, the two men featured in it are quiet and companionable and their dog, is a loyal and sensitive mountain dog which tries to rescue the older man when he gets lost in the snow. Mistaking the dog's howls to be let in for the ghostly cries of his lost companion, the younger man, unable to cope with his own loneliness, drinks himself into insanity.

While 'L'Auberge' does not resemble the story Doyle was constructing, it does poignantly evoke the story of his own father which he was, perhaps, trying to shut out. Books for Doyle uncannily evoke those borderland passes where an author might transform into a sandman and try to blind his reader to the substitutions he is making. It was during this trip to Switzerland that Louise Doyle apparently picked up 'the wretched microbe' that was diagnosed as consumption. Interestingly, the third victim of 'L'Auberge', the innkeeper's daughter, is also called Louise, Louise Hauser, or 'Holmes' perhaps! The story concludes with her nearly dying of consumption: 'Little Louise Hauser nearly died that summer of decline, which the medical men atributed to the cold air of the mountains.'[83] Those medical men, perhaps, had a lot to answer for. Rather than preventing him from writing a story, 'L'Auberge' seems to have provided him with one to tell. Whatever the familial renegotiations of 1893, the nervous bodies of his father and his wife became, from this date onwards, a silenced part of his own narrative.

Sighting solutions

Where Thomas Trotter had studied nervous disorders at a time of national crisis and under the threat of French invasion, Doyle was becoming increasingly preoccupied by the deteriorating relationship between Britain and Germany. Dr Cullingworth's last words in *The Stark Munro Letters* refer to certain war between the two nations, as he prepares to sell his latest military invention to the Germans. In the mid-1890s Doyle created a new character to replace Sherlock Holmes, one through whom he could resymbolize the antagonisms of Anglo-French history as a ludic interaction whose main aim was not conquest but political definition and masculine display. An escapologist of almost infinite nervous flexibility, Brigadier Gerard is a French soldier for whom the story of pain has no meaning.

Set in the Napoleonic period which Doyle knew intimately through his grandfather's political cartoons, the *Brigadier Gerard* stories represent Doyle's writing at its most convivial. They were accompanied by two full-length novels, *Rodney Stone* (1896) and *Uncle Bernac* (1897) which drew on the same historical context but represented it from different sides. Far from illustrating Trotter's thesis about nervous disorder, Doyle's reconstructions of the early nineteenth century celebrates an iron duke and a masculinity of empassioned steel. In *Through the Magic Door*, Doyle had devoted a chapter to this period, citing with pride his collection of Napoleonic military memoirs as offering the best possible model for masculine writing 'There is no better writing, and no easier reading, than the records of these men of action.'[84] He describes the Napoleonic soldiery as 'even more interesting than their great leader, though his must ever be the most singular figure in history'.

Doyle's admiration for the French soldiery, as well as for French standards of culture and civilization, carries with it an unease about the poor partnership mentality of the British:

> It must be admitted that, looking back upon history, we have not always been good allies, nor yet generous co-partners in the battle-field ... . No; I do not think that we are very aimable partners, but I suppose that all national history may be open to a similar charge.[85]

While partnership and the celebration of strange alliances was a main theme of all Doyle's writing, he identified France as the glamorous 'double' of nineteenth-century Britain. Believing himself descended from the Anglo-Norman D'Oil family, France was, for him, 'insider' territory in a literary sense too. France was, he claimed, peculiarly the land of memoir. Unlike the reticent English, the French made personal records of whatever happened to them, aware of the glory that surrounded their exploits:

> French literature, which is so rich in all its branches, is richest of all in its memoirs. Whenever there was anything of interest going forward there was always some kindly gossip who knew all about it, and was ready to set it down for the benefit of posterity. Our own history has not nearly enough of these charming sidelights. Look at our sailors in the Napoleonic wars, for example. They played an epoch-making part ... . And what have we in literature

to show for it all? ... No doubt our sailors were too busy to do much writing.[86]

Once the youngest colonel in Napoleon's army of liberation, but now 'a fragment of history', and a garrulous grey-beard, Brigadier Gerard describes himself as a type of manhood always lost from one generation to the next:

> In me you see one of the last of those wonderful men, the men who were veterans when they were yet boys, who learned to use a sword earlier than a razor, and who during a hundred battles had never once let the enemy see the colour of their knapsacks. For twenty years we were teaching Europe how to fight.[87]

For all Doyle's commitment to accurate historical detail, these short stories are brilliant dramatizations, not so much of the period itself, but of the comic diaspora of individuals enmeshed in the grand narratives and nationalities of nineteenth-century history. Escaping from history through immersement in it, these cartoons reconstruct the major events of early nineteenth-century European history as oddly collaborative – a literal playing into each other's hands on the part of the contending nations. The stories celebrate manhood in a fantasy scenario of entrapments from which survival flows along its erratic, serendipitous course.

This liberation from physical or political finality is particularly visible in *The Exploits of Brigadier Gerard* (1896), ingenious stories written in praise of accident and disaster from which the pains of the nervous narrative have been altogether excised. While physical injury abounds, its corollary is not anguish but increased mental and circumstantial dexterity. As the Brigadier concludes: 'One lesson which I have learned in my roaming life, my friends, is never to call anything a misfortune until you have seen the end of it. Is not every hour a fresh point of view?'[88] This hypothesis is tested in the first story of the collection, 'How the Brigadier Came to the Castle of Gloom', as Gerard demonstrates an unKafkaesque ability to turn the punitive resources of the Castle – round cheese, in this instance, followed by the powder magazine – into agents of his own survival. In the second tale, the young lieutenant of hussars is chosen for a special mission to protect the Emperor Napoleon during a dangerous secret meeting with two vengeful members of a Corsican secret society, the 'Brothers of Ajaccio'. Adversity results, in this instance, in a promotion to the rank of captain. In the third tale, Doyle draws on his own Byronic resources in an escapade where Gerard, now a colonel, falls into the hands of the Spanish guerrilla leader, El Cuchillo, while trying to rejoin his regiment in the Pyrenees.

What is startling about the entrapment of this story is the degree of vividly realized violence which sustains it. Attacked by a supposed priest who drives a brad-awl into his eye, this wound to his eyesight, as the Brigadier admits, gives him more trouble than any of the seventeen wounds he sustained afterwards. Lamed and half-blinded, Gerard is dragged before the terrible guerrilla chief in his cave in the mountains. El Cuchillo, despite his appalling reputation for cruelty, turns out to be something of a surprise. Sitting at a table looking like 'a well-to-do grocer of the Rue St Antoine', the brigand and the brigadier confront each other:

> I was left with my three guards, waiting to hear my fate. He took up his pen, and tapping his forehead with the handle of it, he pursed up his lips and looked out of the corner of his eyes at the roof of the grotto.
>
> 'I suppose', said he at last, speaking a very excellent French, 'that you are not able to suggest a rhyme for the word Covilha.'[89]

The poetical evening pursuits of these aspiring corsairs, however, are the accompaniment, not the annulment, of the most sinister cruelties and the move from horror to humour is quickly reversed. Outside the cave, Gerard notices a tall fir tree with a clump of bushes in front of it, from which is hanging a pair of riding boots with the toes upwards. He realizes with horror that the boots are not empty but contain a man nailed upside down over a burning fire.

The origins of tree worship being what they are – a fetishism of the phallus – the Brigadier faces an even worse ordeal when his ankles are fastened to two young trees both bent in opposite directions so that their release will rip him in half. As a young English soldier, attracted by his cries, arrives at the scene in time to save him, Gerard gratefully surrenders himself to the enemy. Having formed an immediate friendship with his arresting officer, whose aristocratic rank he mistakes for his name, Gerard and his pleasant young captor sit down to play a deciding game of cards on the question of whose prisoner is whom. Just as Gerard wins his horse, sword, saddle, bridle, stirrups and freedom in a lively game of ecarte with 'the Bart', he finds his winning king trumped at the last moment by the arrival of the Duke of Wellington. Gerard, a prisoner once more, ends by pleading the cause of his now disgraced English rescuer, 'the Bart', and is sent to Dartmoor as a prisoner of war for his pains.

Gerard's escape from Dartmoor, hampered and helped by a series of obstacles, leads him round in a huge circle, until he finds himself back at the prison gates inadvertently bearing his own order of release. Doyle's recycled narratives turn tortured, overstretched nerves into ingenious devices for Gallic self-assertion. The torments endured with such nervous elasticity by Etienne Gerard signal the magical resourcefulness of a body able to shift its own cultural paradigm and produce a spirit equal to every context and occasion.

For Doyle this was the Empire body, undeterred by alien circumstance, its powers of endurance celebrated by Kipling in his famously titled poem, 'If'. While the Brigadier represents a French autobiographical impulse, the Duke of Wellington, who won the affection of his soldiers by constantly referring to them as 'the scum of the earth',[90] belongs to the British biographical tradition. Representing all that was repressive, wrongheaded and conservative in English culture, it was Wellington's prerogative, like that of Samuel Johnson, to get everything wrong. Doyle claims 'he fiercely opposed Catholic Emancipation, the Reform Bill, and everything upon which our modern life is founded … . Neither in war nor in politics did he rightly judge the future.'[91]

But if the English had been poor readers of signs in the past, they had possessed a flexibility with regard to their use which had protected them from revolution. Wellington could turn a good phrase as well as a sharp flank. In one of his letters, he had remarked on 'that extraordinary caprice which always pervades the English character … . Nothing but English caprice can account for it … our noblemen associate with stage-coach drivers, and become stage-coach drivers themselves.'[92] This concept of the sporting interchangeability of masculine signs across the boundaries of the British class system is an essential part of its mid-Victorian stereotyping, a device that served the interests of both nation and empire. The American, William Emerson, who derived many of his ideas about the English from his conversations with Thomas Carlyle, presented this interchangeability as integral to British character formation. British culture generated a 'great ability' that was:

> … not amassed on a few giants, but poured into the general mind, so that each of them could at a pinch stand in the shoes of the other … they are more bound in character than differenced in ability or rank. The labourer is a possible lord. The lord is a possible basket maker.[93]

For Doyle, the Regency boxing ring was one fulcrum for a potential democracy which avoided class conflict by ring-fencing an arena of working-class strength:

> No man who looked upon that motley crowd could deny that, for good or evil, the love of the Ring was confined to no class, but was a national peculiarity, deeply seated in the English nature, and a common heritage of the young aristocrat in his drag and of the rough costers sitting six deep in their pony cart.[94]

In *Rodney Stone* (1896) and in its French counterpart, *Uncle Bernac* (1897), Doyle explores the rival masculinities of Britain and France, and redraws the lines of conflict between them as a debate over models of masculine power. While *Rodney Stone* dramatizes the diverse masculinities of English Romanticism, in which aristocrats and highwaymen, dandies and prizefighters share a levelling passion for sporting competitions of all kinds, *Uncle Bernac* illustrates the opposing manhood of France, its power concentrated in one great man, Napoleon, and the soldiers who reflected back his image.

Talking, boxing and war are the main arenas of British manhood in *Rodney Stone*, each supporting its own all-male community of passionate discussion. The verbal contests of the dandies are as hard-hitting as those of the boxing ring, and crowds gather to watch them. The retiring dandy, Charles Tregellis, gracefully acknowledges the superiority of Beau Brummel: 'That young man is destined to take my place ... . He is quite young and of no descent, but he has made his way by his cool effrontery ... . There is no man who can be impolite in so polished a fashion.'[95]

The Napoleonic age, for Doyle, significantly combined strength of arms with Scottish pens: 'We were great in arms, and were soon to be great in literature, for Scott and Byron were in their day the strongest forces in Europe.'[96] While the strength of the age derived from the energy of its competition, the constantly rivalry of its political factions allowed power to be manifested through the various professional and sporting communities which are the novel's real centre. The contests and the conversations that arise from them create a masculine enterprise whose ultimate purpose, as the book makes clear, is military power. At Fladong's in Oxford Street, the supper house reserved for the navy, this communitized masculinity is immediately visible to Rodney Stone:

> I remember that what did cause me some astonishment was to observe that all these sailors, who had served under the most varying conditions in all quarters of the globe, from the Baltic to the East Indies, should have been moulded into so uniform a type that they were more like each other than brother is commonly to brother.[97]

For nearly forty years after its publication, *Rodney Stone* was a book specifically used and remembered as an item of male exchange, inscribed as a fitting present between male friends in the war years, or a book passed from father to son as a good thing to read. It is a deliberately decentred novel. The eponymous narrator is an ordinary village lad from a naval family, who is brought to town by his glamorous uncle, Beau Tregellis. Describing himself as 'one of the smallest and weakest men' in a book about male strength, Rodney Stone's function is largely to admire masculinities other than his own. He says of himself:

> I have always seen things as they are, myself included, which should count in my favour now that I sit down in my mature age to write my memories. With your permission, then, we will push my

own personality as far as possible out of the picture. If you can conceive me as a thin and colourless cord upon which my would-be pearls are strung, you will be accepting me upon the terms which I should wish.[98]

True to his word, Rodney Stone does and says nothing of any note for the duration of the novel. Self-effacingly, he chronicles the deeds that define the masculinity of his age. It is only in the final paragraph of the novel, where he periphrastically mentions that he was one of Nelson's men at the Battle of Trafalgar, that the book's hidden agenda becomes visible.

As a participant-narrator, Rodney Stone images both the role of the common man in history and the peculiarly British notion of narrative self-effacement, of representing masculinity as that which is wordless and does not speak of itself. The antithesis of the delightfully boastful Brigadier Gerard, Rodney Stone's lack of self-discourse, his amputation of himself from his own story, allows him to figure the characteristic and colourless culture of British manhood. His public history asserts the power of his own personal absence from the fictional action: a veteran of Trafalgar does not need the nervous assertion of self-expression.

Lord Nelson himself, on the other hand, the embodiment of a 'virile Puritanism' which makes him 'the greatest living Englishman'[99] is represented in the private sphere as effortlessly subjugated by the crude flattery of Lady Hamilton. In a novel of pugilistic masculinities, Lady Hamilton is an interesting figure for her lavish praise of Nelson reflects directly on that patriotic flattery of British manhood which is the novel's own project.

As a boxing novel, Rodney Stone is particularly concerned with the tension between public name and personal effacement. Beautiful male faces are repeatedly punched into unrecognizable forms; one working-class contestant is so battered in the story's main contest that his wife can only recognize him by his overcoat. The issue of self-effacement inscribed throughout the narrative of Rodney Stone is particularly channelled through the young boxing heroes of 'the Fancy', admired as 'glorious lads' but facing the destruction of their own beauty as the price of fame.

This concern for the fate of both young and old faces reiterates the novel's formal division between the Regency manhood of its subject and that of its late-Victorian readership. Although nostalgia for the days of the Ring is offset by recognition of its brutality and the dishonest profiteering that came to control it, Doyle reminds his readers of the standard set and the purpose served by this ruthlessly masculine sport:

It was a time of war, when England with an army and navy composed only of those who volunteered to fight because they had fighting blood in them, had to encounter, as they would now have to encounter, a power which could by despotic law turn every citizen into a soldier. If the people had not been full of this lust for combat, it is certain that England must have been overborne ... . Brutal it was, no doubt, and its brutality is the end of it; but it is not so brutal as war, which will survive it. Whether it is logical now to teach the people to be peaceful in an age when their very existence may come to depend upon their being warlike, is a question for wiser heads than mine ... the Ring may, as I have said, have served a national purpose.[100]

Published the year after the trial of Oscar Wilde, *Rodney Stone* concludes with a tribute to the dandy aristocrats of England, that 'strange breed of men which has vanished away from England – the full-blooded, virile buck, exquisite in his dress, narrow in his thoughts, coarse in his amusements, and eccentric in his habits ... . The world has outgrown them, and there is no place now for their strange fashions ... . And yet ... Wellington picked his best officers from among them.'[101] Although closely related to one, the plain and very English Rodney Stone insists that he has no understanding of the effeminately virile mentality of the dandy fraternity.

Whereas *Rodney Stone* employs a de-centred narrative structured around separate but intersecting masculine communities, *Uncle Bernac*, set in 1805, is powerfully centred not on the man named in its title but on his employer, the terrible Napoleon, the 'man who stood for France' and, as such, was 'the very personification of Destiny'.[102] Doyle's portayal of Napoleon takes the great icon of Romanticism, the demonized enemy of England, and domesticates him in a fictional narrative. Best approached through the man who supplies the writing to greatness, his secretary Monsieur de Meneval, Napoleon is described as possessing an energy resembling creative inspiration:

> He wears everybody out around him. Even the soldiers cannot keep up with him. I assure you that I look upon it as the very highest honour to have charge of his papers, but there are times when it is very trying all the same. Sometimes it is eleven o'clock at night, Monsieur de Laval, and I am writing to his dictation with my head aching for want of sleep. It is dreadful work, for he dictates as quickly as he can talk, and he never repeats anything. 'Now, Meneval,' says he suddenly, 'we shall stop here and have a good night's rest.' And then, just as I am congratulating myself, he adds, 'and we shall continue with the dictation at three tomorrow morning.'[103]

Embodying France's need for strong leadership after revolutionary change, Napoleon is represented as ecomical, hardworking, and temperate, a man of action with a marvellous grasp of fact and a capacious, well-organized mind. His only weakness, however, is a crucial one in the indices of Doyle's writing for he is a visionary with poor eyesight: 'his sight was so weak that he always needed a single glass indoors and binoculars outside.'[104] With a myopia linked directly to his meglomania, Napoleon's genius lies in the architecture of his own life, as he harnesses the prophetic vision of the Romantic poet to the scaffolding of historical circumstance. A marvellous monologist, Napoleon's conversation silences other men. As he leaves the room after a social engagement, there is 'a long sigh of relief from everyone'[105] and the narrator, de Laval, has difficulty resuming his own narrative: 'As I draw his words and deeds I feel that my own poor story withers before them.'

Ambivalent in his representation of Napoleon's greatness and the revolutionary history behind it, Doyle was, in the early 1890s, becoming increasingly involved in the cultural debate over 'the New Imperialism'. Emerging a decade earlier, this debate over the relationship between Britain and her colonies was a consequence of the changing balance of power in Europe following the Franco-Prussian war. In *The Imperial Experience* (1996) C. C. Eldridge has summarized the aims of this debate as an attempt to find a 'new justification for empire', one that replaced 'the older props of autocratic government and mercantilism' with 'the idea of a great imperial destiny to plant British people and institutions overseas.' The empire, he claims, was seen as a way of remedying ' the social ills of the mother country'.[106]

Doyle responded strongly to Gladstone's notion of empire as a Liberal federation of English-speaking peoples, but he also entered into the more militaristic enthusiasms of Disraeli's Tory Party which fed patriotism with the stories and glories of empire. Doyle could produce novels like *Rodney Stone* which conform closely to J. A. Hobson's definition of the jingoistic text as a combination of 'hero-worship and sensational glory, adventure and the sporting spirit: current history falsified in coarse glaring colours, for the direct stimulation of the combatative instincts'.[107] Such, however, was the stuff of Doyle's historical fiction, based on his recycling of Romantic memoirs. His contemporary engagement with issues of empire, whether in fiction, propaganda or philippic, shows an altogether different focus.

In 1895 Doyle had gone to Egypt with his wife believing that the dry climate would improve her health. As a place of prolonged competition between British and French political and financial interests, Egypt was perhaps an inevitable destination for the man who had just written *Rodney Stone* and *Uncle Bernac*. He found himself in a desert landscape that uncannily resembled that of his first Holmes story, *A Study in Scarlet*. In the same way that Holmes had been able to read the right sequence of signs to reconstruct a retrospective narrative, Doyle began to perceive in his own writing figures that might conceivably be able to forecast the future. Recurrent human and geometric figures set in a landscape of sand act as the fragile signs of both his own greatness and that of the empire whose thoughtful advocate he now became.

Egypt in 1895–96 was a nation contested by imperial powers. Still nominally part of the Ottoman Empire, its finances were in dual Anglo-French control and the politically unstable regime supported by the British had been facing a Sudanese revolt led initially by a Muslim religious leader known as the Mahdi. His forces had defeated the British-led Egyptian army in 1883 and, even more conspicuously, had murdered Governor General Gordon in Khartoum two years later. The Mahdi was suceeded by Khalifa Abdullah in 1885 and it was not until the Conservative ministry of Lord Salisbury ten years later that a British reconquest of the Sudan was contemplated.

On a Nile expedition to Wadi Halfa, the boat in which Doyle and his party were travelling was moored at a village that had recently been attacked by the Mahdi's dervishes. Doyle noted in his journal: 'If I were a Dervish general, I would undertake to carry off a Cook's excursion party with the greatest ease.'[108] Two months later, war was declared and Doyle offered his services as a volunteer war correspondent. It was after these experiences in the Sudan that Doyle, in 1896, wrote what was arguably his best novel, one set on the borders between Egypt and the Sudan. No longer recycling the memoirs of other men, *The Tragedy of the Korosko* had, for once, its genesis in his own. Describing the original tourist excursion, Doyle records his strong impression of the party's vulnerability to terrorist kidnap:

> I thought that the managers of these tours took undue risks, and when I found myself on one occasion on the rock of Abousir with a drove of helpless tourists, male and female, nothing whatever between us and the tribesmen, and a river between us and the nearest troops, I could not but think what an appalling situation would arise if a little troop of these far-riding camel men were to appear. We had four negro soldiers as an escort, who would be helpless before any normal raiding party.[109]

Initially presented as an important international incident which had not been reported in the newspapers, the story of the Nile cruiser, the *Korosko*, has, the reader is told, been suppressed for both personal and political reasons. It is this suppression of the account which most powerfully authenticates it, the narrative being compiled from sworn statements, letters and evidential oral accounts given by the party of travellers on board the cruiser. This compilation of small voices rather than the rock inscriptions of individual greatness was Doyle's method of representing the difference between the British Empire and that of the French or the ancient Egyptians.

In the novel, the party of Western hostages kidnapped by the dervishes comprises a range of character-types and ideological positions. The English group consists of an army officer, Colonel Cochrane; a young diplomat 'slightly tainted with the Oxford manner', Cecil Brown; a Manchester lawyer recovering from influenza, James Stephens; and the Reverend John Stuart, a fat non-conformist clergyman from inauspicious Birmingham. The American tourists include a Boston feminist, Miss Adams, and her niece, and John H. Headingly, a Harvard graduate who 'stood for the best type of young American ... serious, eager for knowledge and fairly free from prejudice'.[110] French culture is represented by an argumentative Parisian, Monsieur Fardet, who repeatedly quarrels with Colonel Cochrane over the illegality of Britain's position in Egypt. Fardet refuses to believe in the military threat of the Mahdi, insisting that the dervishes 'were an invention of Lord Cromer in the year 1885' to justify British presence.[111] The final couple involved in the kidnap are Mr and Mrs Belmont from Dublin, the wife a devout Catholic and her husband a crack marksman.

The night before the fatal expedition, the party sit up late discussing the pros and cons of Britain's involvement in Egypt. The viewpoints canvassed see it variously as a pointless and unjustifiable expense, a predatory act of appropriation, a cultural mission to bring justice and law into ungoverned regions, an act of a guiding providence 'which is for ever getting the best out of each nation' or, alternatively, 'a whimsical freak of fortune which has sent men from a little island in the Atlantic to administer the land of the Pharaohs'.[112] The discussion rehearses the main lines of cultural debate over the question of empire during the last thirty years of the nineteenth century. Cecil Brown, the Oxbridge diplomat, argues for the transience of colonial power and its records:

> it is not an Anglo-Saxon custom to write their deeds upon rocks. I daresay that the remains of a Cairo drainage system will be our most permanent record, unless they prove a thousand years hence that it was the work of the Hyksos kings.[113]

The sightseeing expedition, with an Egyptian dragoman as their travel guide, begins in high spirits as the party attempt to read the hieroglyphic writing on the wall of an ancient temple. Reverend Stuart asks for clarification of a particular inscription and receives a less than Deleuzian account of 'nomad art' in reply. It is not the shape of desert space but the crude delineations of power that inform this representation:

> 'What's this?' ...
> 'That is a hippopotamus,' said the dragoman; and the tourists all tittered, for there was just a suspicion of Mr. Stuart himself in the carving.

'But it isn't bigger than a little pig,' he protested. 'You see that the King is putting his spear through it with ease.'

'They make it small to show that it was a very small thing to the King', said the dragoman. 'So you see that all the King's prisoners do not exceed his knee – which is not because he was so much taller, but so much more powerful. You see that he is bigger than his horse, because he is a king and the other is only a horse. The same way, these small women who you see here and there are just his trivial little wives.'[114]

The feminist Miss Adams ripostes by asking for a magnifying glass through which to view the king's soul.

As the figure of the great man appears in the risible inscriptions of a different culture, the tourists, themselves constituting 'an absurd procession', visit the pulpit rock of Abousir. As their guide points out, it is a prime site for the inscription of masculine spiritual power:

'Now, ladies and gentlemen, we are arrived for the so famous pulpit rock of Abousir. From the summit you will presently enjoy a panorama of remarkable fertility. But first you will observe that over the rocky side of the hill are everywhere cut the names of great men who have passed it in their travels, and some of these names are older than the time of Christ.'

'Got Moses?' asked Miss Adams.[115]

It is at this point, looking out across the Libyan desert, that the tourists get their first picturesque glimpse of some red-turbaned figures on camels emerging from a nearby ravine.

In a desert landscape which is simultaneously the realm of Doyle's literary ophthalmics, consciousness moves through a dream-like transposition into a shocking exchange of one reality for another. At this contested edge of empire, the Western sightseers encounter a place where the nature of seeing, as well as the meaning of what is seen, undergoes a radical transformation. The crossing of this invisible boundary between interpretive paradigms and different modes of cultural perception is signalled by the death of one of the party's four black guards:

The soldier next them had sat down abruptly, and leaned forward over his knees. His movement and attitude were so natural that it was hard to realise that he had been shot through the head. He neither stirred nor groaned.[116]

The shock deepens with the death of the young Harvard graduate who literally completes his education in the desert sand: '"I'm done!" he whispered ... and then he lay still, with his china-white cheek against the black stones.'[117]

In the dervish attack upon the tourists that follows, Doyle shows identity, power and status suddenly unhinged by this fierce encounter.

Bizarrely, it is the fat clergyman from Birmingham who puts up the most resistance, moving in an instant from trance-like inertia to berserk fury:

> It may have been the mania of fear, or it may have been the blood of some Berserk ancestor which stirred suddenly in his veins; but he broke into a wild shout, and, catching up a stick, he struck right and left among the Arabs with a fury which was more savage than their own.

This extraordinary moment of spiritual transformation, when the comic figure is changed into one of heroic wrath, is inscribed in the narrative along with its own truth claim:

> One who helped to draw up this narrative has left it upon record that, of all the pictures which have been burned into his brain, there is none so clear as that of this man, his large face shining with perspiration, and his great body dancing about with unwieldy agility, as he struck at the shrinking, snarling savages. Then a spear-head flashed from behind a rock with a quick, vicious, upward thrust, the clergyman fell upon his hands and knees, and the horde poured over him to seize their unresisting victims.[118]

Once captured, it is only the Reverend Stuart who is kept bound by his captors, 'for the Arabs, understanding that he was a clergyman, and accustomed to associate religion with violence, had looked upon his fierce outburst as quite natural, and regarded him now as the most dangerous and enterprising of their captives'.[119]

Through these sudden discontinuities of perspective, a chasm opens up for the tourists 'between their old life and their new' as the main-stays of their shared culture collapse beneath a different order: 'Humanity, reason, argument – all were gone, and there remained the brutal humili-ation of force.'[120] The novel explores the effect of this discontinuity on the different individuals subject to it. While the respectable Presbyte-rian, Miss Adams, finds herself hunched on a camel and contemplating murder, it is the metamorphosis of the 'gross and vulgar' clergyman, described as 'a good preacher from radical platforms', that is the most dramatic. Wearing a turban made out of Colonel Cochrane's red silk cummerbund and looking ridiculously like 'a man who had dressed up to amuse the children',[121] the radical Reverend displays a spiritual strength and serenity that enables his upper-class companions to pre-serve some semblance of normal identity.

Touching though this image of a re-energized Christianity is, it can-not compete with the power of the desert sun. Growing delirious from the heat and the wound in his leg, the Reverend Stuart is finally aban-doned in the desert, left to the devices of his own delirium. Doyle's account of his fate stresses the kindness of Nature's defences against pain and injury, as consciousness is coaxed away from its uninhabitable body. Returned to the sphere of the comically pathetic, the Reverend Stuart is too feverish to know his own suffering for what it is. Lying on the desert stones, he is left chuckling as if 'at some joke' in his own brain cells which 'those busy little cell-workers had come across in their repairs'. As the camels move off across the sand, the last his devastated friends hear of him is the sound of his 'strong, droning, unmusical voice' singing hymns to himself 'in that huge inarticulate wilderness ... Gradually the voice died away into a hum, and was absorbed once more into the masterful silence of the desert.'[122]

This image of the silent desert as the ultimate masculine landscape, powerfully absorbing the strength of other men and other cultures, is repeatedly reinforced in the Europeans' experience. Cecil Brown, the sophisticated Oxbridge aesthete, turns emotionally savage and helpless under attack, hitting out 'like a girl' before being stabbed to death. Once used to command, Colonel Cochrane is humiliated by contemptuous gestures and the butt of a Remington in his ribs. The props and stays of these powerful masculinities are gradually revealed. The colonel manages to absorb the blow of the rifle not because, as his companions imagine, he is 'a man of steel' but because he has taken to wearing a corset to support his military carriage:

> 'Stays, be Jove!' cried the astonished Irishman.
> 'Well, some slight artificial support,' said the Colonel stiffly, and switched the conversation off to the chances of the morrow.[123]

While the dry-as-dust English lawyer finds himself almost disturbingly in his element (having for the first time in his life fallen in love with the young American girl, Sadie), it is only the Irish couple who bear their misfortunes without suffering any major deconstruction of identity. Their Roman Catholicism is itself a form of stay, 'an excellent prop in hours of danger'.[124]

In his essay, 'Nomad Art: Space', Gilles Deleuze describes the desert as the crucial landscape for the grounding of major religions: 'the great imperial religions need a smooth space like the desert, but only in order to give it a law that is opposed to the *nomos* in every way, and converts the absolute.'[125] Similarly, as the Christian travellers and the Muslim warriors assess each other's physical and spiritual strength, the novel affirms, as the common core of all religious faith, a 'calm, essential fatalism' which can sustain and direct the writing of human lives by 'whispering always that the worst which the world can do is a small thing, and that, however harsh the ways of Providence may seem, it is, on the whole, the wisest and best thing for us that we should go cheerfully whither the Great Hand guides us'.[126]

For Doyle, the connundrum of the desert is the figuring of the spirit, the crucial point of connection between masculinity and religion. While Christianity is troped through the comic and childish contradictions of the Reverend Stuart, the novel asserts the specifically masculine power of the Muslim religion. Describing 'the hour of Arab prayer', Doyle admires the earnestness of the hostage-takers who 'pray with their backs to the sun':

> Who could doubt, as he watched their strenuous, heart-whole devotion, that here was a great living power in the world, reactionary but tremendous ... who shall say that this may not be the besom with which Providence may sweep the rotten, decadent, impossible, half-hearted south of Europe, as it did a thousand years ago, until it makes room for a sounder stock?[127]

As the hostages face death or conversion to an alien religion, Doyle questions the role of the ego in making this decision, imaging investment in selfhood as an ideological affect which keeps the body politic from going on strike:

> Is it the fear of losing the I, that dear, intimate I, which we think we know so well, although it is eternally doing things which surprise us? Is it that which makes the deliberate suicide cling madly to the bridge-pier as the river sweeps him by? Or is it that Nature is so afraid that all her weary workmen may suddenly throw down their tools and strike, that she has invented this fashion of keeping them constant to their present work?[128]

With Nature suddenly constructed as a skilful propagandist averting strikes in the body politic, Doyle's writing suddenly finds itself on dangerous ground, at a place where language must be swallowed. Even in the desert, which exposes the props and stays of apparent power, there are lines to be drawn and silences maintained. There are limits to the revolutionary otherness that can be tolerated and endured; there are limits to the possibilities of personal transformation; there are lines in the sand which permit no transgression. As Doyle's metaphor raises the notion of political strike and class rebellion in a novel decentring the privileged vision of its Western tourists, one of those lines is suddenly drawn. A camel stops in the sand and refuses to move.

The recurrent landscape of Doyle's early work – the swampy landscape of disappearance briefly reinvoked and left behind in the revolutionary politics of *Uncle Bernac* – suddenly and paradoxically reasserts itself in the middle of the Libyan desert. Dying for water, the caravan finds itself on the edge of 'drift sand', the sinking ground of the desert. The Arabs halted 'like men upon the brink of an unfordable river'. This man-eating, story-swallowing terrain is as unpassable in the desert as anywhere else in Doyle's fiction: 'An Arab will sometimes have to go fifty or a hundred miles to go round a drift. Suppose he tries to cross, his camel breaks its legs, and he himself is sucked in and swallowed.'[129] As always, this landscape of disappearance is a place of forgotten language and story-loss where books and bodies vanish to reappear as spirits on another level of representation, or simply as recycled writing turning up in a new context. In the middle of *The Tragedy of the Korosko*, a lengthy passage from *A Study in Scarlet* suddenly appears. Doyle's description of the bone road first encountered by the Mormons in the Nevada desert is reinstated verbatim in the Libyan desert and recrossed by the hostages of the *Korosko* before they reach a resting point at an oasis. This is the place where two stories cross – the sign of masculine presence in Doyle's writing.

As the 'unhomely harshness' of the desert is replaced by the feminized beauty of Nature 'to whose bosom they were about to return', Doyle emphasizes the oasis as a site of disconnection where body and spirit loosen their ties in 'that most mysterious and least understood of miracles' – dream. The exhausted hostages have their first chance to sleep: 'So the spirits went their several ways, wandering back along strange, untraced tracks of the memory, while the weary, grimy bodies lay senseless under the palm-trees in the Oasis of the Libyan Desert.'[130]

This re-encounter with his own early writing and the image of spiritual release that concludes it is a turning point, not just in the plot, but also in Doyle's relationship to British imperialism. A change of spirit affects the hostages too. Faced with conversion to the Muslim religion, it is the turn of the rationalist Frenchman to experience a moment of self-definition. An unlikely martyr for the Christian faith, the atheistical Parisian performs 'miracles' in the guise of some rather crude conjuring tricks which, on board the *Korosko*, had not been 'skilful enough to deceive the critical European intelligence'.[131] They are not skilful enough to deceive the Arabs either but the time gained by his perfomance is crucial for his fellow hostages. In the event, Monsieur Fardet decides to kneel down with an ostentatious sign of the cross to die beside his companions when the Emir decides to take only the four richest hostages any further through the desert.

This conjuring motif recalls a similar moment of identity exchange and narrative substitution in Doyle's early Theosophical novel, *The Mystery of Cloomber*. The similarity in the writing is more than merely superficial. In *The Mystery of Cloomber* a British army officer had encountered a Buddhist Holy Man in a place of ambush and, when addressed by that early figure of the spirit, had made a brutal response. In *The Tragedy of the Korosko*, the representative of the British army, Colonel Cochrane, undergoes a similar encounter with the power of the spirit when a curious figure impinges on his field of vision. 'Good God!' he cried, 'I am going off my head.'

> On this pinnacle stood a solitary, motionless figure, clad entirely in black, save for a brilliant dash of scarlet upon his head. There could not surely be two such short sturdy figures, or such large colourless faces, in the Libyan Desert. His shoulders were stooping forward, and he seemed to be staring intently down into the ravine. His pose and outline were like a caricature of the great Napoleon.[132]

In his new guise as a caricature of the masculine sublime, the Reverend Stuart re-enters the story, having been picked up by a rescue party who were guided to him by the sound of his singing. His appearance, incongruous as always, is now augmented by a thick lance which he uses as a crutch to support his wounded leg, 'like a sheep which had suddenly developed claws'[133] or like the Arthurian knight, Sir Perceval, finding his way across the wasteland of the Grail Quest. His reappearance signals the rescue and redemption of his fellow travellers. Doyle uses a significant imagery of deadened nerves to convey the inner pain of the hostages' returning hope:

> The dull routine of misery through which they had passed had deadened all their nerves until they seemed incapable of any acute sensation, but now this sudden return of hope brought agony with it like the recovery of a frost-bitten limb.[134]

In one of the most surprising substitutions of his career, Doyle uses this pantomime figure to reimage the Napoleonic monolith of masculine greatness and to appropriate its absurdity in a convincing image of Christian power. By using a hybrid singing figure in which the great man is also part child and part clown to represent Christianity's voice in the silent desert, Doyle redraws the figure in the sand which had presided over his writing of masculinity until this point. The novel's emphasis on the remodelling work of the desert finds expression in the hostages' assessment of their traumatic experience: 'they had been swept out of that placid stream of existence, and dashed against the horrible, jagged facts of life … . Great hands had closed suddenly upon them, and had moulded them into new shapes, and fitted them for new uses.'[135]

This imagery of hands, whether those of God, Allah or the French atheist trying to buy time with the 'obvious palming' of his crude conjuring tricks, is repeatedly invoked in the novel as the physical site of a writing which is both providential and literary. While Monsieur Fardet claims that all providence has done is to heal 'the wound which its own hand inflicted',[136] Reverend Stuart quotes Tennyson's lines: 'I stretch lame hands of faith' to reaffirm the hand as a site of the spirit in a landscape of death. The novel concludes with the hands of lovers meeting 'under the shadow of the table'. The hands of the author had, at the time of writing, made a similar set of contacts.

The torture of the desert finds its justification in the reshaping of a spiritual experience out of which new models of the body emerge. Those hostages who survived the experience all agree that they had risen 'to a greater height during those days in the desert'.[137] The new image of the 'master spirit' that emerges from this ordeal is significantly non-gender-specific. Doyle refers to the Irish Catholic, Mrs Belmont, as 'masterful' in her steady refusal to fear the death with which she is threatened, her masculinity of spirit matched by the courage of her husband. The cost and shock of this spiritual reshaping is minimized both by the text and by the unemotional Anglo-Saxon, Colonel Cochrane, who refers to it as merely 'a good shake up'. Far from a jingoistic foregrounding of military exploits, the battle between the dervishes and the military rescue corps is described at long distance, minimizing its physical significance: 'In that perfectly dry and clear light, with the unvarying brown tint of the hard desert as a background, every detail stood out as clearly as if they were toy figures arranged upon a table within hand's touch of them.'[138]

The final perspective on colonialism offered by the novel is that of a torture inflicted upon bodies so that they may adapt themselves to the inexorable process of cultural change. Just as the Mormons in *A Study in Scarlet* had been represented as unsound in their polygamous marital practices, so too the religion of the dervishes, devout, aggressive but exclusively male, falls short in its failure to encompass the developments of modern civilization and the spiritual masculinity of nineteenth-century womanhood. Between the drift sand and the bone road where this desert action takes place, between Gladstonian views of colonial 'drift' and the militarism of the British conservatives, Doyle inscribes both the newly spiritualised figure of the Empire, the heroically wounded body associated with it and the future direction of his own writing. From the nervous body of *The Stark Munro Letters* to the competitive pugilism of *Rodney Stone* and the agile escapology of the *Brigadier Gerard* stories, Doyle's novels of the 1890s map a hardening physique which understands its own suffering as building a body upon which the differences within a unifiable culture are deeply impressed. The inspiration of the farseeing spirit which has the capacity to interpret them all is neither liberal nor conservative. However ridiculous its trappings, its vision is a radical one.

Doyle might, perhaps, have been a major novelist of empire but to travel that route he would have had to face the drift sands of the masculine unspeakable. As the best of the Holmes stories about empire had so graphically illustrated, on the subject of the masculine body to articulate everything was forbidden. To articulate even some of it was difficult, as the 'pessimistic' Thomas Hardy and the 'decadent' Oscar Wilde, had both discovered. *The Tragedy of the Korosko* marks the limits of Doyle's adventures in realist territory.

The marriage question

Like Hardy, Doyle closed his career as a Victorian novelist with a novel about marriage: one which was neither pessimistic, unmanly or decadent. *A Duet* (1899) is a domestic novel which describes a courtship conducted at the great shrines of masculine and marital representation: 5 Cheyne Row, the home of Thomas and Jane Welsh Carlyle, and the tomb of Samuel Pepys and his wife at St Olaves Church. For Doyle, Pepys, with his cipher-ridden *Diary*, remains the man who, uniquely, found a way of telling the inner story of manhood.

Writing about marriage was not necessarily any easier than writing about imperialism, as Hardy had discovered with the publication of *Jude the Obscure* in 1895. Doyle's *A Duet* is an attempt to replace the bleak pessimism of Hardy's masterpiece with a novel which tries to establish the groundrules for a successful cross-class partnership. In writing about the private sphere, Doyle sought to represent a normative and shareable masculine experience, often with considerable success. One of his earliest contributions to the Society of Authors had been a reading of his short story about childbirth, 'The Curse of Eve', which drew on his medical experience in its account of a wife dying in childbirth. However, the story was not well received in its original form and had to be toned down for publication, a safe delivery taking the place of an agonizing death. Robert Blatchford, the socialist journalist, refers to this particular story in his autobiography as speaking for a definitive moment in a man's private life: 'If you are not a father, gentle reader, get Sir Arthur Conan Doyle's story, "The Curse of Eve," and ponder it well'.[139]

In *Through the Magic Door* Doyle had argued that the love story 'must be handled by some great master who has courage to break down conventionalities and to go straight to actual life for his inspiration'.[140] His own novel, *A Duet*, takes none of these risks. Light and funny and firmly middle class, using the image of duet to emphasize the harmonized music of conjoined lives, the novel addresses two issues: what are the agreements that stabilize marriage and what is the best way to commemorate a marriage after the death of one of the partners. Forms of memorial discussed in the novel range from the medieval to the modern, from the line of crosses built by Edward I to mark the sad journey of his wife's coffin from the North of England to Westminster Abbey, to the maudlin *Reminiscences* of Thomas Carlyle. This double project connects Doyle's own declining marriage to Touie to his developing relationship with Jean Leckie.

The marriage at the centre of *A Duet* is one situated both within a cultural history of marriage and within the power relations of British imperialism. The 'Twenty Maxims for the Married'[141] upon which the couple agree are intended to reflect similar agreements about the use of power throughout the British Empire. The architecture of Westminster Abbey is used to symbolize the right spirit of British imperial power, despite its less auspicious modes of manifestation:

> How anything so graceful came to be built by this tasteless and utilitarian nation must remain a marvel to the traveller. The sun was shining upon the gold-work of the roof ... like some gorgeous palace in a dream. It was a fit centre for the rule to whose mild sway one fifth of the human race acquiesces – a rule upheld by so small a force that only the consent of the governed can sustain it.[142]

Working within these large frameworks of orthodoxy, however, Doyle's writing is shot through with subversive inscriptions and deviant perspectives which offer a counter-image of English culture to that inscribed in its formal records and memorials. The monuments of Westminster Abbey carry schoolboy graffiti. The Carlyle Museum in Cheyne Row enshrines not only a major literary marriage but small memorials of other lives spent within its walls and cleaning its windows. At the outset of his career, Doyle had publicly championed Carlyle, bemoaning only 'the strange and obscure style ... which ... prevented his works from reaching the lower classes'.[143] Revisiting this site of literary influence, Doyle defends Carlyle as a husband but not as an employer. Carlyle's treatment of 'that long succession of serving-maids of whom we gain shadowy glimpses in the *Letters* and in the *Journal*' is 'the worst thing I have against him'.[144]

Doyle's career as a novelist can be partly put into context through his dialogue with the major novelist of his age, Thomas Hardy, who also saw himself as a man of defining visions. Hardy's longsighted view of the ideological fissures in contemporary culture was offset by none of the short-term solutions to which Doyle directed his attention. Partly because of his Scottish education, Doyle situated literature in a more dialogic and communicative relationship with legal, medical and religious discourse than Hardy was able to contemplate. The differences between them are instructive. Hardy published *Jude the Obscure*, repeatedly denying that he intended the novel to be an attack on the institution of marriage. Indeed, in his autobiography, he went to considerable lengths to present himself as a man of close marital partnerships. While Doyle's *A Duet* discusses marriage as a set of groundrules and agreements, the pragmatic moderateness of this view is offset by his vigorous public campaigning to improve the laws relating to divorce. In his subsequent role as president of the Society for the Reform of the Divorce Laws, he campaigned for the dissolution of harmful or non-consensual partnerships, arguing convincingly that it is not the family, but the *happy* family, which forms the basis of national life.

Notes

1. Doyle, A. C., *Memories and Adventures*, London: John Murray, 1930, p. 117.
2. Doyle, A. C., *Beyond the City*, London: George Newnes, 1891, p. 192.
3. Ibid., p. 5.
4. Ibid., p. 89.
5. Ibid., p. 82.
6. Ibid., p. 190.
7. Ibid., p. 170.
8. Ibid., p. 18.
9. Doyle, A. C., *Through the Magic Door*, London: Smith Elder & Co., 1907, p. 139.
10. Doyle, *Beyond the City*, op. cit., p. 28.
11. Ibid., p. 161.
12. Doyle, *Memories and Adventures*, op. cit., p. 117.
13. Doyle, A. C., *The Great Shadow*, Elstree, Hertfordshire: Greenhill Famous Authors, 1987, p. 9.
14. Ibid., p. 208.
15. Ibid., p. 48.
16. Ibid., p. 215.
17. Ibid., p. 220.
18. Ibid., p. 43.
19. Ibid., p. 56.
20. Hardy, T., 'Preface', *The Dynasts*, London: Macmillan, 1965, pp. xxiii–xxvii.
21. Doyle, *Memories and Adventures*, op. cit., p. 116.
22. Ibid., p. 117.
23. Doyle, A. C., *The Refugees* in *The Historical Novels*, vol. 2, Poole: New Orchard Ltd, 1986, p. 661.
24. Ibid., p. 774.
25. Ibid., p. 702.
26. Ibid.
27. Green, R. L. and Gibson, J. M. (eds), *A Bibliography of A. Conan Doyle*, Oxford: Clarendon Press, 1983, p. 68.
28. Doyle, *The Refugees*, op. cit., p. 768.
29. Ibid., p. 767.
30. Ibid., p. 770.
31. Ibid., p. 794.

32. Ibid., p. 799.
33. Doyle, *Memories and Adventures*, op. cit., p. 306.
34. See Knight, S., 'The Case Of The Great Detective' in Hodgson, J. A. (ed.), *Arthur Conan Doyle; Sherlock Holmes: The Major Stories with Contemporary Critical Essays*, Boston: St Martins Press, 1994, p. 372.
35. Logan, P. M., *Nerves and Narratives: A Cultural History of Hysteria in 19th-Century British Prose*, Berkeley: University of California Press, 1997, p. 171.
36. Ibid., p. 5.
37. Ibid., p. 168.
38. Ibid., p. 169.
39. Doyle, A. C., *The Parasite*, Westminster: A. Constable & Co., 1984, p. 97.
40. Ibid., p. 11.
41. Ibid., p. 63.
42. Ibid., p. 100.
43. Ibid., pp. 75–6.
44. Ibid., p. 121.
45. See Basham, D., *The Trial of Woman: Feminism and the Occult Sciences in Victorian Literature and Culture*, London: Macmillan, 1992, p. 179.
46. See Pearson, H., *Conan Doyle: His Life and Art*, London: Methuen & Co., 1943, p. 23.
47. Doyle, *Memories and Adventures*, op. cit., p. 71.
48. Doyle, A. C., *The Stark Munro Letters*, London: Smith Elder & Co., 1912, p. 341.
49. Ibid., p. 67.
50. Ibid., p. 119.
51. Ibid., p. 144.
52. Ibid., pp. 62–3.
53. Ibid., p. 149.
54. Ibid., p. 66.
55. Ibid., p. 51.
56. Green and Gibson, *A Bibliography of A. Conan Doyle*, op. cit., p. 89.
57. Doyle, *The Stark Munro Letters*, op. cit., p. 65.
58. Ibid., p. 133.
59. Ibid., p. 14.
60. Ibid., p. 171.
61. Ibid., pp. 147–8.
62. Ibid., p. 331.
63. See Logan, *Nerves and Narratives*, op. cit., p. 16.
64. Ibid., p. 23.
65. Doyle, *The Stark Munro Letters*, op. cit., pp. 75–6.
66. Ibid., p. 73.
67. See Logan, *Nerves and Narratives*, op. cit., p. 29.
68. Doyle, *The Stark Munro Letters*, op. cit., p. 83.
69. See Logan, *Nerves and Narratives*, op. cit., p. 28–9.
70. Ibid., pp. 29–30.
71. Doyle, *The Stark Munro Letters*, op. cit., p. 155.
72. Ibid., p. 156.
73. Ibid., p. 330.
74. Ibid., p. 326.

75. Ibid., p. 336.
76. Ibid., pp. 329–30.
77. Newey, V. and Shaw, P. (eds), *Mortal Pages, Literary Lives: Studies in Nineteenth-Century Autobiography*, Aldershot: Scolar Press, 1996, p. 126.
78. Doyle, *The Stark Munro Letters*, op. cit., pp. 341–2.
79. Ibid., p. 210.
80. Doyle, *Through the Magic Door*, op. cit., p. 122.
81. Ibid., p. 123.
82. Ibid., p. 124.
83. Maupassant, G. de, 'L'Auberge' in *88 Short Stories*, London: Cassel, 1950.
84. Doyle, *Through the Magic Door*, op. cit., p. 171.
85. Ibid., p. 169.
86. Ibid., pp. 199–201.
87. Doyle, A. C., *The Exploits of Brigadier Gerard*, London: John Murray, 1917, p. 7.
88. Ibid., pp. 101–2.
89. Ibid., p. 67.
90. Doyle, *Memories and Adventures*, op. cit., p. 184.
91. Doyle, *Through the Magic Door*, op. cit., pp. 185–6.
92. Ibid., p. 187.
93. Emerson, R. W., *English Traits*, Riverside edn, London: George Routledge & Sons, 1902, pp. 99–100.
94. Doyle, A. C., *Rodney Stone* in *The Historical Novels*, vol. 2, op. cit., p. 1031.
95. Ibid., p. 953.
96. Ibid., p. 955.
97. Ibid., p. 998.
98. Ibid., pp. 856–7.
99. Ibid., p. 1011.
100. Ibid., p. 863.
101. Ibid., pp. 1107–8.
102. Doyle, A. C., *Uncle Bernac*, London: John Murray, 1924, p. 152.
103. Ibid., p. 158.
104. Ibid., p. 178.
105. Ibid., p. 264.
106. Eldridge, C. C., *The Imperial Experience: From Carlyle to Forster*, Basingstoke: Macmillan, 1996, p. 31.
107. Ibid., p. 96.
108. Green, and Gibson, *A Bibliography of A. Conan Doyle*, op. cit., p. 106.
109. Doyle, *Memories and Adventures*, op. cit., p. 151.
110. Doyle, A. C., *The Tragedy of the Korosko*, London: Smith, Elder & Co., 1910, p. 8.
111. Ibid., p. 24.
112. Ibid., p. 40.
113. Ibid., pp. 40–41
114. Ibid., p. 55.
115. Ibid., p. 61.
116. Ibid., pp. 72–3.
117. Ibid., p. 75.

118. Ibid., pp. 79–80.
119. Ibid., p. 90.
120. Ibid., p. 92.
121. Ibid., p. 93.
122. Ibid., pp. 130–31.
123. Ibid., p. 132.
124. Ibid., p. 123.
125. Deleuze, G., 'Nomad Art Space' in Boundas, C. V. (ed.), *The Deleuze Reader*, New York: Columbia University Press, 1993, p. 168.
126. Doyle, *The Tragedy of the Korosko*, op. cit., p. 124.
127. Ibid., p. 127.
128. Ibid., pp. 147–8.
129. Ibid., pp. 153–4.
130. Ibid., pp. 168–9.
131. Ibid., p. 19.
132. Ibid., pp. 221–2.
133. Ibid., p. 334.
134. Ibid., p. 194.
135. Ibid., pp. 237–8.
136. Ibid., p. 252.
137. Ibid., p. 254.
138. Ibid., p. 239.
139. Blatchford, R., *My Eighty Years*, London: Cassell & Co., 1931, p. 167.
140. Doyle, *Through the Magic Door*, op. cit., p. 265.
141. Doyle, A. C., *A Duet,* London: Grant Richards, 1899, pp. 126–7.
142. Ibid., p. 47.
143. Quoted in Stavert, G., *A Study in Southsea*, Portsmouth: Milestone Publications, 1987, p. 72.
144. Doyle, *A Duet*, op. cit., p. 309.

CHAPTER FIVE

Figures in the Sand: Histories, War Correspondence and Legal Campaigning

Egypt and the Sudan

In his study of Victorian tourism, *The Mediterranean Passion* (1987), John Pemble claims that the establishment of the British protectorate in 1882 and an improved railway system made Egypt one of the favourite winter resorts for British tourists in the 1880s and 1890s. Cairo, where Doyle had taken Touie for her health in 1895, had become established as 'a meeting-place of the British Empire and the British metropolis' and was described by a Thomas Cook brochure as 'no more than a winter suburb of London'.[1] Its popularity derived in part from the beneficial therapeutic effects which its climate and calm dry air appeared to offer sufferers from pulmonary tuberculosis. The Doyles stayed at one of the newly opened health resorts, the Mena House Hotel near the Great Pyramid. As Touie began to feel well enough to enjoy a social life in the company of her sister-in-law, Lottie, Doyle 'joined in male society ... a good deal and learned to know many of the great men who were shaping the new destinies of Egypt'.[2]

As he had illustrated in *The Tragedy of the Korosko*, those new destinies were linked to the political instabilities of the neighbouring Sudan. In 1883 British imperial power had been challenged by the revolt of the Mahdi who had proclaimed a Jihad to end Anglo-Egyptian control of the Sudan. By the time of Doyle's visit, these desert terrorists had inflicted a series of sharp defeats on the British-led army. Colonel William Hicks with 10 000 Egyptian troops had been defeated and killed by the Mahdists at El Obeid in 1883. His fellow general, Valentine Baker, had been demoted to the level of the *gendarmerie* following a humiliating conviction for indecent assault. In 1884 the Anglo-Egyptian army suffered another defeat at El Teb forcing a decision from Gladstone's government to evacuate the Sudan. These defeats famously culminated in the death of General Gordon who had been sent to Khartoum to supervise the British withdrawal and who was killed there in January 1885, two days before the arrival of the relief expedition. In 1895, following his gradual reconstruction of the Anglo-Egyptian army,

Major General Kitchener was given the task of reconquering the Sudan by Lord Salisbury's Conservative government. As Doyle put it, 'Egypt had suddenly become the storm centre of the world, and chance had placed me there at that moment'.[3]

The moment was important both in terms of the assembly of personnel who were to play a part in later, larger scenarios of European history and for its reinscription of the British imperial spirit in the sands of the desert. Confronted with the religious commitment of the Mahdists, however, the task of defining that spirit was not an easy one. Although General Gordon had been hailed as a Christian hero, British perceptions of manliness were being shaped by a Protestant, but increasingly secularized culture. In the historiography of Queen Victoria's 'little wars', 'modernity' was the key word. Battles, if the British won them, were described as an encounter between the ancient and the modern, not just in terms of weaponry but also in terms of manhood.

Previous disasters affecting British military morale spoke strongly to Doyle's sense of vocation. In the Holmes stories he had defined as his own those territories where the representation of British manhood seemed most in need of a champion. Amid the swampy politics of *Uncle Bernac* he had invoked that 'curious saint-like trait in our natures which draws us most strongly towards that which involves the greatest sacrifice'.[4] His emphasis on sacrifice struck a strong contemporary note. The publication in 1897 of *The Tragedy of the Korosko* had provided a timely forecast of the reassertion of British military power in the Sudan. As his sense of vocation clarified, so Doyle found himself in geographical regions which confirmed his own literary topographies. The symbolic landscapes he had constructed in his fictional dramas of masculine disappearance and identity exchange became a reality in the years between 1896 and 1918 as he travelled the war zones of the Sudan, South Africa, France and Flanders. The often uncanny match between Doyle's literary locations and the regions of military encounter intensified that sense of providential mission that provides so strong a theme of his autobiography: 'Providence one way or another gets a man's full powers out of him, but ... the man himself should co-operate to the extent of putting himself in the way of achievement .... If your path lies elsewhere, then you have got your sign through your failure.'[5]

But there were other destinies at work in Egypt besides the political and the military. Concentrated here, too, were health-seeking bodies and faith-seeking spirits. Just as General Gordon had seen in the desert regions round the Nile a land which confirmed the authenticity of the scriptures and intensified religious belief, so too, according to John Pemble, Victorian tourists commonly experienced a renewed religious faith in regions which made real their readings of the Bible. Pemble claims that the healing effects of the desert derived less from the dry air than from this reaffirmation of faith. In the desert, he claims, 'medicine and religion met; for when the Victorian doctor sent his patients into the wilderness he became identified ... with the Old Testament Deity, summoning his votaries from the flesh pots to a new life'.[6]

With Doyle, it was the doctor rather than his patient who appears to have received the summons. Although he had officially rejected the faith of his fathers, biblical tropes, disguised, submerged and secularized, structure his writing about Egypt even in the smallest detail. In keeping with the sacerdotal tendency of late-Victorian tourist writing, *The Tragedy of the Korosko* had centred itself on the prophetic impulses of Christianity as figured by Reverend Stuart. If medicine and religion met in Egypt, so too did spirituality and war. The tension between these opposing poles of masculine representation is the context for the next phase of Doyle's writing.

The Sudan represented a border at which the limits of Englishness, empire and Christianity were situated. It had become not merely a geographical and historical site but also a biographical one – a place where biographical subjects from Christ himself to General Gordon could be situated in a modernized and secularized, but still Christian tradition, of iconography. Protestant biography had become the secular equivalent of canonization. According to Jon Hohenberg, it was partly the effect of this hagiography and 'the "great man" theory of history' associated with it[7] which had led to Gordon's appointment to the Sudan in the first place. He was the magical figure who 'could change the deteriorating situation' merely by his presence. By the time of Doyle's visit, the Sudan had become a site not so much for lives as for life-writing. General Gordon himself had illustrated this perception of the place shortly before his own death. Hearing that a Frenchman had been captured by the Madhists, he became irrationally convinced that the man in question must be Ernst Renan, the secularizing biographer of Christ.

General Gordon's ideological importance has been extensively discussed in recent studies of Victorian masculinity. Typifying imperial virtue, Gordon's military manhood was canonized as 'the highest mode of masculine service to King and Empire'. Eva Hope's 1885 biography of Gordon offered him as a lesson to the young in how 'to make the best of their lives', telling her readers 'to discover in him the qualities out of which all heroes are made'.[8] According to Graham Dawson in *Soldier Heroes*, Gordon's murder at Khartoum by the Mahdist forces 'was invested as the ideal type of Christian forbearance in the face of suffering and death'.[9] It is this paradoxical image that George Joy had aimed to present in his famous 1893 painting *The Last Stand of*

General Gordon. Joy saw Gordon's death as a betrayal by the British government 'of all that was highest and best in our national instincts, life, and traditions' as well as a betrayal 'of one of the greatest men we ever possessed; of the anti-slavery cause in the Soudan; as well as of the doomed inhabitants of Khartoum, who had trusted to us, and to our plighted word, to help and protect them.'[10]

It is this representational background, rather than any direct experience of war, that makes Egypt and the Sudan the vital territory in Doyle's still ambivalent interpretation of his own vocation. Significantly, one of the best known accounts of the Sudanese war was written by a young lieutenant attached to the 31st Lancers who was already beginning to construct his own reputation as 'the greatest living Englishman'.[11] Winston Churchill's dispatches for the *Morning Post* later formed the basis for his book *The River War* (1899) and provided a model of manly writing about war that was constantly, but unsuccessfully, contested by Doyle in his own work.

By 1896 when the British reconquest of the Sudan under Major General H. H. Kitchener began, the topography of these regions was beginning to acquire its own discourse. Influential in this was the writing of G. W. Steevens, war correspondent for the *Daily Mail*. In his book *With Kitchener to Khartoum* Steevens had described the desert landscape in terms of its equivalence to a certain stage of masculine development:

> Perhaps to Englishmen – half-savage still on the pinnacles of their civilisation – the very charm of the land lies in its empty barbarism. There is space in the Sudan. There is the fine, purified desert air, and the long stretching gallops over its sand ... . You have gone back to the spring water of your infancy. You are a savage again ... . You are unprejudiced, simple, free. You are a naked man, facing naked nature.[12]

Often constructed as the ultimate territory for masculine representation – so devoid of comfort and resources that it tested and made visible the spirit – the desert provided the landscape against which the shape of the masculine became peculiarly visible. Where Steevens saw it as a place of exchange between primitive freedom and the civilized spirit of British imperialism, Doyle wrote of it as a site of performance for a clown who has yet to become a magician. His own horsemanship was severely tested by one of 'the weird steeds provided by the livery stable' which bolted, threw him and then 'pawing about with his front hoofs, struck me over the eye, and made a deep star-shaped wound which covered me with blood'.[13] This 'black devil' of a horse marked him for life, but not in the Romantic fashion of Byron's *Mazeppa*. Needing five stitches for the wound, he adds, 'I was thankful, for ... I might have lost my sight'.

Into this landscape of great men and Christian propaganda, Doyle introduced a plethora of comedic animals whose task was to deflect the lure of masculine self-aggrandizement. The threat to sight averted, Doyle learns from his fall how to 'see' the desert. Where T. E. Lawrence, according to Edward Said, sought to construct and represent the Orient through a form of 'masquerade' in which he masochistically entered the realm of the racial and social Other,[14] Doyle attempts to hang on to his horse and his heterosexuality. Repeated falls from unaccommodating animals teach him to resist the lure of a Romanticized, overrepresented desert masculinity. He writes the desert by keeping his eyes quite literally to the ground, creating a masculine literature which parodies its own authorship as fallen. Reading the signs of the sand, he also alters his own mode of representational practice, letting animals carry all that is unspeakable in the human story.

In keeping with the language system of the ancient Egyptians (and, incidentally, of the Doyle family themselves), the Egyptian chapters of Doyle's autobiography resort to an animal hieroglyphics in which creatures act as the units of a parodic narrative. Being in Egypt allowed him to assert a providential vantage-point of vision, conferring on him that 'privileged access to "truth" which', according to David Alderson, 'manliness claimed in England over the course of the nineteenth century'.[15] The animals, on the other hand, ensured that that vision was kept close to the ground. In becoming an Empire-writer, Doyle began to modify the English identity that he had been carefully forging for himself since the inception of the Holmes stories.

The closer to the centre of British culture he moved, the more these animal bodies with their countermessages are at work in his text, signifying evasion and suppression of discourse. His account of the Sudan concludes with his return to London and a banquet at Burlington House at which he watches the eggs laid by the poisonous jiggers of the Nile begin to hatch out in his wrists. In contexts where the lie is the condition of masculinity, animal anecdotes become Doyle's truth-signals, indicating a second-level discourse that articulates repressed or censured material. The repeated fall motif associated with these anecdotes suggests hidden confessions relating to his own body history. Egypt for Doyle is everywhere a body story. Where books trope, and substitute for, hidden emotional content in his work, animals signify problems in the representation of physical masculinity.

In what turns out to be the transformative episode of his autobiography, Doyle describes a 'sight-seeing' excursion to a Coptic monastery fifty miles from Cairo in the company of Colonel Lewis of the Egyptian army. The only conveyance the two men can find for their trip is 'a most amazing vehicle ... a sort of circus coach, all gilding and frippery' which turns out to be the state coach prepared for Napoleon III on the chance that he would come and open the Suez Canal.[16] With wheelmarks across the sand as their only guide, Doyle, Lewis and their Nubian driver set out across the desert, the surreal nature of their transport emphasized by the fact that Lewis is a fitness fanatic who prefers to run behind the coach rather than travel in it. A latter-day Tamburlaine in a parody of imperial grandeur, Doyle recalls: 'I remember saying to him that in my wildest dreams I never thought that I should drive across the Libyan Desert in an Emperor's coach with a full colonel as carriage dog.'[17]

Cursed by a thirsty native to whom they have denied water, a sudden, uncanny fall of rain rapidly erases the tracks they are following. As night falls, his party realize they are lost without food, water or direction. Doyle is eventually able to track a route by using the stars as an aid to navigation and by holding lighted matches to the sand to read its surface. Suddenly, to their great relief, they see a light ahead shining from the tent of a surly German surveyor who is camping in the desert. He directs them towards a halfway house where they can rest for the night. But this is more Childe Roland's pilgrimage rather than Childe Harold's and his directions send them round in a circle until, after a further two hours' travel, they come for a second time 'to a tent with a florid bearded man seated outside it ... drawing by the light of a lamp'.[18]

'We had moved in a circle.' Throughout his career, Doyle indicated moments of particular significance in his writing through a recurrent trope of bodies, like that of the German surveyor, situated in an alien sand. The first Holmes story had begun with this motif. Identifying a place where vision and identity suddenly shift their foundations, these figures represent, for Doyle, a counter-emotional crossing point, marking points at which the signs of the future are made visible.

After such a journey, the Coptic monastery, when they finally reach it, is an anti-climax, consisting of a huge outer wall of hardened clay, with 'no doors or windows save one little opening which could be easily defended against the prowling Arabs'.[19] The anecdote illustrates a comic confusion of the military and the spiritual which affects both inmates and visitors. The Brothers seem equally devoid of courage or spirituality, Doyle commenting acidly, 'it was said to be fear of military service which caused many of the monks to discover that they had a vocation'. This configuration of the soldier and the monk, the fighting flesh and the retreating spirit, connects Doyle with what he sees. He also shares the confusion of the monks, mistaking a supply of Holy Bread for a barrel of light stones to throw at the enemy. In the end, it is the doctor in Doyle rather than the fighter or the writer who is of most use in this context of problematized masculinity. Despite his advanced spirituality, the Coptic Abbot has a weak chest and is deeply grateful to be examined and treated by the Western doctor.

Doyle's journey into the wilderness, for that is what the episode inscribes, concludes with eyesight, identity and vocation restored as he compares his field of perception with that of the monks: 'As I looked from the walls and saw the desert on all sides ... it was strange to consider that this was all which these men would ever see of the world, and to contrast their fate with my own busy and varied existence.'[20] This busy, varied, worldly vision is the point of affirmation in Doyle's encounter with the desert. Returning to Cairo, Doyle and Lewis hear that war has been declared, that the British reconquest of the Sudan is under way and that, in the march on Dongola, Colonel Lewis has been placed in command of an advanced brigade. Hearing this in the cloak-room of the Turf Club, Lewis, no self-absolving Pontius Pilate, drops the soap with which he had been washing his hands. Doyle concludes: 'Thus it was that we learned of the next adventure which was opening up before both us and the British Empire.'[21]

The new writing adventure opening up for Doyle was the result of his cabling the *Westminster Gazette* and asking to be employed as an honorary war correspondent. The newspaper's acceptance of his offer led him away from fiction writing towards the more declaratively masculine work of dealing with reality and chronicling the wars. In Doyle's autobiography, this tourist visit to the Coptic monastery is written as a symbolic journey full of quest-like ambiguities with regard to different vocations and conflicting archetypes of the masculine. The Egyptian chapters of *Memories and Adventures* hold the secret of Doyle's writing identity, demonstrating that simultaneous capacity for double vision celebrated in the Holmes stories. Beneath a shortsighted physical buffoonery lies a long-range scrutiny of logical structures which the clowning comedically represents. The future is figured through the incongruous images of the present, while comedy itself becomes a vehicle of spiritual vision. The dream-like images of the travel narrative carry a carefully structured resymbolization of Doyle's entire career path, as he moves through war towards his controversial Spiritualist mission.

At the Coptic monastery, Doyle had seen books strewn across the library floor, prefiguring, in his usual substitution, the scattered bodies of the Sudan. Some of these bodies can still be seen in vivid photographs of Kitchener's victories at Atbara and Omdurman, the Mahdist capital opposite Khartoum, in 1898. The body of the Khalifa himself, killed at Um Diwaykarat in 1899, was photographed with some of the thousand dervishes who died with him in this relatively minor battle. The tomb of the Mahdi was desecrated and his bones thrown into the

Nile. At Khartoum, a funeral service for General Gordon was held at his ruined palace which flew both the British and Egyptian flags. In his account of the funeral, G. W. Steevens acknowledged the legend of General Gordon but commemorated him as a version of the unfallen Englishman:

> Gordon had become a legend with his countrymen, and they all but deify him dead who would never have heard of him had he lived. But in this garden you somehow came to know Gordon the man, not the myth, and to feel near to him. Here was an English-man doing his duty, alone and at the instant peril of his life; yet still he loved his garden. The garden was a yet more pathetic ruin than the palace.[22]

As Steevens's eulogy illustrates, representations of Victorian manhood were still contextualized within a Christian, biblical tradition. Once that context was removed, the representation of masculine military behaviour became increasingly problematic. Before being sent to Khartoum, General Gordon had been preparing for service in the Congo under King Leopold of Belgium. In Doyle's hard-hitting monograph of 1909, *The Crime of the Congo*, King Leopold is figured as the ultimate incarnation of an evil imperial regime. However overrun, Gordon was fortunate in his garden. In the iconography of the Congo, halos tended to be made of burning rubber.

War correspondence

Events in the Sudan during the 1880s and 1890s illustrated, not only the new power of the press in influencing foreign affairs, but also the role of the war correspondent in generating and perpetuating masculine reputations. Preparing the first draft of history, war correspondents vied with biographers in the process of monumentalizing male names and masculine achievement. They contributed significantly to that cult of the celebrity which, Roger Stearn argues, was a creation of nineteenth-century journals such as *The World* and *The Strand*, which carried mass-produced photographs of culturally significant people along with biographical sketches. War correspondence was part of a system of celebritization associated with the career opportunities peculiar to war. In the Sudan Doyle met an amateur correspondent who was 'destined later to be the naval historian of the Great War'.[23] Doyle himself followed a similar trajectory.

The ability of war correspondents to control reputations and make or break careers had first been made apparent in the Crimea when *The Times* correspondent, W. H. Russell, exposed the inadequacies of

British military provision – an exposure which prompted the collapse and death of Lord Raglan. The situation in the Sudan was even more dramatic, for it was already a place haunted by that kind of legend which comes into being when celebrity encounters mortality, as General Gordon had done at Khartoum. The work of the war correspondents had been crucial to the making of this legend and it, in turn, had helped to glamorize the risk-taking masculine writing associated with the profession. In 1883 when the Mahdi's forces had defeated the Egyptian army at El Obeid, two war correspondents from the *Daily News* and the *Graphic* had been killed with the soldiers. The *Times* correspondent in Khartoum, Frank le Poer Power, who had missed the battle through a fortunate attack of dysentery, had been the first to report the story. When Gladstone attempted to pursue a policy of disengagement in the Sudan, the press argued that Khartoum at least must be defended against the Mahdi and it was W. T. Stead who suggested General Gordon as the man for the job. Frank Power himself was murdered during his attempted escape from Khartoum, and four more war correspondents were killed in battles prior to the fall of Khartoum and the decapitation of Gordon on the steps of the governor's palace in January 1885.

War correspondence showed the construction of Victorian masculinity in its most immediate, enthusiastic, patriotic and self-promulgating form. Doyle practised war correspondence as he had practised fiction, by recycling the work of other men, however, within that formulaic system he found ways of expressing difference of viewpoint. A comparison between Doyle's account of the reconstruction of the Anglo-Egyptian army and that of one of his mentors, Bennet Burleigh of the *Daily Telegraph*, illustrates this difference. Burleigh, one of the most authoritative of the new breed of correspondents, combined an apparently dispassionate understanding of military science with a fervently British perspective. He had, for example, blamed the native Egyptian troops for the failure of 'Hicks Pasha':

> I knew several members of Hicks Pasha's Staff, and a more efficient body of officers never accompanied any Egyptian force afield. What the real cause was of the fate that befell Hicks Pasha's army near El Obeid, we shall possibly never know. Perhaps it was due to the one fatal defect that pertains to all Egyptian troops composed of fellaheen – want of courage, or martial ardour. There is no disguising the fact, that as a soldier the Egyptian fellah is worthless. He cowers at alarms, and shrinks from a contest involving physical suffering to himself ... . No amount of personal example and European officering will prevail upon them to offer stubborn and desperate battle.[24]

While Doyle's account paraphrases Burleigh's opinions, his phrasing restructures the understanding of the relationship between British officers and native troops. The fear of the Egyptian soldiers facing Mahdist forces appears, in Doyle's account, altogether reasonable:

> The great question at the opening of the campaign was whether the native fellah troops would stand. The five negro battalions were as good as could be, but the record of the eight or nine Egyptian ones was not reassuring. The Arab of the Soudan is a desperate fanatic who rushes to death with the frenzy of a madman, and longs for close quarters where he can bury his spear in the body of his foeman, even though he carries several bullets in him before he reaches him. Would the Egyptians stand such onslaughts as these? It was thought improbable that they would.[25]

While Burleigh praises the supreme model of European officering, Doyle writes of the relationship between officers and native troops as one based on a paternalistic 'Father Christmas' model. Officers of black troops, visiting Cairo, would come back with pillowcases stuffed with candies for their men. The Egyptian troops, however, tended to be unresponsive to this Christian paternalism and the public school ethos it encoded:

> The Egyptians were more inscrutable, less sporting and less lovable, but none the less their officers were very loyal to them and bitterly resented the distrust shown by the rest of the army. One British officer at some early battle seized the enemy's flag and cried 'Well, the English shall not have this anyhow!' It is this spirit, whether in Egypt or in India, which makes the British officer an ideal leader of native troops. Even at the great Indian Mutiny they would not hear a word against their men until they were murdered by them.[26]

In a memorable phrase, G. W. Steevens, described by Churchill as 'the most brilliant man in journalism',[27] had referred to British involvement in the Sudan between 1882 and 1899 as 'the fight of half a generation for such an emptiness'.[28] Certainly Doyle saw little enough to fill it. Arriving in Sarras on the way to Dongola, he had what he described as 'a glimpse of the actual outpost of civilisation, all sandbags and barbed wire, for there was a Mahdi post at no distance up the river'. He continues: 'It was wonderful to look south and to see distant peaks said to be in Dongola, with nothing but savagery and murder lying between. There was a whiff of real war in the little fortress but no sign of any actual advance.'[29]

The emptiness of this distant vision of war is at the centre of Doyle's Egyptian experience and it contrasts graphically with the cartoon-like sharpness of his close-range descriptions of the various 'beasts' and 'brutes' who shared the forum of war. Camels, mules, donkeys, horses and oxen were, of course, essential for the conduct of warfare at that time and dogs commonly fought alongside their owners in battle but, in

Doyle's recollections, war correspondents themselves were the kings of carnage. Doyle says of the Sudan 'The big pressmen had now arrived – "Where the carcass is there shall the eagles, etc."'[30]

Doyle uses animal stories to image the hybridity of war-writing, the complex negotiations with different interested parties – editors, readers, generals, soldiers, politicians, colleague networks, the enemy – out of which it was inevitably composed. His memories of war correspondence are punctuated with monster pictures which 'rise in his mind' as he remembers his fellowship with the pressmen. He slides from descriptions of the correspondents themselves to descriptions of lizards, death-adders and the tarantula squashed 'into a square foot of filth' when it was jumped on by Francis Scudamore of *The Daily News*.[31] In death, the squashed body of the spider comes to resemble the newspaper for whom its assassin worked.

Instead of discussing the difficulties of war correspondence, Doyle condenses its negotiations and deceptions into a description of camel-purchasing as practised by Francis Scudamore, from whom he learnt the basics of his new profession. The art of cutting the right figure in the sand is the crucial secret of writing about this war. Doyle's comic account of Scudamore's haggling occurs in the middle of his description of the professional war correspondents, but it is a digression whose fundamental ambiguities contain a cartoon-like critique of this mode of writing. Whether victims or villains, Doyle's animal bodies represent the subversive truths of an inside story not signified in the formal discourse of the narrative. As physical signs, camels are as little to be trusted in appearance as would-be soldiers or their war-writing.

In his autobiography, Winston Churchill described the major battle of the Sudanese campaign as the last of its kind in terms of its high-profile glamour:

> Nothing like the Battle of Omdurman will ever be seen again. It was the last link in the long chain of those spectacular conflicts whose vivid and majestic splendour has done so much to invest war with glamour. Everything was visible to the naked eye.[32]

Doyle's experience in the Sudan was valuable precisely because he learnt from it and from his new colleagues how to describe the increasingly invisible men engaged in increasingly invisible combat in South Africa, France and Flanders. The manhood of war during this period was perceptibly a vanishing one and Doyle's task was to make that manhood visible at its point of disappearance. Of the success of Doyle's Sudanese war correspondence, Richard Lancelyn Green writes:

> The use to which he put such experiences shows authorial skill of a high order, for however slight they were in reality, they assumed

epic proportions in print – and often in the eyes of those who had been present. Many people, for example, won glory on the Dongola advance, and many correspondents spent months in the desert, whereas Conan Doyle spent only a few days; and yet it was to him that someone wrote shortly afterward asking if he had received a medal for his war services. He may not have realised how potent were his descriptions.[33]

On the other hand, he may have done. Doyle, in his own war correspondence, was able to draw upon and utilize that absolute mastery of the truth genres, diary, statement, memoir, testimony, eyewitness account – that had informed his fiction since the writing of his historical novel, *Micah Clarke*. As a fiction writer, Doyle had a superlative ability to sound authentic. He also understood the networks and all-male communities by which masculine professional praxis reinforced its own identity. When it came to the representation of manhood, Doyle was, in the terminology of the time, a 'boomster' – someone who reinforced the principle of masculinity by joining the masculine chorus of praise of itself. And as Alfred Harmsworth, the proprietor of the *Daily Mail*, told his star correspondent, G. W. Steevens, he should write up noise-makers like Churchill and 'Boom the Boomsters'.[34] Since Fortinbras ordered the kettle drums to sound so that the pusillanimous Hamlet might have a soldier's funeral, the noise of war has been a problematic but constant signifier of masculine identity.

The representation of contemporary manhood in war brought with it a field of professional debate to which Doyle was no stranger. Churchill describes a quarrel between himself and Steevens on their return voyage to England about how the story of the Sudanese War should be told. At one point Steevens took over Churchill's manuscript and, told to finish it himself, wrote 'Pop-pop! pop-pop! Pop! Pop!' in his tiny handwriting, and then at the bottom of the page printed in big letters 'BANG!!!' Churchill was relieved when the famous correspondent abandoned flippancy and produced articles on the British Empire which sounded impressively as if they had been 'lifted bodily' from Gibbon's *Decline and Fall of the Roman Empire*.[35]

The debate on how the soldier's body should be represented in the sonorities of war writing depended on its ability to signify cultural supremacy. The physical image of the soldier, however, was changing dramatically during these years as their scarlet uniforms gave way to khaki, as soldiers became literate rather than illiterate, as war photography developed and as mechanized transport and weapons gradually took the place of animals in the field of operations. In Doyle's autobiography General Kitchener's career offers a cartoon-like illustration of this crisis of representation around the figure of the warrior. Initially portrayed as the red-faced, indefatigable, organizational genius of the Sudan, Kitchener became less visible as Lord Robert's chief of staff in the rescue operations in South Africa. In Lloyd George's War Cabinet, he has become a mind adrift – a blind, insensitive dictator whose grip on physical reality has been impaired by 'long tropical service'. Reinstated as a hero after his death by drowning on the way to France, Kitchener is finally summed up for Doyle in the words of Lord Asquith's daughter: 'If he is not a great man he is a great poster.'[36]

In his book, *The Adventurous Male* (1993), Martin Green contends that the generation of adventure writers to whom Doyle belonged replaced the mimetic claims of Victorian realism with an aesthetic of trickery rather than of truth. Offering themselves as artists of 'game', 'joke' and 'play', they were masters of 'illusions, and prestidigitation'.[37] This emphasis on conjuring and trickery has already been illustrated in Doyle's fiction but game, joke and play found their grim apotheosis in the representation of real war, just as the games ethic of mid-Victorian Christian manhood found a context for its muscularity. Historians of late-Victorian masculinity following J. A. Mangan have stressed the importance of the games ethic and its institutionalization in the public schools as a mode of training for 'the practical business of spreading the interests of that nation'. According to David Alderson, a contempt for luxury and an emphasis on 'bodily denial', and the imperative of 'discipline ... remained the central moral features of this institutionalisation'.[38] Doyle's anecdotes of British officers in the Sudan conform to this stereotype while simultaneously conveying its fundamental self-estrangement from everything except the ethos of its validating institutions:

> Self-abnegation of this sort is general. The British officer at his best is really a splendid fellow, a large edition of the public schoolboy, with his cheery slang overlying a serious purpose which he would usually die rather than admit. I heard of three of them at rail-end, all doing essential work and all with a degree of fever on them which might well have excused them from work altogether. Every evening each of them dropped a dollar into a hat, they then all took their temperatures and the highest got the pool.[39]

The only time Doyle saw these men display any sign of anxiety and excitement in the Sudan was when they crowded round the noticeboard to read a telegram giving an 'account of the Oxford and Cambridge Boat-race'.

While Alderson argues that the idealized Christian body in late nineteenth-century representation contains in its musculature 'the ideological embodiment of class, race and empire',[40] Doyle's writing about the British bodies in the Sudan – particularly those surrounding Kitchener – portrays them as exhausted, feverish, zealous and unmarried. For Doyle, the idealized body is native and potentially enemy, and its territory is a space between dream and the exotic geography of an unfamiliar region. Camping out in a grove of palm trees close to the Nile, Doyle awakens to such a figure:

> I awoke, and, lying in my blankets, I saw an amazing man riding along this path. He was a Negroid Nubian, a huge, fierce, hollow-cheeked creature, with many silver ornaments upon him. A long rifle projected over his back and a sword hung from his side. A more sinister barbaric figure one could not imagine ... . I have no doubt that he was really one of our own native tribesmen ... but had he been the other thing our fate would have been sealed.[41]

This body is the inspiration for his short story about the Sudan, 'The Three Correspondents', in which British war journalists see a similar man emerge from behind a rock and shake a rifle at them. Describing him as a 'picturesque ruffian', the correspondents are initially more inclined to photograph, rather than shoot, him. When he attacks at close range, the new journalist is unable to comprehend the reality of the threat because the excitement takes him back to sports day 'when he held the tape for the hurdle race ... . He lay staring as if this were a show and he a spectator.'[42]

This picturesque black body is more of an ideal sporting opponent than an enemy. Each bullet wound that kills him is described as 'rosetted with its circle of flies' as if in reward for his participation.[43] In this game of trickery, however, the idealized body of the soldier is relatively unimportant compared to the correspondent's race to relay the news of this 'battle' to their waiting editors. For Doyle, the British body, even when riding his enemy's camel, still serves the dictates of the spirit and this spirit is located, not in the killing or the competition, but in the complex language exchanges of its communication network. His description of the telegraph station emphasizes the work of decipherment as the climax of a story concerned with the legitimacy of a profession whose writing practices otherwise resemble 'horse-stealing and lying':[44]

> With its bare walls and its packing-case seats it was none the less for the moment one of the vital spots upon the earth's surface, and the crisp, importunate ticking might have come from the world-old clock of Destiny. Many august people had been at the other end of those wires, and had communed with the moist-faced military clerk ... . Cipher telegrams had nearly driven the clerk out of his wits, for of all crazy occupations the taking of a cipher message, when you are without the key to the cipher, is the worst. Much high diplomacy had been going on all day in the innermost chambers of European chancelleries, and the results of it had been whispered into this little corrugated iron hut.[45]

The contemporary aesthetic of trick and game is more fully realized in the figure of the war correspondent than in the picturesque body of the warrior. The glamorous cult of their profession as the androgynous epitome of contemporary masculinity had been fostered around the work and lifestyles of men like W. H. Russell, Archibald Forbes, Bennet Burleigh, the American R. H. Davis and Doyle's mentor in the Sudan, Francis Scudamore. In his essay, 'War correspondents and Colonial War 1870–1900', Roger T. Stearn calls them 'Tough protagonists of a "romantic" profession', who 'romanticised themselves and their own mythology'.[46] Philip Knightley, writing of the 'Golden Age' of war correspondents in The First Casualty, takes a slightly different view, claiming 'it is hard to escape the impression that they were all slightly mad'.[47] Claiming to combine toughness and sensitivity, they saw themselves as heroic crusaders for a better world, as well as adepts at trickery and resourceful deception.

Doyle's fascination with this group of men is not difficult to fathom. His fiction had prepared him for one of the most saleable features of war correspondence: its depiction of the injured and agonized male body. Novelists like Archibald Forbes and Doyle himself were given jobs as war correspondents on the strength of their convincing descriptions of fictionalized battles. In turn, Philip Gibbs, one of the most renowned correspondents of the First World War, prepared himself for his job by making a study of Doyle's historical fiction. Despite this training, Gibbs emphasized the authenticity of writing so close to the rawest source of history:

> Reading my own chronicles of these battles ... I am staggered by the stuff that is in them. It is the real stuff as told to me at the time by these men of ours – their own authentic words, their own spirit coming through them ... . I say so not because I wrote it – God forbid – but because here is the raw material of history, told by the men who made it whilst their wounds were still open and while mud and blood were still upon them. Such stories could never be recaptured.[48]

The Boer War

In Male Subjectivity at the Margins, Kaja Silverman has argued for 'the centrality of the discourse of war to the construction of conventional masculinity'.[49] According to Germaine Greer, masculinity 'requires the creation of dangerous situations, actual or symbolic'.[50] Discussing the 'male subject's aspirations to mastery and sufficiency', Silverman discusses the trauma of defeat in battle and notes how 'masculinity is particularly vulnerable to the unbinding effects of the death drive because of its ideological alignment with mastery'.[51] She argues that 'male mastery rests upon an abyss' and argues for the experience of 'living with lack'.[52] This was in fact very much the experience of the British soldier during the first few months of the Boer War.

In December 1899 the British army in South Africa lost three battles in one week – at Stormberg in the Cape under General Gatacre, at Magersfontein on the border with the Orange River Colony under Lord Methuen, and at Colenso in Natal under General Buller. These defeats renewed debate in Britain about the causes and justifications of an already controversial war. The pre-war diplomacy and correspondence of the high commissioner, Alfred Milner, and Joseph Chamberlain, the colonial secretary, combines a fair and principled analysis of political justice with a determination to win 'the great game between ourselves and the Transvaal for the mastery in South Africa'.[53] It was a game surrounded by a great deal of anti-British propaganda in which the Crown stood to lose its British colonies to the Republican ambitions of President Kruger.

After the still remembered British defeats of 1881, when the Boers had proclaimed their republic in the Transvaal, a drama of revenge was already shaping itself for performance. Milner conceptualized the problem in terms of 'two absolutely conflicting social and political systems' contending for control of one people:

> ... the two principal white races are everywhere inextricably mixed up; it is absurd for either to dream of subjugating the other. The only condition on which they can live in harmony and the country prosper is equality all round.[54]

Milner could also invoke the political disenfranchizement and heavy taxation of the foreign workers, the Uitlanders, many of them British, as a legitimate and longstanding grievance under the terms of a democratic state.

On the other hand, that faction of public opinion influenced by W. T. Stead, a former colleague of Milner, believed that the British were playing a predatory role with regard to the South African Republics. Two months before the British disasters of 1899, Stead had argued:

> The story of our dealings with the Transvaal in the last few weeks displayed all the familiar characteristics of the dealing of the wolf with the lamb. Its chief characteristic has constantly been shifting the ground for quarrel whenever it seemed likely that our victim would escape.[55]

By December, however, it had become apparent that the lamb itself was something of a wolf in sheep's clothing and the British defeats prompted an enthusiastic volunteer effort across the empire. Doyle writes of 'the dark hour' which prompted enlightenment and reinforcement:

> In the British Islands and in the empire at large our misfortunes
> were met by a sombre but unalterable determination to carry the
> war to a successful conclusion and to spare no sacrifices which
> could lead to that end. Amid the humiliation of our reverses there
> was a certain undercurrent of satisfaction that the deeds of our
> foemen should at least have made the contention that the strong
> was wantonly attacking the weak an absurd one. Under the stimu-
> lus of defeat the opposition to the war sensibly decreased.[56]

Of these two responses to defeat, the enthusiastic reinforcement of
the war effort was more in evidence than any clarification of its causes
or justification for its conduct. Upper-class English autobiographies of
the period uniformly recall an ignorant enthusiasm for participating in
the war. Churchill thought it 'very sporting of the Boers' to take on the
British army.[57] Sir Patrick Hastings recalls:

> If I had been older I should certainly not have fought against the
> Boers. I had not the slightest idea what I was fighting about and I
> was ashamed to say I did not very much care. I rather think ... I
> regarded the whole thing very much as a prolonged day's hunt-
> ing.[58]

Hastings, who was to become attorney-general under Ramsay
MacDonald in 1923, remembered the Boer War as part of an adventure
culture, a rite of passage into manhood he was happy to have passed
through:

> There must come a moment in the life of every human individual
> when he becomes obsessed by a passionate desire for adventure
> .... As a rule, it is as well to get over that experience at as early an
> age as possible. Adventures, if unduly prolonged, can become a
> dull business.[59]

Hastings had, like Doyle, gone out to South Africa following the
early disasters of the British campaign. As he put it:

> No particular qualification seemed to be required; provided that a
> man could ride and shoot he would be received with open arms;
> his Country needed him. As nobody had ever expressed a need for
> me before, it seemed too good a chance to miss.[60]

Doyle, forty years old at the start of the war, tried unsuccessfully to
enlist in the Middlesex Yeomanry, arguing his case for a commission on
the grounds that he had led an adventurous life and had 'seen a little of
military operations in the Soudan'.[61] In the event, he accepted an invitation to join a volunteer hospital unit sponsored by his friend, John
Langman, and went to South Africa ostensibly as a doctor and unofficial overseer of hospital personnel. His plan, however, combined medicine
with literature, for his intention was to write an instant history of the
war.

Doyle's writing of the Boer War is the focal point of his career and his was the voice which spoke for that phase of masculinity and of manhood which it embodied. Herbert Sussman has drawn a useful, if limited, distinction between these terms:

> ... manhood differs from masculinity, since the latter represents an inner, potent (possibly sexual) force which threatens anarchically to burst through restraints and precipitate madness and disorder, while manliness is the precarious process by which this essence is subdued and channelled into purposeful activity.[62]

Manhood and masculinity, however, were joined in the glamour of historical representation and in writing, like that of the war correspondents, which simultaneously affirmed a lettered manhood and an endangered, fighting body. The encounter between an animal, evil or patriarchal masculinity and a manhood that had been subject to both ideological formation and its written resymbolization was at the centre of Doyle's work, and the Boer War was its main text. To this context belongs not just his history of *The Great Boer War* but also the literary masterpiece of the Holmes canon, *The Hound of the Baskervilles*.

In 1902, while this new Holmes novella was being serialized in *The Strand*, Doyle embarked on a work of propaganda, *The War in South Africa: Its Causes and Conduct*, which subsequently earned him a knighthood. Backed by Foreign Office money and also sponsored by his publisher, Smith, Elder & Co., this widely distributed volume attempted to answer the intense criticisms and 'misrepresentations' of the British campaign which had appeared in the European press. These internationally influential works, to which history, propaganda and fantasy contribute equally, produced a definition of British manhood which is both more pronounced and more fully articulated than anywhere else in his writing. With this body of work should also be placed Doyle's first legal campaign – his effort to clear the name of a West Midlands' solicitor, George Edalji, who had been imprisoned for cattle-maiming and horse-ripping. Doyle's book, *The Story of Mr. George Edalji* (1907) serves as a coda to his work on the Boer War.

Travelling to South Africa, Doyle was conscious that some providential force had matched him with this hour. He was aware, too, that he needed to be in South Africa in person, partly to write his projected history, partly to give a lead to the newly recruited yeomanry for whose presence he had argued persuasively in the press. His first and most significant battle had been against his formidable pro-Boer mother. Mary Doyle had insisted that her son was both metaphorically and literally too big for the war – 'your very height and breadth would make you a simple and sure target ... . There are hundreds of thousands who can fight for *one* who can make a Sherlock Holmes or a Waterloo!

You owe it to us all to care for your life as a *great* treasure' – and Doyle had replied in a manner strikingly at odds with his usual modesty but in a style that matched her own grandiosity:

> I wrote a letter to *The Times* advising the government to call upon the riding, shooting men. They did so, and of course I was honour-bound as I had suggested it, to be the first to volunteer ... . What I feel is that I have perhaps the strongest influence over young men, especially young athletic sporting men, of any one in England (bar Kipling).[63]

Richard Lancelyn Green sees this letter as an example of Doyle's hidden conceit:

> It was a claim perhaps justified only in a private letter to his mother, as his fame rested mainly on his work as an author, for he had not yet been much in the public gaze or held any positions of great responsibility. It was more of an aspiration ... than a fact.[64]

Green perhaps does less than justice here to Doyle's inspiring contribution to that adventure culture through which the manhood of the late nineteenth century so enthusiastically realized itself. Critics reviewing Doyle's patriotic collection of poems, *Songs of Action,* identified the sporting fraternity as peculiarly his own. *The Bookman* claimed that, if Kipling was the first favourite of the soldiers, Doyle was their laureate's lieutenant. Huntsmen and golfers both apparently had his songs in their hearts and upon their lips!

In his recruitment verse, 'A Ballad of the Ranks', Doyle draws an emotive map of local masculinities as 'lads' from different parts of the country become in turn 'carriers of the gun'. Significantly, the first soldier comes from Scotland:

> Who carries the gun?
> A lad from over the Tweed.
> Then let him go, for well we know
> He comes of a soldier breed.
> So drink together to rock and heather,
> Out where the red deer run,
> And stand aside for Scotland's pride –
> The man that carries the gun![65]

Doyle's writing of the Boer War realigned him with the Scottish literary heritage with which his career had begun. It is also brought him into direct contact with his own readership, as he met, in hospital, the men whose sense of adventure had been stimulated by his own fiction. Many of these readers were the newly literate generation who had been beneficiaries of the the 1870 Education Act and had encountered Doyle's short stories in papers like *Boys Own Magazine*. Doyle wrote about the war by placing this newly acquired literacy at its interpretive centre.

The problematic constellation of masculinity and language had been Doyle's subject in his fiction of the mid-1890s and it was an issue he used to image the meaning of the war itself. A well-known Boer War photograph showing a drummer boy writing a letter home using his drum as a writing desk makes the same point.[66] This newly acquired literacy could also bring with it a sense of self-estrangement, as identity was reconstituted in the language system and thought processes sequenced and restructured through contact with a written grammar. An unexpected side-effect for promoters of the adventure culture was the newly identified syndrome of homesickness – a phenomenon immortalised in Thomas Hardy's famous Boer War poem, 'Drummer Hodge'. When the Boer guerrilla leader, Christian De Wet, captured a supply train carrying food, clothing and mailbags at Roodeval station, he ordered the letters to be burnt. Narrating this incident, Doyle stresses how this 'unsportsmanlike action' was worse than physical atrocity: 'Fifty thousand men to the North of him could forego their coats and their food, but they yearned greatly for those home letters, charred fragments of which are still blowing about the veldt.'[67]

Literacy created a body of soldiers who carried a degree of cultural investment with their weapons. According to Paul Usherwood, this caused a shift in military representation away from the portrayal of aristocratic heroism to depict 'officers taking a personal interest in their men':[68] the common soldier came to share in the cultural ideal of manliness. Since *Micah Clarke*, Doyle's writing had enlisted under this new representational banner. *The Great Boer War* reiterates his theme of the enriched 'spirit of free man, whose individualism has been encouraged rather than crushed':

> The clerks and miners and engineers who went up Elandslaagte Hill without bayonets, shoulder to shoulder with the Gordons, and who, according to Sir George White, saved Ladysmith on January 6th, have shown forever that with men of our race it is the spirit within, and not the drill or the discipline, that makes a formidable soldier.[69]

Doyle, at this stage in his career, still saw 'spirit' as something generated within the body mainly through the ideological effects of reading. Books made a man, he claimed in *Through the Magic Door*. But while books made a man, they also tended to make him slower. Recollecting his own experiences in South Africa, General Sir Ian Hamilton confirmed the improved relations between officers and men that literacy – 'the quickened grasp and receptivity of the mind of the English recruit' – had brought about. However, he also observed that an instinctive quickness of eye and hand had been lost in the acquisition of these new skills:

> The first generation to be educated were spoilt as soldiers rather than improved ... . But when the children of the educated men became recruits in 1905, as I wrote in a report to the War Office, they mastered their military alphabet in one third less time than it had taken in the year 1872. Since 1905 there has been further improvement, though the swift, spontaneous reactions of the illiterates are now forever gone, unless we were to breed individuals for the purpose.[70]

As a young officer in 1881, Hamilton himself had been through something of a learning experience in South Africa. Doyle says of him:

> A distorted and half-paralysed hand reminded the observer that Hamilton, as a young lieutenant, had known at Majuba what it was to face the Boer rifles. Now, in his forty-seventh year, he had returned, matured and formidable, to reverse the results of that first deplorable campaign.[71]

He was not the only one. Doyle himself had known something of the hazards of Africa in 1881. In November of that year, as a ship's doctor on board the *Mayumba,* a cargo boat headed for the Gold Coast, he had gone down with typhoid fever and nearly died. He remembered Africa as a place where he overcame the weaknesses and temptations of the flesh and met Henry Highland Garnet, 'one of the most famous black advocates of the abolition of slavery'.[72]

Ian Hamilton had been made a colonel of the Gordon Highlanders in 1891, his paralysed hand symbolizing the crippled manhood of the 1880s which Doyle, through Dr Watson, had attempted to write back into health and vigour. The early months of the Boer War offered little opportunity for such a revision. Instead, they uncannily dramatized the blind vulnerability of that moment when an illiterate masculinity first encountered its letters. It was no accident that George Meredith called Doyle's history of the war 'the most luminous narrative I have read on this matter',[73] for Doyle's professional interest in ophthalmics combined with his narrative gifts to present this war as the ultimate test of that superior sightedness upon which Victorian literary masculinity was grounded. Doyle made this war visible both physically and morally by using the tropes of his own writing career as an underlying lens, so that a reading of the war was simultaneously a rereading of his fiction.

When the British took possession of the Cape in 1814 for the sum of six million pounds, the northern boundaries of the new colony, valued only as 'a house of call upon the way to India',[74] were left undefined. A Dutch farmer was hung for ill-treating a slave two years later, causing friction between the Dutch and the British whose government in South Africa had 'always played the unpopular part of the friend and protector of the native servants'.[75] When, in 1835, the crude compensation mechanism for former slave owners left the Boer farmers with a deep sense of moral and financial injury, they loaded up their wagons and headed north, seeking self-determination and a new homeland. In the beginning was Holmes. Locating the start of his war narrative in the Boer exodus from the Cape, Doyle invokes the analogous exodus that launched his own literary success: 'It was a strange exodus, only comparable in modern times to the sallying forth of the Mormons from Nauvoo upon their search for the promised land of Utah.'[76]

Using *A Study in Scarlet* as its starting point, Doyle tells the history of the Boer republics in the Transvaal and the Orange Free State and their frustrating encounters with the omnipresent British flag. Moving from British recognition of Boer independence at the Sand River Convention, their reannexation in 1877 and the Boer rebellion against this reannexation in 1880, Doyle's prehistory culminates in the British defeat at Majuba Hill and the Liberal government's hasty surrender, with all the anomalies and lack of clarity over British 'suzerainty' inscribed in the Convention of Pretoria. In 1884, a deputation from the Transvaal gained further concessions in the rewritten 'Convention of London' from which the term 'suzerainty' was dropped altogether. Two years later, the vast and accessible gold reserves of the Rand became apparent, attracting to them huge numbers of European workers whose accumulating grievances as an unenfranchized (white) majority led to the ill-conceived Jameson Raid. In April 1899, twenty-one thousand of these Uitlanders sent a petition to Queen Victoria asking for her protection. In October of that year, war was declared. Doyle writes:

> And so we have come to the end of the long road, past the battle of the pens and the wrangling of tongues, to the arbitrament of the Lee-Metford and the Mauser. It was pitiable that it should come to this. These people were as near akin to us as any race which is not our own ... . Brave, too, they were, and hospitable, with those sporting instincts which are dear to the Anglo-Celtic race. There was no people in the world who had more qualities which we might admire, and not the least of them was that love of independence which it is our proudest boast that we have encouraged in others as well as exercised ourselves. And yet we had come to this pass ... . We cannot hold ourselves blameless in the matter.[77]

Past the arbitrament of the Lee-Metford and the Mauser, of course, Doyle returns once more to the 'battle of the pens and the wrangling of tongues', which, like a Holmes summary, his history aims to finalize and silence. While Doyle's public persona may have emphasized his Watsonian normality, as a historian, Doyle was Holmesian in his panoptic vision, the clarity of his war-writing matching the scientific ideal of Victorian ophthalmics. Resembling photography in its instantaneous representation of the war, Doyle's history also explains itself with a pedagogic lucidity that defines the masculinity of its own seeing. Doyle left for South Africa in February 1900 and returned in July with his instant history already well advanced. *The Great Boer War* was published later the same year, Doyle commenting in his Preface:

> The book was begun in England and continued on board a steamer, but the greater part was written in a hospital tent in the intervals of duty during the epidemic at Bloemfontein. Often the only documents which I had to consult were the convalescent officers and men who were under my care.

His views, judgements and criticisms he claimed were made 'without fear or favour', and this unbiased seeing found the book favour with British and Boer alike. Recommended by one Boer leader for its impartiality, it was also used to provide 'the spine' for the official British history of the war.[78]

Beneath the careful exactitudes of Doyle's historiography, the devices of his fiction structure its interpretation. In *A Study in Scarlet* and *The Sign of Four* a powerful but primitive masculinity learns to exchange its partnerships with the animal and the patriarchal for the ideological sign-play of Sherlock Holmes and the higher libidinal energies of game. In Jonathan Small, the figure of the soldier is tautly positioned between masculinity and manhood. This was also the case in the Boer War where the same formula of exchange structures its story. Losing the war under the primitive patriarchs, President Kruger and General Cronje, the Boers re-enter the story in triumph under the sporting guerrilla leadership of Christian de Wet. Another veteran of 1881, the mobile de Wet understands the games ethic on which diverse masculinities can enter a common manhood and be written into a shared story. He has, however, an unBritish defect of vision. Metonymically represented throughout *The Great Boer War* as 'the man with the tinted glasses', Doyle explains the connection between de Wet's eyesight and his anti-British attitude:

> His military experience dated back to Majuba Hill, and he had a large share of that curious race hatred which is ... inexplicable in a Freestater who has received no injury from the British Empire. Some weakness of his sight compels the use of tinted spectacles, and he now turned these, with a pair of particularly observant eyes behind them, upon the scattered British forces.[79]

Doyle's emerging sense of himself as a corrector of the damaged eye of masculinity also involved correcting inaccurate perceptions of British manhood, grounding that manhood in his own ability to represent and explain the perceptual challenge of war. While it is 'difficult to make a modern battle intelligible when fought ... over a front of seven or eight miles'[80] as the 'scrambling, inconsequential, unsatisfactory action' is 'as difficult to describe as it must have been to direct',[81] Doyle, as a historian, faced the particular problem of the British soldiers: that of locating an enemy who, in their use of smokeless bullets, left no trace of their own position. While officers commanding batteries 'should be provided with the coolest heads and the most powerful glasses of any men in the service',[82] the close vision of the historian was required to spot the position of the enemy, and especially the enemy within.

For Doyle, Christian liberalism was the initial enemy, an idealization situated in the British public eye. After the defeat at Majuba Hill in 1881, popular opinion had been opposed to the continuation of the war for the sake of a military revenge, and 'the motive was undoubtedly a moral and Christian one'. The result of this idealism, Doyle argued, had 'not been such as to encourage its repetition'.[83] Liberalism could easily be misconstrued as fear with the paradoxical consequence of generating a doubled commitment to military solutions. History, for Doyle, was both a science of repetitions and a narrative imprinted with the moral values of the future. Of the abolition of slavery in 1834, he writes:

> It was a noble national action, and one the morality of which was in advance of its time ... . If any special grace attends the virtuous action which brings nothing but tribulation in this world, then we may hope for it over this emancipation. We spent our money, we ruined our West Indian colonies, and we started a disaffection in South Africa, the end of which we have not seen. Yet if it were to be done again we should doubtless do it. The highest morality may prove also to be the highest wisdom when the half-told story comes to be finished.[84]

War correspondence was a different matter. War correspondents were not only required to report war, they were becoming increasingly necessary to sustain it as a staged event, the audiencing of which was as political as its enactment. Since the Crimean War, a rapid complicity had been established between the generals and the press. As Doyle put it in 'The Three Correspondents', 'No sane modern general would ever attack until the Press is up'.[85] He makes the same point in *The Great Boer War*: 'The war correspondent, like Providence, is always with the big battalions.'[86] In South Africa Doyle renewed friendships with correspondents he had met in Egypt, travelling with them and the army on the first stage of its march from Bloemfontein to Pretoria. The Glaswegian, Bennet Burleigh, in particular, was a major influence on Doyle, illustrating the particular complicity that existed between the correspondents and the famously colourful Highland Scots regiments. One of the earliest military photographs ever taken shows two men of the Gordon Highlanders nonchalantly embracing their own cannon. Doyle's most vivid memory of South Africa was of a night journey by train to Bloemfontein in which he discovered that he was travelling alongside the Camerons: 'Wonderful is the atmosphere of war,' he declares. 'When the millennium comes the world will gain much, but it will lose its greatest thrill.'[87]

Joseph Kestner in *Masculinities in Victorian Painting* has discussed at length 'the representation of Celts in Victorian battle imagery'. 'Particularly attractive in this iconographic construction' was the Highland soldier with his picturesque dress, bagpipe and 'renowned courage'.[88] Kestner examines the photographs and paintings identifying Scots regiments with climactic moments of military history. In a profession dominated by Scottish and Irish writers who built up impressive military reputations for Scottish and Irish troops, the manhood of the celt was doubly defined as a capacity to represent manliness in words or war. Two Scotsmen in particular, Archibald Forbes and Bennet Burleigh, had an extensive knowledge of their subject, writing as specialists in military history and strategy as well as journalists whose 'wounds proclaimed their power of engagement with the making as well as the writing of British history'.[89] The Scots regiments they wrote about were defined in terms of their legendary comradeship. They were often inscribed as 'heroic rescuers', constituting groups who, having lost independence themselves, 'fight to maintain British hegemony over other colonised groups'.[90] During the First World War, the Gordon Highlanders acquired their own particular scribe in Philip Gibb. However, these carefully orchestrated representations of Scottish manhood experienced an awkward setback at the start of the Boer War.

At the Battle of Magersfontein in December 1899, the Highland Brigade were led on a night attack by Brigadier Wauchope, without this commanding officer having informed the brigade of his plan. Even the principal officers were kept in absolute ignorance of what they were doing. Walking straight into Boer fire, seven hundred of the Highlanders were massacred in five minutes and when Wauchope himself was shot, the remainder of the brigade disintegrated and fled. Caught in the wire defences, many were found in the morning hung up 'like crows' and riddled with bullets. In the aftermath, Wauchope's dying words fuelled an angry controversy. According to camp rumour, his final words were 'Don't blame me, my lads, it was not my fault'.[91] Doyle, however, discountenances this unsoldierly report:

> Wauchope was shot, struggled up, and fell once more for ever ... .
> Rumour has placed words of reproach upon his dying lips, but his nature, both gentle and soldierly, forbids the supposition. 'What a pity!' was the only utterance which a brother Highlander ascribes to him.[92]

The ignominy of the repulse at Magersfontein damaged not only the lives of the men but the power of a whole representational tradition and it was in response to this week of disasters that Doyle decided to go to South Africa. In *The Great Boer War* this episode draws from him a powerful piece of writing in which strength of emotion finds supernatural expression:

> Never has Scotland had a more grievous day than this of Magersfontein. She has always given her best blood with lavish generosity for the Empire, but it may be doubted if any single battle has ever put so many families of high and low into mourning from the Tweed to the Caithness shore. There is a legend that when sorrow comes upon Scotland the old Edinburgh Castle is lit by ghostly lights and gleams white at every window in the murk of midnight. If ever the watcher could have seen so sinister a sight, it should have been on this, the fatal night of December 11th, 1899.[93]

Tackling this episode, another instant historian, Harmsworth's H. W. Wilson, felt the need to explain to his reader how such a collapse of masculinity could occur:

> Those who have read of 'heroism,' of 'fearlessness of death,' and all the popular phrases which describe the bearing of the soldier on the field of battle, may deem the true story ... ignominious and dishonourable to the Highland Brigade. Yet when the truth is told, such incidents happen on every battlefield, and the best and bravest of men are subject to sudden collapse ... . At dawn it is a physical fact that the intellectual force known as *morale* is at its feeblest. The men were hungry, drenched, cold, confused, surprised, exposed to a more than decimating fire. Death had come suddenly amongst them at an unexpected moment.[94]

The day after the battle, Lord Methuen added to the controversy by making a speech to the Highlanders in which he exonerated himself from responsibility by blaming them for their failure to advance at the crucial moment. While Wilson is evenhanded in his report of this speech: 'No doubt there was this much in what he said ... . But ... The Highland Brigade was not composed of automata ... '[95], Doyle supplies the humiliated soldiers with language, and places the communication failure squarely back with the brigadier and the general:

> Lord Methuen is said to have given deep offence to the Highland Brigade by laying the blame of the failure upon them ... .The reply to this is the obvious one that the brigade had certainly not been prepared for the attack, and that it is asking too much that unprepared men after such terrible losses should carry out in darkness a scheme which they do not understand. From the death of Wauchope ... no one seems to have taken the direction. 'My lieutenant was wounded and my captain was killed,' says a private. 'The General was dead, but we stayed where we were, for there was no order to retire.' That was the story of the whole brigade.[96]

'Where are the bosses?' cried a fusilier at a similar moment of disaster at Spion Kop and 'the historian' says Doyle, 'can only repeat the question'.[97]

A new hero was needed to resymbolize the manhood emerging from this crisis. In the Boer War, Colonel Hector A. MacDonald was iconised as the embodiment of a Scotsman who combined communication skills with a cool-headed physical courage. One of the 'heroes' of the Sudan, MacDonald was not only renowned for leadership, he also enjoyed a particularly good relationship with the war correspondents. Knightley quotes him as saying, 'Gentlemen, I am delighted to welcome you. I think I can give you good sport'.[98] MacDonald is a particularly interesting example of the war hero from this period. Eulogized by his personal correspondents as 'fighting Mac', he became the revitalized embodiment of the celtic warrior.

MacDonald brought language, as well as fighting spirit, to the rescue of a demoralized group of men. Summoned from India to take command of the Highland Brigade at what was considered one of the worst moments in its history, he became one of the heroes of the Boer War. Like Hamilton, he had already experienced defeat as a lieutenant in the Gordon Highlanders at Majuba in 1881, but his hands had not been paralysed. Even though disarmed, he had reportedly tried to rally his men by knocking down three Boer opponents with his bare fists. The enemy so admired his courage that the Boer leader, General Joubert, having taken him prisoner, returned his sword to him.[99]

For Doyle, MacDonald stood for an emboweringly unEnglish spirit within the British army. He had the ability not just to fight but to penetrate systems of exclusion while still speaking to his men in their own language. Beginning life as a draper's assistant, 'Mac' had enlisted under Lord Roberts in Afghanistan and been rapidly promoted. At Omdurman in the Sudan, he had been distinguished in his command of the the newly reconstructed First Egyptian Brigade. Doyle describes him as an embodiment of a distinctively Scottish manhood:

> 'Fighting Mac' as he was called by his men, had joined his regiment as a private, and had worked through the grades of corporal, sergeant, captain, major, and colonel, until now, still in the prime of his manhood, he found himself riding at the head of a brigade. A bony, craggy Aberdonian, with a square fighting head and a bull-dog jaw, he had conquered the exclusiveness and routine of the British service by the same dogged qualities which made him formidable to Dervish and to Boer. With a cool brain, a steady nerve, and a proud heart, he is an ideal leader of infantry, and those who saw him manoeuvre his brigade in the crisis of the battle of Omdurman speak of it as the one great memory which they carried back from the engagement. On the field of battle he turns to the

speech of his childhood, the jagged, rasping, homely words which brace the nerves of the northern soldier.[100]

Within two months of their demoralization at Magersfontein, Macdonald had sufficiently revived the spirit of the Highlanders for them to 'take without flinching the very bloodiest share' of the Battle of Paardeberg, in which they faced not only the fire of the enemy but also that of their own comrades who mistakenly shot at them from the other side of the river.[101] Wounded in the foot at Paardeberg, MacDonald sent a note from hospital asking Lord Roberts to allow the Gordons to be the regiment to attack and force the surrender of General Cronje on the anniversary of Majuba Day. In the event, the task of avenging the earlier British defeat was given to the Canadians, as the oldest colonial regiment, with the Gordons providing the covering fire. Apparently mistaking them for Boers, the Gordons accidentally bayoneted thirteen of these Canadians when they took cover in their trenches.[102]

For Doyle, the poor communication that led to the disaster of Magersfontein is a recurrent issue of both the war and of an English masculine culture that was perhaps 'too proud', 'too negligent' and too unprofessional to use its main resource effectively and to put its own case with clarity and conviction. Bad writing had, in his opinion, been largely responsible for the outbreak of war. Discussing the 1881 Treaty of Pretoria with its vague preamble about British suzerainty, Doyle concludes that 'our political affairs were as badly conducted as our military in this unfortunate year'. The war was, in effect, 'a fitting punishment for the carelessness of the representative who failed to make our meaning intelligible'.[103]

Doyle's concern with how English-speaking men used language came to define his own sense of vocation. His writing attempted to fill, or in some instances to signal, the gaps and failures in British self-representation and to embody British culture to the world in writing whose clarity guaranteed what it represented. This project is evident in his account of the propaganda work he undertook in the wake of his history of the war, the internationally circulated 'statement', *The War in South Africa: Its Cause and Conduct*. Realizing that world opinion was biased against the British cause as a result of an upper-class inexperience in the art of explanation, Doyle received a 'direct imperative call' to correct the misperceptions and atrocity stories surrounding the British army:

> To anyone who knew the easy-going British soldier or the character of his leaders the thing was unspeakably absurd ... . And whose fault was it that our side of the question was not equally laid before the jury of the civilised world? ... How *could* they know our case? ... Nowhere could be found a statement which covered the whole ground in a simple fashion ... .

> The next instant I was on fire with the idea. Seldom in my life
> have I been so conscious of a direct imperative call which drove
> every other thought from the mind ... . Before I reached London all
> my programme was sketched out in my head. There was no item of
> it, I may add, which was not eventually carried through.
> Fortune was my friend.[104]

Written in a week, at a rate of 16 hours a day, Doyle's statement
explained, as his history had done, the issues for which the war was
fought from the British point of view, defended the British conduct of
the war by explaining the gallantry and liberalism of the British cultural perspective and hit back with counter-allegations about Boer
atrocities. One of the lessons of the war which Doyle himself felt
equipped to teach concerned the effective use of public relations: 'our
Government does not use publicity enough in stating and defending its
own case'.[105]

Translated into every major European language including Welsh, *The
War in South Africa* emphasized the versatility of Doyle's communication skills by carrying a 'special foreword' designed to address each
nation individually in politically appropriate terms. His Scottish education was given the credit for this undertaking. With part of the proceeds
from the book, Doyle decided to 'bring some benefit to natives of South
Africa' through the channel of his own university by endowing bursa-
ries to reward 'the South African student who acquitted himself with
most distinction'. Though not quite what he intended, he claimed to
have received one of his earliest letters of application from an eligible
'full-blooded Zulu'.[106]

The Boer War not only consolidated the reputations of both Macdonald
and Doyle but it also stimulated a process of change in the representation of British manhood. Sir Patrick Hastings identified it as a war that
erased the face of masculine greatness:

> War is the creation of individuals not of nations ... . There have
> been too many so-called great men in this world... history groans
> with details of their exploits. ... In more recent years the world has
> suffered from a plethora of these monstrosities. I wonder if the
> Almighty will ever present us with a new kind of man to leave his
> mark upon the universe; quite an ordinary man, who is able to
> preach the doctrine of loving-kindness leavened with a good deal
> of humour and a little common sense.[107]

Returning from the war, Doyle contemplated, on Dartmoor, a problem
in the depiction of manhood caused by the breached class barriers and
increased intimacy between officers and men. As for Macdonald, the
embodiment of Scottish military manhood, a tragic silence descended
on his reputation when, in 1903, facing a court martial for homosexuality, he committed suicide in a Paris hotel room.

Reading of 'Mac's' suicide, Roger Casement, a member of the British consular service who had been awarded the Queen's medal for 'special services' in the Boer War, sadly recorded the event in his journal. He hoped that the case might 'awaken the national mind to saner methods of curing a terrible disease than by criminal legislation'.[108] But Macdonald had always been an example to other men. From that year on, Roger Casement's journal began recording homosexual practices of its own. A famous instance of a representational tradition that had come adrift from its referencing of masculine identity, Casement's diaries would, in 1916, become one of the most controversial sites of British manhood when he was tried and found guilty of treason. The contents of the diaries were made public as a way of undermining support for him although their authenticity was repeatedly challenged. Some of the explicit detail contained in them had, it was suggested, been information about 'sexual perversion among the Putumayo Indians' which Casement had been amassing at the request of Doyle himself.[109] Heading the main petition for his reprieve from execution, Doyle argued that Casement, like Kitchener, had spent too long in the tropics to be responsible for his manhood. The tradition of masculine representation that dated from Pepys and Boswell had suddenly become imprisoned in its own writing.

A strange war

Doyle frequently referred to the Boer War as a 'strange war ... to chronicle',[110] one full of strange meetings. Behind the war itself was one of the most extensive investigations into coincidence ever undertaken, and synchronicity became part of its mode of recall. This 'uncanny' dimension in memories of the war was one of an estranged doubleness, whether located in the nature of the enemy, the effects of a new literacy, or the new communications technology of the battlefield – particularly the biograph camera and the heliograph. When the war correspondent G. W. Steevens died of enteric fever at Ladysmith, Mr Dickson, the first man to take biograph pictures on the battlefield, had himself photographed significantly standing by the grave.[111] Doyle's firmly rational history of the war alludes to uncanniness in footnotes on names and name-loss, such as the note on the death of Major Childe at Spion Kop:

> His curious presentiment of coming death may be added to the many well-attested examples of such prescience. He discussed it with his comrades on the night before, requesting, as a play of words upon his own name, that the inscription 'Is it well with the child? it is well', should be placed upon his grave. It was done.[112]

Freud, in his essay, 'Thoughts for the Times on War and Death', argued that the concept of 'spirit' derived from a 'conflict of feeling at the death of loved yet alien and hated persons': 'It was beside the dead body of someone he loved that he invented spirits ... . His persisting memory of the dead became the basis for assuming other forms of existence and gave him the conception of a life continuing after apparent death.'[113]

In the category of 'loved yet alien and hated persons', the Boers ranked very high. For those, like Doyle, who had been in Africa in 1881, the Boer War of 1899 carried an even stronger dimension of the uncanny – one full of suppressed memories, forgotten texts and estranged body parts. There was also a close identification with the enemy. After what Doyle calls the 'barbarian campaigns' of the Victorian era, the Boers were uncannily familiar as a white imperial force with a strong racial resemblance to the British. Enhancing the familiarity and self-estrangement of the war, the conflation of British and Boer identity became a deliberate feature of war tactics, with Boer soldiers dressing up as British officers and using British bugle calls to mislead and command their enemy. So strong was this fascination that many participants and correspondents changed sides and sympathies during the war – most famously, the American war reporter, Richard Harding Davis. The admiration was mutual. By the end of the war, a year later than Doyle had anticipated, five thousand Boers, including the brother of General de Wet, were fighting on the British side.[114]

Designated as 'sporting', this collaboration of New and Old Testament masculinities was, by agreement, 'a white man's war' with no dangerous armaments put in the hands of the native Africans. The Boer general, Piet Cronje, protested in outrage when Baden-Powell infringed this agreement at Mafeking:

> It is understood that you have armed Bastards, Fingos and Baralongs against us – in this you have committed an enormous act of wickedness ... disarm your blacks and thereby act the part of a white man in a white man's war.[115]

The shadowy double of this war was not the enemy who, by and large, subscribed to the same code of manliness. It was to be found, rather, in those excluded from the war zone: European onlookers, blacks, Boer women and visiting British feminists. In significant ways, it was a spectators' war as well as a war of uncanny spectres.

For Doyle, the Boer army embodied those admired attributes of Protestant manhood he had celebrated in *Micah Clarke* and *The Refugees*. These fictional heroes had become the 'enemies' of his history: 'The men were brave, hardy, and fired with a strange religious enthusiasm. They were all of the seventeenth century, except their rifles.'[116]

The Boer leader, Piet Joubert, even had the predictable 'French Hugue-
not blood' which, in its chivalry and generosity, 'made him respected
and liked even by his opponents'.[117] Just as the Boers represented these
early stages of Doyle's writing career, so the war was a conflict between
a modern manhood and and the masculinity of an earlier cultural
phase. Paraphrasing Winston Churchill, Doyle's interpretation of what
the Boers 'unconsciously' stood for borders on parody:

> From above the Boers were flooding down, as Churchill saw them,
> dour, resolute, riding silently through the rain, or chanting hymns
> round their camp fire – brave honest farmers, but standing uncon-
> sciously for medievalism and corruption, even as our rough-tongued
> Tommies stood for civilisation, progress, and equal rights for all
> men.[118]

For all their seventeenth-century religious enthusiasm and lack of
personal hygiene, the Boers also possessed a more advanced military
technology than the British and a more versatile, less convention-
ridden, military intelligence. Their use of smokeless fire coupled with
cunning entrenchment made them an army of physically invisible men,
whose presence was only represented metonymically. Attempting to
cross the Modder River to reach Kimberley, Lord Methuen's infantry
'fired and fired – but what was there to fire at? An occasional eye and
hand over the edge of a trench or behind a stone is no mark at seven
hundred yards.'[119] The British, by contrast, were still fascinated by the
obvious splendours of military display – particularly the ornate insignia
of class and rank which made the officers a prime and easy target for
Boer guns. The Boers fought as citizens rather than as soldiers and their
lack of uniform made killing them seem like murder. As an enemy, they
had a great deal to teach. In Doyle's history that lesson comprised the
slow and painful formation of modern manhood, with both sides contributing equally to its pedagogy.

The first stages of the war, until Doyle's own arrival in South Africa,
are represented through a familiar trope of the enemy as patriarch and
problematic father. Just as the 'disappearance' of his own father in
1879 had coincided with the first signs of his writing career, so Doyle's
arrival in South Africa replayed an uncanny drama figured around the
defeat of Piet Cronje. Having arrived in Bloemfontein to chronicle the
wars and tend its wounded heroes, Doyle found himself in the middle of
an enteritic epidemic, nursing men with chronic diarrhoea who needed
swaddling like babies. Amid this horrific pantomime of unreconstructed
manhood, Doyle found himself back once more amid the sinking grounds
of the masculine story. His early solution to these in his own writing
had been the counter-emotional dryness of Sherlock Holmes. But in the
uncanny context of the war, such dryness was a sign of the problem,

not its solution. Langman's poorly resourced, makeshift hospital had been erected on a sportsfield with its main ward in the cricket pavilion. Doyle comments:

> The first intimation of trouble came to me in a simple and dramatic way. We had a bath in the pavilion and I had gone up to it and turned the tap, but not a drop of water appeared ... . This small incident was the first intimation that the Boers had cut the water supply of the town, which caused us to fall back upon the old wells, which in turn gave rise to an outbreak of enteric which cost us 5, 000 lives.[120]

Doyle represents this month of hardship in pictorial terms, as a horror worthy of the Russian war painter, Verestschagin, whose famous series, the 'Apotheosis of War' (1869–73) had used the sand brown of the desert as its emotional colouring. Here, that colour had a different connotation:

> The outbreak was a terrible one. It was softened down for public consumption and the press messages were heavily censored, but we lived in the midst of ... death in its vilest, filthiest form ... . The worst surgical ward after a battle would be a clean place compared to that pavilion. At one end was a stage with the scene set for 'H.M.S. Pinafore.' This was turned into latrines for those who could stagger so far. The rest did the best they could, and we did the best we could in turn.[121]

Doyle had sailed for South Africa the day after the surrender of General Cronje at Paardeberg on Majuba Day, 27 February 1900. Whatever his capacities as a general, however, Cronje had a remarkable ability to image back the criminal and crime-inducing fathers of Doyle's early fiction. Described as 'capable, crafty, iron-hard, magnetic' but unhampered 'by the chivalrous uses of war', Cronje represented the blind side of the Boer cause and its unreconstructed masculinity. An autocrat and a patriarch, the virile Cronje is simultaneously uncommunicative, 'dark' and 'the minister of death'.[122] The connection between Cronje's 'passing out of history' and Doyle's writing is directly made. It was the filth from Cronje's *laager* on the Modder River which had, in Doyle's opinion, infected the water at Bloemfontein; the enteritis 'had its origin in the Paardeberg water'.[123] Doyle writes of Cronje's camp:

> Already down there, amid slaughtered oxen and dead horses under a burning sun, a horrible pest-hole had been formed which sent its mephitic vapours over the countryside. Occasionally the sentries down the river saw amid the brown eddies of the rushing water the floating body of a Boer which had been washed away from the Golgotha above. Dark Cronje, betrayer of Potchefstroom, iron-handed ruler of the natives, reviler of the British, stern victor of Magersfontein, at last there has come a day of reckoning for you![124]

Doyle intensifies his description of this pest-hole until it re-images the Great Bog of Cree, the place of patriarchal disappearance in *The Mystery of Cloomber*:

> Strong-nerved men came back white and sick from a contemplation of the place ... . From end to end it was a festering mass of corruption, overshadowed by incredible swarms of flies.[125]

In Doyle's method of chronicling the war by matching it to the masculinity parables of his own fiction, Cronje personifies the dark energies of the 'paranoid gothic', a form set in opposition to the rational scientific empiricism whose discourse on empire Doyle could also command. Symbolizing his own containment of sadistic, revenge-seeking energies, Doyle uses the surrender of Cronje to locate the Boer War as that moment of emergence from patriarchal history already celebrated in his early novels. As Cronje vanishes from history, he leaves behind him a residual poison, while Doyle reassumes his familiar task of using both his literature and medicine to reinvigorate a sick and demoralized manhood.

As the revenge drama of Majuba Hill was enacted at Paardeberg by the British troops, the spiritual legacy of the evil father reappeared in Doyle's imagination too, pitting its power of gothic disturbance against the controlling rationalism of Sherlock Holmes. In the Great Grimpen Mire in *The Hound of the Baskervilles*, Doyle recalled the location of Cronje's pest-hole on the Modder River. One of the dangerous features of the Modder for the British army had been its treacherous, boggy banks. Animals, particularly cows, not infrequently became 'bogged' as they attempted to reach the water. In the Harmsworth illustrated history of the Boer War which appeared at the same time as Doyle's, a picture of a bogged cow being drowned in the mud[126] is followed by a photograph of 'Dr Conan Doyle, the creator of "Sherlock Holmes", attending sick Canadians in the club house at Bloemfontein'.[127] While Doyle used the conflicts of masculinity in his own writing to provide the interpretive structure of his history, he also knew that there were bones within it that only Holmes could pick and he threw them to him as soon as *The Great Boer War* was finished. In a way not even Churchill could rival, the Boer War carried the imprimatur of Doyle's writing and his patriotic resistance to the new homoerotic logic of the adventure culture.

Cronje's defence of the Modder River had barred Lord Methuen's road to besieged Kimberley. While Cronje is elided with the dark energies of Doyle's horror stories, Lord Methuen, with his stilted language, represents 'the good old murderous obsolete heroic tactics of the British tradition'[128] and his own historical fiction. The adventure story found its apotheosis at Mafeking. Presided over by the familiar figure of

Baden-Powell, Mafeking, in the northern Cape, is for Doyle 'the visible sign' of the war: 'From a mere tin-roofed village Mafeking had become a prize of victory, a stake which should be the visible sign of the predominating manhood of one or other of the great white races of South Africa.'[129] What triumphs here is that combination of play, resourcefulness and hawk-eyed vigilance that Doyle had inscribed in the figure of Sherlock Holmes. Robert Stephenson Smyth Baden-Powell had himself been a war correspondent in the Sudan in 1895 and, like Doyle and Churchill, was an expert in fashioning heroes. Doyle's description of him displays a certain coy familiarity:

> Colonel Baden-Powell is a soldier of a type which is exceedingly popular with the British public. A skilled hunter and an expert at many games, there was always something of the sportsman in his keen appreciation of war ... . There was a brain quality in his bravery which is rare among our officers ... it was as difficult to outwit as it was to outfight him ... . An impish humour broke out in him, and the mischievous schoolboy alternated with the warrior and the administrator ... he had that magnetic quality by which the leader imparts something of his virtues to his men.[130]

Baden-Powell shares with Holmes an ambidextrous, androgynous manhood grounded in the rituals of play but possessing a sightedness which partakes equally of the divine plan and advanced ophthalmic technology.

The same could not be said of Sir Redvers Buller, the senior British general in Natal who, at his fourth attempt, was responsible for the relief of Ladysmith. A monolithic figure whose name had all the conquering potential of the great man, Buller is, for Doyle, the embodiment of a dilemma at the centre of the war. In his attempt to solve its main strategic problem, he remained, for Doyle, a deeply problematic figure. His slow and ponderous attempts at solution symbolized the difficult lesson of change in Victorian notions of the masculine which were rooted in a hymnology of the rock-like and the unchanging.

Although Buller was a 'heavy, obdurate, inexorable man', his stolid demeanour restored serenity and confidence to his demoralized troops. Unlike the diminutive Lord Roberts, a tiny man with a massive wife in the manner of Doyle's Sir Nigel, Buller had a strong and reassuring masculine presence which 'conveyed an assurance of ultimate victory to those around him'.[131] It seemed a long time coming. Doyle writes of the Natal campaign at the beginning of December, 1899: 'In club, and dining room, and railway car – wherever men met and talked – the same words might be heard: "Wait until Buller moves." The hopes of a great empire lay in the phrase.'[132] Those hopes were soon to be disappointed. Buller's task was to a find a way of crossing the well-defended Tugela River. The Battle of Colenso, his first attempt to do so, was a disaster, in the wake of which the war effort was intensified, bringing Doyle along with the newly formed 'classless' yeomanry to South Africa. Overall command of the campaign was given to Lord Roberts and his chief of staff, Lord Kitchener, but even with these heartening reinforcements, Sir Redvers Buller was still struggling with his task. He tried a different approach to the Tugela, crossed it, lost two thousand of his men on Spion Kop, and returned to the other side, still retaining the confidence of his troops. A slow reader of situations, he tried again with an attack on Vaalkranz and then fell back on the defensive.

To Doyle, literacy skills are key to interpreting the war. At Spion Kop General Buller's forces, after an initial blindness, finally became adept in the new art of condensing their bodies into moving signs which resemble the writing of war. Doyle comments on this moment of transformation into sign as the artillery become 'an irregular fringe of crawlers, wrigglers, withers, crouchers, all cool and deliberate, giving away no points in this grim game of death'.[133] As this literate soldiery learn at last how to exchange physical presence for intelligent sign, they join forces with the writing of manhood, a representational tradition itself much harder to destroy than the physical body, and one repeatedly invoked in the history. Doyle's literary contests with Winston Churchill, whose judgement he constantly both applauds and undermines, flag the same issue. Churchill had been present in person at Spion Kop, but presence was no guarantee of anything in a place where the visible body signalled only the archaic showiness of the English class system. In response to Churchill's argument that British guns could have been taken to the top of Gun Hill, Doyle comments: 'Without venturing to contradict one who was personally present, I venture to think that there is strong evidence to show that it could not have been done … .'[134]

Slow, deliberate but pertinacious, Buller faced 'the hardest problem of the war' and, at the fourth attempt, finally solved it, using the Irish Brigade to fight their way from Colenso to Ladysmith. Doyle found Buller, who was liked by his men as much as he was discredited by the staff, a disturbing figure because the man and his reputation were so squarely at odds. Renowned for being 'a downright John Bull fighter, who would take punishment or give it, but slog his way through without wincing', Buller turns out to be a gifted strategist, but one with 'a disinclination to take a risk or to endure heavy punishment'.[135] From first to last, the soldier's general had shown 'a great – some said an exaggerated – respect for human life'. He had 'no intention of winning a path by mere slogging, if there were a chance of finding one by less bloody means'.[136]

Doyle's account of the relief of Ladysmith is powerful and emotive. The event touched the deepest feelings of his generation so that even 'sober unemotional London found its soul for once and fluttered with joy'. This joy, he insists, was not triumphalism but a celebration of escape from humiliation. He describes the two thousand emaciated men of the Ladysmith garrison who, the day after the siege was lifted, and with barely the strength to lift their rifles, set out on their starving horses in pursuit of a still formidable foe. These ghostly men on their spectral horses so strongly reminiscent of his father's paintings continued to trouble Doyle. While Buller had solved the practical problem of the war, he had also exposed a central problem in the sphere of masculine representation. He had drawn attention to the fact that men in whom some cultural investment has been made had something to lose by dying and seemed less willing to do so. In the Sudan, it was only the unreconstructed Egyptians who had displayed this fear.

As the manhood of the soldier changed, so too did the nature of his oldest enemy. Previously represented as a moment of spiritual affirmation which bestowed upon the Protestant heroes of British culture the final signatory of an enduring name, death was too final for a secularized adventure culture in which resourcefulness was the key signifier of masculinity. When the body of the soldier could vanish into sign rather than spirit, the encounter with death on which the masculinity of the warrior was predicated seemed to be more an issue of class than of courage. As the patriarchal narrative of the past was rewritten, the encounter with death was in danger of losing its privileging masculine status. Embodying an alternative sporting spirit of a ludic culture were British officers like dashing General Pole-Carew, who approached 'a field of battle as a light-hearted schoolboy approaches a football field'. Of one of Pole-Carew's daring flanking manoeuvres outside Bloemfontein, Doyle writes smoothly: 'Every requisite for a great victory was there except the presence of an enemy.'[137]

Doyle compares two encounters in which the British were forced to surrender, one involving a troop of privileged ex-public school men:

> There were all the materials there for a stand which would have brought glory to the British arms. The men were of peculiarly fine quality, many of them from the public schools and from the universities, and if any would fight to the death these with their sporting spirit and their high sense of honour might have been expected to do so ... . The casualty lists ... do not permit us to call the defence desperate or heroic.[138]

In contrast, the manhood of the working class was affirmed by an inexperienced militia regiment who heroically resisted their own survival. Knowing less perhaps about mining and farming than the 4th Derbyshires knew about warfare, Doyle describes their predicament:

... it was a horrible ordeal for raw troops. The men were miners and agricultural labourers, who had never seen more bloodshed than a cut finger in their lives ... . In desperate straits, which would have tried the oldest soldiers, the brave miners did well. They never from the beginning had a chance save to show how gamely they could take punishment, but that at least they did ... they came out of it with death, mutilation, and honour.[139]

Most, even so, preferred to settle for mutilation. Adventure fiction celebrated the mutilated body – a manhood identified by wounds and missing body parts, as in the wooden leg of Long John Silver, the sightlessness of the blind Pugh, or Ian Hamilton's paralysed hand. It was not just fiction. The numbers of men reported wounded were halved at times of high morale when 'only those who were very severely wounded reported themselves wounded at all'.[140] Doyle's history never misses an anecdote of body parts cheerfully surrendered and replaced by verbal jokes, like the leg and foot of Lieutenant Egerton which were carried off as he lay dying upon the sandbag parapet watching the fight. '"There's an end of my cricket," said the gallant sportsman, and he was carried to the rear with a cigar between his clenched teeth.'[141]

The Harmsworth historian, H. W. Wilson, also writes of the silent unselfishness of wounded soldiers, like this defaced survivor of Spion Kop for whom the games ethic provided an entire structure of feeling:

> One poor fellow had been shot in the face by a piece of shell, which had carried away his left eye, the left upper jaw with the corresponding part of the cheek, and had left a hideous cavity at the bottom of which his tongue was exposed. He had been lying hours on the hill. He was unable to speak, and as soon as he was landed at the hospital he made signs that he wanted to write. Pencil and paper were given him, and it was supposed he wished to ask for something, but he merely wrote, 'Did we win?'[142]

The truth-affirming body in Doyle's history does not conform to the shape of its injured adventurers but is rather that of the British Empire itself. Troped as a 'great body whose nerves are the telegraphic wires', its members become connected as 'an organic whole' for the first time through the adversities of the Boer War.[143] Doyle's history is a celebration of a unity of vision around which cohered the colourful pluralities and diversities of the ultimate all-male community:

> Who has seen that army and can forget it – its spirit, its picturesqueness – above all, what it stands for in the future history of the world? ... On the plains of South Africa, in common danger and in common privation, the blood brotherhood of the Empire was sealed.[144]

Picturesque though this Victorian brotherhood was, the picture was intended to carry a clear warning to the readership of a hostile

European press. Connected through the 'spine' of his history, for Doyle the meaning of the war lay in this living body and its hidden, strategic intelligence.

In this battle of masculine archetypes, the war itself is safely under the sign of the magician. While de Wet is the brilliant trickster, Lord Roberts is cast as the mature 'magician' whose 'masterhand had in an instant turned England's night to day, and had brought us out of that nightmare of miscalculation and disaster which had weighed so long upon our spirits'.[145] In this war of men vanishing into representation, 'Bobs', as his nickname itself signifies, had the gift of metonymic disappearance, able at the crisis of the war, to vanish 'entirely from the public ken only to emerge dramatically as victors at a point three hundred miles distant'.[146] In the guerrilla war that followed Lord Methuen's entry into Pretoria and delayed the agreement of peace terms until May 1902, this capacity to disappear and resist closure offered a lesson both in modern warfare and modernist narrative that troubled its climax-seeking historian.[147] The question of finding the right ending for the masculine adventure story of the Boer War was one which Doyle would re-encounter when he wrote his own autobiography. Meanwhile, the solution to that closure was yet to arrive and, as the ending of his war story was kept open, the interpretation of it began to change.

In the two texts that followed *The Great Boer War*, Doyle encoded two further sets of perspectives on the gigantic footprints it had left behind. In *The Hound of the Baskervilles*, serialized in *The Strand* between August 1901 and April 1902, his history acquired its own shadow, one haunted not by a supernatural dog but by memories of the war itself. Naturalizing the Kopje-crests of South Africa as the tors of Dartmoor, the novella resymbolizes the trauma of the war and its recall. Holmes is described as looking 'like a general who is planning a battle with his chief of staff'[148] and is given that peculiar and nearly fatal reluctance to communicate his plans which, under Lord Methuen, had caused such disaster to the Highlander brigade at Magersfontein. In the same way that Doyle had built up the military capacity of the Boer army, so Holmes repeatedly emphasizes the formidable nature of an opponent which turns out to be a half-starved mongrel belonging to a throw-back from the seventeenth century. As signalled by the glorification of its title, *The Great Boer War* emphasized the heroics of masculine encounter while excluding from its field of vision the often more complex issues posed by native blacks, Boer women, British feminists and the European socialist movement.

These issues provided the phenomenal motive energy for Doyle's propaganda writing. *The War in South Africa: Its Cause and Conduct* asserts a privileged masculine interpretation of British manhood against the critical female gaze of Emily Hobhouse, and a reasoned representation that opposed the sensational journalism of W. T. Stead. Emily Hobhouse had visited the British concentration camps set up from November 1900 and reported on the conditions encountered by the Boer women and children who were forced to inhabit them. A relative of the radical MP, Charles Hobhouse, who later distanced himself from her findings, Miss Hobhouse lobbied throughout Britain on her return, using the lecture platform and the support of journalists and editors such as W. T. Stead to expose these war atrocities.

What should we do with the womenfolk of Boer soldiers while the guerrilla war is in progress? That was the question that the camps were trying to address. Boer families, the British found, tended to be 'treacherous', taking up arms to protect themselves and shooting General French's soldiers. A surprisingly large number of women simply fought in the Boer armies. Left to cope in their farmhouses without their menfolk, they might disturbingly have been able to do so. On the other hand, they might also have fallen prey, in a white man's war, to black masculinities. Left at home, the women lent aid to the Boer soldiers; left behind as the guerrilla war moved north, their provision ceased to be a burden to their own side but contributed to the war effort by putting further strain on already inadequate British resources. Pro-Boer in her opinions, Emily Hobhouse's report about British atrocities in the camps not only inflamed controversy at home, it was seized upon by the European press for anti-British propaganda.

So sensitive was the issue that, within six months, the British government had responded by establishing a Ladies Committee to report more objectively from a better informed perspective. This committee under the suffragette, Millicent Garrett Fawcett, was sent out in July 1901, but Doyle does not use the material of this report in his Statement. Instead, he corrects perceptions by explaining anew the British position and by citing accumulated evidence from a range of firsthand sources which contradicted the findings of the Hobhouse report. Doyle argued:

> ... it was the duty of the British, as a civilised people, to form camps of refuge for the women and children, where, out of reach, as we hoped, of all harm, they could await the return of peace ... .
> The British nation would have indeed remained under an ineffaceable stain had they left women and children without shelter upon the veldt in the presence of a large Kaffir population.[149]

He claimed that the high death rate among the children was due to a measles epidemic and the Boer mothers' mistrust of British medical science. The making of his case is a lesson in lucid logic:

> ... the death of these numerous children lies heavy ... upon the heart of our nation ...

> ... we cannot deny that the cause of the outbreak of measles was the collection of the women and children by us into the camps. But why were they collected into camps? Because they could not be left on the veldt? And why could they not be left on the veldt? Because we had destroyed the means of subsistence. And why had we destroyed the means of subsistence? To limit the operations of the mobile bands of guerrillas. At the end of every tragedy we are forced back to the common origin of all of them.[150]

Doyle concludes by pointing out that the British also housed their own colonial refugees in the concentration camps and that the Boer women and children received better rations there than the private soldiers did in the army. By a characteristic perversion of Christian liberalism, he maintained, 'we have looked after our enemies far better than our friends'.[151]

The Edalji case

Doyle's career derives its meaning from those years between 1880 and 1920 when the figure of the British soldier was subject to a relentless process of representation. Just in case they were needed, Doyle followed his Boer War writing with another collection of Brigadier Gerard stories – perhaps the most fantastic and delightful soldier stories ever written. In an essay entitled 'Making the New Soldier', General Sir Ian Hamilton enthusiastically promoted the army as a career for adventurous boys who want, above all, to belong:

> No other career, not even the Church, can vie with the Army in offering to a boy while still in his 'teens the chance of becoming friend and adviser to a delightful set of young adventurers called recruits. The boy who aims at making for himself a million pounds will miss all the fun of the fair just when he can best enjoy it: the boy who aims at having a million good comrades should, with any luck, hit the bull's eye of happiness plumb centre.[152]

This continual propagandizing of the good soldier led to some bizarre contrasts with the unreconstructed bodies of the actual soldiery. None was more bizarre than Doyle's involvement with a case in which, as in *The Hound of the Baskervilles*, animals were made the scapegoat for human aggression. Following the death of his wife in 1906, Doyle went through a period of depression in which there appears to have been a strong element of guilt. According to *Memories and Adventures*, what helped him to emerge from his depression was his legal campaign on behalf of one of his own readers, George Edalji, a young half-caste lawyer who had been imprisoned in 1903 under the Malicious Damage Act of 1861 on a charge of animal maiming. The case had a long history of local malice behind it.

Edalji came from an unusual family. His father Shapurji Edalji had been reared as a Parsee but, on marrying an English woman, had, with the help of her relatives, become an Anglican vicar in the farming and mining community of godless Great Wyrley, near Walsall. In 1888 the family began receiving poison pen letters, and a servant girl, Elizabeth Foster, was dismissed. Anonymous letters and malicious pranks were again directed at the family in the early 1890s and these were renewed in 1903, accompanied by a spate of attacks on animals in the neighbourhood. They began with the ripping of a horse belonging to a man named Holmes. Other animals were also attacked until, following the death of a pit pony, the police arrested George Edalji. On very slender evidence, he was convicted and sentenced to seven years' imprisonment. Yet the maimings continued. A petition was set up on Edalji's behalf and, after three years, he was released but not pardoned. Being a devotee of Sherlock Holmes who had solved the mystery of animal-maiming in 'Silver Blaze', Edalji then sent a statement of his case to Doyle asking for his help in finding the true solution to the Mystery of Great Wyrley Cattle Rippings.

In 1907 following Doyle's articles on the case in the *Daily Telegraph*, public pressure forced the home secretary to set up a committee of inquiry which resulted in a pardon for Edalji and his reinstatement on the Roll of Solicitors. He was, however, awarded no compensation and Doyle continued to write on his behalf, eventually submitting to the Home Office his own extraordinary solution to the mystery. His 'Statement of the Case Against Royden Sharp' identified the man he believed to be guilty of both the horse-maimings and the letter-writing. To his intense frustration, no action was taken by the police.

Richard and Molly Whittington-Egan, who produced a reprint of the investigation in 1985, believe that Doyle's own 'absolutism about Royden Sharp's guilt' was the consequence of his own 'state of emotional disequilibrium' and that he 'manoeuvred himself into a tight corner. Contact with Edalji edged him towards a wilderness of his own.'[153] If so, it was a wilderness that had chosen its own voice with particular care. Whereas Holmes in *The Hound of the Baskervilles* had had reservations about taking on the 'Father of Evil himself', Doyle had no qualms in dealing with a writer who signed his letters, 'I am Satan'. His involvement in this case has all the signs of his Boer War writings, for the patterns of his own inner story formed a curious liaison with the bizarre materials of his investigation. In his history and propaganda he had tried to correct faulty perceptions of the British at war. Now he began to correct the faulty vision of British justice itself.

Doyle was insistent that no guilt could attach to the highly literate young lawyer who had read his own Sherlock Holmes stories with such close attention and such poor eyesight. His Special Investigation began with this reminder:

> The first sight which I ever had of Mr. George Edalji was enough in itself to convince me both of the extreme improbability of his being guilty of the crime for which he was condemned ... . He had come to my hotel by appointment, but I had been delayed, and he was passing the time by reading the paper ... . He held the paper close to his eyes and rather sideways, proving not only a high degree of myopia, but marked astigmatism ... . There, in a single physical defect, lay the moral certainty of his innocence, and the reason why he should become the scapegoat.[154]

If Doyle was at his most chivalric in this championship of one of his readers, his determination to identify the real villain skews disturbingly back into his own life. Examining the anonymous letters, Doyle designates their writer as a man of double identity, one side of him exhibiting 'remarkable qualities', 'grim humour, wild imagination, and a maniacal turn of mind', while the other displayed 'no fancy and no madness' and appeared 'particularly practical'.[155] Why, it might be a description of Watson! Concluding that these two styles may well have coexisted in one man who had a younger brother as his partner, Doyle summarizes the history of his suspect, Royden Sharp. It was a history with some curious parallels.

Sharp had come into being with Doyle's writing career in 1879. Good at drawing and lying, he was by 1892 being 'caned daily', becoming, like Doyle at Stoneyhurst, the most beaten boy at school. Perhaps his bad behaviour was a response to his father's death, Sharp's father, like Doyle's, dying in 1893. By that time Sharp had begun to forge letters and initials, showing a talent for literary impersonation which Doyle's *Boy's Own* story, 'Cyprian Overbeck Wells' had recommended to its readership in 1886. Apprenticed to a butcher, Sharp, like many another difficult young man, had been sent away to sea – an experience through which, according to Doyle 'his natural brutality was probably not lessened'.[156] He returned, like Doyle from the Arctic, full of ingratitude, aggression and deviantly lettered aspirations. This was the profile of the semi-literate working-class man Doyle named as the villain responsible for attacking Mr Holmes's horse and making Edalji his scapegoat.

Where Edalji had studied law and gained distinction with his treatise on railway legislation, Sharp had early declared his intention of running away from school to join the army and became involved with a group of young men from the local yeomanry. A mediation between law and the masculine body had always been the main focus of Doyle's fiction. Although he had been designated the muse of the yeomanry, the masculinities that emerge from these local testimonies are considerably less colourful than those eulogized in *The Great Boer War*. One young trooper, Harry Green, confessed to disembowelling his own horse following Edalji's arrest, with an eye to the insurance money. He subsequently withdrew his confession and left the country with a ticket for South Africa. Sharp's older brother, Wallie, also left for South Africa, dying there in 1906. This story of matching guilts should perhaps be seen as the shadow-writing of Doyle's own knighthood.

The more Doyle penetrated the British system of power and privilege into which he had written himself by his defence of it, the more he used fierce pamphleteering to attack its limitations of vision, justice and truth. His belief in the British Empire contrasted starkly with his fierce exposure of the corrupt colonialism of other European countries. In his pamphlet *The Crime of the Congo* (1909), inspired by his work and friendship with Roger Casement and E. D. Morel, he provided a horrifying exposure of the 'dark story' of the rubber trade. Illustrated by photographs of severely mutilated children and by strings of quotations from victims and eye-witnesses, the story of the Congo, that 'huge massacre', was, for Doyle, the most appalling story in the world: 'It stands alone, colossal in its horror, colossal, too, in its effrontery.'[157] As a narrative, it was soon to have company.

The First World War

Doyle's carefully planned and researched six-volume history of *The British Campaign in France and Flanders* (1916–19) has few of the interlocking autobiographical and fictional devices apparent in his Boer War writings. On the contrary, the relatively unimpressive performance of the British army in the Boer War is presented as contributing to the build-up of German aggression prior to 1914. This grim and detailed history begins with one note of agreement in its Anglo-German relations. The year 1902 is cited by both British and German authorities alike as the first date that the British contemplated war with Germany as a serious, if undesirable, possibility. Providing his usual clear account of the balance of power and aspiration in pre-war Europe, Doyle emphazises the chaotic design that underlay the actual outbreak of war. Of the assassination of the Austrian archduke in Sarajevo, he comments 'Politics takes fantastic shapes in this south-eastern corner of Europe'[158] and madness, delusion and the bankruptcy of reason inform his version of what followed. While his own project is ambitious and well-executed, the great writing of his career inscribes an enemy culture unable to contain its own tendency towards the primitive, the bloodthirsty and the grotesquely oversized.

Despite his year of happiness there, Doyle felt that Germany had chosen to follow an ideological path that obliterated and dissolved the spiritual and legal contracts and the moral codes that gave civilization its name. His instant history of the First World War is told from the British perspective and presents what he frankly acknowledges as 'a partial record of those crowded and heroic days'.[159] From one of the great masters of concise writing, this culminating history grimly prolongs the formulaic repetition of its main unit of narrative:

> No finer force for technical efficiency, and no body of men more hot-headed in their keen desire to serve their country, have ever left the shores of Britain. It is a conservative estimate to say that within four months a half of their number were either dead or in the hospitals.[160]

If *The Great Boer War* had been for Doyle a war of writing, a battle for the signs of modern manhood, his account of the First World War describes an epic attempt on the part of Germany to tear that writing up. Brave and energetic though they were, the Germans had no code of honour, were not 'gentlemen' and 'could not understand the British Government making such a fuss about a mere scrap of paper'.[161] Britain, bound to the masculinities of its written culture, could not countenance watching its political guarantees being 'treated as waste paper'.[162] Doyle concludes that German culture carried a different imprint of signs to that of the English-speaking world, one which would brand it as 'a nation of monsters so long as history is read'.[163] Monstrosity was bred through the grotesque 'tribal deity' of Prussian militarism and its rejection of the writing of manhood:

> Nietzsche's doctrines were a ... defence ... of violent brutality against everything which we associate with Christianity and Civilisation. The whooping savage bulked larger in this perverted philosophy than the saint or the martyr ... . The typical brute whom he exalted was blonde, but a brute of any other tint would presumably suffice'.[164]

Looking back to the Sudan from this new theatre of war, he writes of the German retreat in March 1917:

> It was considered the last possibility of savagery when the Mahdi's men cut down the slow-growing palm-trees in the district of Dongola, but every record upon earth has been swept away by the barbarians of Europe.[165]

In six volumes of battle plans, bad weather, slaughter and endurance, Doyle re-employs one device to commemorate his own road through the writing of a history which produces ever more exact copies of its own masculine death narrative. His account of the Third Battle of Ypres and its culminating horror of Passchendaele is quirkily prefaced by a detailed description of what happened to two battalions of General Strickland's First Division, the 1st Northamptons and the 2nd King's Rifles, at the little seaside town of Nieuport. As the 3rd Ypres campaign was commonly known as the battle of the mud, the sand-figured story of Nieuport is in striking contrast to what it replaces. For Doyle, as for most participants and historians, the 3rd Ypres was an indefensible campaign. He refuses to summarize its significance or to describe its more disturbing details, resorting instead to quoting the 'measured words of the Field-Marshal in Command':

> This offensive, maintained for three-and-a-half months under the most adverse conditions of weather, had entailed almost superhuman exertions on the part of the troops of all arms and services. The enemy had done his utmost to hold his ground, and in his endeavours to do so had used up no less than seventy-eight divisions.[166]

The significance of 1917 was inscribed elsewhere in Doyle's history, in the impact of the Russian Revolution and in Russia's withdrawal from a war initially precipitated by the honouring of alliances. This betrayal of partnership is synonymous for Doyle with the collapse of manhood itself. The war correspondent, Philip Gibb, had famously invoked the deathly resurrections of the mud-soaked Ypres battlefield as wounded men 'struggled back yard by yard, plastered with mud, so that they looked like the dead who had crawled out of their graves'.[167] Doyle's missing descriptions of Passchendaele resurface instead in his visualization of Russia as a dissolving man. 'It was', he says of the country's withdrawal, 'as though a robust man had suddenly softened into liquid putrescence before one's eyes.'[168]

This image of revolution and masculine dissolution is checked by the preceding account of Nieuport, a small incident in the field of operations but one which tropes for Doyle the meaning of manhood. In an alien landscape of sand, British and Australian troops figure with exemplary coolness and courage the ideological and spiritual victory of their encounter with death:

> For hour after hour the men lay motionless in the midst of these terrific ear-shattering explosions, which sent huge geysers of sand into the air and pitted with deep craters the whole circumscribed area of the position. It was a horrible ordeal, borne by both battalions with the silent fortitude of veterans.[169]

Communications cut off, dug-outs blown in, strafed by machine guns mounted on German aircraft and sprayed with liquid fire, those who could still move sat in an unfinished tunnel trying to protect their weapons from the 'all-pervading sand' while the Germans dropped bombs down the three ventilation shafts. While some of the division's officers and men managed to escape by swimming across the river, others remained buried like human sculptures. Describing it as 'an experience which can have had few parallels even in this era of deadly adventure', Doyle is fascinated by the classical heroism of this act of suffering and endurance: 'Like the Spartans at Thermopylae the men of Northampton and the Riflemen had died where they had been posted. Heroism could do no more.'[170]

The significance of these dead soldiers huddled in their sand tunnel is clear. They represent the last moment of that adventure culture which, for Doyle's generation, had answered the question of what it meant most to be a man. They, rather than the thousands killed at the 3rd Ypres, stood – or rather sat – for British manhood facing its definitive ordeal. Doyle draws attention to the personalized inscription in this incident as he apologizes for the detail and length of its telling: 'Such was the deplorable affair of Nieuport, a small incident in so great a war, and yet one which had an individuality of its own which may excuse this more extended account.'[171]

The individuality of the 3rd Ypres campaign, on the other hand, was hard to find. Doyle condensed it into the death of Private Ellis H. Evans of the 15th Welsh Fusiliers, winner of the Bardic chair at the last Eisteddfod. Doyle comments: 'An empty Bardic chair was afterwards erected over his grave.'[172] The death of Ellis Evans symbolizes the lost poetry of manhood in a battle which cancelled the essential contract of masculinity – its capacity to generate meaning. After the rain started in October and the battle of the mud began, Doyle relied on the anecdotes of the Australian correspondent, Mr Bean, for odd notes of heroism and occasional humour.

In his letters from the Somme and from Passchendaele, the war correspondent, Hugh Quigley, identified a moment when he could no longer use the vocabulary of heroism and adventure to report the war. Initially describing his experiences at Passchendaele as 'rather good fun',[173] he quickly changes perspective to reflect on the shame, disgust and incomprehension that accompany painful memory:

> Now that the business is over, the soldier cannot look back on shell-holes and acres of dead Germans as monuments to the heroism of the British Army: he has a dim sense of shame as at some unnatural, disgraceful thing he was forced to do, which neither instinct, sentiment, nor reason could invest with pride. With that comes the ironic feeling of sacrifice to the political intrigues of worthless statesmen we could not explain the Passchendaele offensive from a military point of view.[174]

In Doyle's first depiction of soldiering, a Buddhist holy man had emerged from a small cave to confront the materialism of the British army. At Nieuport, the British soldiers themselves were in the place of the spirit, displaying a courage that Doyle's writing had helped to underpin. When Colonel Abadie told the riflemen to sit down in the sand-filled tunnel, they did so with perfect discipline. Never such obedience again! As these well-trained dogs of war sat on command, they took with them the secret writings of their identity: 'Even at this crisis the military code was strictly observed, and the confidential documents of the battalion carefully destroyed.'[175] Nieuport was, for Doyle, the moment when the writing of British manhood found its vanishing point. Was it for this the clay grew tall? For Doyle, the answer to Wilfred Owen's famous question was 'Yes'. The ideological mission of late-Victorian manhood had modelled its own memorial.

Notes

1. Pemble, J., *The Mediterranean Passion*, Oxford: Oxford University Press, 1988, p. 47.
2. Doyle, A. C., *Memories and Adventures*, London: John Murray, 1930, p. 151.
3. Ibid., p. 158.
4. Doyle, A. C., *Uncle Bernac*, London: John Murray, 1924, pp. 23–4.
5. Doyle, *Memories and Adventures*, op. cit., pp. 234–5.
6. Pemble, *The Mediterranean Passion*, op. cit., p. 255.
7. Hohenberg, J., *Foreign Correspondence: The Great Reporters and Their Times*, New York and London: Columbia University Press, 1964, p. 123.
8. Dawson, G., *Soldier Heroes: British Adventure, Empire and the Imagining of Masculinities*, London and New York: Routledge, 1994, pp. 48–9.
9. Ibid., p. 48.
10. Kestner, J. A., *Masculinities in Victorian Painting*, Aldershot: Scolar Press, 1995, p. 216.
11. Ramsden, J., '"That Will Depend on Who Writes the History": Winston Churchill as His Own Historian" in Louis, W. R. (ed.), *More Adventures With Britannia*, Austin: University of Texas Press, 1998, p. 242.
12. Quoted in Kestner, *Masculinities in Victorian Painting*, op. cit., p. 217.
13. Doyle, *Memories and Adventures*, op. cit., p. 150.
14. See Silverman, K., *Male Subjectivity at the Margins*, New York and London: Routledge & Kegan Paul, 1992, p. 299.
15. Alderson, D., *Mansex Fine: Religion, Manliness and Imperialism in Nineteenth-Century British Culture*, Manchester: Manchester University Press, 1998, p. 13.
16. Doyle, *Memories and Adventures*, op. cit., p. 153.
17. Ibid., pp. 153–4.
18. Ibid., p. 155.
19. Ibid.
20. Ibid., p. 156.

21. Ibid., p. 157.
22. Quoted in Giddings, R., *Imperial Echoes: Eye-Witness Accounts of Victoria's Little Wars*, London: Leo Cooper, 1996, p. 201.
23. Doyle, *Memories and Adventures*, op. cit., p. 163.
24. Quoted in Giddings, *Imperial Echoes*, op. cit., pp. 188–9.
25. Doyle, *Memories and Adventures*, op. cit., p. 159.
26. Ibid., p. 160.
27. Churchill, W. S., *My Early Life*, London: Odhams Press Ltd, 1930, p. 209.
28. Quoted in Hohenberg, *Foreign Correspondence*, op. cit., p. 130.
29. Doyle, *Memories and Adventures*, op. cit., p. 167.
30. Ibid., p. 162.
31. Ibid., p. 165.
32. Churchill, *My Early Life*, op. cit., p. 170.
33. Green, R. L., 'His Final Tale of Chivalry' in Lellenberg, J. L. (ed.), *The Quest for Arthur Conan Doyle: Thirteen Biographers in Search of a Life*, Carbondale and Edwardsville: Southern Illinois University Press, 1987, p. 53.
34. Churchill, *My Early Life*, op. cit., p. 210.
35. Ibid.
36. Doyle, *Memories and Adventures*, op. cit., p. 423.
37. Green, M., *The Adventurous Male: Chapters in the History of the White Male Mind*, University Park, PA: Pennsylvania State University Press, 1993, pp. 202–4.
38. Alderson, *Mansex Fine*, op. cit., pp. 58–60.
39. Doyle, *Memories and Adventures*, op. cit., p. 161.
40. Alderson, *Mansex Fine*, op. cit., p. 56.
41. Doyle, *Memories and Adventures*, op. cit., pp. 165–6.
42. Doyle, A. C., 'The Three Correspondents' in *The Conan Doyle Short Stories*, London: John Murray, 1929, p. 204.
43. Ibid., p. 206 .
44. Ibid., p. 196.
45. Ibid., p. 210.
46. Stearn, R. T., 'War Correspondents and Colonial War' in *Popular Imperialism and the Military*, Manchester: Manchester University Press, 1992, p. 153.
47. Knightley, P., *The First Casualty: The War Correspondent as Hero, Propagandist and Myth Maker*, London: Quartet Books, 1982, p. 43.
48. Gibbs, P., *The Pageant of the Years: An Autobiography*, London: William Heinemann Ltd, 1946, p. 207.
49. Silverman, *Male Subjectivity at the Margins*, op. cit., p. 62.
50. Greer, G., *The Whole Woman*, London: Doubleday, 1999, p. 293.
51. Silverman, *Male Subjectivity at the Margins*, op. cit., p. 61.
52. Ibid., p. 65.
53. Milner, A., 'Reform in the Transvaal or War?' in Caldwell, T. C. (ed.), *Problems in European Civilization: The Anglo-Boer War*, Boston: D. C. Heath & Co., 1965, p. 96.
54. Ibid., p. 97.
55. Stead, W. T., 'How the British Government Caused the War' in Caldwell, T. C. (ed.), *Problems in European Civilization: The Anglo-Boer War*, Boston: D. C. Heath & Co., 1965, p. 46.

56. Doyle, A. C., *The Great Boer War*, London: Smith, Elder & Co., 1901, pp. 196–7.
57. Churchill, *My Early Years*, op. cit., p. 229.
58. Hastings, Sir P., *The Autobiography of Sir Patrick Hastings*, Melbourne, Toronto and London: William Heinemann, 1948, pp. 50–51.
59. Ibid., p. 30.
60. Ibid.
61. Doyle, *Memories and Adventures*, op. cit., p. 179.
62. See Sussman, H., 'Introduction', Youngs, T., *Travellers in Africa: British Travelogues, 1850–1900*, Manchester: Manchester University Press, 1994.
63. Quoted in Nordon, P., *Conan Doyle*, trans. F. Partridge, London: John Murray, 1966, pp. 45–6.
64. Green, *His Final Tale of Chivalry*, op. cit., pp. 52–3.
65. Doyle, A. C., 'A Ballard of the Ranks' in *Songs of Action*, London: Smith, Elder & Co., 1900, p. 40.
66. See Pakenham, T., *The Boer War*, London: Weidenfield and Nicolson, 1979, p. 195.
67. Doyle, *The Great Boer War*, op. cit., pp. 465–6.
68. Usherwood, P., 'Officer Material Representations of Leadership in Late Nineteenth-Century British Battle Painting' in MacKenzie, J. M. (ed.), *Popular Imperialism and the Military 1850–1950*, Manchester: Manchester University Press, 1992, pp. 162–76.
69. Doyle, *The Great Boer War*, op. cit., p. 393 .
70. Hamilton, I., 'Making a New Soldier' in Trevelyan, G. M. (ed.), *Fifty Years: Memories and Contrasts: A Composite Picture of the Period 1882–1932*, London: Thornton Butterworth Ltd, 1932, p. 140.
71. Doyle, *The Great Boer War*, op. cit., p. 399.
72. Edwards, O. D., *The Quest for Sherlock Holmes*, Edinburgh: Mainstream Publishing, 1983, p. 256.
73. Nordon, *Conan Doyle*, op. cit., p. 54.
74. Doyle, *The Great Boer War*, op. cit., p. 5.
75. Ibid., p. 7.
76. Ibid., p. 9.
77. Ibid., p. 79.
78. Ibid., Preface.
79. Ibid., p. 459.
80. Ibid., p. 180.
81. Ibid., p. 113.
82. Ibid., p. 171.
83. Ibid., p. 20.
84. Ibid., pp. 8-9.
85. Doyle, 'The Three Correspondents', op. cit., p. 189.
86. Doyle, *The Great Boer War*, op. cit., p. 316.
87. Ibid., p. 187.
88. Kestner, *Masculinities in Victorian Painting*, op. cit., pp. 207–8.
89. Stearn, 'War Correspondents and Colonial War', op. cit., p. 143.
90. Kestner, *Masculinities in Victorian Painting*, op. cit., p. 207.
91. Wilson, H. W., *With the Flag to Pretoria: A History of the Boer War of 1899–1900*, vol. 1, London: Harmsworth Bros Ltd, 1900, p. 186.
92. Doyle, *The Great Boer War*, op. cit., p. 155.
93. Ibid., p. 161.

94. Wilson, *With the Flag to Pretoria*, vol. 1, op. cit., p. 187.
95. Ibid., p. 203.
96. Doyle, *The Great Boer War*, op. cit., p. 162.
97. Ibid., p. 264.
98. Knightley, *The First Casualty*, op. cit., p. 45.
99. Wilson, *With The Flag To Pretoria*, vol. 1, op. cit., p. 225.
100. Doyle, *The Great Boer War*, op. cit., p. 308.
101. Ibid., p. 332.
102. Ibid., p. 338.
103. Ibid., p. 24 .
104. Doyle, *Memories and Adventures*, op. cit., pp. 222–3.
105. Ibid., p. 233.
106. Ibid., p. 232.
107. Hastings, *The Autobiography*, op. cit., p. 52.
108. Montgomery Hyde, H., *Famous Trials 9: Roger Casement*, Harmondsworth: Penguin Books Ltd, 1964, p. 175.
109. See ibid., p. 172.
110. Doyle, *The Great Boer War*, op. cit., p. 515.
111. Wilson, H. W., *With the Flag to Pretoria: A History of the Boer War of 1899–1900*, vol. 2, London: Harmsworth Bros Ltd, 1901, p. 520.
112. Doyle, *The Great Boer War*, op. cit., p. 25.
113. Freud, S., 'Thoughts For the Times on War and Death (1915)' in *Civilization, Society and Religion*, vol. 12, The Penguin Freud Library, London: Penguin Books, 1985, pp. 82–3.
114. See Pakenham, *The Boer War*, op. cit., p. 282.
115. Ibid., p. 205.
116. Doyle, *The Great Boer War*, op. cit., p. 66.
117. Ibid., p. 83.
118. Ibid., pp. 215–16.
119. Ibid., p. 143.
120. Ibid., p. 188.
121. Doyle, *Memories and Adventures*, op. cit., p. 189.
122. Doyle, *The Great Boer War*, op. cit., pp. 139–40.
123. Ibid., p. 371.
124. Ibid., p. 335.
125. Ibid., p. 340.
126. Wilson, *With the Flag to Pretoria*, vol. 2, op. cit., p. 560.
127. Ibid., p. 57.
128. Doyle, *The Great Boer War*, op. cit., p. 87.
129. Ibid., p. 418.
130. Ibid., pp. 405–6.
131. Ibid., p. 247.
132. Ibid., p. 175.
133. Ibid., p. 255.
134. Ibid., p. 260.
135. Ibid., pp. 296–7.
136. Ibid., p. 266.
137. Ibid., pp. 296–7.
138. Ibid., pp. 460–62.
139. Ibid., pp. 464–5.
140. Ibid., p. 392.

141. Ibid., p. 209.
142. Wilson, *With the Flag to Pretoria*, vol. 1, op. cit., p. 305.
143. Doyle, *The Great Boer War*, op. cit., p. 72 .
144. Ibid., pp. 515–16.
145. Ibid., pp. 341–2.
146. Ibid., p. 310.
147. Ramsden, '"That Will Depend on Who Writes the History"', op cit., p. 243.
148. Doyle, A. C., 'The Hound of the Baskervilles' in *The Penguin Complete Adventures of Sherlock Holmes*, London: Penguin Books, 1981, p. 751.
149. Doyle, A. C., *The War in South Africa: Its Cause and Effect*, London: Smith, Elder & Co., 1902, p. 94.
150. Ibid., p. 98.
151. Ibid., p. 99.
152. Hamilton, 'Making a New Soldier', op. cit., p. 141.
153. Whittington-Egan, R. and Whittington-Egan, M. (eds), *The Story of Mr. George Edalji by Sir Arthur Conan Doyle*, Kent: The Lowfield Printing Company, 1985, p. 21.
154. Ibid., p. 35.
155. Ibid., pp. 97–9.
156. Ibid., p. 116.
157. Doyle, A. C., *The Crime of the Congo*, London: Hutchinson & Co., 1909, p. 53.
158. Doyle, A. C., *The British Campaign in France and Flanders, Vol. 1: 1914*, London: Hodder and Stoughton, 1916, p. 13.
159. Ibid., p. 30.
160. Ibid., p. 51.
161. Ibid., pp. 21–2.
162. Ibid., p. 32.
163. Doyle, A. C., *The British Campaign in France and Flanders, Vol. 5: January to July 1918*, London: Hodder and Stoughton, 1919, p. 5.
164. Doyle, *The British Campaign in France and Flanders, Vol. 1*, op. cit., p. 8.
165. Doyle, A. C., *The British Campaign in France and Flanders, Vol. 4: 1917*, London: Hodder and Stoughton, 1919, p. 9.
166. Ibid., p. 233.
167. Gibbs, *The Pageant of the Years*, op. cit., p. 206.
168. Doyle, *The British Campaign in France and Flanders, Vol. 4*, op. cit., p. 235.
169. Ibid., p. 125.
170. Ibid., p. 129.
171. Ibid., p. 130.
172. Ibid., p. 145.
173. Quigley, H., *Passchendaele and the Somme*, London: Methuen and Co. Ltd, 1928, p. 148.
174. Ibid., p. 178.
175. Doyle, *The British Campaign in France and Flanders, Vol. 4*, op. cit., p. 128.

CHAPTER SIX

Beyond Auto/biography: Spiritualism and Travel Writing

Re-imaging masculinity

Doyle's history of *The British Campaign in France and Flanders* concludes with a grim picture of a post-war Europe:

> Laden with debt, heart-heavy for its lost ones, with every home shaken and every industry dislocated, its hospitals filled with broken men, its hoarded capital all wasted upon useless engines.[1]

This is the background to Doyle's Spiritualist campaign and his attempt, through it, to find a new interpretive centre for masculine intelligence. No longer located in the capital city of a vast empire or in the intellectual control of the brain, Doyle's writing in the last phase of his life travels towards a region of consciousness more 'in rapport' with the signs of the body and the flow of the emotions. When Sherlock Holmes, in 'The Adventure of the Cardboard Box' from *His Last Bow* (1917), gives his customary display of privileged intelligence, these are the signs that constitute his 'small essay in thought reading'. He tells Watson:

> ... your face grew sadder; you shook your head. You were dwelling upon the sadness and horror and useless waste of life. Your hand stole towards your old wound and a smile quivered on your lips which showed me that the ridiculous side of this method of settling international questions had forced itself upon your mind.[2]

In making public his conversion to Spiritualism in 1916, Doyle appeared to have surrendered his 'masculine' reason and fundamentally revoked the identity he had scripted for himself as a war historian and the creator of Sherlock Holmes. As Freud observed, European civilization seemed to have contradicted 'the basis of its own existence'[3] through the barbarism of the warfare on which it embarked in 1914, and Doyle in this new statement of belief appeared to have done the same. As he became the increasingly indiscriminate champion of seance mediums, fairies and spirit photographers, he moved in a direction that many of his readers found inexplicable. Initially, however, Doyle's Spiritualism was more a continuation of his war-writing by other means than a repudiation of it. Closely connected to his interest in codes, ciphers and secret intelligence, his Spiritualism was, in its early stages, a strategic attempt to realign the British Empire with a revised and modernized version of Christianity.

Doyle had concluded *The British Campaign in France and Flanders* (1919) by arguing for a radical reshaping of the inner stories of men and empires:

> Not to change rival frontiers, but to mould the hearts and spirits of men – there lie the explanation and justification of all that we have endured. The system which left seven million dead upon the fields of Europe must be rotten to the core.[4]

In his introduction to the war, Doyle had compared British and German cultures and had located the root difference between them in a disagreement over the role of the New Testament in the ideological construction of manhood. German culture promoted a masculinity whose prophet was Nietzsche rather than Christ. Where Victorian Protestantism had laid a strong emphasis on Christian sacrifice and gentlemanly conduct, the Nietzschean superman regarded 'the everyday Christian' as 'a pitiful figure, a man who really cannot count up to three'.[5] Nietzsche's attack on Christian manhood and his 'mischievous philosophy, which grew the more rapidly as it was dropped into the favourable soil of Prussian militarism'[6] led Doyle to re-image and refortify the Christian model. This new model of manhood was presented in the two Spiritualist tracts which he published immediately after the war, *The New Revelation* (1918) and *The Vital Message* (1919).

Both in *Memories and Adventures* and *The British Campaign*, Doyle's account of German culture emphasizes grotesque, oversized images of the masculine body – his own (during his year in Feldkirch) briefly included. The neglected gifts of the spirit, on the other hand, he identified as humour, proportion and judgement.[7] Doyle's attempt to strengthen the spiritual definition of British manhood found a further motive in the tarnished image of science and scientific research that had resulted from its deadly deployment in the war zone. In his essay on 'The Disillusionment of the War' (1915) Freud comments on the loss of scientific idealism it occasioned:

> We cannot but feel that no event has ever destroyed so much that is precious in the common possessions of humanity, confused so many of the clearest intelligences, or so thoroughly debased what is highest. Science herself has lost her passionless impartiality; her deeply embittered servants seek for weapons from her with which to contribute towards the struggle with the enemy.[8]

Doyle himself had already begun to caricature the arrogant and aggressive rationalism of Victorian science through the Neanderthal figure of Professor Challenger. Describing the readjustments in his own thinking in an essay on posthumous survival, he admitted: 'It is hard when a man has taught all his life that the brain governs spirit, to have to learn after all that it may be spirit which acts independently of the human brain.'[9]

This reconceptualization involved a paradigm shift away from an Enlightenment philosophical tradition which, for two centuries, had identified the reasoning and controlling brain with male power. As Peter Middleton has observed in *The Inward Gaze* (1992), both Freud and Doyle had iconized the gentleman-investigator in the privileged space of his study as the epitome of late nineteenth-century manhood:

> The gentleman investigator's interior world is entered by someone with a disturbing story to tell, a story whose disturbances of sanity, order and law are strongly contrasted with the tidy masculine enclave of the study/consulting room ... . Freud uses the idea of a mystery to be solved and the image of the man's study as a metonymic sign of the masculine rationality that will enable this to happen, and to help legitimise his innovative blend of medical consultation, confession and detection.[10]

Typically, the scientific intellect of the professional man – whether novelist, doctor, lawyer or detective – would resymbolize as character, diagnosis or crime the confused inner stories with which they were presented. In his advocacy of Spiritualism, Doyle, while still employing Enlightenment modes of thought, stepped across a crucial threshold into a domain of vulnerability and self-exposure, where few of his male readers were willing to follow him. Doyle was no longer aligning himself with the powerful investigative stance of the Society for Psychical Research, although he retained his membership until the year of his death. Instead, he had joined the ranks of the ridiculed and the investigated.

Throughout his Spiritualist crusade, Doyle repeatedly insisted that investigators were themselves as suspect and as partial as the mediums over whom they assumed such power. Investigators were not sites of objectivity and detachment but had personal agendas and political relativities of their own. Evident amongst these was a suspicious assessment of the new cultural power of the USA and, in particular, its emergent feminism. Many European scientists distanced themselves from any investigation of seance phenomena because of their low-status association with Americans, Red Indians, women and the poor. Huxley is reported to have said that Spiritualism was merely an additional argument against suicide: 'Better live a crossing-sweeper than die and be made to talk twaddle by a "medium" hired at a guinea a seance.' When the spirit of grammarian, Lindley Murray, was summoned to a seance and asked if he was present, the spirit, perhaps trying to reconcile the imperatives of grammar with the multiplex nature of spirit identity, replied 'I are'. Relaying this incident in his essay, 'Natural Science in the

Spirit World' (1878) Friedrich Engels noted contemptuously, 'The medium was from America'.[11]

In *The History of Spiritualism* (1926) Doyle included a chapter on 'Spiritualism and the War' which interpreted ghostly phenomena as a dramatization of that process of masculine relocation in which, for him, the war's spiritual significance lay. He writes:

> In this chapter only brief reference can be made to the different ways in which the spiritual world intermingled with the various phases of the war. The conflict itself was predicted over and over again; dead soldiers showed themselves in their old homes, and also gave warnings of danger to their comrades on the battlefield; they impressed their images on the photographic plate; solitary figures and legendary hosts, not of this world, were seen in the war area; indeed, over the whole scene there was from time to time a strong atmosphere of other-world presence and activity.[12]

Contemporary historians, such as Jay Winter in *Sites of Memory, Sites of Mourning* (1995), now acknowledge that Spiritualism did serve an important cultural function in helping to deal with the massive scale of bereavements after the First World War. When all other forms of public commemoration had proved inadequate to contain the disaster, the consolations of spiritual communication – and, in particular, spirit photography – provided a trail of continuity across that post-war wasteland of loss. Even this limited historical acknowledgment of the importance of the movement has, however, been late in finding supporters. For Doyle, these widely reported apparitions of war trauma signalled a disturbance in the root processes of male identity and the imagery through which it was formed. Forty years of research had, he claimed, given him 'an absolute conviction that the change of vibration which we call death did not destroy our personality and that communication was still possible'.[13]

To most of Doyle's biographers, his Spiritualism and his 'surrender to the supernatural' – to use Jon Lellenberg's phrase – have posed a recurrent problem. Lellenberg claims 'The Spiritualist episode probably set back his chances of gaining a serious reputation as a writer for decades.'[14] To these biographers, a trusted voice – trusted precisely because it had always been able to speak in the tongues of other men – suddenly began to champion ideas and convictions at odds with the rationality paradigm of post-Enlightenment masculinity. Their sense of puzzlement was fuelled in part by a decontextualized reliance on Doyle's own autobiography for the interpretation of his life. *Memories and Adventures* was written at the height of his Spiritualist crusade but, having supplied the perceptual frame for his own image, he himself appeared to have slipped out of it, leaving his biographers unable to make sense of this last phase of his career. This note of biographical puzzlement has deepened with time.

Doyle's first and family-authorized biographer, the Reverend John Lamond, is a notable exception to this trend. Lamond not only shared Doyle's Spiritualist beliefs, he was a worshipper of his biographical subject and committed to a hagiography that Doyle's second family and Doyle himself would have approved. He speaks of Doyle in terms of the ultimate and the exceptional, a leader whose oratory, in particular, proclaims him 'A man – a real man'. The 'reality' of Doyle's manhood is, for Lamond, grounded in his ability to confer the status of reality on his own beliefs. He writes:

> It has been my privilege, during a life far extended beyond the normal limit, to meet with many gifted men alike in the service of the Church and State. Many of these men were of outstanding intellectual gifts ... . I have seen these men in their homes, discussed with them the special objects they had in view ... . But never have I met anyone to whom his life purpose was so real as Sir Arthur Conan Doyle ... . He beheld the New Jerusalem arising not only in England, but in every land.[15]

While all biographies of Doyle have relied heavily on his own cleverly crafted autobiography, subsequent biographers and critics of Doyle have been unable to share Lamond's perspective. The more it has been discussed, the more a community of response has pronounced his Spiritualism as problematic. Philip A. Shreffler addresses this issue of Doyle at 'what one might consider his silliest' in his essay, 'A Spiritualist Crusade', in Jon Lellenberg's *The Quest for Sir Arthur Conan Doyle*:

> To a modern reading public, which might wish the author of the Sherlock Holmes stories to reflect Holmes' scientific skepticism and logical positivism, virtually any author's account of the last years of Conan Doyle's is likely to sound mildly absurd. For the man who invented Holmes to believe in ghosts ... is somewhat disappointing.[16]

A French commentator, Jean Dorsenne, expresses the same sense of dismay:

> Here is a man who, to judge from his mentality and his previous writings, seems scarcely inclined to believe in spiritualism. Yet he has become its most eloquent spokesman. Is this not a remarkable phenomenon?[17]

Richard Lancelyn Green, who otherwise provides such a complete account of Doyle, declares that it is hard to know how best to deal with his Spiritualism, admitting that the words 'queerness' and 'madness' spring to mind when describing it:

It is hard to understand how a man who had stood for sound common sense and healthy attitudes could sit in a darkened room watching for ectoplasm or be convinced by psychic photographs or fairies.[18]

Eden Phillpotts's observation that Spiritualism was 'a creed the antithesis and opposite of his former, intellectual standpoint'[19] is perhaps the most helpful formulation of this problem arising from Doyle's resituation of his masculine identity in the unexplored regions of the spirit rather than in the intellectual hegemony of the mind.

More recently, Daniel Stashower has tried to readjust the balance of opinion by defending the honesty of Doyle's belief and the energy of his commitment to it. While Stashower's biography, *Teller of Tales* (1999), offers a well-researched account of Doyle's psychic interests and the important social connections they established for him, he shares that unexamined investment in the masculine model of Doyle's life which is common to his biographers. As Doyle apparently reported from the after-life, accurate self-encounter and self-judgement only really begin with death:

> In this judgment a man is introduced to a precise record of every outer and inner event of his life on earth ... since the traveller is likely to have misjudged himself, perhaps very seriously, whilst on earth, how does he acquire the insight to make the judgment correctly? To see himself as he really is and was itself requires enhanced powers of judgment and self-analysis.[20]

Stashower quotes a review article in the *Sunday Express*, 'Is Conan Doyle Mad?', in which a contemporary journalist, James Douglas, reassured himself of Doyle's sanity after the publication of *The New Revelation* in 1918 on the grounds that his arguments for Spiritualism contained such 'vigorous common sense'. 'If ever there was a well-balanced mind in a well-balanced body, it is his.'[21] Stashower is more generous than his predecessors but he still attempts to fit Doyle's Spiritualism into the same outdated paradigm of masculine rationality.

The problem with Doyle's conversion to Spiritualism is not the issue of private belief but the fact that Doyle made such a public restatement of his identity through his commitment to the Spiritualist cause. The connotations of a public name were altered by this highly publicized realignment, giving good grounds for the sense of betrayal expressed by his biographers. In the earnestness of the post-war period, Doyle began to produce a new mode of writing whose voice and personality had disconcertingly little in common with that previously associated with his name. He appeared to have created a concept of professional authorship only to betray its use, employing his literary fame to publicize his peculiar religious beliefs. In his conversion to the relatively low-status creed of Spiritualism, Doyle was effectively renouncing all that had previously identified him as a model for masculinity, including institutionalized systems of recognition and legitimization. In the conclusion to his war history, power itself has become 'grotesque', and cultural destruction the 'crop reaped from those navy bills and army estimates, those frantic professors and wild journalists, those heavy-necked, sword-trailing generals, those obsequious, arrogant courtiers, and the vain, swollen creature whom they courted'.[22]

In converting so publicly to Spiritualism, Doyle had made a name associated with masculine thought-modes, activities and enjoyments suddenly stand for something else.

After writing *Memories and Adventures* (1924), Doyle claimed that he had completed his literary work and would 'write no more works of the imagination'.[23] He devoted the last fourteen years of his life to his Spiritualist mission and, apart from two collections of Holmes stories and his science fiction novellas, his writing during this time was essentially devoted to expounding and defending his new faith. The last ten years of his life were spent in organizational activity for the international Spiritualist Association, whose president he quickly became, and in highly publicized excursions to Australia and New Zealand, North America, Africa and, finally, Scandinavia and Holland. These journeys combined missionary work with political propaganda and the celebrity tour. There was something penitential about them too. He travelled to exhaustion, working so relentlessly for his new cause that he once rather touchingly confided to a stranger that sitting in the darkened room of the seance was the only rest he got. Eventually he died of Spiritualism, claiming in his last months that the work had now been too much for him, weakening his heart and leaving him disabled.

After his two post-war tracts, Doyle's Spiritualist writing consisted mainly of descriptive accounts of these voyages but with this body of work too should be placed the late ghost stories: the Professor Challenger novels and the brief biographies and innumerable prefaces he wrote to introduce the Spiritualist texts of other, often very obscure, people. In his sixties, he wrote four travel books. *The Wanderings of a Spiritualist,* recounting his lecture tour of Australia and New Zealand in 1920–21, was followed by two books about America. *Our American Adventure* covered the eastern states which he and his family visited in 1922 while *Our Second American Adventure* dealt with his adventures on the West Coast and in Canada in 1923. *Our African Winter* (1929) describes his final visit to South Africa in 1928 and his lecture tour of Kenya and Rhodesia. These tours were a form of cultural diplomacy in which his fame was used to reconnect an empire shocked and shattered by European war. He travelled to promote Spiritualism as a religion whose ideological cohesion could repair the damage of the war and bind the English-speaking world into a stronger cultural unity. He was convinced that the First World War had not completed the necessary process of spiritual and political change and that another war would shortly follow.

Humour, that gift of the spirit, had always been an integral part of Doyle's literary personality but in his early Spiritualist tracts and travels, the spirit in his own writing appeared to have been silenced. Where Holmes had been a controller of masculine jokes, Doyle himself had suddenly become their target, and humour his enemy. In *Memories and Adventures*, he recounts an anecdote concerning Henry Irving in which the famous actor sat listening to a Scotsman earnestly discoursing late into the night on the subject 'of the Deity or the Universe or some other tremendous topic':

> Irving sat with his intense eyes riveted upon the speaker's face, which encouraged Hamilton to go on and on. When at last he had finished, Irving remarked:
> '*What* a low comedian you would have made!'[24]

Fearing the American sense of humour on his tours of the United States, Doyle admitted that 'no subject can be more easily made humorous than this'.[25] It was, however, on this American tour that his humour returned to him, restoring something of the doubled masculine vitality which had informed all his best writing. In his late Spiritualist novel, *The Land of Mist* (1926), written to expose the archaic laws by which mediums could still be prosecuted, he was able briefly to get humour back on his side. In a novel where the 'solemn and the comic' achieve a happy synthesis, two investigative journalists move through 'the humorous angle'[26] towards a more informed appreciation of Spiritualism and its ability to unlock the frozen places of the inner being.

Doyle's autobiography, *Memories and Adventures*, was written in the middle of his Spiritualist years and stands in striking contrast to the texts that surround it. Its model manhood is constructed through one principal comedic device, the narrative repeatedly placing Doyle in mirroring encounters with other men and with other identities that might have been his. The episode detailing his friendship with Dr George Budd is the most expanded example of this comedic mode which figures a potentially aggressive encounter with a loved but rival masculine identity. After quarrelling with Budd, Doyle arrives in Portsmouth and immediately becomes involved in a street fight with a man who then becomes one of the first patients at his newly established medical practice. Many of his comedic encounters with other men contain an element of bizarre visuality. Sitting in a Turkish bath in a private house with a huge towel wrapped round his head, Doyle sees the door open and the prime minister, Arthur Balfour, walk in. Promptly raising his head towel in a gesture of deferential greeting, Doyle comments 'I can remember the amazement with which he gazed at me ... I felt that he went away with the impression that this was my usual costume'.[27] Incorrect clothing, or the lack of it, is a recurrent motif in these encounters with public authority, while father figures like George Meredith tend to fall over when he meets them. These comical encounters act as a recurrent reinforcement of identity in an autobiography full of missing links between the public and the private man.

Doyle's Spiritualist writing abandons this masculine doubling, replacing its humorous mirroring with images of successful marital partnership and a masculinity constructed partly through a familial role. As a Spiritualist, he initially had no real rival. As a historian he had unsuccessfully contested the pre-eminence of Winston Churchill whose literary heritage and social resources he could not match. As a novelist, he had had the prescient originality of Thomas Hardy with which to contend. As a doctor he had been outshone by the flamboyant charisma of George Budd. Even in the short story in which he excelled, he had had the laurels and limelight stolen from him by a character of his own creation. On failing to enter politics after the Boer War, Doyle realized, rather humorously, that his oratorical gifts marked him out as a potential religious leader.

In a field relatively empty of competitive laughter, Doyle decided to bind the scattered forces of Spiritualism into an organized 'Church', and he travelled from London to Brisbane literally laying the foundations. He wrote of this decision: 'When immortal forces are behind you, your real personality counts for nothing ... The churches had to be spiritualised. Mankind had to face its problems.'[28] In undertaking this work, Doyle positioned himself rather clumsily and self-consciously in that radical tradition of alternative spirituality that went back to Joanna Southcott, Swedenborg and William Blake. Half body-theatre, half religious creed, Spiritualism offered a spectacular revelation, one based less in the book and the word, than in the voice and the visual image. The Victorian seance moved climactically as well as cinematically towards visual materialization, although the Cambridge-based SPR continued to privilege its more veridical and literary manifestations.

Spiritualism re-established, for Doyle, a lost emotional contact with that artistic, Catholic, family background which underlay his literary career. His uncle, Richard Doyle, had shown a pronounced interest in Spiritualism and left a psychic legacy of his own in the coincidences and premonitions surrounding his death in 1883. Unexpectedly struck down by apoplexy at the Athenaeum club, he had left on the easel in his studio an unfinished black-framed painting of an old man mowing long grass in a graveyard.[29] Many instances in Doyle's Spiritualist writings suggest a belief that his own father, Charles, had made contact with him, both through automatic writing and, appropriately, through spirit photography.

Doyle's medical specialization in the human eye, allied to the artistry of the Doyle family, finally lead him to a place where seeing is deceiving. In spirit photography he found what his own writing had always lacked, a representational form where hidden interiorities could make themselves visible. He had learnt in Africa something of the uncanny power of the photograph in depicting the blindspots of masculine interiority. In an immature and racist essay from his 1881 sea voyage along the West Coast of Africa, Doyle described having photographed a native prince at Duke Town. The native prince rejected the photographic likeness:

> His highness did me the honour of informing me that it was wonderfully unlike him. The delight of his retinue, however, at seeing the ugliness of their lord so faithfully represented more than assuaged my wounded photographic feelings.[30]

Forty years later, Doyle would publish a spirit photograph taken by a Scottish churchman in the same location. In this photograph, a black mother and child appear surrounded by a psychic aura as ' spirit-extras' in a group picture of native Africans. In the dark exchanges of photographic identity, Africa remained a place of lost bodies and uncanny spiritual doubles.

Doyle's conversion to Spiritualism remarkably fits together two logics in a way which resembles the match of private and public narratives to be found in his Boer War writing. In a frequently cited account, Doyle became a convert to Spiritualism in 1916, the catalyst for conversion coming from within his own family circle. His second wife Jean's close friend and bridesmaid, Lily Loder Symonds, had been living with them during the war, ostensibly to help with the children, though her own fragile health made her more the stereotypical Victorian sensitive or invalid medium. Forced to rest, Lily began to explore her talents for automatic writing. Her scripts sometimes seemed to carry messages of knowledgeable clairvoyance. One script predicted the sinking of the *Lusitania*, an event which, in influencing America's entry into the war, made a deep impression on Doyle. Her writing had other veridical successes, predicting the arrival of a telegram on a certain day and accurately foretelling the unlikely person who would deliver it. Most characteristically, however, Lily's scripts bore the imprint and handwriting of her brothers, three of whom had already been killed in the war.

Conviction came finally in the handwriting of Jean's brother, Captain Malcolm Leckie of the Medical Corps, who had been killed in 1915 at the Battle of Mons while giving first-aid to the injured as the army retreated. Doyle records this death in his war history as an instance of the most noble self-sacrifice.[31] The automatic writing script produced by his wife's best friend contained details of what Doyle believed to have been a private conversation between himself and Malcolm Leckie. Jean, too, became convinced by this episode, later remarking:

> It was the death of my brother at Mons that brought me to believe in Spiritualism ... . I frankly confess that, before that, I was sceptical. It was the only subject upon which my husband and I did not see alike. But in this very room ... the spirit came to us of my brother, and I knew that I had got in touch with him.[32]

This Christianized return in spirit of the self-sacrificing healer is one side of the conversion story, but the mysterious communication link with Lily Loder Symonds's brothers was a two-way process. While Doyle was receiving the spirit-writing, he was also sending cipher messages to Lily's surviving brother in a prisoner-of-war camp. *Memories and Adventures* contains this account:

> It was in 1915 that I managed to establish a secret correspondence with the British prisoners at Magdeburg. It was not very difficult to do, and I daresay others managed it as well as I, but it had the effect of cheering them by a little authentic news, for at that time they were only allowed to see German newspapers. It came about in this way. A dear friend of my wife's, Miss Lily Loder Symonds, had a brother, Captain Willie Loder Symonds, of the Wiltshires, who had been wounded and taken in the stand of the 7th Brigade on the evening before Le Cateau. He was an ingenious fellow and had written home a letter which passed the German censor, because it seemed to consist in the description of a farm, but when read carefully it was clear that it was the conditions of himself and his comrades which he was discussing. It seemed to me that if a man used such an artifice he would be prepared for a similar one in a letter from home. I took one of my books, therefore, and beginning with the third chapter – I guessed the censor would examine the first – I put little needle-pricks under the various printed letters until I had spelled out all the news. I then sent the book and also a letter. In the letter I said that the book was, I feared, rather slow in the opening, but that from Chapter III onwards he might find it more interesting ... Loder Symonds missed the allusion altogether, but by good luck he showed the book to Captain the Hon. Rupert Keppel ... . He smelled a rat, borrowed the book, and found my cipher.[33]

This two-way communication established by Lily's automatic writing and Doyle's own ciphers helps to explain how he became so deeply involved in deciphering of automatic scripts after the war. He had become fascinated by the possibility that these scripts contained some kind of private code which resembled his own. This indeed had been the conclusion of the SPR researchers investigating their famous

'Cross-Correspondences', where mediums in different countries produced scripts linked by a common pattern of often literary allusions.
Careful reading of the hidden code apparently operating in these unco-
ordinated scripts suggested to the SPR that they offered evidence of the
post-mortem survival of their own founding fathers, particularly
Frederick Myers. Spirit communicators appeared to speak most directly
through the use of esoteric ciphers unrecognized by the mediums who
produced them and only apparent to a coordinating eye. The spirits
wrote like prisoners of war attempting to outwit the controlling censorship of the mind and their own letters. T. S. Eliot famously encrypted
this use of occultism for the purposes of political intelligence in the
figure of the 'SOS' signalling 'Madame Sosostris' in *The Waste Land*.
Doyle's initial interest in Spiritualism inscribes espionage and surveillance as high on the agenda of its religious practices.

According to the recollections of Julian B. Arnold, Doyle began col-
lecting automatic scripts shortly after the First World War and, having
made an exhaustive study of them, came to the 'conclusion that they all
agreed in indicating another universal war late in 1939 or early in
1940'. Mr Arnold quotes the last letter that Doyle wrote to him in 1927
about the scripts which he had borrowed, adding 'it is strange to recall
the famous novelist's prescience and the correctness of his readings of
the scroll of fate'.[34] Doyle's letter reads:

> You can have no idea what a concentration of evidence there is, in
> the automatic writings, upon the world disaster, nor how remark-
> ably consistent the various accounts are.
> I have, I should think, 50,000 words (in automatic writings) on
> this subject, all carefully copied out and extending over three years.
> Then I have about sixty independent testimonies of the coming
> of a world disaster. Time is their difficulty but the general impres-
> sion is that it is at the end of the next decade.

According to Arnold, Doyle's Spiritualism was part of his political
propaganda against this coming event: 'it was the endeavour of my
gifted and occult friend to cultivate amicable relations among all the
English-speaking peoples, so that in the day of trial they should not be
afraid to stand against their enemies at the gate'.[35]

Apart from German culture, there were at first two main enemies at
the gates of Doyle's Spiritualist mission. One was socialism, an uneasily
recurring subject in his fiction from *The Firm of Girdlestone* and *Micah
Clarke* to *The Stark Munro Letters*. In placing himself at the head of a
Spiritualist church, Doyle was not only publicizing its beliefs, he was
also effectively depoliticizing it, for Spiritualism was beginning, particularly in the North of England and in Glasgow, to define itself as the
Word of an emergent British and international socialism. A religion of

Utopian potential and class-free perspectives, Spiritualism had the ability to convert men of dangerous calibre into its fold, as it had done with the Chartist poet, Gerald Massey, and later the best-selling socialist journalist, Robert Blatchford. Significantly, it is Gerald Massey whose words Doyle quotes at length as the conclusion to his first Spiritualist tract, *The New Revelation*:

> Spiritualism has been for me, in common with many others, such a lifting of the mental horizon and letting in of the heavens – such a formation of faith into facts that I can only compare life without it to sailing on board ship with hatches battened down and being kept a prisoner, living by the light of a candle, and then suddenly, on some splendid starry night, allowed to go on deck for the first time. ...[36]

The Spiritualist movement under Doyle's championship shed its radical political agenda while attracting to itself a widespread media interest as a result of its celebrity spokesperson. It could be argued that Spiritualism lost its political edge in acquiring such a prestigious and respectable leader. As Russia in 1917, and Germany a year later, succumbed to revolution, the British government at the nadir of the war may have found, in its favourite propagandist, an inspired mode of diversion, pacification and counter-revolution. The year of Doyle's conversion, 1916, was also the year of the Battle of the Somme, when British morale was at its lowest. In writing his history of the Boer War, Doyle had attempted to explain the otherwise inexplicable conduct of Sir Redvers Buller by suggesting that he might, heroically, have been following instructions damaging to his own reputation. Certainly the pattern of Doyle's career suggests that, in becoming the figurehead of British Spiritualism when he did, Doyle was acting 'in the interests of the nation' and with the complicity and aid of its government.

A popular but apolitical figure, who had a dialogue both with his extensive readership and with key figures in the political, military and social establishment, Doyle's was an ideally unEnglish-sounding voice to convey a reassuring message across the class divisions of English society and throughout the British Empire. Radical in some respects but in no way a revolutionary, Doyle described Spiritualism as offering a new 'Charter' like the one for which Massey had earlier been imprisoned – a creed of 'seven well-defined principles' whose adoption 'would mark a very great advance in human thought'.[37] The seven points in this Charter were 1) the Fatherhood of God, 2) the brotherhood of man, 3) the survival of personality, 4) the power of communion, 5) personal responsibility, 6) compensation and retribution, 7) eternal progression. Doyle carefully identified his icons of this New Revelation, Christ and Joan of Arc, with the working class. He writes:

Each was sprung from the labouring class. Each proclaimed an inspired mission. Each was ... acclaimed by the common people and betrayed or disregarded by the great ... . Finally, each spoke with the same simple definite phrases, strong and short, clear and concise.[38]

Throughout his Spiritualist mission, Doyle expounded a tentative and simplified socialist programme in which, as with Spiritualism, unselfishness and a decent place to live were the key concepts:

Surely, it is a palpable truth that no one has a right to luxuries until everyone has been provided with necessities, and among such necessities a decent environment is the first. If we had spent money to fight slum land as we spent it to fight Germany, what a different England it would be.[39]

In *The Wanderings of a Spiritualist* the Labour Party is described as having his 'full sympathy' – if not his membership – on the grounds that British culture has many 'anomalies and injustices, and it is only a people's party which can set them right'.[40] Democracy, he felt, had two faces: one which offered the equality he espoused, another whose codes of conduct were as yet undeveloped. Though travelling first-class himself, he insisted that the spiritual meaning of a culture came from its common people and was not imposed through the ideology of its rulers. Brooding over the guilts of imperialism, Doyle discusses the victimization of indigenous people such as Maoris and Aborigines while simultaneously deploring the immense invasion of rabbits to which Australia had been subject.

In America, it is the Labour Movement, strikes, racial injustice, the condition of prisons and the length of the working day to which he turns his attention but, at this stage in his travels, his political reflections are quickly subsumed in the sensationalism of his Spiritualist encounters. He comments with almost equal enthusiasm on the exotic animal life and the extraordinary spirit performances he witnesses there, making contact with eleven deceased members of his family through various seances. At one conducted by the American medium, Ada Besinnet, he recognized from a distance of three foot the spirit of his mother, complete with familiar wrinkles. Trumpet mediums, materializers, healers, animal psychics, arithmetical dogs, Atlanteans and enthusiasts with messages from Charles Dickens in the middle of the night are all, with the exception of the latter, courteously reviewed in the course of these volumes. Among the 'floating fringe of mystics' attracted to Spiritualism was an American poet whose masterpiece on the creation of the world was reviewed in the press – perhaps, Doyle suggests, by the poet himself – as 'a decided improvement upon the earlier and cruder effort of John Milton'.[41] At a seance in Winnipeg,

Canada, a medium who came from the Western Highlands of Scotland specialized in exciting tables to the point where they rapped out quotations from Robert Louis Stevenson. Doyle's late alignment with this visionary and radical tradition is uncritically manifest in these good-tempered, unapostolic volumes.

John Lamond presents Doyle as the embodiment of Victorian chivalry in his romantic espousal of a misrepresented, but fundamentally working-class, cause:

> Alas! in the chasm of misrepresentation and vituperation that has risen in connection with Spiritualism it is not the life of one knight, but the lives of many that are being demanded before any hope can be entertained that the chasm will close. Sir Arthur was not afraid of it. He was fifty-eight years of age. He had at least twelve good years before him ... . A man is no longer deemed on his way to the asylum simply because he has announced that the facts of Spiritualism interest him ... .
>
> As for the Spiritualists of that period they welcomed the accession of Sir Arthur to their ranks with joy. It was a repetition of Cinderella and her Prince. Cinderella had been sitting among the ashes, and her proud step-sisters eyed her with disdain. But it was this forgotten Cinderella that won the heart of Sir Arthur.[42]

Despite its brief vogue as an upper class entertainment, Spiritualism won most of its serious converts from 'the splendid lower middle class folk' whom Doyle described as 'the spiritual peers of the nation'.[43] In *The Land of Mist*, he described them as a 'type' that was 'not distinguished nor intellectual, but ... was undeniably healthy, honest and sane'.[44]

For Doyle, the appeal of his new position lay in the fact that it gave him an arena for that 'aggressive fighting for the right' which had increasingly became part of his own self-definition. His fictional figure of medieval chivalry, Sir Nigel Loring, had deliberately chosen an unattractive wife so that he might have more opportunities of championing her beauty. Doyle, in his espousal of Spiritualism did much the same, claiming to have brought to the cause a combative and aggressive spirit which it lacked before. He saw Spiritualism as part of an ongoing fight against materialism, one that offered 'a challenge to our manhood to attack and ever attack in the same bulldog spirit with which Foch faced the German lines'.[45]

One other factor informing his Spiritualist mission may have been the happiness of his marriage. Whereas Touie had been a creative muse, Jean Leckie was by all accounts his soul mate. Michel Leiris, the French autobiographer of *Manhood*, concludes his discussion of sadism and masochism with the following judgement: 'In love, everything always seems too gratuitous, too anodyne, too lacking in gravity; the punishment of social disgrace, of blood or death must intervene to make the game worth the candle'.[46] No longer unhappily married or creatively inspired, Doyle seems to have reached the same conclusion. The Spiritualist movement gave him a platform for leadership but significantly shifted the grounds of 'greatness' into this marginal domain so resistant to codification by the master discourses of Victorian science, law or theology.

Doyle's overt aim in his Spiritualist mission was to reclaim the church for masculinity, just as, in his fiction, he had attempted to reclaim literature. In this respect, Spiritualism was the final manifestation of his lifelong interest in biography. The experience of the war had shown that Christianity had failed disastrously to 'control ... the morals of Europe'.[47] Germany, from Goethe to Nietzsche, was emerging as a culture gradually shaking itself free of belief in New Testament Christianity, its version of materialism grounded in the findings of its advanced biblical scholarship. Comparing British and German culture, Doyle, in *The British Campaign*, had acknowledged German supremacy in chemistry, music and 'some forms of criticism', especially biblical exegesis. In poetry, biology, travel and moral manhood, however, Britain had the advantage of greater names:

> What name had [Germany] in poetry to put beside Tennyson and Browning, in zoology to compare with Darwin, in scientific surgery to excel that of Lister, in travel to balance Stanley, or in the higher human qualities to equal such a man as Gordon?[48]

It was an advantage that Doyle, with a little help from biblical exegesis, intended to press. In his first travel book, *The Wanderings of a Spiritualist*, he redirects Freud's famous question about the wants of women towards Germany. Having every visible attribute of masculine power, what was it Germany lacked?

> You had everything, numbers, discipline, knowledge, industry, bravery, organisation, all in the highest – such an engine as the world has never seen ... . What was it wanting in you to bring you to such a pass? Was it not spirituality? ... All other life was at its highest, but spiritual life was dead.[49]

In his early tracts Doyle directly addresses the question of the failed dialectic between masculinity and Christianity. In *The Vital Message*, he wrote of Christianity:

> It has not been an active controlling force upon the minds of men. And why? It can only be because here is something essential which is wanting. Men do not take it seriously. Men do not believe in it. Lip service is the only service in innumerable cases, and even lip service grows fainter. Men, as distinct from women, have, both in the higher and lower classes of life, ceased ... to show a living interest in religion.[50]

Of his own experience of church-going, he comments bluntly and in rationalist mode:

> Personally, I can never remember since I reached manhood feeling myself the better for having gone into one ... . Verily, there is something deep down which is rotten. It is want of fact, want of reality, words instead of things. Only last Sunday I shuddered as I listened to the hymns, and it amazed me to look round and see the composed faces of those who were singing them. Do they think what they are saying, or does Faith atrophy some part of the brain?[51]

For Doyle, masculine religious experience centred on the notion of communication with intelligent power. Spiritualism, he believed, met this desire 'to communicate direct without intermediary with that tremendous centre of force from and to whom all things radiate or return'.[52] As Jay Winter has pointed out in his study of Spiritualism and the war generation, the movement under Doyle's leadership tried 'to create a new synthesis between Darwinian evolution and humanistic Christianity'.[53] While Victorian science offered one form of this communication through its gradual deciphering of the enigmatically animal text of evolution, Doyle sought access to another through his reading of the coded scripts of the spirit mediums. Believing that the biologist, Alfred Russel Wallace, was his spirit-guide, Doyle attempted to provide a blueprint for the spiritual, as opposed to the evolutionary, development of the species.

Observing a decentred Christianity in which 'something essential is wanting', Doyle nonetheless believed that Christianity provided a necessary continuity of structure for religious belief. In opposition to the main trends of modernism, Doyle insisted there should be no more radical breaks after the painful discontinuities of the war. In his attempt to inscribe a new masculine figure in the spiritual void of post-war Europe, he represented Christ as 'an extremely powerful man', a natural healer with 'redundant health and strength to give to others'.[54] Aligning him with the 'Great Men' of the nineteenth century, Doyle invokes Napoleon's view of Christ as not, mercifully, a model for other men to follow, but as an exception to the human rule: 'It is different with Christ. Everything about him astonishes me. His spirit surprises me, and His will confounds me ... . He is really a being apart.'[55] As Christ was a spirit too remote to imitate, what was required was a new model life, one set in a providentially-ordered discourse of moral engagement, but ambitiously secular, adequately scientific and, above all, easy to read. In his attempt to model a Christian life whose emphasis did not fall on its subject's unmanly defeat at the hands of his enemies, Doyle turned first to his gift for case-making, then to the writing of his own autobiography.

The new model 'Life'

Doyle's conversion to Spiritualism was publicized with his usual power-ful clarity in *The New Revelation* (1918) and *The Vital Message* (1919), the two explanatory texts which underpinned his lecture tours of Great Britain between 1918 and 1920. *The New Revelation* begins with a coincidental and magical encounter which affirms the continuity of his writing self. Picking up a copy of the Spiritualist newspaper, *Light*, in 1917, he finds that he is reading a letter written by himself in 1887:

> There is a column in that excellent little paper, *Light*, which is devoted to what was recorded on the corresponding date a genera-tion – that is thirty years – ago. As I read over this column recently I had quite a start as I saw my own name, and read the reprint of a letter which I had written in 1887, detailing some interesting spir-itual experience which had occurred in a seance. Thus it is manifest that my interest in the subject is of some standing, and also ... that I have not been hasty in forming my opinion. If I set down some of my experiences and difficulties my reader will not, I hope, think it egotistical upon my part, but will realise that it is the most graphic way in which to sketch out the points which are likely to occur to any other inquirer.[56]

Doyle's method of Spiritualist case-making is to devote the first chap-ter of *The New Revelation* to a brief outline of his own psychic history, recording the incidents that began to unsettle the medical materialism of his early years and transform his belief in an intelligent but anti-humanist force behind the operations of Nature into a commitment to Christian Spiritualism. First, he discusses the memoirs, reminiscences and biographies of famous scientists, lawyers and clerics who had al-ready testified to the reality of the spirits. The biography of Alfred Russel Wallace held particular fascination for him and he came to believe that Wallace was guiding him in spirit, as his book, *Darwinism*, had clearly done in thought. Equally important to Doyle was the biog-raphy of the famous Edinburgh medium, D. D. Home, written by his second wife in 1863 and issued in abridged form with an introduction by Doyle in 1921. A British war correspondent in the Franco-Prussian War, D. D. Home not only shared Doyle's Scottish background, he had also been the medium responsible for the conversion to Spiritualism of the Scottish literary entrepreneur, Robert Chambers. According to a lecture in 1919, it was reading *D. D. Home: His Life & Mission* that finally convinced Doyle that Spiritualism dealt with facts he could accept as proven.[57]

As a young doctor, Doyle had regarded Spiritualism as a vulgar delusion of the uneducated, and had considered the communications of the seance as a feeble-minded joke. His Southsea friend in the 1880s, the astrologer General Drayson, had a moderating influence on his scepticism, and he then experienced for himself evidential or veridical seance communications from a man who had died on the Dongola Expedition in the Sudan in 1896. More reading led him to the Society for Psychical Research which he joined in 1893, impressed by F. W. H. Myers and his systematized account of the multiplex nature of human identify in *Human Personality and its Survival of Bodily Death*. This book provided a detailed discussion of telepathy, on which Doyle comments:

> If the mind, the spirit, the intelligence of man could operate at a distance from the body, then it was a thing to that extent separate from the body. Why then should it not exist on its own when the body was destroyed?[58]

Acting with Frank Podmore as an investigator for the SPR in a poltergeist case in the 1890s, Doyle was startled by the phenomena and concerned by the SPR's account of the investigation which seemed to him an inaccurate, oversceptical summary of their experiences. In a motif that subsequently haunted his writing, he later learnt that the bones of a child had been dug up in the garden of the house. Blocked or unused life-energy was, he believed, responsible for many uncanny displacement phenomena. A biographer might speculate here on Doyle's handling of the abortion issue during his medical practice in naval Portsmouth where prostitution and contagious diseases were a major concern. Had the Catholic-educated doctor been required to perform abortions? If so, a residual guilt might have informed this aspect of his Spiritualist beliefs.

Doyle continued to attend seances and 'might have drifted on ... as a psychical researcher' had the experience of the war not brought 'earnestness into all our souls' and forced him to examine his beliefs. Further personal experience and some of the 'wonderful literature' which had sprung up around Spiritualist phenomena, particularly Oliver Lodge's *Raymond* (1916), moved him to a public declaration of conversion: the phenomena of the seance were actual and the Spiritualist hypothesis for them sound. Sixty years of rapping, table-turning and pencil tapping had scribbled its way across Victorian culture and finally attracted a well-known writer as its theorist and interpreter.

For Doyle, the collective phenomena of the seance were the attention-seeking signs – the telephone bells – of a new revelation. Unimportant in their own right, the strange phenomena of mediumship only existed to usher in a new set of spiritual meanings. No longer a parlour game or a questionable scientific novelty, Spiritualism had reached the stage of requiring a definite system – the construction of a new scheme of thought which could combine human reason with spirit inspiration.

Doyle's aim in his first two tracts was to provide a structure of explanation that fitted the new psychic phenomena into a comprehensible body of thought. Despite the changed citadels of masculine intelligence he was beginning to explore, his first instinct was to contain within a logical 'masculine' framework or system of interpretation some of the predominantly female performances of the seance room. What the spirits had to say was simple: the human personality did not cease with death but survived the transition in recognizable form and could, given the right conditions, still communicate with those living on earth and help the process of bereavement and cultural reconstruction. Men in the future, might, he believed, need to listen for this information.

His second tract, *The Vital Message*, is Doyle's attempt to read the needs of the future. Positioning himself as a seer who looks 'into the future of the human race' and 'sees more clearly and broadly what our new relations with the Unseen may be',[59] he announces the two adjustments of religious vision necessary for its achievement. First, the Old Testament must be discarded from the Bible. Then, having separated the Testaments, emphasis must be placed, not on the death of Christ, but on his life as the real source of masculine meaning. Doyle minimized the significance of death and dying. Anyone, he claimed, could die for a belief, as thousands were currently doing in France. It was the question of how to live that mattered most. His description of the Christian life is one which came to determine his own self-definition in *Memories and Adventures*:

> It was a life which even in those limited records shows us no trait which is not beautiful – a life full of easy tolerance for others, of kindly charity, of broad minded moderation, of gentle courage, always progressive and open to new ideas, and yet never bitter to those ideas which He was really supplanting.[60]

Christ himself, though responsible for human souls, was obviously too busy to act as a personal host to the after-life. When crossing the divide, anyone who was not Tennyson was likely to be disappointed: 'He does not, save in most rare and special cases, meet us when we die. Since souls pass over, night and day, at the rate of about 100 a minute, this would seem self-evident.'[61]

In life, Christ had demonstrated a manly scepticism. He had 'critically examined religion as He found it, and brought His robust common sense and courage to bear in exposing the shams and in pointing out the better path.'[62] Robust common sense was indeed the main quality of His own teaching. Living a purposeful life of unselfishness, courage and reason, Christ also exhibited in extreme form, the magical skills and spiritual gifts of the divine medium. To Doyle, these gifts derived from an ability to negotiate a path between conflicting imperatives in a space between the sexuality and appetites of the body and the moral judgements and sanctions by which it was constrained. Somewhere between the word and the flesh was the realm of the spirit – a zone which drew on the attributes of both sexes for its pronouncements. The New Testament story which particularly attracted Doyle was that of Christ's dealing with the woman taken in adultery:

> One [incident] which appeals to me greatly is the action of Christ when He was asked a question which called for a sudden decision, namely the fate of the woman who had been taken in sin. What did He do? The very last thing that one would have expected or invented. He stooped down before answering and wrote with His finger in the sand. This He did a second time upon a second catch-question being addressed to Him ... . I hazard the opinion that amongst the many forms of mediumship which were possessed in the highest form by Christ, was the great power of automatic writing, by which He summoned those great forces which were under His control to supply Him with the answer ... He opened a channel instantly for the knowledge and wisdom which were preterhuman.[63]

In Doyle's psychic bookshop in Westminster, he kept a gallery of psychic paintings, particularly liking to be photographed against one entitled 'The Divine Medium' which represented this moment of configuration. Caught in an impossible dialectic, Christ did the unexpected thing: He did what Doyle had always done in his writing, he drew a figure in the sand and called on Holmes for the answer. The higher intelligence of the spirit is accessed not through the reasoning power of the brain but through the sensitive intelligence of the hand which can read and replicate the writing of the spirit. The later Holmes explicitly possesses this spiritual gift:

> Holmes leaned forward and laid his long, thin fingers upon the woman's shoulder. He had an almost hypnotic power of soothing when he wished. The scared look faded from her eyes.[64]

While Christ had been able to access a preternatural wisdom and knowledge, he had not, however, always been fortunate in attracting a good class of biographer:

> It speaks much for education in the Roman province of Judea that these fishermen, publicans and others could even read or write. Luke and Paul were, of course, of a higher class, but their information came from their lowly predecessors.[65]

The records of Christ's life had, as a result, been full of contradictions and inconsistencies. Writing of the problems arising from the New Testament, Doyle concludes:

> One other consideration must be urged, Christ has not given His message in the first person. If He had done so our position would

be stronger. It has been repeated by the hearsay and report of earnest but ill-educated men.[66]

By contrast, Doyle's Spiritualist writing is remarkable for its deliberate foregrounding of the autobiographical 'I'. He begins his first travel book, *The Wanderings of a Spiritualist*, by emphasizing this change in his literary identity:

> Should the reader have no interest in psychic things ... then this is the place to put the book down. It were better also to end the matter now if you have no patience with a go-as-you-please style of narrative, which founds itself upon the conviction that thought may be as interesting as action, and which is bound by its very nature to be intensely personal. I write a record of what absorbs my mind.[67]

This autobiographical impulse in a writer who had formerly rejected the autobiographical genre is a strategic attempt to forestall the inconsistencies of Christian biography. In writing *Memories and Adventures*, Doyle successfully ensured that his own 'Life' would be blessed with a biographical following which seldom departed far from his own testimony. In what is the most remarkable sleight of hand in his career, Doyle's writing reinscribes a Christian Spiritualist manhood within the covers of a secularized, comedic, masculine adventure story. Through the humorous exchanges of its joke system, the reading of this book guarantees immediate conversion to its more or less hidden spiritual creed.

The early Christian church was, for Doyle, fundamentally a Spiritualist church, and the promise of life after death the basis of all religion. His account of the after-life, correlated from a plethora of independent accounts, emphasizes the emotional continuity of the human personality and its survival, its identifying limitations intact, in a dimension that 'is preeminently a life of the mind, as this is of the body'.[68] Dying, we become thought-material, still bound up in our own concerns as we were during earth life, but able to retain contact with the thought processes of the living. The continuity of personal development through a spatial dimension as fluid as thought is Doyle's version of the 'pleasant condition of life in the beyond'.[69] As part of the thought-energy of the living, the Spiritualist after-life is itself the future, and spirits register the stress and well as the benefits of their hopefully improved material conditions.

Sometimes disturbingly and sometimes with great difficulty, in the post-mortem world we carry on where we left off, working on the next bit of our familial puzzles and passing on our solutions to our descendants through the medium of their dreams. Dreams for Doyle were a vital repository of ancestral wisdom. Our forebears who, in spirit, can see further than we, can utilize this channel to offer us vital information, like the spirit dream which gave Doyle the Italian place name, 'Piave', as a turning point for the British campaign during the First World War.

Doyle concludes his first tract, *The New Revelation*, with a section on the problems and limitations of this account of the after-life. The problem of identity remains, he admits, the most difficult to resolve, followed as a close second by the enigmatic nature of spirit communication. What recognizable form does survival take? 'Are we', he asks, 'to be mere wisps of gaseous happiness floating about in the air?'[70] Rejecting this attractive idea, he argues instead that we need the specific signification of a thought-body for survival to be meaningful in human terms. But how can a thought-body be recognized when the mind itself 'seems to be like a rope which can be unravelled into its various threads. Then each thread is a different personality which may take dramatic form, and act and speak as such.'[71] Names, anecdotes and jokes identify us in a way that thought, consciousness and even the changeable body do not. But the greatest of these is undoubtedly names.

To the intense puzzlement and frustration of psychic investigators, most spirits seem to have great difficulty remembering their own names, let alone those of other people. While they could signal presence, they could not say who they were. The question of names, so crucial a test of human intelligence and identity, was a nettle repeatedly grasped by the SPR in its investigation of purported communications. In an article in *The Journal of the SPR* in 1919, Dr L. P. Jacks puzzled over a spirit who had communicated with him and identified himself through the means of an old coat: 'I am very sure that my friend of the seance when on this earth was as far from thinking of himself in terms of his old coat as he was from identifying himself with the sound of his name. Yet the coat was manifested and the name was not.'[72] Doyle, who had given so much attention in his fiction to the right models for masculine speech, was forced to conclude that spirits were nominally-challenged:

> The spirits have the greatest difficulty in getting names through to us, and it is this which makes many of their communications so vague and unsatisfactory. They will talk all round a thing, and yet never get the name which would clinch the matter ... . I do not know if the earth name is a merely ephemeral thing, quite disconnected from the personality, and perhaps the very first thing to be thrown aside.[73]

While the need for names and significant selves is a relentless requirement of Western cultural systems, the spirits had been liberated from that assertive, individualized hierarchy. By and large spirits were team-players. Lacking both body and language, they, like the dreams that are their element, particularly enjoyed jokes about the nature of identity.

Death is a joke they have already seen. Tentative and unconfident speakers, who prefer circumlocution to direct exchange, spirits enjoyed playing games with the more linguistically-circumscribed living.

These problems of name and identity are addressed by Doyle in his second tract, *The Vital Message*. It is a moot point, however, whether the vital message in question is one sent by the spirits or that which Doyle himself was hoping to conveying to his future biographers. Endeavouring to 'show what is the purpose of the Creator in this strange revelation of new intelligent forces impinging upon our planet', Doyle simultaneously remarks that this subject is so important that anyone who could explain it 'would rank before Christopher Columbus as a discoverer of new worlds, before Paul as a teacher of new religious truths, and before Isaac Newton as a student of the Universe'.[74]

If Doyle came to be described as 'the St Paul of the Spiritualist Movement', it was because that was how he had chosen to identify himself in writing which constantly seeks alignment with the apostle. On his way to Australia, he describes himself as having 'taken advantage of the voyage to reread the *Acts* and Paul's *Epistles*'.[75] In Canada he spent 'his lonely days reading Renan's *Vie du St. Paul*'[76] as he worked on the manuscript of *Memories and Adventures*. Whereas St Paul had an unfortunate gift for making clear things obscure, Doyle shares with Christ, the clarifier, 'a genius for making an obscure thing clear'.[77] With the four countries of Great Britain as his evangelists, Doyle constructs an identity for himself which plays on the unreliable signification of names while encoding deeper patterns of spiritual identity in the image-structures of his text.

These deeper, often predictive patterns had already appeared in his fiction. In 1912, for example, Doyle, a former Liberal Unionist in Anglo-Irish politics, had became converted to Home Rule. In the same year he had published his first Professor Challenger novel, *The Lost World*. Both the novel and the political conversion owed much to Doyle's friendship with Roger Casement whose work in conducting a humanitarian investigation into atrocities perpetrated by a British-registered company in the Putumayo River region of the Amazon Basin he admired. Doyle's science fiction novel, which uses this setting, also uses Casement as the model for its hero, Lord Roxton. Under the guise of a prehistoric conflict between ape-men and bird-men on an island plateau in a time warp in South America, the novel explores the long history of Anglo-Irish hostilities. Two differently evolving branches of a species which share the same geography and language, the ape-men and the bird-men have developed through 'the feuds of countless generations, all the hatred and cruelties of their narrow history'.[78] The 'lost world' of the title is simultaneously that of the dinosaurs, of the narrator's Irish past and of male societies freed from the requirements of truth and civilization. Coinciding with the birth of his second daughter, the novel celebrates male bonding and the masculine embrace of a lost, but tantalisingly rediscoverable, world.

Uncannily, the prehistoric landscape and Irish subtext of the lost world images more than the life adventures of Roger Casement. It also images his death. The ultimate fate of this gallant 'gallows bird' hovers disturbingly over the novel through its persistent trope of bird-men and gigantic birds resembling those painted obsessively by his own father. The novel's culminating image of a pterodactyl swooping from the rafters of a London lecture hall to fly loose over the city reiterates an earlier motif of bird-men being catapulted to their doom by ape-men bent on their extinction. The novel's hidden source of horror is finally located in those 'jumping off' places where the dominant ape-men force their enemies off the steep cliffs of the plateau on to the spikes below. Lord Roxton explains the executionary topography of ape-town:

> ... that's the jumpin' off place of their prisoners. I expect there's heaps of skeletons there, if we looked for 'em. They have a sort of clear parade ground on the top, and they make a proper ceremony about it. One by one the poor devils have to jump, and the game is to see whether they are merely dashed to pieces or whether they get skewered on the canes.[79]

At the start of the expedition to South America, the Irish narrator, Malone, writes in his journal: 'It was August 2nd when we snapped our last link with the outer world ... tomorrow we disappear into the unknown'.[80] By a curious coincidence which would not have been lost on Doyle, 2 August was also the date on which Casement, in 1916, heard that the reprieve for which Doyle had petitioned had not been granted. Snapping his last link with the outer world, he made his first confession as a Roman Catholic, before jumping off 'into the unknown' from Pentonville Prison the following day. Doyle's conversion to Spiritualism was announced in a letter to *Light* three months later.

Re-imaging the body

Doyle's re-evaluation of autobiography as a mode of masculine writing was accompanied by a change in his thinking about the body and its inner, nervous story. His later writing on Spiritualism replaces the religious earnestness of the early tracts with an interest in alternative forms of healing and in the body's ability to challenge the epistemic discourse that controls it. This belief is reiterated in the Preface he wrote for J. W. Herries's *Other-World People* (1926):

> We are spirits here and now, though grievously held down by
> matter. What a spirit can do we can do if we can get loose. I am
> just as sure that the explanation of many mediumistic phenomena
> lies in this direction as I am that there is a large residue which
> could only come from external intelligent beings.[81]

To clarify his belief that 'we are spirits here and now', Doyle returned
to the double map of which, he believed, body is composed, its out-
ward, physical surfaces containing within itself a second spiritual, or
etheric, body, planned along the routes of the nervous system. This
double body with its hidden, hinged interiority had always fascinated
both the writer and the doctor in Doyle. He had used it as the sign of
his own double professional identity – a doubleness reinscribed through
the truth–fiction dialectics of his stories. His early research into 'locomotor ataxy', a disease of the spinal cord, stimulated a professional
interest in the spine and the nervous system, which produced some
dramatic anecdotes in *Memories and Adventures*. The only surgical
operation he records in detail is one to remove shrapnel from the spine
of the Dutch attaché, Lieutenant Nix, during the Boer War. Trapped
cerebro-spinal fluid rose from the incision, forming 'a column of clear
water 2 feet high, feathering at the top like a little palm tree' before the
patient died.[82] Doyle's own closest encounter with death came when a
motoring accident left him trapped under his own car:

> ... the weight of the car settled across my spine just below the neck,
> pinning my face down on the gravel ... . I felt the weight getting
> heavier moment by moment, and wondered how long my vertebrae
> could stand it ... . I should think there are few who can say that
> they have held up a ton weight across their spine and lived
> unparalysed to talk about it.[83]

The spine, for Doyle, articulated the structural meaning, or 'truth', of
the body and his stories of torture, twistedness and evil illustrate the
perversities to which that structure could be subject or liable. In its
attempt to generate a discourse about the inner nervous body, Spiritualism revived his interest in medicine as well as his literary career.

For opponents of Spiritualism like the German socialist, Friedrich
Engels, the whole movement derived its spurious credibility from the
objectifying tendencies of British empirical thought. In his essay, 'Natural Science in the Spirit World' (1898), Engels claimed that a lack of
dialectical theory made British scientists an easy target for American
fraud:

> ... it is not to be wondered at if in recent years English empiricism
> in the person of some of its representatives – and not the worst of
> them – should seem to have fallen a hopeless victim to the spirit
> rapping and spirit seeing imported from America.[84]

Identifying Alfred Wallace as the first serious scientist to fall prey to 'mediocre charlatanism', Engels ridicules spirit photography and physical mediumship for its reliance on the body as a source of meaning. He is derisive, too, about German mathematicians who consulted spirit mediums for their work on the fourth dimension, unaware that Henri Poincaré himself was an eager devotee of psychic research. He concludes contemptuously:

> In short, all the miracles of the fourth dimension are said to have been performed by the spirits with the utmost ease ... it obviously signifies a new era both in the science of spiritualism and that of mathematics ... . All previous mathematics and natural science will be only a preparatory school for the mathematics of the fourth and still higher dimensions, and for the mechanics, physics, chemistry, and physiology of the spirits dwelling in these higher dimensions ... we even have the physiology of the spirit bodies.[85]

Elementary, my dear Engels! The body, and in particular 'the physiology of the spirit body', is one of the problematics at the centre of the Spiritualist movement. Just as fourth-dimension mathematics could, in Engels's words, turn space 'inside out like a glove', so Spiritualism attempted to do the same with the human body. While Freud had used his hysterical women to explore the hidden workings of the mind, Spiritualism addressed itself to the inside stories of the body, a narrative domain for which there was no medical discourse available. This was the issue that Doyle attempted to explain in *The Vital Message*, one dating back to the early years of his medical practice and his dissatisfaction with the prevalent materialism of his own beliefs.

In no area of science was the materialist paradigm so inadequate as in the medical account available for the discussion and treatment of pain caused by injury to the nervous system and by missing limbs. When Doyle concludes his second Spiritualist tract with advice to the Christian church to 'cut away from their own bodies all that dead tissue which is but a disfigurement and an encumbrance',[86] his surgical metaphor figures the medical impasse in his thinking about the spirit. This image recalls the episode in *Micah Clarke* where a Puritan soldier amputates his own injured arm with his battle sword.

It was, however, field surgeons working with wounded soldiers in the American Civil War who first began to face the problem posed by amputation and the syndrome now known as 'phantom limb pain'. In *The Great Boer War*, Doyle had lingered over accounts of war wounds and the shocked painlessness with which soldiers had lost arms, legs and feet. As he tries, in *The Vital Message*, to describe the physiology of the spirit, this is the issue that haunts his writing. The etheric body, he insists, is 'a perfect thing':

This is a matter of consequence in these days when so many of our heroes have been mutilated in the wars. One cannot mutilate the etheric body, and it remains always intact. The first words uttered by a returning spirit in the recent experience of Dr. Abraham Wallace were 'I have got my left arm again.'[87]

Dr Wallace was not the only person to have this experience. If returning spirits had trouble remembering their names, they had no difficulty at all in recognizing their lost body parts. One of the most remarkable investigations conducted by the SPR involved the alleged spirit of an Icelandic man, Runolfur Runolfsson (1828–79), who lost a leg at the time of his death and was still searching for it through seances in Reykjavik sixty years later.[88]

The return 'in spirit' of lost limbs after the shock of separation had posed a problem for medical science which the work of Max von Frey in the mid-1890s had begun to address. Von Frey's work on receptors suggested the possibility that the nervous system in the spine holds what amounts to a complete map of the whole body – a map to which nerves continue to relate, even when their endings and the damaged limbs that contain them have been removed. While many medical researchers agreed that limbs could be severed without any immediate sensation of pain, the suffering caused by the so-called 'phantom limb' continues to haunt the body often for years after the separation.

According to Ronald Melzack and Patrick Wall in their modern medical classic, *The Challenge of Pain* (1982, 1996), it is only recently that medical research has been able to provide a detailed account of how loss is sustained and pain activated. Melzack and Wall describe how early research into pain studies conflicted with the mechanistic and materialistic account of the body available to, and accepted by, Doyle's medical contemporaries at the end of the nineteenth century. A hundred years later, the account of 'phantom limb pain' is still incomplete, although it is now accepted that lost body parts continue to haunt their former place of attachment. Melzack and Wall give the following description of this syndrome:

> Phantom limb pain is one of the most terrible and fascinating of all clinical pain syndromes ... .
>   The proportion of amputees with phantom limb pain is astonishingly high ... . Amputees report feeling a phantom limb almost immediately after amputation of an arm or a leg (Simmel, 1956). The phantom limb is usually described as having a tingling feeling and a definite shape that resembles the real limb before amputation ... . At first, the phantom limb feels perfectly normal in size and shape – so much so that the amputee may reach out for objects with the phantom hand, or try to get out of bed by stepping onto the floor with the phantom leg. As time passes, however, the phantom limb begins to change shape. The arm or

leg becomes less distinct and may fade away altogether, so that the phantom hand or foot seems to be hanging in mid-air. Sometimes, the limb is slowly 'telescoped' into the stump until only the hand or foot remain at the stump tip. Amputation of a limb, however, is not essential for the occurrence of a phantom. A painless phantom is often reported by subjects or patients who have a local anaesthetic block of a sufficiently large part of the body.[89]

This account of limb loss has a clear correlate in the psychic experience of families who had lost members of their circle in the First World War. As described by Oliver Lodge in *Raymond, or Life after Death* (1916) the whole of post-war culture was, in this sense, affected by a family phantom limb syndrome, unable to acknowledge physical loss as also spiritual absence. Lodge describes a Christmas and an Easter day at which his dead son, Raymond, was present in spirit, joining in the conversation and, in particular, the family music through the means of a wooden table. Using the table as an artificial limb, the spirit became so excited by the music that it started banging against the pianist and a black satin cushion had to be held up 'as a buffer' against Raymond's exuberance.[90] The table continued to bang until it had made a hole in the satin whereupon it sat down with an alphabet to communicate through that instead. Psychic affects frequently attend breaches of the somatic body, a fact perhaps signalled by those Victorian seance mediums who specialized in the production of disassociated limbs, especially hands and feet. Spiritualism, with all its ambiguities, was preferable to the mutilating absences perpetrated by medical science and what Oliver Lodge described as its alternative, 'the selfish creation of silence to deaden pain'.[91] Death, Lodge suggested, should be seen as a process of gradual dissociation rather than of sudden extinction.[92]

For all its bizarre, fraudulent and comic elements, it is a mistake to relegate Victorian Spiritualism to the rubbish bin of history, if for no other reason than the fact that it rewrote the Victorian sense of ending and removed the dread finality of its judgements. By establishing a needed forum for interclass dialogue, it allowed new speakers access to quasi-public platforms and it gradually informed and improved social conversation itself, providing an enhanced vocabulary for intersubjective exchange. In particular, it began to address some of the deep silences surrounding the body in Victorian culture, supplying a crude but powerful bereavement therapy while amusing, compelling and consoling its contemporary audience. If it did not communicate with the dead, it certainly communicated with much that was cut off in the living and from mainstream culture.

On the other hand, Spiritualism was also a threat to established categorizations, including, and especially, those of gender. Particularly perhaps for its masculinity-conscious investigators, Spiritualism signalled vulnerability and spoke from and to places of wound, breach and loss in a manner that threatened and opposed the guarded power systems which protected that masculinity. The spirits needed weakened points of access to make their revelations heard, their messages often viewed by medical men and psychic researchers alike as one of the signs and articulate affects of menstruation. Spirits made contact through old wounds and psychic vulnerabilities. The strain on Doyle's spine from his car accident may have made him particularly open to such influxes, especially as there were as many gaps in his emotional history as there were breaks in his memory. It was a vulnerability he recognized and decided to act upon.

His account of the soul or 'surviving spirit' is very close to Melzack's notion of the inner nerve map of the body:

> ... the soul is a complete duplicate of the body, resembling it in the smallest particular, although constructed in some far more tenuous material. In ordinary conditions these two bodies are intermingled so that the identity of the finer one is entirely obscured.[93]

With death, Doyle believed, came a separation of these bodies, life being continued by the thought-body encoded in the nervous system. This imagined relationship between the inner and the outer man was the main territory of Doyle's fiction and of his life story; his Spiritualism was a solution to longstanding problems in his identity discourse. In *The History of Spiritualism*, he distinguishes the two potentially contradictory directions of Spiritualist enquiry:

> Very many psychic phenomena ... may, in the opinion of the author, be referred to the etheric body and may be classed under a higher and subtler materialism than under Spiritualism. They are in a class quite distinct from those mental phenomena such as evidential messages from the dead, which form the true centre of the spiritual movement.[94]

Inscribing a new 'vista of medical possibilities', Doyle's most graphic anecdote of the nervous body linking inner and outer man is given in *The Wanderings of a Spiritualist*, where it carries uncanny familial, as well as colonial, connotations. In Brisbane, he met a kinsman, another 'Dr Doyle', who was a skin specialist and who, like himself, had recently lost a son, Eric, in the war. This other Dr Doyle had had a dream premonition of his son's death. In the dream, Eric's face had been held very close to his own so that he could see the skin was suffused with acne. He told his wife of the dream and of the spots which were the recurrence of an old condition and said he feared Eric was dead. Not only did this prove true but the following day the parents received a letter from Eric, written before his death, in which he asked his father to send some special ointment, as his old acne had returned.[95]

If the dead could contact the living from an after-life of disassociated thought imagery, that after-life itself appeared to be locatable, not in the cosmos, but in the linguistics of the nervous system. In *The Land of Mist*, Professor Challenger's scientific protegée, Dr Ross Scotton, author of 'The Embryology of the Sympathetic Nervous System', eventually falls victim to an agonizing disseminated sclerosis, complaining of 'the cramps when my body – like a badly articulated skeleton – would all get twisted into one rigid tangle'.[96] He is cured by a spirit doctor who, to the horror of Professor Challenger, manifests through the mediumship of a young female nurse. A hidden emotional vulnerability in his own past makes Challenger himself the last convert of a novel eager at last to discuss its own painful interiority.

The re-opening of old wounds and the trauma of pain is the subject of a masculine ghost story Doyle wrote after his conversion but set in 1878 at the time of the Franco-Prussian war. 'The Bully of Brocas Court' (1921) is the story of a moonlit boxing match between Alf Stevens of Kentish Town, the only man able to stand up to Slogger Burton of the South Midland Yeomanry, and an uncanny opponent. This hideously mutilated Bully of Brocas Court turns out to be the ghost of a prizefighter from 1822, the 'Gasman', Tom Hickman. In an international contest of masculinities, old and new, physical and ghostly, the eventual victor turns out to be neither the great, living dragoon or the ghostly bully with the broken head. Instead, the fight is broken up by an unexpected animal mnemonic. In dramatic contrast to the aristocratic supernaturalism of *The Hound of the Baskervilles*, this psychic intervention takes the form of a small white terrier. The sudden sound of an inarticulate, high-pitched cry as 'if from a child or some small woodland creature in distress' is enough to make the ghostly 'Gasman' reel back in terror from the fight he is winning against his living opponent:

> 'It can 'urt me! It will 'urt me!' screamed the fighting man. 'My God! I can't face it! Ah, I see it! I see it!'
>
> With a scream of fear he turned and bounded off into the brush wood ... .
>
> Then from among the bushes there ran a small white terrier, nosing about as if following a trail and yelping most piteously ... .
> Then it also vanished into the shadows.[97]

The complete demoralisation of the fighting men, both living and dead, at the sight of this tiny, avenging working-class terrier is caused by its capacity to re-create trauma. When the Bully had drunkenly broken the dog's back with a poker in 1822, he had swaggered out of a tavern only to be run over and have his head crushed by a wagon wheel. This wound to the brain is the ultimate castration:

Stevens gave an exclamation of surprise and horror. The removal
of the beaver hat had disclosed a horrible mutilation of the head of
his antagonist. The whole upper forehead had fallen in, and there
seemed to be a broad red weal between his close-cropped hair and
his heavy brows.[98]

Although the ghost of the Gasman continues to seek human opponents
to overpower, his arrogant ego collapses in terror at the sight of the
sleeping dog he did not let lie. The terrier itself, a breed renowned for
its aggression, is part of a continuum of masculine combat which stretches
back through a hundred years of European history, but the story of pain
articulated through the wounded spirit of its broken spine can no
longer be silenced.

These wounds to masculinity let women into the writing. According
to John Lamond, it was 'really the bereaved mothers of Great Britain'
that 'made London the greatest centre in the world for Spiritualism',
asking questions about the death of their sons that the Church was
unable to answer.[99] Doyle's Spiritualist mission encouraged them to
seek a solution through him. Mediumship, so controversial a performance arena for Victorian women, was for Doyle a phenomenon associated
with possession and control of the body, one that duplicated women's
sexual passivity and their willingness to submit to external control:

> The whole secret of mediumship on this material side appears to lie
> in the power, quite independent of oneself, of passively giving up
> some portion of one's bodily substance for the use of outside
> influence.[100]

'Nearly every woman', he claims, 'is an undeveloped medium.'[101] Significantly, the most successful male mediums tended to be associated
with marginal cultures which allowed them to represent qualities of
sensitivity not associated with the dominant Anglo-Saxon male. D. D.
Home, whom Doyle described as 'a man of swift emotions and feminine
susceptibilities',[102] came from Scotland. Evan Powell, the medium who
inspired Doyle's Spiritualist travels, was a Welsh coalminer. Erich Weiss,
'Houdini', was a mid-European Jew.

The ironic tragedy of Doyle's life was that, having realigned himself
with his missing father through his Spiritualism, he lost contact with his
own oldest son. Kingsley died of pneumonia in 1918 after being wounded
on the Somme. It was Kingsley who, through the mediumship of Evan
Powell at a seance in Merthyr Tidffyl, not only spoke directly to Doyle
but provided the motive for the journeys that occupied the last ten years
of his life. Like Tennyson's 'Ulysses', Doyle found he could not rest
from travel and, like James Joyce's *Ulysses*, he travelled as a mythic
father in search of the son he had lost. The prolonged nature of this loss
was perhaps evidenced by his second daughter, Jean. Known as Billy, it

was only on her tenth birthday that she ceased to sign her notes to him, 'Your loving son'.[103] Doyle eventually found his lost son in the person of Houdini.

The final figure

From the seance in Wales where he believed he had made contact with Kingsley, Doyle travelled as a fellow colonial to places in Australia and New Zealand that reminded him of the Scotland of his youth. 'Nowhere', he remarked, 'is Spiritualism more firmly established now than in Scotland'.[104] Australians generally reminded him 'more of the Scotch than the English, and Melbourne on a Sunday ... is like the Edinburgh of my boyhood'.[105] Appropriately perhaps, his mother, the presiding force of his childhood, died while he was away on this trip. Describing her rather impersonally in *The Wanderings of a Spiritualist* as a 'world-mother mourning over everything which was weak and oppressed', Doyle concludes his paragraph on her death by referring to her lack of sympathy and understanding for his own mission. While she could not, in life, understand the spiritual needs of others, 'She', as he rather grimly put it, 'understands now'.[106]

The forging of new identities both for himself and across the empire is the project of Doyle's travel writing, its perspective as ideologically decentred from London as from the reasoning brain. All four books quote liberally from the 'kind reception' given him by the press in reporting his lecture successes and the size of his audiences. Acknowledging that he is throwing bouquets to himself in citing these journalistic reports, his travel-writing combines an itinerary of places visited and lectures given with reflections on societies, both temporal and spiritual, still seeking their own grounds of definition.

Perhaps because Spiritualism was originally an American phenomenon and the sign of its growing cultural and political power, the most engaged and engaging of the four travel books is *Our Second American Adventure*. Here he visits and discusses the places whose culture and technology had excited his imagination from the beginning. The encounter brings out the Englishman in him in unexpected ways, as in his vitriolic rejection of Wrigley's Chewing Gum. Referring to that 'horrible habit of chewing which does much to disfigure American life in the eyes of the traveller', he insists that 'Venus would look vulgar if she chewed, and Shakespeare a lout. There never was so hopelessly undignified a custom ... the woman who chews becomes all animal at once'.[107]

Rochester, home of the Spiritualist movement, should, he feels, have been renamed 'Kodak Town' on account of the photographic industry which dominates it. New York State generally he defines as a centre of modern revelations for from it came, between 1820 and 1850, the seer, Andrew Jackson Davies, Mormonism and the Spiritualist Fox sisters with their informative poltergeist. America was full of encounters with the cultural material which had supplied his own literary identity. In Salt Lake City, he returned to the old Holmes territory of the Mormons, discussing at length Joseph Smith's 'statement' and his record of the revelations vouchsafed to him through the sacred writings discovered at Palmyra:

> The most interesting document ... and the one of most value to the historian is Joseph Smith's own account of the whole matter. I think it is impossible for anyone with a discriminating mind to read a long narrative without understanding whether it is written honestly or not. Here is a long, plain statement by a man who finally sealed his faith with his blood. I am prepared to take it up to a point at its face value, but I am also prepared to maintain that the writer, from his ignorance of psychic matters, lost all sense of proportion and misinterpreted to a great extent the evidence which was put before him.[108]

To members of the SPR, Doyle's Spiritualism itself could not have been better summarized.

Leaving the Land of the Saints, Doyle and his family went on to the 'Land of the Sinners – the famous home of the cinema industry'.[109] To his apparent surprise, his Arabian spirit-guide, whole troops of fairies and the spirit of his mother were still pursuing him through the materializing seances. Doyle had begun his American tour with the disclaimer that he was 'not a simple minded person who has been deceived by fakers'[110] but the manner of his response to spirit materializations laid him particularly open to the charge. As a spirit who was visibly not either of the usual communicators (his brother, Innes, or his son, Kingsley), stepped out of a cabinet, Doyle asked it if he were Captain Cubitt, a young officer who had been killed in action. Clearly glad to be recognized as anyone, the materialization nodded. When Doyle asked him if his Spiritualist views on the after-life had proved correct, this spirit, like so many others, obligingly confirmed that they were. Deprived of the significant men in his own family, Doyle was looking desperately through the seances for someone to disagree with him.

His final travel book, *Our African Winter*, returned him to the scenes of some of his best writing, and to his life as an army doctor in Bloemfontein. Already in 1900 a place of repressed memory, Africa in 1928 proved as uncanny as ever. Doyle prefaces his travels with the story of the extraordinary death of the Boer leader, General de la Rey, a death which went 'beyond the range of coincidence', for he was accidentally shot in mistake for a bank robber who was driving an identical grey Talbot car. Doyle saw the anecdote as a sign of the 'direct intervention of Providence to prevent the disruption of the British Empire'.[111] On another occasion in Nairobi, when Doyle was exhibiting a spirit photograph taken in a haunted house in Nottingham, a local dentist in the audience stood up and claimed that the photograph was a fraud, as he himself had impersonated the ghost to play a trick on his companions. He did, however, admit, that when the real ghost turned up to repossess its territory, he immediately regretted what he had done. Hidden agendas could appear out of the blue. A spirit caught hovering in a tree turned out, on closer inspection, to be a picture of Keir Hardie.

The most uncanny and significant incident of Doyle's travels, however, was undoubtedly his friendship and eventual quarrel with Houdini. Whereas Doyle represented a masculinity figured through reason and spirit, Houdini exhibited it through trickery and physical courage. In the course of this dramatic friendship, both men enacted a version of 'the Musgrave Ritual', that problematic transmission of manhood between father and son. Despite the physical contrast between them, there were hidden similarities in their backgrounds which set up a strong mutual fascination and respect. Both had had to create their own masculinity from the absence of a paternal model, in a close relationship with the mother and through a persecuted but powerful faith. Both represented and publicized the masculinity-ideals of their chosen cultures. But where Doyle's memories of Dr George Budd had been associated with the successful performance of manhood in the public sphere, his tragi-comic final friendship with the magician, Houdini, situated the close of his life story in a private sphere of confused emotional interiority. The encounter with Budd in Plymouth perversely helped Doyle to define and develop his career and realign his own inner and outer man; the friendship–rivalry with Houdini, on the other hand, re-opened the seam between them, exposing the contradictions which held Doyle's concept of manhood together. The fault-line lay along the intimate borders between the public and the private man, a space for the exchanged identity between men and their women.

Doyle had, since his friendship with Budd and *The Stark Munro Letters*, defined himself as a man whose vision and version of events could be trusted, an eye specialist whose professional life had been spent in the correction of misaligned images and perceptions. Whereas Budd had been born inside the machine of the medical profession and understood its mechanisms, Houdini was an insider in the fraternity of magic. His extraordinary acts of escapology specialized in collapsing concepts of spatial confinement, mystifying the boundaries between 'inside' and 'outside'. A man of extraordinary psychic sensitivity, Houdini was obsessed with the exposure of spirit mediums, particularly if they were women. Doyle, the rational expounder of a psychic religion, who had always covered or excised the female voice with his own writing, was now the champion of their public mediumship.

The real opposition in this friendship did not come from the men themselves who formed, between them, a striking continuum of literary, psychic, spiritual and physical prowess. They were both magicians, publicists, propagandists and entertainers within the variants of their shared culture. While Houdini defied death one way, using his body as a performative site, Doyle defied it in another, offering the power of written, spoken and spiritual intelligence as the sign of post-mortem survival. The opposition came instead, as it had come with Budd, from the two women on whom their performance of masculinity depended. In the contestation between them it was suddenly the performance of women that mattered. And with the women came the spirits.

The lost energy and humour of Doyle's Spiritualist writing returns with the entrance of Houdini and the self-mirroring tensions which his presence activated. Spiritualism, Houdini claimed, was a fraud from start to finish. There were for him only two kinds of medium – those who were mental degenerates, and ought to be under medical observation, and those who were deliberate cheats and frauds. Doyle, on the other hand, considered Houdini himself one of the greatest mediums of the age. He had 'the essential masculine quality of courage to a supreme degree',[112] had a highly developed psychic intelligence and represented everything that Doyle, in his attempted relocation of masculinity, was looking for. In the public sphere, the controversy between them was of benefit to both, for they were well-matched opponents in a publicity-seeking quarrel. In the private sphere, it was a different matter. What they quarrelled about was written language and the different configurations by which identity could claim to be represented.

Two episodes in *Our American Adventure* dramatize the psychological rivalries of these two famous men, each in the last decade of their lives. After delivering a matinee lecture in Philadelphia, Doyle had an experience which his audience, at least, found immensely amusing. Having concluded his talk on the after-life, he was unable to find a way off the stage:

> I spoke with a huge drop-curtain of canvas behind me. When I had made my bow I walked off, but found that there was no exit on the right side. I turned and walked across the proscenium, but again, to my surprise, was faced with a rigid canvas. I then concluded I was mistaken in my first venture, so I again crossed but found it quite impassable.[113]

Doyle then wandered down the face of the curtain amid sympathetic laughter from his audience until at last he saw a slit with an agitated hand waving at him through it and gratefully followed its signal. In contrast to his own failure to find the exit, he describes a typical triumph of Houdinis. After a lecture in New York, Houdini escorted Doyle's wife down a passage which ended in a padlocked door. 'Houdini put out his big right hand, and by some cantrip gathered up the padlock as one picks a plum from a tree'.[114] The lecture in question involved a man with an inner demon whose advice and instructions he was compelled to obey, as Houdini always obeyed the inner voice which instructed his own death-defying movements. These two 'exit' anecdotes image Doyle's anxieties about his own public performance. The spirit in his writing significantly appears, not as part of his formal discourse on Spiritualism, but through the comedic sign that directs and guides it: in this instance, the disembodied hand frantically signalling to him behind the curtain.

On a similar occasion in America, Doyle made his entrance on to a lecture platform clutching a pile of books, tripped over a small ledge at the stage door and appeared before his audience spilling all of them before him in a literal burst of premature ejaculation.

Rivals on the question of death and the definition of spirit identity, Doyle and Houdini sought and found unexpected allies in each other's wives. Houdini had a habit of seeking intimacy with Spiritualists, the better subsequently to expose their practices. Whereas Jean Conan Doyle preferred, as Doyle put it in *Our American Adventure* 'not to speak in public',[115] Bess Houdini was a vital and accomplished participant in her husband's acts. From the anecdote already recorded, Doyle appears so impressed by Houdini's ability to solve problems as physically challenging as the intellectual knots unpicked by Holmes, that he feared he might carry Jean with him. Doyle certainly seems to have become eager to demonstrate her own psychic commitment and spiritual abilities.

Of all the figures in the sand cast by Doyle's career, perhaps the most controversial was the one inscribed on the beach in Atlantic City in 1922, a moment preserved in an often reproduced photograph of the two families. Either at his request or that of Houdini, Jean Doyle agreed to demonstrate her newly acquired powers of automatic writing by holding a private seance for Houdini through which she hoped to make contact with his dead mother. Doyle shortly afterwards published the intimate details of this seance in *Our American Adventure* as prestigious propaganda for Spiritualism, forcing Houdini to counterattack by denying the authenticity of Jean's mediumship. According to Doyle's account, Jean rapidly produced pages of automatic script written in English under the sign of the cross, which purported to be an impassioned communication from the Jewish Mrs Weiss. Houdini himself was apparently deeply moved by what he read. At the end of the seance, he borrowed the automatic writing pencil from Jean and, as if in contact with the spirits himself, produced a script of his own. Significantly it was composed of just one word, the name 'Powell'.[116]

As Doyle had a Spiritualist friend of that name, Ellis Powell, who had recently died and promised to make contact with him, he was convinced that Houdini had himself been the recipient of a genuine message and had unwittingly revealed his mediumship powers. Houdini explained that he was thinking of a different Powell, a fellow magician from Texas, F. E. Powell, who had recently consulted him for advice on a delicate professional matter. His wife, who was also his assistant, had had a stroke. Should he, or should he not, take a new one to fill her place? On this issue of public and private performance Bess and Houdini had disagreed over the answer, Bess arguing that a wife's place should not be taken by a girl, as perhaps Touie's place had been taken by Jean Leckie. Houdini found a letter from F. E. Powell waiting for him on his return from Atlantic City and he posted it on to Doyle, remarking on the coincidence.[117]

In one of his last works, *The Edge of the Unknown* (1930), a collection of essays and short biographies on psychic subjects, Doyle returns to this controversy and gives a more detailed, and more contradictory, account of his dealings with Houdini. By this time, the incident had come and gone as a public controversy, Houdini having denied the validity of the spirit message, rejecting as embarrassingly inauthentic the wordy emotionalism and non-specificity of Jean's script. Defending the 'purity' of his wife's mediumship, Doyle describes both the seance and Houdini's protracted grief for his mother:

> He had spoken in a touching manner of his mother, so my wife, who has the great gift of inspired writing – that is, of writing which appears to be quite disconnected from her own mentality – tried to see if she could get any message for him. It was done at my suggestion, and I well remember that my wife needed much persuasion.[118]

Doyle remembered it so well that two pages later, he remembered it differently, claiming that the seance had been held entirely at Houdini's 'own urgent request'![119]

Houdini's account of the genesis of this ill-fated seance is significantly different in emphasis. According to Houdini, he, his wife, Bess, and Doyle 'were sitting on the sand skylarking with the children'[120] when Doyle left to take an afternoon nap. He came back shortly afterwards with a message from Jean saying she would hold a special seance for him that afternoon. Bess Houdini, a former stage medium, who had talked intimately to Jean the night before, was requested not to attend.

The figure left in the sand after the dust of these different accounts had settled is that of Bess Houdini herself.

The quarrel was never resolved. Fulfilling Spiritualist prophecies of his imminent doom, including some through the mediumship of Jean Conan Doyle, Houdini died in 1926, forced to drop the curtain on his own act at the age of fifty-two. Calling him 'the greatest publicity agent that ever lived',[121] Doyle paid tribute to him as 'the most curious and intriguing character whom I have ever encountered'. In claiming him as a medium, Doyle made a careful proviso:

> ... we have to remember that we are ourselves spirits here and now, and that a man may well be producing psychic effects without going beyond his own organism. It is in this sense that I suspect the Houdini results as being psychic, and I do not at all insist upon the interposition of outside forces.[122]

The text of *Our American Adventure* which had contained the first account of the seance proved to have something of a life of its own. It had become a further source of contention between the two men when, after its publication, Houdini claimed that Doyle had promised to give him the manuscript, and wrote reminding him of the promise. Doyle replied that he had forgotten making it and felt, in any case, that the manuscript should belong with his descendants, as his mission of 'altering the religious opinion of the world'[123] might make it very valuable. Could Houdini remember the exact conversation in which Doyle had made the promise? Houdini unfortunately could, and Doyle therefore agreed to honour his promise, thus allowing Houdini to position himself as his son and spiritual heir. Houdini himself had been keeping a day-book of Sir Arthur's sayings and doings which he was considering making public in the future. As this quarrel by correspondence deepened into serious mistrust, the friendship broke down altogether in May 1924.

In 1927, a year after Houdini's death, the quarrel was finally run to earth when Bess Houdini sent Doyle a book from her late husband's library. It was an illustrated collection of letters produced as a young man by Doyle's father, Charles, which had found its way into Houdini's collection. Doyle wrote to Bess with gratitude and surprise, saying 'it really seems like a series of miracles – first that it should exist still, then that it should cross the Atlantic, and finally that it should come back to me. I accept it as a peace-offering from your husband, and thank him as well as you.'[124] It was Bess Houdini, with those familiar initials 'HB', who had been the real medium to complete the last stage of this magical exchange between father and son.

The encounter with the Houdinis had one other literary consequence for Doyle. Three months after Houdini's death in 1926, Jean Conan

Doyle obviously changed her mind about performing in public, and Doyle published *Pheneas Speaks*, a selection of her spirit mediumship by automatic writing and direct voice, edited and introduced by himself. As Jean seems astutely to have realized when she began to preside as a medium over the family seances, only Doyle's spirit guide, Pheneas, could address the masculine losses and subsequent vulnerability in his intimate circle. Unlike Houdini, Pheneas was full of praise for Jean's mediumship:

> She is a Medium of rare and wonderful vibration, through whom I can work in perfect harmony of one accord. It is like virgin soil. You put the plant in, and it grows a beautiful specimen. So with our power, the vibrations between us of harmony are complete. Therefore I can come to you without fear of any outside force polluting or touching my channel.[125]

A former Arabian physician, Pheneas combined flowing desert robes with an interest in cooking, sagely advising Doyle's son, Denis: 'You can't get an apple dumpling till you have the apples.'[126] Pheneas had first manifested in 1922, after the seance with Houdini, and the spirit seemed determined that Doyle's final figure in the sand should be his own. Desert metaphors were a speciality of Jean's mediumship. 'Faith in the desert when you are very hungry does not satisfy your hunger',[127] Pheneas remarked through her on one occasion. He likened the Doyle home seance circle to people toiling across a desert, not quite sure of their road. In the aftermath of the war, his teaching was the 'oasis' which gave them hope.

As a boy at Stonyhurst, Doyle had discovered through being beaten that he had a 'literary streak' which included a talent for poetry. As he records it in *Memories and Adventures*, the discovery allowed him to 'realise himself a little'.[128] Like all Doyle's efforts at self-realization, it involved the drawing of figures in the sand. The poem through which his literary talents had first become apparent had as its theme the crossing of the Red Sea by the Israelites. Stretching from his first Holmes story to his last novel, *The Maracot Deep* (1930), a love story set in the ocean kingdom of Atlantis, these figures in the sand represent the continuity and integrity of Doyle's writing and the deepest direction of his thought.

In their debate over the nature of spirit which was simultaneously an argument over its masculine control, neither Doyle nor Houdini could be the winner. While the sensitive Houdini had reason on his side, he had the spirits against him and, after the controversial seance in 1922, they did not seem best pleased with Doyle either. So at least he thought when the seance house he had bought for Jean in the New Forest caught fire and was burnt to the ground in 1928. Nearly a century later, the argument over psi phenomena in which Doyle and Houdini involved themselves has been neither concluded or resolved by the SPR.

Those figures in the sand at the Atlantic City seance had, nonetheless, inscribed a cryptogram in which opposing concepts of identity–representation confronted and cancelled each other out. If Jean's automatic writing was, like so many other messages from the circumlocutionary spirits, vague, emotional, over-long and unspecific, the one name, 'Powell', with which Houdini immediately countered it, was concise, to the point, but equally devoid of powerful identity. 'Powell' was the name of *both* a fellow magician *and* of a fellow Spiritualist. It was also the name of the medium who had first inspired Doyle's travels and the name too of the man who had hanged Roger Casement. Performing under the name of the French magician 'Houdin', whose magic he had written a book to expose, Erich Weiss knew that spirit is brought into being only through the magical continuity and continual celebration of masculine names. As the nineteenth-century biographical tradition which had shaped Doyle's entire career had always affirmed, the meaning of masculinity itself lay in the reinforcement of this nomenclature.

But the audiencing spirits of the late nineteenth- and early twentieth-century seance thought differently. They did not participate in this system of names and name making. They rejected as false and inauthentic the coinages of celebritized individuality and cultural greatness. The champions, in particular, of under-representation, the spirits are the natural enemies of biography as a form.

Doyle used his celebrity status to allow these spirits to speak, not through the master-discourses of the late nineteenth century, but through the directing humour of his often subversive anecdotes. His own identity grounded in contradictions which he had spent his life trying to bind into a masculine unity, he was the natural spokesperson not just for the unions of the British empire, but also for their disintegration.

If there was a genuine revelation in the Spiritualist movement, it is one directed towards the private lives and emotions of ordinary individuals, not a platform for public performance and the making of great men's names. Three years after his death, in one of the many spirit communications purportedly sent by him, Doyle relayed his experience of undergoing, not just the first, but the second death in which everything of the earth-life is finally relinquished. At the first death, we take things with us, still particularizing our identity. After the second death, the message we send back to the living could be from anyone:

> We do not pass naked into the astral, but rather bear with us many an earthly treasure of knowledge, strength and pride of accomplishment.

And then ... crown and climax of all our striving, comes utter relinquishment – such is the marvel and miracle of the human soul and spirit.[129]

In his final work, *The Edge of the Unknown* (1930), Doyle returned for the last time to the life-writing genre that had shaped his career. After his many changes of literary identity, it is here, in a collection of short 'lives' of the prophets of Spiritualism – Andrew Jackson Davies, D. D. Home, Thomas Lake Harris and Harry Houdini – that he finally places himself. But does the creator of Sherlock Holmes belong in this company? The author of the great problem-solving detective had himself, after a lifetime of supplying rational explanations, finally become part of the puzzle.

Like many of the earnest but relatively obscure men who accepted him as their leader, Doyle finally found in Spiritualism a way of belonging to his own culture that did not require him to submit either his intellect or his interiority to a higher power. Holmes too had been happier investigating powers that were lower than his own, as if in recognition of the alternative career paths he might have taken. Burglary, as he observed in his final case, *The Retired Colourman*, had always been an alternative profession!

Spiritualism thus represents the vital component in any evaluation of Doyle's work or his cultural significance. In any narrow or exclusively literary definition of the term, Doyle cannot be described as a great writer but his career is interesting and instructive for its synthesizing, multi-disciplinary account of the cultural mechanisms by and through which the masculine meanings of his age were produced. As a movement and an organisation, Spiritualism was a curious parody of these mechanisms, for it was, by definition, always able to generate ideas beyond and outside its own institutional rituals and ideological framework. This, apart from the comfort it brought and the craziness it channelled, was its particular importance during the challenging early decades of the twentieth century. As evidenced by the Holmes stories, Doyle's writing is also remarkable for its ability to image space and narrative outside his chosen systems of logical enclosure and to render as a textual presence the prohibitions of his own discourse. His own quasi-mythical status as a postmodern character and a literary magus suggests that what will survive of him is, in part, this gift for colourful and suggestive silence.

In the later stages of his career, Doyle saw himself as a practical messiah and a great clown whose writing recast Christian spirituality in contemporary idioms while continually preparing his readership for war. His Celtic background gave him a natural ear for marginal voices and modes of expression and although he acquired the accents of a hegemonic Englishness, his deepest self-identification lay elsewhere. He figured the complex tensions of a British identity at the height of empire and saw in the after-life a new dispensation for his native Scotland.

Notes

1. Doyle, A. C., *The British Campaign in France and Flanders: July to November 1918*, vol. 6, London: Hodder and Stoughton Ltd, 1919, p. 304 .
2. Doyle, A. C., 'The Adventure of the Cardboard Box' in *His Last Bow* in *The Penguin Complete Adventures of Sherlock Holmes*, Harmondsworth: Penguin, 1981, p. 889.
3. See Freud, S., 'Thoughts for the Times on War and Death (1915)' in Freud, S., *Civilization, Society and Religion*, The Penguin Freud Library, vol. 12, Harmondsworth: Penguin Books, 1991.
4. Doyle, *The British Campaign in France and Flanders* vol. 6, op. cit., p. 305 .
5. Nietzsche, F., *Human, All Too Human*, Harmondsworth: Penguin Classics, 1994, p. 86.
6. Doyle, A. C., *The British Campaign in France and Flanders 1914*, vol.1, London: Hodder and Stoughton Ltd, 1916, p. 8.
7. See Doyle, A. C., *The Edge of the Unknown*, New York: Berkley Publishing Corporation, 1968, p. 69.
8. Freud, 'Thoughts for the Times on War and Death (1915)', op. cit., p. 61.
9. Doyle, A. C., *Psychic Experiences*, London: and New York: G. P. Putnam and Sons, 1925, p. 112.
10. Middleton, P., *The Inward Gaze: Masculinity and Subjectivity in Modern Culture*, London and New York: Routledge, 1992, p. 80.
11. Engels, F., *Dialectics of Nature*, Moscow: Progress Publishers, 1934, pp. 50–61.
12. Doyle, A. C., *The History of Spiritualism*, vol. 2, 1926, London: Psychic Press, 1989, pp. 225–6.
13. Doyle, A. C., *Memories and Adventures*, London: John Murray, 1930, p. 439.
14. Lellenberg, J. L., *The Quest for Arthur Conan Doyle: Thirteen Biographers in Search of a Life*, Carbondale and Edwardsville, IL: Southern Illinois University Press, 1987, p. 16.
15. Lamond, J., *Arthur Conan Doyle: A Memoir*, London: John Murray, 1931, pp. 170–71.
16. Lellenberg, *The Quest for Arthur Conan Doyle*, op. cit., p. 94.
17. Jean Dorsenne, 'A French View of Conan Doyle' in Orel, H. (ed.), *Arthur Conan Doyle: Interviews and Recollections*, London and Basingstoke: Macmillan, 1991, p. 263.
18. Green, R. L., 'His Final Tale of Chivalry' in Lellenberg, J. L. (ed.), *The Quest for Arthur Conan Doyle*, op. cit., p. 61.
19. See Orel, *Arthur Conan Doyle*, op. cit., p. 226 .
20. Beard, P., *Living On: A Study of Altering Consciousness After Death*, London: George Allen and Unwin, 1980, pp. 97–8.

21. Stashower, D., *Teller of Tales; The Life of Arthur Conan Doyle*, New York: Henry Holt & Co., 1999, p. 344.
22. Doyle, A. C., *The British Campaign in France and Flanders*, vol. 6, op. cit., p. 304.
23. Orel, *Arthur Conan Doyle*, op. cit., p. 265.
24. Doyle, *Memories and Adventures*, op. cit., p. 298.
25. Doyle, A. C., *Our American Adventure*, London: Hodder and Stoughton, 1923, p. 11.
26. Doyle, A. C., *The Land of Mist*, large print edn, London: Chivers Press, 1987, pp. 25 and 16.
27. Doyle, *Memories and Adventures*, op. cit., p. 286.
28. Doyle, *Our American Adventure*, op. cit., p. 10.
29. See Everitt, G., *English Caricaturists and Graphic Humorists of the Nineteenth Century*, London: Swan Sonnenschein and Co., 1893, pp. 393–4.
30. Gibson, J. M. and Green, R. L. (eds), *The Unknown Conan Doyle: Essays on Photography*, London: Secker and Warburg, 1982, p. 21.
31. Doyle, *The British Campaign in France and Flanders*, vol. 1, op. cit., p. 82.
32. Orel, *Arthur Conan Doyle*, op. cit., p. 241.
33. Doyle, *Memories and Adventures*, op. cit., p. 372.
34. Orel, *Arthur Conan Doyle*, op. cit., p. 266.
35. Ibid., p. 267.
36. Doyle, A. C., *The New Revelation and the Vital Message*, London: Psychic Press, 1981, p. 61 .
37. Doyle, A. C., *Our Second American Adventure*, London: Hodder and Stoughton Ltd, 1924, p. 41.
38. Preface to Dennis, L., *The Mystery of Joan of Arc*, trans: A. C. Doyle, London: John Murray, 1924.
39. Doyle, A. C., *The Wanderings of a Spiritualist*, Berkeley, CA: Ronin Publishing, 1988, p. 55.
40. Ibid., p. 217.
41. Doyle, *Our Second American Adventure*, op. cit., p. 41.
42. Lamond, J., *Arthur Conan Doyle: A Memoir*, op. cit., p. 164.
43. Doyle, *The Wanderings of a Spiritualist*, op. cit., p. 20.
44. Doyle, *The Land of Mist*, op. cit., p. 17.
45. Doyle, *Psychic Experiences*, op. cit., p. 98.
46. Leiris, M., *Manhood*, London: Jonathan Cape, 1968, p. 182.
47. Doyle, *The New Revelation*, op. cit., p. 149.
48. Doyle, *The British Campaign in France and Flanders*, vol. 1, op. cit., p. 29.
49. Doyle, *The Wanderings of a Spiritualist*, op. cit., p. 32.
50. Doyle, *The New Revelation*, op. cit., p. 149.
51. Doyle, *The Wanderings of a Spiritualist*, op. cit., p. 38.
52. Doyle, *The New Revelation*, op. cit., p. 24.
53. Winter, J., *Sites of Memory, Sites of Mourning: The Great War in European Cultural History*, Cambridge: Cambridge University Press, 1995, p. 59.
54. Doyle, *The New Revelation*, op. cit., p. 87.
55. Ibid., p. 82.
56. Ibid., p. 11.
57. See Doyle, A. C., 'A Full Report of A Lecture on Spiritualism', *The Worthington Gazette*, 1919, p. 3.

58. Doyle, A. C., *The New Revelation*, op. cit., p. 22.
59. Ibid., p. 75.
60. Doyle, *Memories and Adventures*, op. cit., p. 35.
61. Doyle, *The New Revelation*, op. cit., p. 85.
62. Ibid., p. 82.
63. Ibid., p. 142.
64. Doyle, 'The Adventure of the Red Circle' in *His Last Bow*, op. cit., p. 902.
65. Doyle, *The New Revelation*, op. cit., p. 83.
66. Ibid.
67. Doyle, *The Wanderings of a Spiritualist*, op. cit., p. 15.
68. Doyle, *The New Revelation*, op. cit., p. 45.
69. Ibid., p. 42.
70. Ibid., p. 48.
71. Doyle, *The Land of Mist*, op. cit., pp. 204–5.
72. Jacks, L. P., 'Personal Appearance of the Departed' in *The Journal of Society for Psychical Research, February–March 1919*, pp. 26–7.
73. Doyle, *The New Revelation*, op. cit., p. 53.
74. Ibid., p. 98.
75. Doyle, *The Wanderings of a Spiritualist*, op. cit., p. 213.
76. Doyle, *Our Second American Adventure*, op. cit., p. 208.
77. Doyle, *The Wanderings of a Spiritualist*, op. cit., p. 84.
78. Doyle, A. C., *The Lost World*, London: John Murray, 1934, p. 232.
79. Ibid., p. 204.
80. Ibid., p. 90.
81. Preface to Herries, J. W., *Other-World People*, Edinburgh and London: William Hodge & Co., 1926, p. xiii.
82. Doyle, *Memories and Adventures*, op. cit., p. 217.
83. Ibid., p. 333.
84. Engels, *Dialectics of Nature*, op. cit., p. 50.
85. Ibid., pp. 58–9.
86. Doyle, *The New Revelation*, op. cit., p. 150.
87. Ibid., p. 124.
88. See Roy, A. E., *The Archives of the Mind*, Glasgow: SNU Publications, 1996, pp. 193–218.
89. Melzack, R. and Wall, P. D., *The Challenge of Pain*, Harmondsworth: Penguin, 1996, pp. 61–2.
90. Lodge, O., *Raymond Revised*, London: Psychic Book Club, 1916, p. 130.
91. Ibid., p. 48.
92. Ibid.,, p. 197.
93. Doyle, *The New Revelation*, op. cit., p. 100.
94. Doyle, A. C., *The History of Spiritualism*, vol. 1, London: Psychic Press, 1989, p. 253.
95. Doyle, *The Wanderings of a Spiritualist*, op. cit., p. 224.
96. Doyle, *The Land of Mist*, op. cit., p. 269.
97. Doyle, A. C., *The Conan Doyle Stories*, London: John Murray, 1929, p. 133.
98. Ibid., p. 130.
99. Lamond, *Arthur Conan Doyle: A Memoir*, op. cit., p. 160.
100. Doyle, *The New Revelation*, op. cit., p. 90.

101. Ibid., p. 60.
102. Doyle, *The Edge of the Unknown*, op. cit., p. 149.
103. Doyle, *Our Second American Adventure*, op. cit., p. 11.
104. Doyle, *The Wanderings of a Spiritualist*, op. cit., p. 206 .
105. Ibid., p. 112.
106. Ibid., p. 215.
107. Doyle, *Our Second American Adventure*, op. cit., p. 121.
108. Ibid., p. 91.
109. Ibid., p. 106.
110. Doyle, *Our American Adventure*, op. cit., p. 19.
111. Doyle, A. C., *Our African Adventure*, London: John Murray, 1929, p. 9.
112. Doyle, *Edge of the Unknown*, op. cit., p. 5.
113. Doyle, *Our American Adventure*, op. cit., p. 96.
114. Ibid., p. 100.
115. Ibid., p. 138.
116. Ibid., pp. 180–89.
117. Brandon, R., *The Life and Many Deaths of Harry Houdini*, London: Secker and Warburg, 1993, pp. 242–9.
118. Doyle, *The Edge of the Unknown*, op. cit., p. 28.
119. Ibid., p. 31.
120. Brandon, *The Life and Many Deaths of Harry Houdini*, op. cit., p. 245.
121. Doyle, *The Edge of the Unknown*, op. cit., p. 7.
122. Ibid., p. 36.
123. Ernst, B. M. L and Carrington, H., *Houdini and Conan Doyle: The Story of a Strange Friendship*, London: Hutchinson and Co., 1933, p. 204.
124. Ibid., p. 221.
125. Doyle, A. C., *Pheneas Speaks*, London: Psychic Press, 1926, pp. 109–10.
126. Ibid., p. 204.
127. Ibid., p. 147.
128. Doyle, *Memories and Adventures*, op. cit., p. 24.
129. Beard, *Living On*, op. cit., p. 127.

Bibliography

Works of Arthur Conan Doyle referred to in this volume

(See notes for editions used)

Doyle, Arthur Conan, *The Complete Works*: see chapter endnotes for editions.

Fiction and poetry

The Adventures of Gerard
The Adventures of Sherlock Holmes
Beyond the City
The Case-Book of Sherlock Holmes
Danger! and Other Stories
The Doings of Raffles Haw
A Duet with an Occasional Chorus
The Exploits of Brigadier Gerard
The Firm of Girdlestone
The Great Shadow
The Green Flag and Other Stories of War and Sport
His Last Bow
The Hound of the Baskervilles
The Land of Mist
The Lost World
The Man from Archangel
The Maracot Deep and Other Stories
The Memoirs of Sherlock Holmes
Micah Clarke
The Mystery of Cloomber
The Parasite
The Poison Belt
The Refugees: A Tale of Two Continents
The Return of Sherlock Holmes
Rodney Stone
Round the Fire Stories
Round the Red Lamp
The Sign of Four
Sir Nigel
The Stark Munro Letters

A Study in Scarlet
The Tragedy of the Korosko
Uncle Bernac
The Valley of Fear
The White Company

Non-Fiction and poetry

The British Campaign in France and Flanders
The Case for Spirit Photography
The Coming of the Fairies
The Crime of the Congo
The Edge of the Unknown
The Great Boer War
The History of Spiritualism
A Lecture on Spiritualism
Memories and Adventures
The New Revelation
Our African Winter
Our American Adventure
Our Second American Adventure
Pheneas Speaks: Direct Spirit Communications in the Family Circle
Songs of Action
The Story of Mr. George Edalji
Through the Magic Door
The Vital Message
The Wanderings of a Spiritualist
The War in South Africa: Its Causes and Conduct

Collections

Essays on Photography
Letters to the Press
Uncollected Stories

Secondary work on Conan Doyle

Baker, Michael (1978), *The Doyle Diary*, London: Paddington Press.
Carr, John Dickson (1949), *The Life of Sir Arthur Conan Doyle*, London: John Murray.
Coren, Michael (1995), *Conan Doyle*, London: Bloomsbury.

Cox, Don Richard (1985), *Arthur Conan Doyle*, New York: Frederick Ungar Publishing Co.

Dennis, Leon (1924), *The Mystery of Joan of Arc*, trans. A. C. Doyle, London: John Murray.

Edwards, Owen Dudley (1983), *The Quest for Sherlock Holmes*, Edinburgh: Mainstream Publishing Co.

Ernst, Bernard M. L. and Carrington, Hereward (1933), *Houdini and Conan Doyle: The Story of a Strange Friendship*, London: Hutchinson & Co.

Gibson, J. M. and Green, R. L. (1982), *The Unknown Conan Doyle: Essays on Photography*, London: Secker & Warburg.

Gibson, J. M. and Green, R. L. (1982), *The Unknown Conan Doyle: Uncollected Stories*, London: Secker & Warburg.

Gibson, J. M. and Green, R. L. (eds) (1983) *A Bibliography of A. Conan Doyle*, Oxford: Clarendon Press.

Gibson, J. M. and Green, R. L. (1986), *Letters to the Press*, London: Secker & Warburg.

Green, Richard Lancelyn (1983), *The Uncollected Sherlock Holmes*, Harmondsworth: Penguin Books.

Hall, Trevor H. (1978), *Sherlock Holmes and His Creator*, London: Duckworth.

Haining, Peter (ed.) (1980), *A Sherlock Holmes Compendium*, London: Warner Books.

Higham, Charles (1976), *The Adventures of Conan Doyle*, London: Hamish Hamilton.

Hjortsberg, William (1995), *Nevermore A Novel*, London: Orion Books Ltd.

Hodgson, John A. (ed.) (1994), *Arthur Conan Doyle: Sherlock Holmes: Contemporary Critical Essays*, Boston: St Martin's Press.

Jahn, Rosemary (1995), *Detecting Social Order*, New York: Twayne's Masterwork Studies.

Jones, Kelvin I. (1989), *Conan Doyle and the Spirits*, Wellingborough: Aquarian Press.

Keating, H. R. F. (1979), *Sherlock Holmes: The Man and His World*, London: Thames and Hudson.

Kestner, Joseph A. (1997), *Sherlock's Men: Masculinity, Conan Doyle and Cultural History*, Aldershot: Ashgate.

Lamond, Revd John (1931), *Arthur Conan Doyle: A Memoir*, London: John Murray.

Lellenberg, Jon L. (ed.) (1987), *The Quest for Sir Arthur Conan Doyle: Thirteen Biographers in Search of a Life*, Carbondale and Edwardsville, IL: Southern Illinois University Press.

McQueen, Ian (1974), *Sherlock Holmes Detected*, New York: Drake Publishers.

Nordon, Pierre (1966), *Conan Doyle*, trans. F. Partridge, London: John Murray.

Orel, Harold (ed.) (1991), *Arthur Conan Doyle: Interviews and Recollections*, London and Basingstoke: Macmillan.

Payne, David S. (1992), *Myth and Modern Man in Sherlock Holmes*, Indiana: Gaslight Publications.

Pearsall, Ronald (1977), *Conan Doyle: A Biographical Solution*, Glasgow: Richard Drew Publishing.

Pearson, Hesketh (1943), *Conan Doyle: His Life and Art* London: Methuen and Co.

Pointer, Michael (1975), *The Public Life of Sherlock Holmes*, London: David & Charles.

Redmond, Christopher (1984), *In Bed With Sherlock Holmes: Sexual Elements in Arthur Conan Doyle's Stories of the Great Detective*, Toronto: Simon & Pierre.

Roberts, S. C. (1953), *Holmes and Watson: A Miscellany*, Oxford: Oxford University Press.

Roden, Christopher and Roden, Barbara (eds) (1996), *The Case Files of Sherlock Holmes: The Musgrave Ritual*, Ashcroft, British Columbia: Calabash Press.

Roden, Christopher and Roden, Barbara (eds) (1999), *The Case Files of Sherlock Holmes: The Blue Carbuncle*, Ashcroft, British Columbia: Calabash Press.

Rodin, Alvin E. and Key, J. D. (1984), *Medical Casebook of Dr. Arthur Conan Doyle*, Malabar: Robert E. Krieger.

Rosenberg, Samuel (1975), *Naked is the Best Disguise*, London: Arlington Books.

Shepherd, Michael (1985), *Sherlock Holmes and the Case of Dr Freud*, London and New York: Tavistock Publications.

Stashower, Daniel (1999), *Teller of Tales: The Life of Arthur Conan Doyle*, New York: Henry Holt & Co.

Stavert, Geoffrey (1987), *A Study in Southsea*, Portsmouth: Milestone Publications.

Symons, Julian (1979), *Portrait of an Artist: Conan Doyle*, London: Wizzard Press/Andre Deutsch.

Weller, Philip (ed.) (1993), *Recollections of Sir Arthur Conan Doyle by Residents of Crowborough*, collected by Malcolm Payne, The Conan Doyle (Crowborough) Establishment.

Contemporary references

Blatchford, Robert (1892), *Autobiographical Reminiscences*, Edinburgh and London: W. & R. Chambers.

Blatchford, Robert (1925), *More Things in Heaven and Earth: Adventures in Quest of a Soul*, London: Methuen.

Blatchford, Robert (1931), *My Eighty Years*, London: Cassell & Co.

Blavatsky, Helena Petrovna (1960), *Isis Unveiled*, Pasadena, CA: Theosophical University Press edn.

Carlyle, Thomas (1881), *Reminiscences*, New York: Harpers & Bros.

Chambers, William (1872), *Memoir of Robert Chambers with Autobiographic Reminiscences of William Chambers*, Edinburgh and London: W. & R. Chambers.

Churchill, Winston (1941), *My Early Life*, London: Odhams Press. First edition 1930.

Clausewitz, Karl von (1832), *On War*, Harmondsworth: Penguin Classics, 1982 edn.

Doyle, Richard (1980), *Journal 1840*, Edinburgh: John Bartholomew.

Duncan, Isadora (1928), *My Life*, London: Victor Gollancz.

Emerson, Ralph Waldo (1902), *English Traits*, London: Routledge & Sons. Riverside edition.

Engels, Friedrick (1934), *Dialectics of Nature*, Moscow: Progress Publishers.

Garland, Hamlin (1908), *The Shadow World*, London and New York: Harper & Bros.

Gibbs, Philip (1946), *The Pageant of the Years*, London: William Heinemann Ltd.

Giddings, Robert (1996), *Imperial Echoes: Eyewitness Accounts of Victoria's Little Wars*, London: Leo Cooper.

Glenconner, Pamela (1921), *The Earthen Vessel: A Volume Dealing with Spirit-Communication in the Form of Book-Tests*, London: John Lane.

Graves, Robert (1929), *Goodbye to All That*, Harmondsworth: Penguin, 1960.

Gutteridge, Joseph (1893), *Lights and Shadows in the Life of an Artisan*, Coventry: Curtis & Beamish.

Hardy, Florence (1994), *The Life of Thomas Hardy*, London: Studio Editions.

Hastings, Sir Patrick (1948), *The Autobiography of Sir Patrick Hastings*, Melbourne, London and Toronto: William Heinemann.

Hawkins, Sir Henry (1904), *The Reminiscences*, ed. Richard Harris, KC, London: Thomas Nelson & Sons.

Herries, J. W. (1926), *Other-World People*, Edinburgh and London: William Hodge & Co.

Hill, J. Arthur (1918), *Man is a Spirit: A Collection of Spontaneous Cases of Dream, Vision, and Ecstasy*, London: Cassell & Co.

Holmes, Oliver Wendell (1889), *The Autocrat of the Breakfast Table*, London: Walter Scott Ltd.

Home, Mme D. D. (1921), *D. D. Home: His Life and Mission*, London: Kegan Paul, Trench and Trubner.

Hyde, H. Montgomery (1964), *Famous Trials 9: Roger Casement*, Harmondsworth: Penguin.

Jerome, Jerome K. (1926), *My Life and Times*, New York: Harper & Bros.

Lang, Andrew (1905), *Adventures Among Books*, London: Longmans, Green & Co.

Lockhart, J. G. (1906), *The Life of Sir Walter Scott*, Dent: Everyman.

Lodge, Sir Oliver (1918), *Raymond Revised*, 3rd edn, London: Psychic Book Club.

Macaulay, Thomas Babington (1889), *The History of England from the Accession of James II*, vol. 1, London: Longmans, Green & Co.

Monkswell, Lady Mary (1946), *A Victorian Diarist: Later Extracts from the Journals 1895–1909*, London: John Murray.

Milne, James (1934), *The Memoirs of a Bookman*, London: John Murray.

Myers, F. W. H. (1904), *Fragments of Prose and Poetry*, London: Longmans, Green & Co.

Myers, F. W. H. (1904), *Human Personality and Its Survival of Bodily Death*, vol. 1, New York and London: Longmans, Green & Co.

Nisbet, J. F. (1889), *Marriage and Heredity A View of Psychological Evolution*, London: Ward & Downey.

Noyes, Alfred (1953), *Two Worlds for Memory*, London and New York: Sheed & Ward.

Pinkerton, Matthew Worth (1898), *Murder in All Ages*, Chicago: A. E. Pinkerton & Co.

Putnam, G. P. (1925), *Psychic Experiences*, London: Putnams.

Quigley, Hugh (1928), *Passchendaele and the Somme*, London: Methuen and Co. Ltd.

Ross, Janet (1912), *The Fourth Generation: Reminiscences*, London: Constable & Co.

Rousseau, Jean-Jacques (1953), *The Confessions*, trans. Cohen, J. M., Harmondsworth: Penguin Classics.

Sawyer, R. (ed.) (1997), *Roger Casement's Diaries 1910: The Black and The White*, London: Pimlico.

Seely, J. E. B. (1930), *Adventure*, London: William Heinemann.

Stead, Estelle W. (1918), *My Father: Personal and Spiritual Reminiscences*, Thomas Nelson & Sons.

Stephen, Leslie (1898), *Studies of a Biographer*, 2 vols, London: Duckworth & Co.

Stephen, Leslie (1919), *Hours in a Library*, vol. 3, London: John Murray.

Stevenson, Robert Louis (1879), *Edinburgh*, London: Seeley, Service & Co.

Stevenson, Robert Louis (1910), *Essays in the Art of Writing*, London: Chatto & Windus.

Stevenson, Robert Louis (1988), *The Lantern Bearers and Other Essays*, ed J. Treglown, London: Chatto & Windus.

Swann, Annie (1934), *My Life*, London: Ivor Nicholson & Watson Ltd.

Trevelyan, George Macaulay (ed.) (1932), *Fifty Years: Memories and Contrasts: A Composite Picture of the Period 1882–1932*, London: Thornton Butterworth Ltd.

Trollope, Anthony (1980), *An Autobiography*, The World's Classics Series, Oxford: Oxford University Press.

Wells, H. G. (1914), *An Englishman Looks at the World*, London: Cassell & Co.

Wells, H. G. (1934), *Experiment in Autobiography*, 2 vols, London: Gollancz Ltd.

Wilson, H. W. (1900–1901), *With the Flag to Pretoria: A History of the Boer War of 1899–1900*, 2 vols, London: Harmsworth Bros Ltd.

Wilson, H. W. (1901–1902), *After Pretoria: The Guerrilla War*, 2 vols, London: The Amalgamated Press Ltd.

Secondary sources

Alderson, David (1998), *Mansex Fine Religion, Manliness and Imperialism in Nineteenth-century British Culture*, Manchester: Manchester University Press.

Amigoni, David (1993), *Victorian Biography: Intellectuals and the Ordering of Discourse*, Hemel Hempstead: Harvester Wheatsheaf.

Bakhtin, M. M. (1986), *Speech Genres and Other Late Essays*, Austin: University of Texas Press, 1986.

Barbanell, Maurice (1959), *This is Spiritualism*, London: Herbert Jenkins.

Barker, Steve (1993), *Picturing the Beast: Animals, Identity and Representation*, Manchester: Manchester University Press.

Basham, Diana (1992), *The Trial of Woman: Feminism and the Occult Sciences in Victorian Literature and Culture*, London: Macmillan.

Beard, Paul (1980), *Living On A Study of Altering Consciousness After Death*, London: George Allen & Unwin.

Beckett, I. F. W. (1988), *Victoria's Wars*, Aylesbury: Shire Publications Ltd.

Beckson, Karl (1992), *London in the 1890s A Cultural HIstory*, New York and London: W. W. Norton & Co.

Bederman, Gail (1995), *Manliness and Civilization*, Chicago and London: University of Chicago Press.

Boundas, Constantin V. (ed.) (1993), *The Deleuze Reader*, New York: Columbia University Press.

Brandon, Ruth (1993), *The Life and Many Deaths of Harry Houdini*, London: Secker & Warburg.

Braude, Stephen (1986), *The Limits of Influence, Psychokinesis and the Philosophy of Science*, London: Routledge & Kegan Paul.

Briggs, Asa (1990), *Victorian Things*, Harmondsworth: Penguin.

Briggs, K. M. (1967), *The Fairies in Tradition and Literature*, London: Routledge & Kegan Paul.

Broughton, Trev Lynn (1999), *Men of Letters/Writing Lives: Masculinity and Literary Auto/Biography in the Late-Victorian Period*, London: Routledge.

Caldwell, T. C. (ed.) (1965), *Problems in European Civilization: The Anglo-Boer War*, Boston: D. C. Heath & Co.

Chandler, Frank Wadleigh (1907), *The Literature of Roguery*, 2 vols, London: Archibold Constable & Co.

Chase, Cynthia (ed.) (1993), *Romanticism*, London and New York: Longman.

Cooke, Ivan (ed.) (1961), *The Return of Arthur Conan Doyle*, Liss, Hampshire: White Eagle Publishing Trust.

Connell, R. W. (1995), *Masculinities*, Cambridge: Blackwell's/Polity Press.

Cornwall, Andrea and Lindisfarne, Nancy (eds) (1994), *Dislocating Masculinity: Comparative Ethnographies*, London and New York: Routledge.

Cummins, Geraldine (1956), *Mind in Life and Death*, London: Aquarian Press.

Dale, Peter Allen (1989), *In Pursuit of a Scientific Culture: Science, Art and Society in the Victorian Age*, Madison: University of Wisconsin Press.

Dawson, Graham (1994), *Soldier Heroes: British Adventure, Empire and the Imagining of Masculinities*, London and New York: Routledge.

Deleuze, Gilles and Sacher-Masoch, Leopold von (1989), *Masochism: 'Coldness and Cruelty' and 'Venus in Furs'*, New York: Zone Books.

Edwards, Owen Dudley (1988), *Macaulay*, London: Weidenfeld & Nicolson.

Edmunds, Simeon (1966), *Spiritualism: A Critical Survey*, London: Aquarian Press.

Eldridge, C. C. (1996), *The Imperial Experience: From Carlyle to Forster*, Basingstoke: Macmillan.

Farewell, Byron (1989), *Armies of the Raj: From the Great Indian Mutiny to Independence 1858–1947*, London: Viking.

Foucault, Michel (1991), *Discipline and Punish: The Birth of the Prison*, Harmondsworth: Penguin.

Gagnier, Regenia (1991), *Subjectivities: A History of Self-Representation in Britain, 1832–1920*, Oxford: Oxford University Press.

Girourd, Mark (1981), *The Return to Camelot: Chivalry and the English Gentleman*, New Haven and London: Yale University Press.

Gissing, George (1961), *The Private Papers of Henry Ryecroft*, New York: The New American Library of World Literature, Signet Classics.

Green, Martin (1993), *The Adventurous Male: Chapters in the History of the White Male Mind*, University Park, PA: Pennsylvania State University Press.

Hogg, James (1924, 1970 edn), *The Private Memoirs and Confessions of a Justified Sinner*, Oxford: Oxford University Press.

Hohenberg, John (1964), *Foreign Correspondence: The Great Reporters and Their Times*, New York and London: Columbia University Press.

Inglis, Brian (1974), *Roger Casement*, Coronet edn, London: Hodder & Stoughton.

Keener, Frederick M. (1973), *English Dialogues of the Dead*, New York and London: Columbia University Press.

Kestner, Joseph A. (1995), *Masculinities in Victorian Painting*, Aldershot: Scolar Press.

Knightley, Philip (1982), *The First Casualty: The War Correspondent as Hero, Propagandist and Myth Maker*, London: Quartet Books.

Logan, Peter Melville (1997), *Nerves and Narratives: A Cultural History of Hysteria in 19th Century British Prose*, Berkeley: University of California Press.

MacKenzie, John M. (1992), *Popular Imperialism and the Military 1850–1950*, Manchester: Manchester University Press.

Mangam, J. A. and Walvin, James (eds) (1987), *Manliness and Morality*, Manchester: Manchester University Press.

Marwick, Arthur (1989), *The Nature of History*, 3rd edn, London: Macmillan.

Mason, Michael (1994), *The Making of Victorian Sexuality*, Oxford and New York: Oxford University Press.

Middleton, Peter (1992), *The Inward Gaze Masculinity and Subjectivity in Modern Culture*, London and New York: Routledge.

Moore, Robert and Gillette, Douglas (1991), *King, Warrior, Magician,*

Lover: Rediscovering the Archetypes of the Mature Masculine, San Francisco: HarperCollins.

Newey, V. and Shaw, P. (eds) (1996), *Mortal Pages, Literary Lives: Studies in Nineteenth-Century Autobiography*, Aldershot: Scolar Press.

Oppenheim, Janet (1985), *The Other World: Spiritualism and Psychical Research in England, 1850–1914*, Cambridge: Cambridge University Press.

Pakenham, Thomas (1979), *The Boer War*, London: Weidenfeld & Nicolson.

Palling, Bruce (1992), *India: A Literary Companion*, London: John Murray.

Phillips, Richard (1997), *Mapping Men and Empire*, London and New York: Routledge.

Rose, Jonathon (1986), *The Edwardian Temperament, 1895–1919*, Ohio: Ohio University Press.

Roy, Archie E. (1996), *The Archives of the Mind*, Glasgow: SNU Publications.

Salmon, Lucy Maynard (1923), *The Newspaper and the Historian*, New York: Oxford University Press.

Salwak, Dale (ed.) (1996), *The Literary Biography: Problems and Solutions*, Basingstoke: Macmillan.

Scott, S. and Morgan, D. (eds) (1993), *Body Matters*, London and Washington DC: The Falmer Press.

Sedgwick, Eve Kosofsky (1985), *Between Men: English Literature and Male Homosocial Desire*, New York: Columbia University Press.

Showalter, Elaine (1992), *Sexual Anarchy: Gender and Culture at the Fin de Siècle*, London: Virago.

Silverman, Kaja (1992), *Male Subjectivity at the Margins*, New York and London: Routledge.

Sinha, Mrinalini (1995), *Colonial Masculinity*, Manchester and New York: Manchester University Press.

Steedman, Carolyn (1984), *Policing the Victorian Community*, London: Routledge & Kegan Paul.

Sussman, Herbert (1995), *Victorian Masculinities: Manhood and Masculine Poetics in Early Victorian Literature and Art*, Cambridge: Cambridge University Press.

Sutherland, John (1996), *Is Heathcliff a Murderer? Great Puzzles in Nineteenth-Century Literature*, Oxford and New York: Oxford University Press.

Symons, Julian (1972), *Bloody Murder: From the Detective Story to the Crime Novel: A History*, London: Faber & Faber 1972. Paperback edition 1992.

Tabori, Paul (1974), *Crime and the Occult*, Newton Abbot: David & Charles.

Theweleit, Klaus (1989), *Male Fantasies*, 2 vols, Cambridge: Polity Press.

Todorov, Tzvetan (1995), *The Morals of History*, trans. Waters, A., Minneapolis: University of Minnesota Press.

Turner, E. S. (1958), *Call the Doctor: A Social History of Medical Men*, London: Michael Joseph.

Vance, Norman (1985), *The Sinews of the Spirit: The Ideal of Christian Manliness in Victorian Literature and Religious Thought*, Cambridge: Cambridge University Press.

Waugh, Charles G. and Greenberg, Martin H. (1981), *The Best Science Fiction of Arthur Conan Doyle*, Carbondale and Edwardsville, IL: Southern Illinois University Press.

Wheeler, Michael (1990), *Death and the Future Life in Victorian Literature and Theology*, Cambridge: Cambridge University Press.

Winter, Denis (1979), *Death's Men: Soldiers of the Great War*, Harmondsworth: Penguin.

Winter, Jay (1995), *Sites of Memory, Sites of Mourning: The Great War in European Cultural History*, Cambridge: Cambridge University Press.

Index